THE NEW CONGRESS

THE NEW CONGRESS

EDITED BY THOMAS E. MANN AND NORMAN J. ORNSTEIN

American Enterprise Institute for Public Policy Research
Washington and London

Library of Congress Cataloging in Publication Data

Main entry under title:

The New Congress.

   (AEI studies ; 305)
   Includes index.
   1. United States. Congresses—Addresses, essays,
lectures. I. Mann, Thomas E. II. Ornstein, Norman J.
III. Series: American Enterprise Institute for Public
Policy Research. AEI studies ; 305.
JK1041.N48   328.73   80-25724
ISBN 0-8447-3415-2
ISBN 0-8447-3416-0 (pbk.)

AEI Studies 305

Printed in the United States of America

Contents

THE NEW CONGRESS

Introduction

Everyone recognizes that much has changed in Congress over the past twenty years. Its members are very different, its rules and internal organization have been restructured, its staffs have greatly expanded. Yet some basic features of Congress have remained stable over this period, anchored as they are in the constitutional separation of powers and in our decentralized political party system. The purpose of this book is to assess what this mix of continuity and change means for the policy process.

This question takes on special significance in contemporary American politics. On the one hand, an increasing number of analysts, most notably Lloyd Cutler, former counsel to President Carter, have argued that the instruments of collective authority and accountability in American politics have been weakened in recent years at the same time that the problems facing government have become more complex. Our inability "to form a government," in Cutler's words, stems in large part from the fact that Congress has become more decentralized and individualized.

On the other hand, we have just experienced one of the most dramatic elections in recent American history, in which an incumbent president was rejected, control of the Senate shifted to the Republicans for the first time in twenty-six years, and conservative forces gained significant strength in the House.

The Reagan administration clearly aspires to change the direction of federal policy, reducing taxes and domestic spending, increasing defense spending, and balancing the budget. What happens when a reformed Congress (including a Republican Senate which shows few signs of "re-reforming" or unreforming) meets a new administration armed with a powerful electoral mandate and intent on changing course?

1

We believe the essays in this book shed some light on these immediate questions, as well as on the broader picture of what has changed—and what has not—in Congress and in the American political system in the past two decades.

We start with a series of essays on forces *outside* Congress. No one who visited Washington in the 1950s and who returns today could ignore the tremendous changes that have taken place in every sense—architecturally, ethnically, socially, and economically—in the broader Washington community. James S. Young's *The Washington Community 1800–1828* makes clear that the structure of the Washington environment affected Congress in its earliest days; recent changes in the contemporary Washington community, as Nelson Polsby's chapter recounts, have influenced the modern Congress. Also, of course, Congress, as it has changed, has had a profound effect on the contours of the District of Columbia.

We cannot discuss Congress without considering members and their constituencies. Mann's essay notes that the *internal* behavior of Congress and congressmen is influenced importantly by the conditions of nomination and election. Many of these conditions—the political parties, the electorate, and the pool of available congressional candidates—have changed in the 1960s and 1970s, precipitating or encouraging reforms and changes in individual behavior inside the House and the Senate.

Few developments in American society have been more dramatic than the advent and expansion of television and the nationalization of the mass media in the past few decades. But as Robinson notes, the local press remains important for Congress and congressmen and is completely different from the national media in its coverage of Congress and its impact on members. Robinson also points out that Congress is not merely "covered" by the media; it uses its *own* media resources to publicize and promote its actions.

In part two, we examine some of the changes that have taken place inside Congress as an institution. Roger Davidson looks more deeply at the upheaval that has occurred in the committee system—particularly at the expansion of power and initiatives to subcommittees. Michael Malbin undertakes an in-depth examination of the new role of congressional staff and its impact on the legislative process. Barbara Sinclair analyzes how policy coalitions have changed in the 1970s and how party leaders are trying, not always successfully, to cope with the changes.

In part three, we move to the policy side of the equation. The Nixon presidency dramatically altered Congress's perceptions and actions in making policy and overseeing the executive. Charles O.

Jones takes us through the Nixon era to the Carter White House and Congress, and beyond. Jimmy Carter tried to change the policy process in at least one controversial area—water projects—and he found Congress angrily insistent on "politics as usual." R. Douglas Arnold asks whether "politics as usual" continues generally to be the byword in the broader scope of domestic policy. Allen Schick and I. M. Destler examine, in a similar vein, post–Budget Act economic policy and post-Vietnam foreign policy on Capitol Hill. As they all note, some things have changed in the policy arena, but much remains the same in operation and outlook as it was in the prereform Congress.

In the concluding section, Ornstein examines how the House and the Senate have responded differently to the changing political environment of the 1970s and whether the overall role of Congress in the American political system has been altered in any fundamental way.

On balance, while the authors acknowledge and document the decentralizing and individualizing trends that critics of the contemporary Congress stress, most of them also see signs of vitality and adaptiveness in a complex and changing environment. While Congress is, in Samuel Huntington's words, "a source of anguish to both its friends and its foes," it is also a remarkably rich and influential institution.

PART ONE
The Context

1
The Washington Community, 1960-1980

Nelson W. Polsby

Most of the events mentioned in the rest of this book occur within the confines of Washington, D.C. And most of the people whose names appear in it live or work in the Washington community, the subject of this essay. The Washington community is also presumably the community to which President Jimmy Carter referred when he complained in his famous speech of July 1979 that Washington was an island, cut off from the concerns of the rest of the country.[1] Washingtonians hear insults of that kind with some regularity from all sorts and conditions of politicians, and so they could not have been surprised when it was said even by a president noted for his difficulty in finding trustworthy top assistants from anywhere but the state of Georgia. Twenty years ago, John Kennedy more good naturedly observed that Washington was a city of southern efficiency and northern charm. In a world of flux, there are some constants.

In fact, like all communities, the Washington community is based on interaction. What is unusual is that who gets to interact consequentially in Washington is determined to a high degree not by internal cooptation but by nationwide recruitment. This makes the Washington community almost absurdly permeable to outside influence: Supreme Court justices and senators, for example, by some reckonings among the most influential people in town, have little

With apologies to James Sterling Young, and thanks for unusual help and encouragement from generous friends at AEI in completing this essay, in particular, Nina Kerstiens, Norman Ornstein, and Tom Mann. Thanks also to Daniel D. Polsby, an early inhabitant, Linda O. Polsby, and Philip Wilson. Charles W. Harris, a leading scholar of Washington local politics, generously guided me away from numerous errors. Those that remain are mine alone.

[1] President Carter's speech is printed verbatim in the *New York Times*, July 17, 1979, p. A15, and *Congressional Quarterly, Weekly Report*, vol. 37 (July 21, 1979), pp. 1470-1472.

or nothing to say about who their closest colleagues will be. Like it or not, they must take whatever presidents and far-flung electorates, respectively, give them. Then they must live and work in collegial intimacy, sometimes for half a lifetime, with the results.[2]

Unlike the communities from which most politicians—including Jimmy Carter—come, Washington is a community that rewards the ecumenical spirit. If Franklin Roosevelt had remained a New York lawyer no doubt he could have passed a life of ease never consorting with the non-Wasp likes of his exact contemporary Felix Frankfurter. In the far more open texture of Washington, however, where politics counts for more than the accidents of birth in throwing people together, it was possible for such an alliance to occur.[3]

So the first and most important lesson to be learned about the Washington community is: it is not an island, not in at least one sense in which virtually every other sizable community in America is an island. What other community in America regularly accords automatic, immediate, unshakable top status to someone from out of town, even if that someone's public conversation consists mainly of unpleasant statements about the community and attacks on its oldest inhabitants? To a degree undoubtedly greater than in most American communities, even ones experiencing growth as rapid as Washington's, leadership in the Washington community consists of people who, like President Carter, originally came from someplace else.[4]

[2] The tensions involved occasionally surface in popular gossip, now known as investigative journalism. Early examples can be found in such publications as Anonymous, *The Washington Merry-go-round* (New York: Liveright-Blue Ribbon, 1931). Or, more recently, see Robert Woodward and Scott Armstrong, *The Brethren* (New York: Simon and Schuster, 1979).

[3] In 1916, during Roosevelt's first tour of duty in Washington as assistant secretary of the navy, leading members of the bar from New York and Boston led the fight against the appointment of a Jewish Justice, Louis Brandeis, to the Supreme Court. See A. L. Todd, *Justice on Trial* (New York: McGraw-Hill, 1964).

[4] An unsystematic racking of the brain discloses only one figure of national reputation in the Washington community in recent history to have been a home-grown Washingtonian: J. Edgar Hoover. Both local newspapers are owned by people who were originally from elsewhere. Until recently, the *Star* was home-owned; it now belongs to Time, Inc., headquarters, New York. Since Eugene Meyer bought the *Post* in the 1930s, he and his successors in the family have lived in Washington. The editors of both papers are from Boston. The famous politicians, journalists, lawyers, and bureaucrats whose names are most often dropped when the idea of Washington as the center of the universe is conjured up in ordinary conversation are invariably from out of town. And of course so are all senators and congressmen, except the District of Columbia's own Walter Fauntroy. A few sample lawyers: Edward Bennett Williams, born in Hartford, Connecticut; Lloyd Cutler, born in New York City; Clark Clifford, born in Fort Scott, Kansas; Abe Fortas, born in Memphis, Tennessee; Joseph Califano, born in

Principles of Aggregation among Political Elites

Thus the Washington community can be regarded as the product of American politics in the largest sense. We shall initially be concerned with the social and demographic consequences for a single locale of processes that have been going on for as long as Americans have come from all over the nation to do their common business there, with particular emphasis on the twenty years since John Kennedy was inaugurated. The political community of Washington consists of a very large population: presidents and their immediate employees; congressmen and their staffs; the people who run the great bureaucracies of the permanent government, career military, workers in the Agriculture Department, and so on; judges and personnel of the Supreme Court, the Appeals Court of the District of Columbia, specialized courts of similar rank, and the District Court; employees of independent regulatory agencies, of the hundred-odd embassies of foreign nations, of the tens of hundreds of interest-group organizations with Washington headquarters or listening posts and doing business with the government; staffs of consulting firms, think tanks, newspapers, magazines, news bureaus, and information services.

All of these people date their experience in Washington according to the same political calendar. Every year and especially after every election a new group of outsiders floats into Washington on the political tide and is deposited in one or another organization in the community, most of which contain strata from previous administrations. During quadrennial presidential transitions, movement from out of town to Washington, and between public and private sectors, is especially busy. In consequence, one way to look at the Washington community is geologically: all over town, there are networks of friendship, enmity, alliance dating from the Truman years, from the Eisenhower administration, and so on.

The geological strata are cross-cut by "issue-networks," "subgovernments," "iron triangles," and similarly described groups of variously situated people who do business with one another because of their common focus on a particular subject matter. And these bonds are further complicated by networks based on state or community of origin.

Brooklyn, New York. The journalists on Agronsky and Company who tell us "what Washington thinks" each week are Martin Agronsky, born in Philadelphia; Hugh Sidey, born in Greenfield, Iowa; James J. Kilpatrick, born in Oklahoma City; Elizabeth Drew, born in Cincinnati, Ohio; Carl Rowan, born in Ravenscroft, Tennessee; and George Will, born in Champaign, Illinois.

These principles of aggregation—by generation, by issue-area, by place of origin—remain significant throughout the careers of political Washingtonians. In this sense it seems to me that Washington, like other one-industry capitals (Canberra, Brasilia, Bonn, and Ottawa are other possible examples), affixes a far less distinctive stamp on its political class than do capital cities that are cities first and capitals second (London, Rome, Paris, and so on). Middle-aged residents are surprised to realize that their children, who have spent most of their lives there, think of themselves as Washingtonians. On the whole, political Washingtonians never do, but rather consider themselves transplanted Texans, Minnesotans, New Englanders, or whatever.

In the last twenty years two significant trends have had a major impact on the composition of this political Washington community. One is the so-called welfare shift in the federal budget. Over a twenty-year period the money newly allocated in the federal budget to various kinds of social amelioration—welfare, occupational health and product safety, regulation of food and drugs, the financing of low-cost housing and model cities, the enforcement of equal opportunity rules, and so on—has been enormous. Much of this followed in the wake of legislation passed during the Johnson administration, but a good part of its programmatic impact was not spelled out in the legislation itself. What happened was that a great chunk of the American population that had traditionally been considered outsiders to government, and special wards of liberal presidents, had government bureaucracies established in their behalf.

"Bureaucracies" means bureaucrats, programs, consultants, justifications, reports, red tape, the creation and servicing of clientele groups. These in turn had to get organized and find processes and agencies of intermediation. During the 1960s and 1970s, as this branch of the public sector was burgeoning, an explosive growth took place in the private sector of Washington. Firms sprang up designed to hook the bureaucracies into their client groups, to discover needs, to monitor the performance of the public sector in relation to needs, and to monitor the performance of the private sector in response to governmental interventions both distributive and regulatory.

One of the striking changes of the two decades has been the progressive decline in the presence of federal bureaucracies in two sorts of activities: direct service delivery on the model of the Post Office or the Social Security Administration—and policy planning and evaluation. The federal bureaucracies are increasingly confined to middle-man functions. They write regulations headed downward and outward to grantees and contractors: universities, private firms, state and local governments. And they write reports for their political superiors, describing how well the regulations are being complied with. The politicians who sit at the tip of these bureaucratic icebergs like to keep control of policy planning and evaluation themselves, and will contest about it, if they must, only with other politicians. Consequently programmatic foresight and planning functions are increasingly kept away from career bureaucrats and given to political appointees and their paid professional consultants.

In the aftermath of World War II the U.S. Air Force wisely decided to maintain and to subsidize a civilian capability in the United States to do strategic planning equal in strength to the capabilities available in the armed services.[5] Defense intellectuals working for think tanks are now complemented by small communities devoted to foreign affairs, welfare policy, housing policy, education, macroeconomic planning, and all the rest of the policy areas that modern central government addresses. These communities, with their warring schools of thought, their Republican and their Democratic affiliates, and their differing tendencies, do in a relatively open and pluralistic way what civil servants in other modern democratic nations do monopolistically and in private.

All of these little communities have outposts across America, wherever there is a major university or a think tank of any size or a cluster of important law firms. The main concentration of all of them, however, is in Washington, where at any given time a fair number of issue-community leaders will be in the government, a fair number will be nearby in think tanks and law firms aiding and abetting the government on a part-time or consultative or temporary basis, and a fair number will be similarly employed in the private sector but politically in opposition.

The 1960 election settled the question whether a Catholic could become president. Now, by 1980, the latest political tides are bringing into high governmental positions a larger number of "public interest" advocates, Americans with Spanish surnames, black officials, and women. In most respects these people are arriving at influence in the Washington community by much the same route as the phalanx of business school types in the Nixon administration, or, for that matter, Frankfurter's "Happy hot dogs" from Harvard Law School in the 1930s—through the political alliances and calculations of the elected officials who make most of the appointments. During the

---

[5] See Bruce L. Smith, *The Rand Corporation* (Cambridge: Harvard University Press, 1966).

New Deal the joke went: "How do you get to Washington? Go to Harvard and turn left." Changes in budgetary priorities over the last twenty years have made that even better advice today than it was then.

After the welfare shift in the budget, with its bureaucratic consequences, the second most significant change in the composition of the Washington community over a twenty-year period has been the explosion in the population of Capitol Hill.[6] This is, on balance, a sad story, though not without its silver lining. The proximate cause of the growth of congressional staffs on an unprecedented scale and the creation of several new congressional bureaucracies was Richard Nixon's war on the Washington community and on Congress in particular. More or less as a result of President Nixon's instruction, the executive branch became untrustworthy as far as Congress was concerned. This gave a whole new dimension to a government divided between the parties, a common enough occurrence in modern times. But where Dwight Eisenhower, Sam Rayburn, and Lyndon Johnson knew how to keep partisan antagonism within bounds and strove to do so, Nixon strove to do the reverse.

Moreover, he succeeded; and piecemeal decisions that were already being made on Capitol Hill to professionalize, upgrade, and strengthen the staffs of committees, to increase the capacities of the Congressional Research Service and the scope of the General Accounting Office, began to accelerate rapidly. The result is an extraordinary array of staff resources placed at the disposal of 535 elected politicians in myriad permutations and combinations. These congressmen and senators now perch precariously atop more than 28,000 employees. Congressional staffs at their best are highly competent and professional. They give members of Congress a means by which they can independently verify the factual premises upon which administration proposals rest. When congressional staffs perform these functions, they narrow the scope of political debate to those matters which are genuinely debatable and provide an incentive for the administration to back its proposals with empirically sound arguments.

Frequently congressional staffs are entrepreneurial as well, seeking out ways to make their principals (and, by extension, themselves) look good, testing the political environment for interest group alliances and for favorable publicity. Because favorable publicity is not rigorously allotted only to activities that are geared to making the legislature function properly, the activities of entrepreneurial staff frequently conflict with corporate goals established by congressional leaders. And

[6] See John F. Bibby, Thomas E. Mann, Norman J. Ornstein, *Vital Statistics on Congress, 1980* (Washington, D.C.: American Enterprise Institute, 1980).

sometimes staff members are allowed such independence by their political principals that it can be said that they are to all intents and purposes unaccountable. It is now common wisdom that Congress has become unmanageable because of this problem.[7] In fact Congress has never in modern times been manageable by the standards of even a loosely run hierarchical organization, but it is fair to say that the reasons for its unmanageability have shifted over a twenty-year period from the problems of working around an ideological impasse among members evenly balanced between liberal and conservative coalitions, to the problems of coordinating the diverse concerns of a large but not terribly cohesive or docile majority—generally liberal in sympathies—backed by an enormous, ambitious, and not terribly accountable staff.

Three Important Groups. Over a twenty-year span, then, the demographic composition of the Washington political community has changed, mostly by expansion. Within that community, three additional constituent groups are of particular interest. Senior bureaucrats have lost ground, massively. It is now rare that they dominate the highest level of planning for the future conduct of government in their lifelong specialties, and in some cases they are not even invited to the meetings that matter.

Another large population—sometimes called in-and-outers—waxes and wanes in importance depending upon who holds the reins of political power. When politicians to whom these people have access are in, they are in; when another faction or another party occupies the executive branch, they return to money making, brooding, or political opposition; some, in the marvelous jargon of Washington locals, may even "disappear"—that is, take up residence some place in the world beyond the beltway.

A third group hardly fluctuates in its status at all as presidents succeed presidents and administrations succeed administrations. This group consists mostly of the mandarins of the high-priced law firms, and the gurus of the Washington press corps, who give continuity and whatever it has in the way of a corporate ideology to the Washington political community. As these James Restons, Joseph Alsops, Clark Cliffords, and Paul Porters grow old and put on weight they form an American equivalent to the House of Lords.[8] They may, by

---

[7] For a compendium of complaints, see Michael Malbin, *Unelected Representatives: The New Role of Congressional Staffs* (New York: Basic Books, 1980).

[8] I once heard a shrewd foreign observer of U.S. politics speculate that an appearance on the cover of *Time* magazine was the U.S. equivalent to membership in the House of Lords. A nice try, but not quite right: Nasser (for example) qualified for one but not the other. It is true, however, that successive editors

mutual cooptation, include in their ranks a few high-born or especially well-connected politically active senior citizens, as, for example, when the law firm of Covington and Burling hired former Senator John Sherman Cooper to decorate its stationery in roughly the position formerly occupied by his fellow Yale man Dean Acheson. At any given time the Washington community boasts a generation of senior oracles who by their patterns of social interaction and their attentiveness to some matters and not to others have a lot to do with which substantive arguments are taken seriously and which disregarded. There are plenty of outlets of appeal from this con'sensus, through the mass media and via Congress (which participates only very slightly in this aspect of Washington life). Indeed, the Washington mandarins alone can rarely prevail in public policy, even when they agree among themselves—as they frequently do not.[9] It is nevertheless useful to know that some sort of extragovernmental consensus in Washington quite frequently forms and gives shape and constraint to such large issues as the need for a Marshall Plan, or the wisdom and timing of granting recognition to the nation a generation of Americans called Red China, or the need to get into, or out of, Vietnam.[10]

Like most groups, this group is generally divided on issues. It has its more liberal (for example, John Gardner) and its more conservative (for example, Arthur Burns) members, and these in turn have ties with different constituencies in the nation at large. But when they unite on a public question, their influence upon the atmosphere within which alternatives are generated and chosen by the government is very significant.[11]

---

of *Time* have made a considerable effort to conceptualize American life as a parade of heroes, and *Time* occasionally prints lists of present or future big shots. President Carter even hired a retired editor of *Time* to sit in the White House and create a "commission" on goals for the 1980s, a real collector's item for people who like old covers of *Time.*

[9] An instance where they did not prevail, for example, was in the prosecution, which they opposed, of Richard Helms for concealing information from a congressional committee. See Thomas Powers, *The Man Who Kept the Secrets* (New York: Knopf, 1979), pp. 52-53, 299 ff. and passim; and William Greider, "Circle of Friends Supports Helms," *Washington Post*, February 2, 1975.

[10] A derogatory term for this consensus is "group think." See Irving Janis, *Victims of Group Think* (Boston: Houghton Mifflin, 1972). On the same thing in its guise as just plain consensus, see Joseph Jones, *The Thirteen Weeks* (New York: Viking, 1955). See also Herbert Y. Schandler, *The Unmaking of a President* (Princeton, N.J.: Princeton University Press, 1977), chap. 14, "The Wise Men," pp. 256-265.

[11] In an earlier day, the principles of aggregation among elites were much the same. See Henry Adams, *The Education of Henry Adams* (New York: Heritage, 1942), first published in 1918. Compare with Laurence Leamer, "Networks," *Washingtonian* (November 1979).

Hometown Washington

So far I have discussed the Washington community as a socio-demographic phenomenon, dealing mainly with significant twenty-year-long changes and stabilities in the composition and disposition of political elites. Because Washington, even today, forty years after it began to become a city of major size, is still essentially a one-industry town devoted exclusively to government, this construction of the term community makes some sense. But this is not the only way to look at Washington as a community, and certainly not the only way in which Washington inhabitants experience it as a community. We can also consider Washington as a community in the sense that any community is a community and ask what it is like to live there, go to school there, grow up there, shop there, how it compares with other places as an advertising market or as a hometown. This is the Washington chronicled by the *Post*'s local columnist, Bill Gold, consisting of people who used to watch the late WMAL weatherman, Louis Allen, and who still listen to Hardin and Weaver, who root for the Redskins and remember Sammy Baugh, who drink National Bohemian Beer and drop a nostalgic tear now and again for the sports page of the old *Times-Herald*, for Arch Macdonald, the Eddie Yost fan club, for Pick Temple and for Jim Henson's Sam and Friends, local precursors to the Muppets. In this community live the children—and sometimes the grandchildren—of the leaders of the Washington political community. About this Washington, the backdrop and scenery against which the drama of national political life is played, there are a number of things to be observed. These include that Washington is a high-growth city, a middle-class city, a southern city, a black city, and a federal city. Each of these facts has important consequences for life in the Washington community.

Since 1940, the Washington, D.C., metropolitan area has sustained high and steady population growth. The growth of the federal government—pretty much a recession-proof industry—has been something of an economic bonanza for the Washington community. Real estate and construction millionaires, many of them self-made within living memory, are the largest part of that small group of local Washingtonians who have struck it rich in a big way. The rest of the group consists mostly of entrepreneurs in a few key service industries: liquor and automobile dealers, for example.

This pattern of financial accumulation has important consequences for the intellectual and cultural life of the city. It is frequently remarked that Washington has no university of the first rank. The foundation of such an institution requires philanthropy on a very large scale, normally the result of a long generation of financial accretion followed by years of dispersion. Local Washington fortunes cannot compare with the fortunes generated by industry or technology in such places as Pittsburgh, Rochester, New York, or Los Angeles, and they are all late on the scene, dating from the boom years after World War II. Thus the people who made them have scarcely had time to die off, never mind to endow higher learning. Virtually all the big money in and around Washington—the Mellon, Harriman, Post, Bliss, and Meyer fortunes for example—was made by out-of-towners whose descendants chose to settle, or keep quarters, in Washington in the manner of Henry Adams, to be near a piece of the political or social action, and much of their philanthropy is sent back home.

The class distribution of Washingtonians is strongly biased toward the middle: the government is mainly a white-collar employer, and professionals who service the government, plus government workers, make up an unusually large proportion of the whole employed population. An example of the symbiosis of government and its attendant professional class: an extremely generous provision for psychiatric treatment in the standard government Blue Cross plan has given Washington the highest proportion of psychiatrists per capita of any city in America.[12] Of the incidence of lawyers and lobbyists one need say nothing. Service workers of all kinds, for example in tourism, the professions, and trade associations, as of 1979 slightly outnumbered government employees—360,300 to 359,700—in the Washington metropolitan area. Blue-collar symbiosis with the government also exists. The principal nongovernmental blue-collar industry is printing and publishing, and among the largest manufacturing establishments are newspapers.[13]

Rapid, steady population growth in the Washington area and the maintenance of a large well-paid middle class to sustain markets for housing and office space have produced some of the best and some of the worst examples of city and regional planning in the world. Bethesda and Silver Spring in Maryland, and Rosslyn, Virginia, are three enormous conglomerates of high-rise buildings adjacent to the

---

[12] In *Fortune*, September 24, 1979, p. 34, Daniel Seligman gives the number of psychiatrists in Washington as 1 per 1,780 people. In San Francisco, the number is 1 per 2,296; New York, 3,240; and Los Angeles, 6,118.

[13] See William H. Jones, "Government No Longer Area's Largest Employer," *Washington Post*, March 24, 1979, p. D9. Also, Martha Derthick, *City Politics in Washington, D.C.* (Cambridge, Mass.: Joint Center for Urban Studies, 1962), p. 20. On the general characteristics of the Washington economy, see Metropolitan Washington Board of Trade, *The Case for Washington: Our Resources* (no date). The latest figures given in this pamphlet are for 1978.

District of Columbia, all without proper street level amenities, that have grown from virtually nothing in thirty years, memorials to greed and indifferent city planning that can compare with the worst civic building anywhere in the world west of Warsaw. On the other hand, Reston, Virginia, and Columbia, Maryland, both communities a little farther out into the countryside, are among the most successful planned towns ever built, maintaining civic amenities on a human scale while, after halting beginnings, even meeting the tests of the marketplace. These triumphs of the last twenty years were forecast by the more modest, but no less successful, Greenbelt, Maryland, a striking planned "garden suburb" that was executed as a project of the New Deal.[14] Unlike many of the structures and other plans of the 1930s, Greenbelt has aged gracefully; in this it is matched in the private sector by Charles Goodman's brilliantly conceived and executed Hollin Hills, Virginia, a postwar residential community, and his more inexpensive version in Wheaton, Maryland.

In Washington, the continuous boom of the last forty years has meant a steady, indeed an expanding, market for good housing and commercial building; alas, the pressure of demand has expanded the market for shoddy as well. Money has rained alike on the just and the unjust in the real estate market.

There has also been a continuous process of renovation in many parts of the inner city, sparked in a few cases by federal funds but mostly by private capital. Georgetown was reclaimed from slum conditions during the 1930s and 1940s, and every year the gentrification of Capitol Hill marches a few blocks further east. In general, piecemeal private sector efforts have preserved amenities more successfully than the larger efforts, although many residents have pleasant things to say about the totally demolished and rebuilt southwest section of the District of Columbia; it is too early to tell if the giant Fort Lincoln project in the far northeast of the city will be a success.

It is impossible to speak of change in the physical plant of the community without discussing how it affects demography. Washington, D.C., has had a black majority since sometime between the censuses of 1950 and 1960.[15] Since Reconstruction—and certainly all during the Jim Crow years, which came to a close only in the late 1950s—Washington (unlike many American cities) has boasted a large, prosperous, settled black middle class, distinguished by many

---

[14] See the Works Progress Administration, Federal Writers Project, *Washington: City and Capital*, 1937, pp. 829-832.

[15] Derthick, *City Politics*, p. 1.

highly educated and cultivated men and women, professionally accomplished doctors, teachers, and, increasingly, public servants.[16] They have on the whole until recently made their homes from the Howard University area to the east side of Rock Creek Park, which roughly bisects the city on a north-south axis. The majority of the black population, however, has never been as prosperous as well-to-do whites, and as urban renewal and private sector gentrification have proceeded, large numbers of black residents have been priced out of parts of town where they once lived. It is not easy to predict when or under what conditions these processes of residential succession become political issues. On the whole, in Washington they never have.[17] This is only one indication, though it is an important one, of the extent to which the middle-class character of Washington is sustained rather than undermined by its black population.

Since its beginnings, northern observers have noted that Washington was a southern town. It is useful to recall that the Mason-Dixon line, which since 1763 has been accepted as the boundary between northern and southern customs—especially in respect to race—runs between Maryland and Pennylvania, perhaps sixty miles north of the District of Columbia. Until the late 1950s black people were unwelcome in Washington restaurants except those specifically catering to them, and want ads in the newspapers for housing and jobs were explicitly segregated by race. The local newspapers always provided a racial designation of persons mentioned in crime stories. No segregation was enforced in public transport, but it was at most places of public assembly including the (privately owned) National Theater and Glen Echo Amusement Park, where black people were not welcome. The worst offender was Constitution Hall, for years the city's biggest auditorium, owned by the Daughters of the American Revolution, who in 1939 refused to permit an unsegregated concert by the contralto Marian Anderson. The event was held at the Lincoln Memorial, a famous public relations coup for the Roosevelt administration.[18]

All this belongs to another era; indeed it seems no more part of contemporary times than horse-drawn ice wagons or the bustle. Yet

---

[16] See Constance McLaughlin Green, *The Secret City* (Princeton, N.J.: Princeton University Press, 1967); Thomas Sowell, "Black Excellence: The Case of Dunbar High School," *The Public Interest*, vol. 35 (Spring 1974), pp. 1-21; and Sowell, "Patterns of Black Excellence," *The Public Interest*, vol. 43 (Spring 1976), pp. 50-53.

[17] See Green, *Secret City*, pp. 233-236, 322 ff.; and Derthick, *City Politics*, pp. 34-35, 123-126.

[18] See Harold L. Ickes, *The Secret Diary of Harold L. Ickes*, vol. 2, "The Inside Struggle, 1936-1939" (New York: Simon and Schuster, 1954), pp. 612-616.

even today Washington is a southern town. Census figures for 1970, which list Washington as a city-state as well as a metropolitan area, show:

- The District of Columbia is still a target for a lot of migration. Only 42.5 percent of its population was born there, compared with an average of 65 percent for the states. Only Florida and a few western states show a smaller percentage of native-born residents.
- Born Washingtonians move out of town at a rate exceeding that of any state, but three-fifths of the migrants move to adjacent states, which undoubtedly means Washington suburbs. An overwhelming number of those moving out have been white.
- Half of all Washington residents in 1970 were born in another state, the vast majority (about three-quarters) from noncontiguous states. This pattern is common in the boom states of the West and the sunbelt, but it is utterly atypical of the northeast.
- The states sending migrants into Washington are predominantly southern. The top four states of origin for Washingtonians of 1970 born elsewhere are North Carolina and Virginia (sending about 50,000 migrants each), South Carolina (34,000), and Maryland (23,000). The next two states—New York (22,000) and Pennsylvania (20,000)—combined do not equal North Carolina's contribution. Georgia and West Virginia rank seventh and ninth.[19]

Southern accents predominate on the streets of Washington. The slightest snowfall ties up traffic instantaneously, although the District of Columbia is for the most part flat and what hills there are, are not steep. Northerners find this puzzling.

The common explanation for Washington's southernness has two parts. In the first place, Washington is located in the South; its location was a sweetener in the political deal that gave Hamilton his assumption bill, thought to be disadvantageous to the South.[20] Second, Washington is a railhead, for a century or more the end of the line for the vast majority of passenger trains from the west, south, or north. With Baltimore only forty miles to the northeast, and then a whole string of cities beyond, Washington's natural hinterland lay southward. Without any marketing effort, the *Washington Post* is

[19] These figures are drawn from official publications of the Bureau of the Census, in particular "State of Birth," *1970 Census of Population*, March 1973.
[20] James Sterling Young, *The Washington Community 1800-1828* (New York: Columbia University Press, 1966), p. 16.

19

the largest selling newspaper in Virginia, an opportunity certainly not available to it in the territory of the Baltimore *Sunpapers*. Washington professional sports teams have frequently gone out of their way to tap this regional market. This has been one reason for the unusually strong resistance to the desegregation of the local professional football team by Washington Redskin management, and the similarly obdurate attitude of the management of the old Washington Senators who, oddly enough, were pioneers in the recruitment of talented Cubans to major league baseball. Nevertheless, bigotry goes a long way toward explaining why Washington was for so long "First in war, first in peace, and last in the American League."

One of the byproducts of the fact that Washington is a southern community, with immigration predominantly from the South, is the nearly total absence of white ethnic minority groups such as populate the low income parts of Baltimore and every other city of the northeast. Few low income white ethnics—Italians, Poles, Irish, and so on—means very little violent disputation over residential turf between black and white populations and a tendency for the pocketbook, not communal sentiment, to determine the demarcation between white and black residential areas. In Washington, there are black neighborhoods and white neighborhoods, but almost no ethnic neighborhoods. This also means not much in the way of ethnic holidays or ethnic restaurants, and speakers of foreign languages in Washington are more often than not connected with an embassy. The major exception is the growing Latino population mostly concentrated in the Mount Pleasant and Adams-Morgan districts.[21]

Because Washington is a middle-class community and has only a small indigenous population of great wealth, large-scale philanthropy suffers, and economic leadership in the community is bureaucratized. Even when the Board of Trade was riding highest in its local political influence in the 1950s, it was dominated not by millionaires but by local private sector bureaucrats who represented the banks, utilities, real estate companies, and department stores.[22] Because it is a middle-class community and has only a small white lower class, there is little ethnic heterogeneity or local color. The large black community is uncommonly infused with middle-class values. Its very large size,

---

21 Between 1970 and 1978 the number of Hispanic children enrolled in the D.C. school system increased by 75 percent. The number of Asians living in Washington also tripled during that time period, to 3 percent or 4 percent of the population. See Eunice S. Grier and George Grier, "Changing Faces of Washington," *Washington Post*, June 17, 1980, p. A17.

22 See Constance McLaughlin Green, *Washington: Capital City 1879-1950* (Princeton, N.J.: Princeton University Press, 1963), pp. 29-34 and passim; and Derthick, *City Politics*, pp. 86-89.

not its militancy, was the threat that turn-of-the-century bigots saw and that accounts for the withdrawal of home rule after 1874 and for the length of the battle that had to be waged before it was finally restored in the 1960s.[23]

Thus, the third great fact of Washington life is that it embraces a very large black population. For the better part of the twentieth century this meant no home rule. Municipal government was dominated by the locally unaccountable southern congressmen who ran the District Committee of the U.S. House of Representatives in coalition with the leaders of the D.C. Board of Trade.[24] The last twenty years have seen this system replaced with one that includes a locally elected mayor, city council, and school board and a local nonvoting representative in Congress. Almost all of these have been liberal, Democratic, and black, more or less as predicted by friends and foes alike of the granting of home rule. This falls short of the full statehood advocated by some Washingtonians, but the present home rule arrangement constitutes a meaningful expansion of the civic rights of District residents.[25]

As the largest landholder by far in the District of Columbia, and the largest local employer, the federal government, which pays no taxes, looms very large in the calculations of local leaders. Washington is entitled to federal appropriations under the same theory that produces federal aid to impacted areas, and the federal appropriation makes up one-fifth of the income in the municipal budget, more than any other source outside the personal income tax. It must be negotiated by local officials with the House District Appropriations Subcommittee (whose members are no longer conservative, segregationist southerners) and with the relevant subcommittee of the Senate Finance Committee; and so congressional influence on city politics, though diminished, remains strong.[26]

The federal influence is thus the fourth great factor in determining the shape of the contemporary Washington community. Of course if it were not a federal city, it is doubtful that contemporary Washington would exist at all. Its location and physical layout—the magnificent avenues punctuated by circles diagonally overlaying a grid lined up according to the points of a compass, the whole system radiating out from the Capitol building—was of course done to a

[23] Derthick, *City Politics*, pp. 169-178.

[24] Ibid., pp. 37-72.

[25] See Charles W. Harris and Alvin Thornton, *Perspectives of Political Power in the District of Columbia since Home Rule* (forthcoming).

[26] See District of Columbia Government, *Executive Budget FY 1981*, October 1979.

master plan, a French master plan at that. It is long on logic and symmetry and has inspired innumerable great piles of insipidly monumental building, erected to house more and more of the bureaucracies that call Washington home. In recent years the legislative branch has spared no expense to litter the landscape with its marble mausoleums as well.[27] By contrast, and as an everlasting reproach to what has happened elsewhere in town, the village of Georgetown, a Potomac port that existed before L'Enfant's planned city and was incorporated into it, has retained a human scale and a fair amount of its Georgian and federal domestic architecture.

The federal influence on Washington's physical planning has on the whole been highly destructive. Survivors of the John Kennedy administration congratulate themselves for not having despoiled the area surrounding Lafayette Park as though they had averted a force of nature rather than a dimwitted set of their own bureaucratic plans. A group just like the saviors of Lafayette Park produced another set of plans to do something about Pennsylvania Avenue that would have made Mussolini proud.[28]

In order to protect the visibility and the civic symbolism of monumental Washington, commercial Washington has been restricted in the heights its buildings may attain.[29] Squat attenuated skyscrapers, vaguely resembling the hulls of mothballed battleships in their gray sameness, now march up Connecticut Avenue and down nearby streets to the west. Provision for a coherent—never mind a colorful or interesting—street and sidewalk life and for pedestrians is at best rudimentary. In all the new public, commercial, and federal building that has gone on in the last thirty years, enclosing hundreds of thousands of square feet of space, perhaps five or six buildings in the entire metropolis merit more than a passing glance.[30]

[27] The rate of building on Capitol Hill appears to be accelerating. Both the Senate and the Library of Congress have recently built monstrosities to rival the House's Rayburn building. And there are plans for more.

[28] See Arthur M. Schlesinger, Jr., A Thousand Days (Boston: Houghton, Mifflin, 1965), pp. 737-738. For an overview of monumental Washington see William Walton's attractive coffee-table book The Evidence of Washington (New York: Harper and Row, 1966).

[29] A good discussion of the consequences of this and other conditions influencing Washington architecture is Howard Means, "Please Don't Shoot the Architect," Washingtonian (March 1980), p. 130 ff.

[30] Anybody can play this game. Here are my nominees: Eero Saarinen's masterpiece, the Dulles Airport Building, thirty miles out of town; Harry Weese's playful and comfortable new home for Arena Stage; I. M. Pei's theatrical addition to the National Gallery of Art; Philip Johnson's rather precious jewelry box that houses exhibitions of the Dumbarton Oaks collection; and one or two of the commercial restorations in Georgetown that imitate San Francisco's Ghirardelli Square.

Outweighing these by far are the hundreds of lost opportunities to build livable public buildings in the District of Columbia. One or two monstrosities have achieved the distinction of public scandal: the $121 million House Office Building grotesquely dedicated to the memory of the unpretentious Sam Rayburn, with its giant cement cornucopias, its endless featureless hallways, its pointlessly bombastic hearing rooms, and its main entryway dominated by a larger-than-life statue of the great Speaker, showing his rear end to the bustling traffic below, is perhaps the best example, but it is not the only example. Two other disasters seem especially poignant to me. On a small scale, the Brookings Institution missed a superb opportunity in the late 1950s to create a building embodying the values of collegial interchange and scholarship that Brookings stands for—and that are in desperately short supply in the anxiety-prone, hierarchical, status-conscious agencies producing the public policies that Brookings exists to monitor, criticize, and improve. Instead what emerged was a building that mimics a federal bureaucracy, its public and communal spaces relegated to back hallways and hidden behind locked doors, its territory for scholars insipidly modularized and badly planned for mutual access.

A far sadder example is the Kennedy Center, a leaky behemoth housing several active theaters and restaurants situated on what should have remained empty park-land along the Potomac, now largely inaccessible, except by automobile, to ordinary citizens. Why could not this enormously undistinguished building have been broken down into its natural components and strategically grouped in what was in the late 1960s the faltering heart of downtown Washington, where buses ran day and night—and where the subway now runs—where stores, restaurants, and other places of public amusement struggled to retain nighttime pedestrian traffic and a respectable clientele?

A blithe disregard for obvious civic requirements of the local population is one of the hallmarks of the federal presence in Washington. This is the counterpoint to the fact that the federal presence brings local amenities in the first place. The National Gallery, originally a Mellon philanthropy, is in Washington because Washington is the federal city. Likewise the Hirshhorn Collection, the Smithsonian Institution, the National Geographic Society, the Library of Congress, and the Folger Shakespeare Library. And the presence of the government guarantees the presence in turn of a highly educated, cosmopolitan upper middle class that is eager to consume the artifacts of high culture—books, art exhibits, plays, and concerts—in sufficient numbers to create a genuine market with considerable commercial potential.

23

In exchange, the government offers its heavy hand: a magnificent, grossly overpriced subway where the trains run infrequently, but on time;[31] a commercial waterfront, urban renewed to within an inch of its life, scoured of character and turned into an uninhabitable, but indubitably clean, wasteland of barnlike restaurants and windswept parking lots; and civic architecture and planning that in its most inspired moments is mediocre.

The result is a civic high culture that local boosters like to compare with New York's, but which falls far short. Only in the realm of public exhibitions of art does the comparison seem worth taking seriously. In architecture, music, ethnic variety, restaurants, the worlds of books (writing, retailing, or publishing), universities, medicine, and the theater, Washington compares with other American cities roughly in its size class, (San Francisco, Boston, Detroit, Cleveland, and Houston) and overall comes out somewhere in the upper half, better on some scales, worse on others.

Three extraordinary civic benefactions give Washington some of its strongest claims to cultural excellence. One is embodied in the decision in 1921 by Duncan and Marjorie Phillips to move out of their home at 21st and Q Streets, NW, and permit the public regular access to the splendid paintings they had assembled there: choice examples of Klee, Degas, Rouault, Daumier, Renoir, and other significant modern artists. Its particular combination of high quality and intimacy of scale makes the Phillips collection one of the most rewarding art galleries anywhere. A second is embodied in the thirty-year career of a remarkable Washington woman, Zelda Fichandler, whose dedication to repertory theater brought into being the Arena Stage, perhaps the finest enterprise of its kind in the United States. The caliber of players, directors, and original productions that have filtered through the Arena Stage since its beginnings in an abandoned skid-row theater, and then in a disused brewery (nicknamed the Old Vat), is remarkable and no doubt owes a part of its viability to the nearby resources of Father Gilbert Hartke's distinguished drama program at the Catholic University of America. The third is the series of gifts to the Library of Congress that brought it a group of superb Stradivarius stringed instruments, the small, comfortable Coolidge auditorium, where they can be heard to good effect, and an endowment permitting the engagement of players of high caliber to play them regularly.[32]

31 See Herman Nickel, "Washington's Metro is the Solid-Gold Cadillac of Mass Transit," *Fortune* (December 3, 1979), pp. 110–124.

32 Any decent local guidebook gives the particulars on these benefactions, along with information about how to enjoy them. See, for example, Laura Longley Babb, ed., *The Washington Post Guide to Washington* (New York: McGraw-Hill, 1976).

These three achievements are worthy of particular notice because they are genuine expressions of an indigenous civic spirit arising locally and not more grandiose expressions of a wish to make a footprint upon the cosmic sands of national notoriety. They also provide civic amenities to Washingtonians that can properly be called unique.

Finally, Washington's civic amenities include those it can claim by virtue of its status as a center of political news, namely, local news publications of more than routine interest. Moviegoers have now heard of the *Washington Post;* the apparent hair-breadth rescue of the *Star* from bankruptcy by Joseph Allbritton and then by Time Incorporated means that Washington is one of the few cities in America served by two serious independent local newspapers of high standards. In addition Washington has its very own general news weekly, *U.S. News,* two superb specialized news weeklies in *Congressional Quarterly* and *National Journal,* a weekly and a monthly journal of commentary in the *New Republic* and the *Washington Monthly,* and even a local slick magazine of unusual merit, the *Washingtonian.* This makes for a very rich news diet for a conscientious consumer. And of course a great many professional Washingtonians are highly conscientious consumers.[33] The result is that these journals, while many of them circulate widely, provide genuine links between members of the Washington community, spanning the generations, bridging the issue-networks, binding together Washingtonians from all their varied places of origin.

Congress in the Washington Community

Within the Washington community the congressional subcommunity has traditionally been an entity apart: congressmen have primarily sought to maintain their links with the localities which sent them to Washington, and this has generally precluded deep or meaningful involvement with Washington as a community—even for those whose children were growing up Washingtonians.[34] In the 1960s, congressmen with "downtown" connections were regarded with some suspicion by their fellows, and marks of high status within the congressional world were far more likely to be accorded to members who stuck close to the floors of their respective houses and sought

[33] As Elizabeth Drew puts it: "Washingtonians do not live like other people. On Sunday, when other people are hiking or sailing or doing nothing, many Washingtonians are earnestly going through the thick Sunday papers and watching 'Meet the Press' and 'Face the Nation.' Washingtonians do this even when there is little going on." *Washington Journal* (New York: Random House, 1975), p. 23.

[34] See Myra MacPherson, *The Power Lovers* (New York: Putnam, 1975).

cordial relations with their colleagues than to those who took their recreation in Georgetown.

Any number of cues to the insulation of Congress from Washington at large were available to the observer. Most obtrusive, perhaps, was the tendency of Congress to work unsocial hours: breakfast was a popular time to have a quiet meeting on the Hill, and the legislative day quite frequently pushed on toward 6 or 7 P.M. After the legislative day was over, the informal gatherings would take place—Sam Rayburn's Board of Education was the most significant of these but not the only one. They could be found in Democratic and Republican Capitol Hill clubs, and private sector watering holes like the Rotunda and the Monocle. The legislative life could, if avidly pursued, consume every waking hour. The aging bachelors who dominated Congress made no concessions to the school vacations of members with growing children either. So the legislative calendar as well as the legislative clock tended to insulate congressmen from those outside the clutches of the institution. No doubt every student of Congress during those years had his own favorite stories illustrating the way Congress was cut off from the rest of official Washington and maintained a world of its own. In the jockeying for the Democratic leadership after the death of Sam Rayburn in late 1961, an "outside" strategy was a distinct handicap; personal friendship meant much more than ideological affinity, and a cosmopolitan world view was far less desirable than a penchant for mingling democratically with one's colleagues on the floor of the House.[35] Insofar as connections "downtown" were held to be an actual disadvantage to a member's congressional career, we could see the workings of a sort of tribal sentiment rather than a rational calculation of political effectiveness in a city where so much of consequence to congressmen was in fact decided downtown in the agencies of the executive branch and at the regulatory commissions. So it was not that members were not expected to know their way around the executive branch: they were simply expected to treat the executive branch instrumentally, and reserve their real loyalties and emotional attachments for the freemasonry of the Hill.

It must have been a reaction to some such set of norms that prompted James Reston, the venerable Washington correspondent of the *New York Times*, once to say within my hearing that he always felt he needed a visa when he crossed Seventh Street on his way to the Hill. The remark was made at an orientation session for freshman

[35] See Nelson W. Polsby, "Two Strategies of Influence in the U.S. House of Representatives," in Polsby, *Political Promises* (New York: Oxford University Press, 1974), pp. 113-148.

congressmen in aid of the extraordinary proposition that the 435 newly elected or reelected members of the House of Representatives were somehow out of touch with the country at large. On reflection, I think Reston confused the rather aggressive corporate parochialism of the Congress of those years vis-à-vis the rest of Washington with isolation from the nation. The same confusion, no doubt, was the source of a similar pratfall by a well-known academic, who proposed as an example of congressional insularity the fact that members had infrequently been invited to appear at the deliberations of the American Assembly.[36]

Despite my own reluctance to accept the makers of American Assembly guest lists as possessors of perfect pitch when it comes to cosmopolitan sophistication, some members of Congress seemed to be making an effort to live up to the stereotype thrust upon them. In one of the few television news specials of the 1960s to focus on Congress, wily old Judge Howard W. Smith of the House Rules Committee could be overheard professing not to know who Walter Lippmann was and disdainfully mispronouncing his name.

Informal interaction among members who were strangers to one another or only casually acquainted—members of different age groups and parties, say, meeting in the gym—strongly emphasized their common immersion in hometown localism. The casual friendliness of the place seized upon the pleasant neutrality of the noncontroversial fact that everybody was *from* somewhere; and that particular somewhere, with its distinctive climate, topography, and economy, could be the basis for nonpartisan, ice-breaking banter. Localism, in short, was rewarded not only at home, where the votes were, but at the Capitol, where it could provide a highly legitimate prop for members' identities.

On the whole, the national news media emphasized the disaggregated and localistic orientations of Congress by treating congressional elections as local rather than as national news stories. The long election-night vigils conducted by the television networks, with their hours of make-weight repetitiveness about the presidential race, spent some time on Senate contests but practically no time at all on significant House elections, even when, as in the otherwise boring landslide of 1964, the composition of key House committees was being remade by the voters, all unnoticed and unremarked by the news media.

---

[36] Samuel P. Huntington, "Congressional Responses to the Twentieth Century," in *The Congress and America's Future*, ed. David B. Truman, 2nd ed. (Englewood Cliffs, N.J.: Prentice-Hall, 1973), p. 18.

The twenty-year trend has shown a blurring of the social boundaries around the congressional component of the Washington community, just one part of a complex set of changes which have had a sizable impact on virtually all of the institutions of American national politics and on the way they do business. In Congress itself, the effects have included drastic changes in the internal clout of show horses, who have gained at the expense of work horses; an expansion of the division of labor in the House and a simultaneous increase in the powers of the Speaker;[37] a transformation in the role of the U.S. Senate from an inward-looking, club-like deliberative body to a major center of publicity, a mobilization point for national interest groups and a launching pad for presidential hopefuls;[38] and the professional-ization and proliferation of staff through Capitol Hill, including those staff who work for individual members, those who work for com-mittees and subcommittees, and those who work for free-standing congressional agencies, both new (like the Congressional Budget Office) and refurbished (like the Congressional Research Service of the Library of Congress).[39]

Not even so well insulated a body as Congress has been able to protect itself against major changes in the conditions of American political life. It is possible, and even illuminating, to dispute about the causes of the manifold changes barely sketched above. Among the most important I should propose the following:

1. *The rise of television.* The thirty-year revolution in news communication in the United States has brought the potential of non-partisan celebrity to congressional politicians. From the crime hear-ings of Estes Kefauver to the impeachment vote of the House Judiciary Committee, whenever television has covered Congress there has been lightning in the air waiting to strike, making an instant celebrity out of an everyday politician. As Michael Robinson's chapter in this volume underscores, it requires very little ingenuity on the part of a politician to discern the usefulness of celebrity in an occupation that requires for survival or advancement the marshalling of mass senti-ment in the form of votes. It is not surprising, then, to see congress-

[37] Norman Ornstein and David Rohde, "Shifting Forces, Changing Rules and Political Outcomes," in R. L. Peabody and N. W. Polsby, eds., *New Perspectives on the House of Representatives*, 3rd ed. (Chicago: Rand McNally, 1977), pp. 186-269.

[38] Nelson W. Polsby, "Goodbye to the Inner Club," in Polsby, ed., *Congressional Behavior* (New York: Random House, 1971), pp. 105-110.

[39] See Malbin, *Unelected Representatives*, and Harrison W. Fox, Jr., and Susan W. Hammond, *Congressional Staffs: The Invisible Force in American Law-making* (New York: The Free Press, 1977).

men and senators festooning themselves with lightning rods, with the indicated cumulative effects on the institutions that house them.

2. *The continued nationalization of politics.* The social and geographic mobility of Americans works against localism as a long-term political posture, not because local ties and sentiments matter less to members of Congress (although, marginally, I believe they do) but because mobility, mass marketing, and national television all are making American localities more and more alike. One chain of causation in which these forces play a major part would run as follows: Social and demographic changes in the South have been replacing conservative Democrats with Republicans in the House.[40] This has weakened the voice of the South and of conservatism in the Democratic Congressional Caucus sufficiently to make the caucus a suitable arena for the occasional assertion of mainstream Democratic party discipline. And from this fact have flowed such procedural innovations as the subcommittee bill of rights, the Speaker's right to appoint members of the Rules Committee, and the shaking if not toppling of the House seniority system.

3. *Bad vibrations between Congress and the presidency.* A large number of changes in the party system affecting presidential behavior have had an adverse impact on presidential-congressional relations, impelling Congress to reduce its dependence upon the executive branch as a source of public policy information and analysis. And so Congress has hired its own staff and upgraded the professional capabilities of the staff it already had. Internal competition among power centers on Capitol Hill has hastened the pace of this trend.

The effect has been to give congressmen independent access to the sort of knowledge that they used to get from the departments, and a capacity to make their own estimates, projections, and assumptions about the impact of policy.[41] It has also brought to Capitol Hill the sort of staff person whose career is tied less to the congressional patron than was common heretofore, and more to the trans-congressional issue-network. The natural tides of the careers of these professionals have done much to remove the distinctiveness of congressional staff service and to bring congressional perspectives into the mainstream of the Washington community.

[40] Nelson W. Polsby, "An Emerging Republican Majority?" *The Public Interest*, vol. 17 (Fall 1969), pp. 119-126.

[41] For an analysis of the situation in 1970, just before these changes began to accelerate, see Nelson W. Polsby, "Strengthening Congress in National Policy Making," in Polsby, ed., *Congressional Behavior*, pp. 3-13.

Thus three big changes in American political life that have reached everywhere have had a notable impact on Congress: the growth of television as a news medium, the nationalization of politics, and the increase in tension between the president and other elements of the national political system.

Conclusion

Over a twenty- or thirty-year span, what are the major changes that have overtaken the Washington community? Surely three are most important: desegregation, a precondition for civic decency; home rule, which gave the community a local political identity; and the continued, unabated growth of the community, due to the growth of federal government and its satellites in the private sector. Washington itself has emerged from its isolation to mirror other cities in other parts of the country—just as Congress has become less isolated within Washington.

I do not know whether these changes are as significant as those witnessed by the previous generation. In 1960, Representative Joe Martin wrote of his early years in Congress:

> Of course there was no air conditioning. Summers seemed even hotter in Washington than they do now. Many of the committee rooms were ill-ventilated, and members would sometimes come to the verge of fainting during long hearings. The installation of air conditioning in the 1930's did more, I believe, than cool the Capitol: it prolonged the sessions. The members were no longer in such a hurry to flee Washington in July. The southerners especially had no place else to go that was half as comfortable.[42]

By 1980, virtually all of middle-class Washington, public and private, was air-conditioned. The excellent local transit system had once been looted of its capital reserves by a private sector buccaneer and the husk in due course had been dropped in the government's lap. Suburbs had multiplied and multiplied again, and freeways, beltways, and subways had arrived, some of them comically overbuilt. Parking became difficult, then impossible, to find downtown and land values began to jump. Vestiges of the medium-sized, tree-clad, rather comfortable southern town of the 1950s remained amid the pretentious workaholic buzz, but the astute visitor had to know where to look.

[42] Joseph Martin as told to Robert J. Donovan, *My First Fifty Years in Politics* (N.Y.: McGraw-Hill, 1960), p. 49.

Because of the way the city had spread out, and because of its dependence on air conditioning, an energy crisis would be felt in the Washington community. But the indexing of government pensions and the perceived need for more government during times of economic and other crises made Washington, by and large, an economically countercyclical city, mostly cushioned against the economic shocks that could visit a manufacturing town. This residual atypicality, and the city's dependence upon the national government, made it possible, despite the links that so many Washingtonians maintained with their roots elsewhere, for frustrated politicians to complain that Washington was an island. But the truth is, as communications technology, mass marketing, social mobility, internal migration, and international networks in the distribution of supplies knit us all together, no American city—not even Miami Beach, which *is* an island—is an island.

2

Elections and Change in Congress

Thomas E. Mann

Some years ago H. Douglas Price observed that "the conditions of entry into a legislative body and of survival through successive terms are a major factor in the behaviour of aspirants and incumbents. . . . An understanding of the risks of the electoral arena is vital for an understanding of Congress."[1] Price is surely correct: no one can fully understand Congress without taking the measure of the manner in which senators and representatives are nominated, elected, and ultimately replaced. By the same token, if Congress has changed in the past twenty years, its electoral environment must have something to tell us about how and why. That, at any rate, is the assumption behind this chapter, which examines the ways in which congressional elections shape the internal ·character of Congress.

First, the electoral strength of the two major parties determines the party balance within Congress. A Congress in which one party enjoys uninterrupted control is likely to develop a set of rules and a culture quite different from a Congress in which control shifts frequently between the two major parties. Moreover, a dramatic shift in party strength in Congress can transform the policy agenda and heighten partisan differences within Congress.[2]

NOTE: Parts of this chapter were adapted from my presentation "Changes in the External Environment of Congress: Implications for Presidential Leadership," made at a conference on The Congress and the Presidency, White Burkett Miller Center of Public Affairs, University of Virginia, January 24-25, 1980. I am indebted to my coeditor, Norman Ornstein, for his very constructive comments on an earlier draft of this chapter.

[1] H. Douglas Price, "The Electoral Arena," in David B. Truman, ed., *The Congress and America's Future*, 2d ed. (Englewood Cliffs: Prentice-Hall, Inc., 1973), pp. 39-62.

[2] See, for example, Walter Dean Burnham, *Critical Elections and the Mainsprings of American Politics* (New York: W. W. Norton and Co., Inc., 1970), and Barbara Sinclair, "Party Realignment and the Transformation of the Political Agenda: The House of Representatives, 1925-1938," *American Political Science Review*, vol. 71 (September 1977), pp. 940-953.

Second, the amount and source of membership turnover has an important bearing on the internal structure of Congress. The seniority system grew up as the nineteenth-century pattern of high membership turnover and short congressional careers gave way early in this century to low turnover and long careers.[3] Similarly, the surge in turnover during the 1970s altered the balance of power between junior and senior members enough to prompt a new revision of the system of allocating positions of authority. In a narrower sense, turnover influences internal structure and policy by altering the composition of committees and congressional leadership.

Third, what type of people are recruited to the House or Senate determines what legislative styles will predominate in each chamber. And the personalities and outlook of new members can themselves be influenced by local nomination systems and the issues or concerns that sparked a desire to run for office in the first place.

Fourth, the structure of competition in Senate and House elections *and* its underlying bases have numerous direct and indirect effects on Congress. Turnover and party balance, for example, are determined partly by the competitiveness of districts and states. Thus, when the distribution of partisan voters across districts and states is uneven, some seats are safe for one party or the other, thereby reducing turnover and lengthening the congressional career.[4] But seats may also be made safe by the actions of individual incumbents running apart from their party—with very different consequences for Congress.

This is related to a fifth connection between elections and the shape of Congress: elections register the relative importance of national and local forces. If changes in district and state returns from one election to the next are set in motion by national candidates or issues, senators and representatives will tend to identify their own electoral fate with their party's—all the more when large numbers of candidates ride to Congress on the coattails of their party's presidential candidate. When changes are locally based, it becomes more difficult to focus attention within Congress on a national agenda.

Finally, the nature of campaigning itself conditions the orientations of members and the organization of Congress. For example, the pervasiveness of party and the aversion to personal promotion in

[3] Nelson W. Polsby, Miriam Gallaher, and Barry Spencer Rundquist, "The Growth of the Seniority System in the U.S. House of Representatives," *American Political Science Review*, vol. 63 (September 1969), pp. 787-807.

[4] The realignment around the election of 1896 made a number of seats safe for one party or the other. See H. Douglas Price, "The Congressional Career—Then and Now," in Nelson W. Polsby, ed., *Congressional Behavior* (New York: Random House, 1971), pp. 14-27.

nineteenth-century congressional campaigns heightened the salience of party within Congress.[5] The candidate-centered campaigns of the 1970s reinforce a very different set of congressional norms.

My intention in this chapter is to explore the most important developments in each of these aspects of congressional elections since the 1950s, to speculate on how they have shaped the internal structure of Congress, and to examine the 1980 election for signs of additional change during the decade of the 1980s.

Party Strength in Congress

Prior to the 1980 elections, Democratic dominance of the Senate and House appeared to be one of the few near permanent features of American politics. The Democrats organized every Congress between 1955 and 1980, and after the 1956 election their margin never fell below 56 percent of the seats in either chamber. Of course, the Democratic hegemony in Congress actually began decades earlier with the New Deal realignment; Republicans managed to wrest control from the Democrats in only two of the twenty-four Congresses leading up to the 1980 elections.

Many factors contributed to the Democrats' dominance, the most important of which was the distribution of party loyalties among the voters. Through most of this period more than twice as many citizens identified themselves as Democrats than as Republicans, and the vast majority of votes cast for senators and representatives were consistent with party identification.

Democrats in the House also benefited from malapportionment, which, quite apart from any partisan gerrymandering in their favor, typically rewards the majority party in single-member-district electoral systems with a higher percentage of seats than of votes: since 1958 the Democratic "majority party bonus" has averaged over seven percentage points.[6]

As the majority party in Congress, the Democrats have been in a position to profit most from the electoral advantages of incumbency. For most of this century, House and Senate incumbents seeking reelection have been highly successful; even before the 1960s, when

[5] Les Benedict, "The Electorate and Congressional Voting Behavior in the 19th Century" (Paper presented at the Conference on Congress, sponsored by Project '87, February 1-4, 1981, Washington, D.C.).

[6] John F. Bibby, Thomas E. Mann, and Norman J. Ornstein, *Vital Statistics on Congress, 1980* (Washington, D.C.: American Enterprise Institute, 1980), pp. 6-7.

the resources available to incumbents increased so dramatically, re-election rates for the House seldom dropped beneath 90 percent. (The reelection rate of Senate incumbents has been much more variable and generally lower.) Clearly the incumbency advantage works to keep the majority party in the majority.

Finally, one cannot overstate the importance of particular elections for long-term party control. In 1958 and 1974, both midterm elections during the second term of Republican administrations, the Democrats registered impressive gains that went unanswered by the Republicans in the subsequent elections. The only big Republican gains during this period came in 1966, but they had little long-term impact since they merely returned the Republicans to their standing before the Democratic landslide of 1964. Thus, it is clear in retrospect that the Eisenhower recession of 1958 and the political and economic troubles of the Nixon/Ford administrations in 1974 were critical, contingent factors in the continued Democratic control of the Congress.

While the Democrats remained firmly in control of both houses throughout this period, the regional composition of the party changed in one important respect. During the 1950s the Democratic party in the Senate and House was dominated by the Deep South, which had almost a majority of the party's seats in both chambers and an even larger share of the committee chairmanships. Beginning with the election of 1958 and continuing during the 1960s, the combination of resurgent Democratic strength in the North and Republican inroads in the South reduced the southern share of the Democratic seats to less than a third, although the party's hold on committee chairmanships remained firm.[7] Changes in the rules for selecting House chairmen in 1971 and the dramatic ouster of three southern chairmen in 1974 were made possible by the regional shift within the Democratic party away from the South.

It is impossible to know whether the seniority system would have come under attack much earlier had the Republicans been in the majority during this period, but there is some historical evidence that the Republicans handle their internal party business very differently from the Democrats. In his study of House leadership change, Garrison Nelson found the Democratic House organization to be "hierarchically arranged in a tightly controlled system which is designed to minimize internal conflict," while the House Republicans were "relatively egalitarian in their leadership succession system, with

[7] Ibid., p. 63.

open competition and a dominant role for the membership."[8] This difference, Nelson insists, distinguishes Democrats from Republicans, not majority from minority, and it appears to reflect a difference in the parties' composition, the Democratic party being the more heterogeneous. Had the Republicans controlled the House during the 1950s and 1960s, the move toward more open, egalitarian, and competitive procedures and norms that swept through Congress during the 1970s might have developed a good deal earlier.

Long-term Democratic strength in the House and Senate had other effects as well. Large, relatively stable majorities tend to become divided and self-centered; they come to take for granted the rewards of majority status and lose sight of the importance of the party's collective performance. Stable majority parties also show relatively little concern for the resources and status of the minority, since they never expect to be in the minority themselves. Minority parties, on the other hand, with their seemingly permanent status, can easily become demoralized and passive, only intermittently offering policy alternatives for voter consumption. All of these tendencies, reinforced by a party system whose critical issues have faded, can be observed to one degree or another in the Congress of the last twenty-five years.

Turnover

Quite apart from determining the number of seats held by each party, elections shape the internal politics of Congress by setting the overall level of membership stability. As Price argued, a low degree of turnover is highly compatible with the seniority system: most members can reasonably assume that they will be around to reap the harvest of their seniority, and there is no large cadre of junior members to question the appropriateness or value of delayed gratification.[9] And while the changes in turnover in recent decades pale in significance beside some in the nineteenth century, they have had considerable political importance.

In the House throughout the 1950s and 1960s, there was a steady increase in the proportion of "careerists," senior members serving ten or more terms, while the proportion of junior members intermittently declined. The 92nd Congress (1971–1972) was the peak of both these trends—the twenty-year club had reached 20 percent of the House

[8] Garrison Nelson, "Partisan Patterns of House Leadership Change, 1789-1977," *American Political Science Review*, vol. 71 (September 1977), p. 939.
[9] Price, "The Congressional Career."

membership, while the proportion who had served six years or fewer had fallen to 34 percent. Both trends were reversed during the 1970s. In the 96th Congress (1979–1980), junior members made up 50 percent of the House: the careerists, only 13 percent. A 1.7-to-1 ratio of juniors to seniors in 1971 had changed to a near 4-to-1 ratio in only eight years.[10]

The pattern of service in the Senate was different in several respects. The increase in the proportion of senior senators began after the 1958 election and continued for most of the 1960s and 1970s. Moreover, junior members were more numerous in the Senate than in the House during the 1950s. But, as in the House, the trend has been reversed: the number of junior senators grew from a low of twenty-seven in 1971 to a post–World War II high of forty-eight in 1979.

As noteworthy as the amount of turnover is its source, particularly the difference between the House and Senate. In recent elections voluntary retirement has become the largest source of turnover in the House, just the opposite of the pattern that existed before the mid-1960s. The number of retirements exceeded the number of defeats only once in the eleven elections between 1946 and 1966; since then, there have been more retirements than defeats in five out of seven elections. The reasons for the increase in retirements since 1972 are diverse: the job is much tougher, the life is less pleasant, the pace is excruciating, the rewards for longevity are reduced, and the financial incentives to leave are greater, particularly since retirement benefits have been sweetened and congressional salaries have failed to keep pace with inflation. By contrast, most senators continue to leave Washington involuntarily; the increase in turnover in the Senate beginning in 1976 is due partly to the number of retirements but mostly to primary and general election defeats.

The relative stability of the membership in the House during the 1950s and 1960s reinforced the existing rules and norms. The first stirrings of reform followed the large influx of northern Democrats in the 1958 elections, but sixteen years passed before an even larger freshman class supplemented the junior ranks to the point where sufficient pressure was generated to weaken committee chairmen and equalize resources within the House. The proportionately larger Democratic gains in the Senate as a result of the 1958 election, on the other hand, led to a somewhat more rapid change in the internal arrangements of the Senate. By the late 1970s, the junior cast of both chambers constituted a bulwark against any effort to recentralize power within the parties or the committees.

[10] Bibby, Mann, and Ornstein, *Vital Statistics on Congress*, p. 41.

Recruitment

The amount of membership turnover is significant, but equally important is the character of those who enter the House and Senate. The individuals recruited to the Congress reflect the local political milieus in which they are nominated. Nelson Polsby has argued that as recently as the 1950s, more than half of all congressmen came from districts with significant party organizations, be they large urban machines, Democratic courthouse rings, or their Republican counterparts in the Northeast and Midwest.[11] The contrast in legislative style between these party-initiated members (or party regulars) and the self-starters was striking, as Leo Snowiss demonstrated in his study of Chicago-area congressmen.[12] Party regulars were likely to be followers and compromisers, while the self-starters tended to be issue-oriented and publicity-conscious. Over the last two decades, the proportion of members elected from districts with some substantial party presence in the nominating process has probably declined to a third or less, which means that the mix in Congress has been altered to include more new-style members with very individualistic perspectives on their careers.

While this is a significant development, it is very clearly not an abrupt break with the past. Since the adoption of the direct primary in the early part of this century, many congressional candidates have been self-starters, putting together their own political organizations in seeking the nomination and succeeding with relatively little help or even downright opposition from local party officials. As Mayhew wrote, "The important point here is that a Congressman can—indeed must—build a power base that is substantially independent of party."[13] To be sure, nomination politics were somewhat more structured in the past, when a limited number of major interests were involved in picking the "right" candidate. The growing political mobilization of diverse groups in recent years and the further atrophy of local party organizations have created many more opportunities for potential candidates operating outside those major interests. And changes in the conduct of campaigns, especially in the use of the media, have worked in the same direction. Different types of indi-

[11] The argument in this paragraph was first made by Nelson W. Polsby at a conference on The Congress and the Presidency, White Burkett Miller Center for Public Affairs, University of Virginia, January 24-25, 1980.

[12] Leo M. Snowiss, "Congressional Recruitment and Representation," *American Political Science Review*, vol. 60 (September 1966), pp. 627-639.

[13] David R. Mayhew, *Congress: The Electoral Connection* (New Haven: Yale University Press, 1974), p. 26.

viduals are attracted to the prospect of being candidates in these more fluid situations, and they may behave differently in office than those recruited in more structured situations.

While this subtle though important change has taken place in the politics of nomination, the politics of renomination has changed very little since V. O. Key examined congressional primaries several decades ago. Between 1956 and 1974 only 20.2 percent of all House primaries with Republican incumbents and 36.8 percent of House primaries with Democratic incumbents were even contested.[14] The percentage of incumbents facing serious primary challengers is much lower; the number who actually lose (typically eight or fewer in the House, three or fewer in the Senate) has been consistently small over the last several decades. This does not mean that members of Congress are free from worry about primaries. As Mayhew argues, congressmen are successful precisely because they worry about elections—primary and general—and take action continuously to increase their probability of success.[15] Moreover, the political importance of primary defeats often outweighs their number. For example, twelve House committee chairmen were defeated in primary elections between 1966 and 1978; four Senate committee chairmen lost their primaries between 1966 and 1974.

In summary, local politics and individual initiative continue to dominate congressional nominations. The direct primary severely limits the ability of party organizations to control the selection of congressional candidates; and as Mayhew reminds us, even where parties are still strong enough to control congressional primaries, they are locally rather than nationally oriented. The important change that has taken place, then, is not that strong parties have suddenly become weak, but that the conditions favoring individualistic politicians have become even more prevalent now than in the past.

What appears to have happened in the Congress of the 1950s and earlier is that those who were nominated in areas with a significant party presence stayed in Congress longer than the others. Their seats were often in safe one-party districts, and they felt comfortable moving slowly up the seniority ladder. Hence, the typical member of Congress during the period resembled the party regular described by Snowiss. He was relatively nonideological, he tended

---

[14] Harvey L. Schantz, "Contested and Uncontested Legislative Primaries: Nominations for the U.S. House" (Paper presented at the Annual Meeting of the Southern Political Science Association, Gatlinburg, Tennessee, November 1-3, 1979).

[15] Mayhew, *Congress.*

to avoid conflict and confrontation, and he was content to defer to committee and party leaders on matters of strategy and substance as long as the interests of his constituency were not abrogated.

The large Democratic class of 1958 began to change the mix of members in Congress, especially in the Senate, where a sizable bloc of liberals arrived with definite ideas about how they wanted to see public policy change. The Johnson landslide of 1964, which swept into office a number of new Democrats in traditionally Republican districts, continued the process of bringing new types of individuals into the Congress. Perhaps the most significant development during the 1960s was the change in the recruitment pool stimulated by the civil rights movement and the war in Vietnam. People whose formative political experience had been participating in mass demonstrations obviously had perspectives on the job of a congressman very different from those of people who had made their way into politics by more conventional routes. During the late 1960s and 1970s, the dominant values brought to the Congress by these waves of new members included a distrust of authority and of existing institutional arrangements and a belief that government must be made more open and participatory. This new ethic combined with the increasingly junior cast of the membership to generate pressure for spreading the action well beyond a handful of committee and elected leaders. The results of that pressure for the internal structure of Congress are chronicled in the other chapters in this book.

The Structure of Competition

The basic pattern of competition in congressional elections in recent decades was set in the New Deal realignment, which, in addition to improving the fortunes of Democratic candidates across the board, left in its wake a majority of districts relatively safe for one party or another, with a smaller though sizable bloc of districts more evenly divided between the parties. Charles Jones found that during the 1930s, 1940s, and 1950s, between 70 and 80 percent of all congressional districts were represented by the same party for five consecutive elections.[16] Dramatic changes in party strength were possible, but they seldom disturbed the vast majority of districts. The New Deal realignment produced a similar pattern in Senate elections, although the greater diversity of states meant that a higher percentage of Senate seats were competitive between the parties.

[16] Charles O. Jones, "The Role of the Campaign in Congressional Politics," in M. Kent Jennings and L. Harmon Zeigler, eds., *The Electoral Process* (Englewood Cliffs: Prentice-Hall, Inc., 1966), pp. 21-41.

The consequences of these patterns of competition were a relatively high reelection rate for House incumbents and a significantly lower success rate for senators. In the seventeen elections between 1946 and 1978, 91 percent of House incumbents who sought another term were successful, while the success rate for incumbent senators was only 68 percent. Senators were more successful than representatives only once during this period—in 1960.[17]

But these averages computed for the entire post–World War II period obscure important changes. While House incumbents have always had a high degree of success in seeking reelection, the margins of their victory increased significantly beginning in the mid-1960s. The number of districts in the competitive zone—where the parties were relatively even and the outcome was vulnerable to strong national tides and to local challengers—declined markedly.[18] About three-fourths of all House incumbents now win with at least 60 percent of the major party vote, an increase over the past two decades of ten to fifteen percentage points. Only a fourth of all incumbents seeking reelection are now sufficiently pressed by their challengers to fall into our loosely defined competitive zone.[19] This "vanishing marginals" phenomenon, as David Mayhew called it, was concentrated in districts with relatively new incumbents running. Open seats remained as competitive as before, and veteran congressmen amassed no special advantage beyond the partisan edge in their districts.[20]

During this period party-line voting declined markedly in House elections, and incumbents became increasingly successful in attracting support from party defectors. The evidence strongly suggests that this decline in party-line voting resulted from the use the new-style candidates made of the considerable resources of incumbency to present themselves in a highly favorable light to their constituents. By the end of the 1970s, it was clear that House incumbents enjoyed an enormous advantage in visibility and popularity over their challengers. The automatic party vote for the challenger had been greatly di-

---

[17] Christopher Buchanan, "Senators Face Tough Re-election Odds," *Congressional Quarterly, Weekly Report*, April 5, 1980, pp. 905-909.

[18] David R. Mayhew, "Congressional Elections: The Case of the Vanishing Marginals," *Policy*, vol. 6 (Spring 1974), pp. 295-317.

[19] Albert Cover and David Mayhew, "Congressional Dynamics and the Decline of Competitive Congressional Elections" in Lawrence C. Dodd and Bruce I. Oppenheimer, *Congress Reconsidered* (New York: Praeger, 1977), pp. 59-72.

[20] Richard Born, "Generational Replacement and the Growth of Incumbent Reelection Margins," *American Political Science Review*, vol. 73 (September 1979), pp. 811-817.

minished, leaving incumbents in a position to extend their victory margin well beyond their natural partisan base.[21]

The contrast with the Senate could not be greater. Voting in Senate elections also became increasingly unhinged from party; the number of states that split their Senate delegation between the two parties increased from fourteen in 1959 to twenty-six in 1979. But starting in 1976 it worked increasingly to the disadvantage of Senate incumbents. The gap in reelection rates between senators and representatives grew to over thirty percentage points, and the percentage of senators seeking reelection who won big—with 60 percent or more of the vote—declined to about half of the comparable figure in the House.

These differences in the competitiveness of House and Senate elections are due in large part to differences in the seriousness of the challenge waged by the opposition party. Evidence from campaign expenditure reports supports the view that no challenge of any consequence is mounted in most House races with incumbents running. For example, in 1978, the mean expenditure by challengers who won less than 40 percent of the vote was $32,564, an insignificant sum compared with the $200,000 budgets of winning challengers and candidates in open seats. In the typical House district, the challenge to an incumbent is so inconsequential that few voters even recognize the challenging candidate, and the largely favorable image of the incumbent prevails. By contrast, few Senate challenges—typically less than 30 percent—are low budget affairs.[22] Senate incumbents are only slightly less popular than House incumbents; they are more vulnerable primarily because they usually face challengers who are widely recognized by the voters.

But why do senators attract consistently more formidable opposition than representatives? Part of the explanation no doubt rests with inherent political differences between states and congressional districts. States are generally more heterogeneous in their economic and social structure and therefore more likely to contain opposing groups which constitute the base for challenges. Partly as a result of this diversity, Senate challengers are better able to raise the large sums of money necessary to mount a serious campaign; they also attract a good deal of attention from the press, giving them much more free media time than is available to House challengers. In addition, the prestige of the Senate—and the six-year term—attracts a

21 Thomas E. Mann and Raymond E. Wolfinger, "Candidates and Parties in Congressional Elections," *American Political Science Review*, vol. 74 (September 1980), pp. 617-632.
22 Ibid., p. 627.

higher caliber of candidate, including a number of House members who have already achieved a substantial public following.

There is something of a self-fulfilling prophecy here. House incumbents are increasingly strong at the polls because potentially strong opponents, perceiving that strength, do not run, thus ensuring a wide margin of victory. In the Senate, the pattern is just the reverse. The recent success of many challengers in defeating incumbents or at least in reducing their margins of victory has made all senators appear potentially vulnerable, which in turn has encouraged more vigorous opposition, making the appearance a reality.[23]

The consequences of the changes in House elections are not as obvious as might first appear. The decline in competitiveness and increase in the advantage of incumbency have not appreciably altered the reelection rates of House incumbents, which in the absence of strong national tides have usually been well above 90 percent. The 1974 election demonstrated that sizable partisan swings are still possible, albeit not of the magnitude of the sweeping seat changes during the 1930s and 1940s. More important, House incumbents do not perceive themselves as more electorally secure or more independent of their constituencies. Their advantage is seen as soft, based not upon enduring party loyalties but rather on voter evaluations that are thin and highly personalized. Feelings can sour, opposition groups in the district can mobilize, serious challengers can surface, suddenly rendering a safe incumbent vulnerable. A good example was Representative Lionel VanDeerlin (Democrat, California), who, after a series of easy reelections, dropped over twenty percentage points in the 1980 returns and was defeated.

Most House incumbents now feel obliged to tend to their districts in a very active way, emphasizing constituent service and projects of local interest, traveling home more often, deploying staff in district offices, cultivating their "home style."[24] Ironically, wider victory margins have led to an increase, not a decrease, in the amount of time incumbents spend mending their political fences back home.

The same uncertainty and concern about reelection is also present among senators, but for more obvious reasons. The immediate effects of increased competition in the Senate have been to accelerate the rate

---

[23] Gary C. Jacobson, "Congressional Campaign Finance and the Revival of the Republican Party" (Paper prepared for delivery at the Thomas P. O'Neill Symposium on the United States Congress, Boston College, January 29-31, 1981), p. 4, and Thomas E. Mann and Norman J. Ornstein, "1980: A Republican Revival in Congress?" Public Opinion, vol. 3 (October/November 1980), pp. 16-17.

[24] Richard F. Fenno, Jr., Home Style: House Members in Their Districts (Boston: Little, Brown, 1978).

of membership turnover and to improve the fortunes of the Republican party. How senators adapt in the long run to this more treacherous electoral environment remains to be seen. Democrats put on the defensive ideologically may try to behave more like representatives, emphasizing constituent concerns and local issues. The ignominious defeat of prominent liberals on the Senate Foreign Relations Committee in recent years, including Dick Clark, Frank Church, Clifford Case, and Jacob Javits, gives pause to those who might aspire to take the lead on controversial national issues.

National versus Local Forces

As Nelson Polsby observed in the last chapter, many forces in society have led to a nationalization of politics; but in congressional elections the balance of national and local forces has shifted in the opposite direction. The amount of local variation in House elections tripled between 1958 and 1978, reflecting the fact that more and more of the changes in district returns from one election to the next are specific to the local candidates, issues, and events, not to what is happening at the national level.[25]

Coupled with this increasing localization has been a decline in the extent to which presidents and legislators have shared electoral fates. Much of the political dynamism in our system has come from popular presidential candidates sweeping into office with them many new congressmen who (at least for a year) give them critical support on their major policy proposals. In recent years, however, the saliency of local races has further separated presidential and congressional electorates, making this much less likely to happen. The contrast between LBJ's Democratic party victory in 1964 and Richard Nixon's personal triumph in 1972 is striking.

This is not to argue that national political forces have no influence on congressional races—the Republican losses in the 1974 election had much to do with Watergate, the Nixon pardon, and the recession. National conditions shape the overall results—which party gains and by how much—but they are of secondary importance in local races, where the mix of candidates and campaigns influences many more votes.

Of course, the importance attached to national factors depends largely on what one wishes to explain. Edward Tufte, being primarily interested in shifts in the national strength of the two parties, found

---

[25] Thomas E. Mann, *Unsafe at Any Margin: Interpreting Congressional Elections* (Washington, D.C.: American Enterprise Institute, 1978), chap. 5.

that the state of the economy and the popularity of the president were very powerful predictors of the size of the midterm loss of House seats by the president's party,[26] although other scholars have searched in vain for traces of the economically rational voter. Jacobson and Kernell provide a partial explanation for this seeming contradiction: national economic and political conditions shape the climate in which potential candidates decide whether to run and donors decide whether to give. When times are bad, the president's party has a difficult time getting its ablest candidates to run and its wealthiest contributors to give, thereby weakening its appeal at the local level, where votes are decided.[27]

From the perspective of the candidates, however, national forces are of secondary importance. Changes in state and district returns are largely a function of the local mix of personalities, issues, and events. Incumbents have more reason to fear an attractive, well-financed challenger than an unpopular president or a deteriorating economy. And while, nationwide, the emergence of candidates is conditioned by the national climate, in most districts and states local considerations remain dominant in candidate recruitment.

The localization of political forces provides an additional electoral base for the increasingly individualized behavior within the House. On the one hand, even a very popular presidential candidate can enter office without a surge in his party's strength in Congress sufficient to provide a working majority, making it much more difficult to "form a government" in the parliamentary sense. On the other hand, the attention of returning members, including the president's fellow partisans, is more easily diverted from a national agenda, both because the message from the public is obscured by the unevenness of the vote and because the incentives in the electoral arena pull his attention back home. The fact that other changes inside Congress have increased their workload on national issues makes this a source of increasing frustration to members. Some decide that the only way out of this bind is retirement.

Campaigns

Most House elections are effectively over before the onset of the fall campaign, since in most districts a decision will have already been made not to wage a serious challenge. The same is true in a much

[26] Edward Tufte, *Political Control of the Economy* (Princeton: Princeton University Press, 1978).

[27] Gary C. Jacobson and Samuel Kernell, *Strategy and Choice in Congressional Elections* (New Haven: Yale University Press, forthcoming).

45

smaller percentage of Senate races. Opposition may be weak or nonexistent for any number of reasons: one-party domination of the district or state, the popularity of the incumbent, the unavailability of resources with which to wage a challenge, an unfavorable national political climate for the opposition party, and so on. In these districts and states, the critical political behavior to explain is neither the campaign nor the attitudes and preferences of voters; instead it is the failure of potentially strong candidates to emerge as serious contenders.

Campaigns are therefore important in two major respects: first, they are an important factor in determining the outcome in races with two major candidates, and, second, the conditions of modern campaigning may influence significantly the calculations of potential candidates. Recent developments in congressional campaigns are relevant to both. These developments include a rapid escalation of the cost of campaigning, an increasing emphasis on the media, greater use of professional consultants, a further personalization of the campaign organization, and more resourceful and active year-round campaigning by incumbents. Congressional campaigns of the 1970s differed from campaigns of the 1950s not so much in kind as in degree. In recent decades few congressional campaigns have come anywhere close to the nineteenth-century pattern of entirely party-based and partisan campaigns.[28]

While prior to the 1970s reliable figures on expenditures were not made available, there is no question that congressional campaigns are considerably more expensive now than in the past. Between 1972 and 1978 the total amount raised for campaigns increased 137 percent for the House and 183 percent for the Senate, both much higher than the rate of inflation.[29] By 1978 prospective House candidates were advised that a serious run for office required a minimum budget of $200,000. The comparable figure two decades earlier was closer to $25,000. And while budgets vary widely in Senate elections, most successful challengers in 1978 spent over $1 million.

The increased cost of campaigning combined with the restrictions imposed by federal legislation have dramatically altered the way in which funds are raised. National political action committees, direct mail solicitation, and candidates' personal contributions have all become more important, while the role of large contributors and parties has diminished. More money is now being raised outside congressional

[28] Benedict, "The Electorate and Congressional Voting Behavior in the 19th Century."

[29] Bibby, Mann, and Ornstein, *Vital Statistics on Congress*, p. 21.

districts and states, and contributions by national groups are playing an increasingly important role in legitimizing local candidates. Paradoxically, national resources fuel a localization of political forces.

As Michael Robinson documents in the next chapter, congressional candidates are relying more upon the media, particularly television, radio, and direct mail, than they used to. Incumbents do so in their official capacity—the in-house media capacity of Congress is well suited for continuous campaigning. The structure of the media market in some districts discourages reliance on television in campaigns, but in these cases highly sophisticated direct mail techniques are available. Media advertising can be very expensive but also essential for challengers striving to become known to voters in their districts or states.

This increasing utilization of the media in congressional campaigns obviously does not escape the notice of those considering whether to run; the effect, as Robinson shows at some length, is to encourage those whose personal style is compatible with a highly charged media existence and to discourage those whose orientation to politics is very different.

Heavy reliance on the media also introduces a great deal of uncertainty into congressional elections for threatened incumbents. With the voters' attitudes and preferences less anchored to party loyalties, new information may sharply alter a candidate's public standing. While little hard evidence on the effects of political advertising exists, candidates increasingly believe that negative advertising can have a decisive impact on their elections and, more important, they are acting upon that belief, in both Senate and House races.

Sophisticated media campaigns require technical expertise, and few cottage industries have flourished in recent years like that of campaign consultancy. The use of outside consultants—for media, polling, targeting, fundraising, and campaign management—has increased dramatically in congressional campaigns, accounting for much of the rise in costs. As Larry Sabato observes, "Political consultants and the new campaign technology may well be producing a whole generation of office-holders far more skilled in the art of running for office than in the art of governing."[30]

As political party organizations have weakened, congressional candidates have substituted their own personal organizations, often staffed with large numbers of volunteers. Even in areas where the party maintains some significant organizational presence, candidate

[30] Larry Sabato, *Political Consultants and American Democracy* (New York: Basic Books, forthcoming).

organizations often take on a very separate existence. This was true in the 1950s; it was even more the case in the 1970s. Moreover, in recent years more and more groups with a Washington legislative agenda have developed grass-roots organizations that can be mobilized for or against House and Senate candidates. One consequence of these and other developments in congressional campaigns is that the substance of the campaign as presented to the voters revolves around the candidate, not the party.

Their continuous campaigning makes incumbents better able to discourage potentially strong challengers and their contributors. While constant politicking is certainly not new to the Congress, in recent years members of Congress (especially representatives) have become better equipped and more resourceful in devising ways of appearing before their constituents that stress their personal concern for and responsiveness to their constituents—town meetings, work days, mobile offices, and large district staffs are especially useful in this regard. In addition, members constantly communicate with their constituents through the mail, in newspapers, and on radio and television; the quantity of these communications has increased dramatically since the 1950s.[31]

These "home styles" differ among members depending upon their seniority and personal predilections and upon the nature of their constituencies.[32] The growing vulnerability of more senior representatives in recent elections may be due in part to their failure to use the resources of incumbency to keep in close touch with the folks back home. Part of the problem experienced by these more senior representatives is similar to that of senators—and part is beyond their control. The effectiveness of continuous campaigning by incumbents is diluted when voters back home have alternative sources of information about those incumbents. Senators and, to a lesser extent, senior representatives, because they are newsworthy nationally, are less able than junior representatives to control the flow of communications to their constituents. The most visible politicians—presidents and senators—are also the most electorally vulnerable. Incumbency is an advantage primarily in settings where information is scarce and controlled.

The rigors of modern campaigning reinforce the individualistic perspectives stimulated by other aspects of the electoral arena. Now, even more than in the past, congressmen feel that their electoral fates

[31] Albert D. Cover, "Contacting Congressional Constituents: Some Patterns of Perquisite Use," *American Journal of Political Science*, vol. 24 (February 1980), pp. 125-135.

[32] Fenno, *Home Style*.

are decided in their states and districts. Members worry about adverse national conditions, particularly when their party controls the presidency, but they realize that they cannot do much about them. The clearest way to cut their losses is not to try to make the president look better or the economy improve—their actions are deemed too marginal to make a difference—but instead to concentrate on their own personal reputations in their constituencies. And these reputations, they believe correctly, are largely independent of the performance of Congress as an institution.

In addition, members worry more about reelection than appears justified by objective measures of their electoral success. They have good reason to worry. Their investment—in personal energy, money, and career choice—is very high yet subject to sudden depreciation. Dramatic shifts in district returns are not uncommon, and members typically think in terms of a sequence of elections, not just the immediate one. Any sign of weakness is likely to attract more serious opposition next time, and the advantages of incumbency wane in the face of a well-known, well-financed opponent. The stories of those who lose are told and retold in the cloakrooms as members try to develop their own early warning systems. Senators have even more reason than representatives to learn the lessons of their fallen colleagues.

As a consequence, members invest considerable energy in seeking to forestall a strong challenge, by acting continuously to enhance their personal reputations and by coming to grips with the major interests that might underwrite such a challenge. The latter might mean writing off interests whose views are diametrically opposed from their own; or it might mean reaching an accommodation. In either case, members are pulled inevitably into conversation and dealings with community leaders and activists and with representatives of national groups on legislative matters that largely escape the attention of the rank-and-file voter.

The 1980 Elections

The 1980 elections departed in several important respects from patterns established in recent congressional elections. The shift of twelve seats to the Republicans in the Senate is very large by any standard and, more important, sufficient to return control to the GOP for the first time since 1954. The magnitude of the Republican presidential and congressional victories coupled with the first serious party effort in many years on behalf of the entire ticket and a relatively clear and consistent set of Republican issues and themes raises the possibility

49

that national forces and presidential coattails are alive and well, perhaps even that we are on the verge of a major political realignment. Finally, while the reelection rate of House incumbents in 1980 remained above 90 percent, many experienced Democratic legislators targeted for defeat by the Republican party or by other groups appeared vulnerable—and a good number actually lost—raising the prospect of increased competition in House elections.

In many respects the most interesting question is whether 1980 will prove to be like 1932, the last realigning election, or like 1952, when a popular Republican presidential candidate led his party to temporary ascendancy in the Congress. An initial reading of the returns reveals that many of the ingredients of a realigning election are missing. The size of the Republican victory beneath the presidential and senatorial levels was quite modest by realignment standards, leaving the party well short of majority status in the House, in the governorships, in the state legislatures, and in local governmental bodies. There is no sign that underlying party attachments shifted significantly to the Republicans in 1980. And finally, the Republicans failed to capture the support of the youngest cohort of voters, a group that has fueled the realignments of the past.

Whether or not it proves to have the makings of a realigning or critical election, 1980 certainly appeared to refute House Speaker Tip O'Neill's favorite aphorism that "all politics is local." The decisiveness of the results, the content of the campaign, the involvement of the national Republican party, all pointed to a national decision by voters that President Carter and his party had failed and that the Republicans—in the presidency and in Congress—deserved an opportunity to govern.

At one level, this argument is surely well taken. The Republicans' net gain—twelve seats in the Senate and thirty-three in the House—was not simply the result of adding and subtracting the outcomes of the hundreds of local contests. A national Republican tide washed across the states and congressional districts, leaving a mark on any number of Senate and House races. But at another level, the local character of congressional elections remained prominent in 1980. Liberal Democratic Senators Alan Cranston and John Glenn had no difficulty in 1980, having scared away any serious Republican challengers many months before November. Republican Senator Barry Goldwater, dean of the conservatives, on the other hand, saw his reputation in Arizona suffer to the point where he barely survived the Democratic challenge. In the House, a number of liberal Democrats, such as Morris Udall of Arizona, actually increased their 1978 margins while other Republicans saw their vote totals decline.

More generally, 1980 saw no reversal of the trend toward a localization of political forces that has been apparent in recent elections. In fact, the variance in swing across districts was actually greater in 1980 than it was in 1976 or 1978. Most voters still made their choice in terms of the local Senate and House candidates in 1980, not of the presidential contest or national issues.

But, as Jacobson and Kernell have argued, the mix of local candidates, resources, and issues is influenced by the national political milieu.[33] President Carter's low estate in 1979 created a mood in which potential Republican candidates were encouraged to compete for seats held by Democrats and in which potential donors—including corporate PACs—were willing to gamble more than usual on Republican challengers. Moreover, this advantage in candidate recruitment and campaign finance during 1979 and 1980 was strengthened by the efforts of the national Republican party organizations.[34]

Traditionally, the national party organizations have stayed clear of local contests for nominations, realizing they would have to live with whoever was elected. Yet in the last several years the national Republican party has lost its reticence in this regard—or at least temporarily overcome it. Under the combined leadership of Republican National Committee Chairman Bill Brock, National Republican Congressional Committee Chairman Guy Vander Jagt, and Republican Senatorial Campaign Committee Chairman John Heinz, the GOP has taken the lead in encouraging strong candidates to run, in providing financial and technical assistance to candidates, in developing a more attractive party image, and in planning a local campaign effort on behalf of state legislative candidates, who constitute the major recruitment pool for Congress. This has meant favoring certain candidates with national party endorsements and resources before their primary election, in order both to get the strongest possible Republican candidate and to give that candidate a head start in the general election campaign. These GOP activities, particularly the infusion of large sums of money into Senate campaigns, considerably strengthened the Republican ticket at the local level.

Finally, there is no sign that the underlying structure of competition in either the Senate or the House was altered appreciably by the 1980 elections. The gap in reelection votes between senators and representatives continued to grow. And only nine of the twenty-five senators (36 percent) running in November 1980 won 60 percent or more of the vote, exactly half the percentage of big winners in the House.

[33] Jacobson and Kernell, *Strategy and Choice.*
[34] Mann and Ornstein, "Republican Revival."

It is too early to say what the consequences for Congress of the 1980 elections will be. The Republican takeover of the Senate, the conservative gains in the House, and the widespread perception in Washington that the country has moved right will all have some effect on policy. But it is instructive to note that one of the first actions of the new Republican majority in the Senate was to increase the number of subcommittees and assignments. The rapid turnover of senators, especially of Republicans, will sustain interest in maintaining a highly decentralized institution.

Conclusion

In assessing the consequences of changes in congressional elections for the internal processes of Congress and for its role in the larger political system, it is easy to overemphasize recent developments at the expense of more stable elements that continue to determine the basic shape of the political process. The fact that the president and Congress have separate electoral bases, which virtually ensures a degree of institutional tension not seen in parliamentary systems, is rooted in the constitution, not in contemporary American history. American political parties, while unquestionably weaker today than in the past, have always been highly decentralized and factionalized, never strong in a European sense; and even when some of their local organizations were robust, this did not necessarily strengthen the hand of the president or improve the prospects for the national party platform.[35] As for turnover, while we may be impressed (and rightly so) by the high level it reached during the decade of the 1970s, the membership of the modern Congress is remarkably stable by nineteenth-century standards; the continuing desire of most senators and representatives to remain in office and to develop politically and personally rewarding legislative careers is terribly important for the internal shape of Congress and for its stature vis-à-vis the executive.[36]

The other danger in concentrating on recent changes in the electoral environment is to assume that trends set in motion during the past decade or so will continue predictably into the future. While in the 1970s we saw a seemingly permanent Democratic majority in the Congress, an enhanced advantage of incumbency in House elections, and a dominance of local candidates over national issues and parties in congressional elections, the 1980s, which began with the Republicans' capture of the Senate, may bring Republican control to both

[35] Mayhew, *Congress.*

[36] Nelson W. Polsby, "The Institutionalization of the U.S. House of Representatives," *American Political Science Review*, vol. 68 (March 1968), pp. 144-168.

houses, the rise of serious challengers in many House as well as Senate races, and heightened attention from individual voters to the record and the image of the two parties. If the decade leading up to the 1980 elections was a period in which the electoral experiences of members reinforced and exacerbated their most individualistic tendencies, the years ahead may see some modest movement back toward concern for collective goals and interests.

The forces fueling the individualistic tone of the present-day Congress remain strong. As far as elections are concerned, senators and representatives are in business for themselves. From the initial decision to seek the nomination and the rigors of the first primary and general election campaigns all the way to eventual retirement or defeat, they are political entrepreneurs in their states and districts, seizing opportunities, generating resources, responding to pressures, shaping the image that voters react to on election day. In this respect, the growing difference between Senate and House elections is more apparent than real: objectively speaking, representatives may be much less vulnerable than senators, but their subjective orientation to the electoral environment (the one that shapes their posture within Congress) is not unlike that of their colleagues in the other house. It is no surprise, then, that Senate and House members pursue their careers within the institution in a similar manner. While legislative styles differ—members are more or less active, ideologically motivated, solicitous of constituency interests, and inclined to defer to their colleagues—they all are likely to view themselves first and foremost as individuals, not as members of a party or as part of a president's team.

Against this backdrop, the 1980 elections showed some clear signs of a countervailing trend. The Republican presidential nominee went out of his way to lead his party ticket, articulating common themes and emphasizing the importance of electing a Republican Congress. The national Republican party organizations played an important role in the election of Republicans to the House and in the takeover of the Senate, financially, organizationally, substantively, and symbolically. Republicans perceive, rightly or wrongly, that they are on the verge of becoming the majority party in American politics and that the record of their party in office will largely determine whether or not they succeed. The Democrats, on the other hand, for the first time in a quarter century, find that their individual careers can be affected by the collective performance of their party. The shift of party control in the Senate, and the prospect of a similar shift in the House, because it means real changes in staff and authority, has focused the minds of Democrats as nothing else could. Much more than in recent years, Democrats in Congress are asking: How can our party help us, and what do we stand for as Democrats?

I do not want to suggest that 1980 will revolutionize the politics of congressional elections or the internal structure of Congress. Republicans face formidable problems in sustaining over the next several years the party cohesion they achieved in 1980. Their disagreements over policy are more likely to surface with their party in power, especially if the economy fails to respond to Republican remedies. Moreover, many of the changes in Congress set in motion under the Democrats—the democratizing reforms that have made the institution more active and independent—will be difficult to reverse, especially in light of the extraordinarily junior cast of the Republicans in both houses. And, of course, most forces for change in congressional elections will probably remain at the local level, where the mix of candidates, issues, and resources will be only partially influenced by party-related factors.

But Congress in the 1980s will respond to a variety of forces, including the norms and values of its newest members. The demands for individual participation that dominated the Congress, state legislatures, other national assemblies, the presidential nominating system, the universities, the family, and other institutions during the 1960s and 1970s may well diminish in the 1980s in the face of heightened concern about the capacity of our political institutions to govern effectively. This is one of the promising signs of change for the coming decade.

Perhaps even more promising is the possibility that a new set of ideas will emerge to give shape and substance to party competition. This revitalization would affect the context within which individuals are recruited to Congress and the climate in which they seek reelection. Above all, such a change in the political atmosphere could improve the conditions for governing, in spite of the fragmented character of our political institutions.

3

Three Faces of Congressional Media

Michael J. Robinson

The press is getting tougher. When I came here four years ago I could send up three press releases a week and get each one of them in the papers. Now I'm lucky if those papers take two.

A House press secretary

Ask anybody on Capitol Hill about the most basic change in the relationship between Congress and the media since 1960 and the response is practically catechistic—the media have become harder, tougher, more cynical. Committee chairmen, senior Republicans, press secretaries, aides in the press galleries and media studios at the Capitol, and members of the Washington press corps express what amounts to a consensus: the biggest change in the relationship between Congress and the media is that the press has grown more hostile to Congress.

Having conducted almost fifty personal interviews and collected some sixty questionnaires from representatives, staff, and reporters between 1977 and 1980, I found that only one person in fifteen thought this toughening was not the major development.[1] One official in the House of Representatives, who has worked personally with congressional correspondents for almost thirty years, put it this way: "The biggest change has been readily discernible—the greater emphasis on the investigative approach. Years ago there was an occasional exposé, but the last six to eight years there has been a shift toward the Watergate approach."

Press secretaries seem particularly sensitive to the change in attitudes. One former reporter, who has now served almost twenty

[1] Unless otherwise noted, the quotations in this chapter are from these interviews.

years as press secretary to a senior House Democrat, expressed his frustration with the "new journalism" he sees in and around the Capitol. The press, he says, has become "bloodthirsty." It has "developed a sickly preoccupation with the negative aspects of government operations, the presidency, the Congress, the administrative agencies." The media "think we're all crooks and it only remains for them to prove it." This man speaks for many of the staff who work directly with the press corps in Congress.

The members themselves seem to be most certain about the new journalism. One senior Republican senator who came to Congress in the mid-1960s (and who has generally enjoyed a good press) sees everything the press secretarial corps has been seeing, and more.

> I think the whole press has been infected with the virus of Watergate and has reacted accordingly. What young reporter doesn't start out now with ambitions of becoming another Woodward or Bernstein?
>
> The term investigative reporting has taken on a new dimension of power. . . . Watergate has tended to magnify what has been a professional cynicism among news media people. It's almost like . . . a field day! We (the press) can all become famous exposing a crooked elite. . . . That is a generalization, but that is the gamesmanship that's evolved . . . since the Watergate era.

Almost two-thirds of the members interviewed expressed opinions not unlike this one.

This conventional wisdom is almost as widespread among the press as it is among elected officials and their staffs. As Leland Schwartz, director of States News Service, a news organization which is itself a spinoff from Ralph Nader's Congress Watch, put it:

> In the post-Watergate era editors are more apt to question members' [information] and the editors are passing that feeling along to reporters. . . . In the old days, members passed through their [information] as if it were coming down from the mountain. . . . Watergate gave reporters new license to get the real story.

The only difference between Schwartz and the members themselves is that what Schwartz regards as journalistic "professionalism," Congress considers "cannibalism" (a word used by a mid-level House Democrat who had started his own career as a reporter). But both sides agree that the press has become much tougher since 1960, and practically everyone agrees that Watergate was the watershed.

So, if one were to rely on interviews alone, the thesis of this chapter would be simple: since Watergate, and because of Watergate, the Capitol Hill press—for good or ill—has come of age, and the media have turned themselves around.

But this chapter would be too short if it ended so soon. Besides, at least three important qualifications to the statements we have reported come to mind: First, to quote Victor Lasky, "it didn't start with Watergate." Modern press relations in Washington began to change as far back as the Kennedy administration and continued to do so rather markedly during the war in Vietnam. Second, the relationship between Congress and the news media is only a small part of the relationship between Congress and the mass media as a whole. The mass media are more than the independent press corps. They include the in-house media—those controlled by Congress and its members—and the campaign media as well. Third, the insiders we have quoted just may have missed their mark. The biggest story may *not* be the coming of an adversarial press to Capitol Hill, but instead the emergence of a press corps that is both hard and soft. The real story may be that the hometown press still does *not* behave much like Woodward and Bernstein—that beneath the new "hardness" at the national level, the old "softness" survives at the local level.

In fact, there is both more and less to developments in Congress's relations with the media than the Woodstein phenomenon. While it may be true that parts of the *news* media have grown more professional (or more cannibalistic), the total package looks, on closer inspection, quite different. And when all three faces of congressional media—in-house, campaign, and news—are considered, the result is not nearly as hostile to Congress, either the people or the institution, as even insiders believe.

Despite the prevailing view, this essay argues: that the mass media, in toto, have *not* hurt the membership electorally, especially in the House; that even the news media have *not* been of a piece in their relationship with Congress; that many of the major changes brought by the media to Congress have been brought *not* by a "new journalism" but by the campaign media or by practices associated with "old journalism"; that change has *not* been fundamental and continuity has *not* disappeared.

Combining these points with what I shall present later in this chapter, I offer these conclusions concerning the changing relationship between the in-house, campaign, and news media and the Congress over the last twenty years:

1. The in-house media in Congress have changed as fully as the news media since 1960, and they have tended to negate much of the

effect that the new, hardened Washington press corps has had on incumbents.

2. The campaign media around Congress have grown at least as fast as the news media in Congress, and under most circumstances they still tend to benefit incumbents, especially in the House.

3. The new toughness of the national press corps is not much in evidence in the local press. In some respects, the local media may have actually become "softer" than they were in 1960.

4. The discrepancy between the "soft" local press and the "tough" national news media has grown wider since 1960, and this widening gap goes a long way toward explaining why people hate Congress but love their congressman.

5. The "media-mix" that has developed in Congress since 1960 helps explain both the increase in safety of House incumbents and the concomitant decline in the safety of incumbents in the Senate.

6. The greatest effect of the new media-mix on Congress as an institution has been to attract a new kind of congressman.

7. The new media-mix has continued the evolutionary process, begun with radio, through which the executive branch grows increasingly more important than Congress as a policy-making institution.

8. *The media, taken together, have not done much to damage the members of Congress* but have damaged the institution of Congress—at least a little.

This last point may be the most important of all. In fact, I believe that the membership has learned to cope very effectively with the modern congressional media—even if the institution and the leadership have not. So, while it may be true that the mass media have proved somewhat detrimental to the institution, their three faces have not looked unkindly on the members per se. The overall pattern is one of change much in keeping with David Mayhew's notions about Congress. One finds, as Mayhew might have guessed, resourceful members who have restricted the impact of the media and adapted beautifully to their new forms, but a disunified institution far less able to restrict or adapt to those very same forms.

To understand all of this, however, one must remember that the congressional media are a mixture of the national, local, and regional press, an in-house press, and an ever-growing campaign media. Any analysis that stresses only the so-called new journalism oversimplifies the changing relationship between Congress and the mass media. One must emphasize the pluralism of congressional media if one takes into account all the major dimensions of modern, mass, political communication.

"In-House" Media—Unambiguous Advantages

The Revolution in Office Technology. In 1960 Senator John F. Kennedy asserted that American public opinion was whatever *Time* magazine told it to be. It is no wonder Kennedy, a senator, should have felt that way: as of 1960 the electronic media had made even smaller inroads into the Congress than they had into American politics generally.

The Senate office of 1960 had neither a Xerox machine nor a WATS line. No Xerox, no "free" phone, should indicate—especially to staff members reading this chapter—how long twenty years can be in the history of mass communication. The typical Senate office had only four electronic communications devices (in-house media) in 1960, all primitive by the standards of 1980. Offices had phones, but long-distance calls were operator assisted and individually billed. Aides had electric typewriters, but they were, of course, *non*-self-correcting. Offices also had thermofax, a primordial word-reproduction machine which provided photostated copies that were both illegible and perishable. The one "modern" device Senate offices had was Flexiwriter, an early machine for mass producing correspondence. But even Flexiwriter, innovative as it was, was nothing approaching the computer-based correspondence equipment available today.

Today's Senate office is a spaceship of electronic communications systems, some of which approach the state of the art. Looking at 1980 in the four areas in which the Senate did have electronic media equipment in 1960—telephone, thermofax, typewriting, and correspondence—one finds a near revolution in gadgetry. Every Senate office by now has Xerox, of course; Congress would almost cease to operate without xerography. Since 1977, every office also has had WATS lines. WATS means immediate, free communication to anywhere in the continental United States—all the time, inside or outside one's district. More important, WATS means a major political asset. In fact, were phone service as fully monitored and recorded as use of the frank, it would probably turn out that WATS has meant as much to Congress as any other recent change in its capacity to deal with constituents. Incumbents and their offices constantly use WATS to reach out and touch someone—especially someone in the district.

But phone service has been improved in more ways than one. The congressional phone of 1980 comes equipped with a telecopier and a set of "alligator phone clips," both of which provide instantaneous news flow back to the district via the Bell system. Telecopiers not only send press releases over phone lines back to the state, they also send local press reports from the state to Washington. Alligator clips serve a similar function for radio communication, providing radio stations with blurbs ("actualities") recorded by the member for use on local radio news reports. Although neither telecopiers nor alligator clips existed in 1960, both are standard electronic equipment now and make office news feeds to local media practically painless—a far cry from the late 1950s when senators like Richard Neuberger used Western Union telegrams to get emergency press releases back to the local press.

Since 1960 the Senate has already been through four generations of memory typewriters—Flexiwriter, Robo, Mag-card, and MTST. The modern Senate mail system, Correspondence Management System (CMS), produces up to forty letters per hour on each in-office computer terminal. CMS letters appear personalized and individually typed, of course, although they emerge mass-produced from the multi-memory bank of the central processing unit which is housed outside the Capitol. With CMS, senators can also sign up for automatic folding, stuffing, and signing machinery—again a relatively new set of routines. An "average" senator now has five letter processors (terminals) working off CMS; a middle-sized Senate office can send 2,500 personalized letters per week to constituents. Senate offices together send approximately 1 million "personal" letters per month to constituents. Twenty years ago that would have been an impossibility.

The ability to communicate more often with more constituents directly through the mail has been one of the most important changes in the in-house media. In fact, much of the technology adorning the new congressional office either produces mail or can be used to facilitate mail. Mail—in its volume alone, which has increased over 300 percent—represents a revolutionary change in in-house communications over the last two decades.[2] Currently, the average American receives two pieces of mail every year from Congress.

The increase in congressional mail can be explained in part by population growth, in part by an increasing national politicization. But the major explanation is the coming of modern computer technology to Congress. In 1960 nobody had a computerized mail system. As of 1979 almost every Senate office and, according to Congressional Quarterly, 300 House offices have computerized mailing facilities.[3] Younger members increasingly consider computerized

[2] Figures supplied by the Senate Appropriations Committee.

[3] Irwin B. Arieff, "Computers and Direct Mail Are Being Married on the Hill to Keep Incumbents in Office," Congressional Quarterly, Weekly Report, July 21, 1979, p. 1451.

mail a political necessity. The House itself found in a study conducted in 1977 that the freshman class was almost twice as likely to employ computerized correspondence as senior members.[4] One can expect "managed mail" to increase rapidly as the seniors leave.

But the new in-house correspondence systems mean more than a greater quantity of mail, and more than efficient mail. The new system can also mean "targeted" mail. Most mail from members is computerized, and most of it is sent in direct response to a constituent inquiry or problem. But more and more "personalized" mail is unsolicited and is sent to types of individuals who might be pleased by what it says: this is "targeted" mail, one of the big new phenomena on Capitol Hill.

The system is simple enough. A member buys or builds a list of his constituents, which is fed into the member's own computer disc space and cross-referenced by any number of characteristics. (Some cross-referencings are illegal, such as reference by party or amount of campaign contribution.) Later his office can run mail through the referencing system and target it according to any of those characteristics. If the member wants to send letters to all Blackfoot Indians who have written to him on ERA and who live on a particular street or block, he can do it without much effort.

In 1972, while seeking reelection, then Senator Robert Griffin decided to use the Senate system to target middle-income white voters in Michigan. Griffin hoped to communicate to these people how staunchly he personally opposed busing and, implicitly, to ask them for their support. Blacks, of course, were targeted out of Griffin's mailing. After Griffin won, his campaign techniques led to an investigation of targeting and eventually to a set of relatively stringent reforms in the Senate. The House also adopted regulations, but these were somewhat less Draconian than the Senate's. In both houses most of the reforms have either been ignored or remain unenforceable, and targeting has in fact expanded.

Computers and targeting, together, have been responsible for much of the increase in the quantity of congressional mail. In fact, the biggest single jump in franked mail came in 1976, the year after the House permitted such systems to be brought in. Although targeting can be overemphasized as a miracle drug for sick incumbents, it is a good example of a modern in-house communications device that has helped take away the sting of a tougher press corps.

But the computers on Capitol Hill do more than process mail.

[4] Dianne O'shetski, "Analysis of Survey on Computer Support Provided to Member Offices, As of April 1977," House Administration Committee Report, August 1977, p. 10.

Since the passage of H.R. 18428 in 1966 both House and Senate have worked to establish comprehensive computer facilities throughout Congress. And since that time Congress has authorized the establishment of dozens of legislatively oriented programs for members, leadership, and committees. Two of the most widely used computer programs are SCORPIO and LEGIS. SCORPIO, which stands unabashedly for Subject Control Oriented Receiver for Processing Information On-Line, provides offices with immediate access to the Library of Congress file. SCORPIO not only provides references to material and information, it also prints out short position papers, pro and con, on dozens of questions of public policy, written almost as mini-speeches for members or staff—Congress's computerized answer to Cliff's Notes.

LEGIS (Legislative Information and Status System) offers complete information, updated every legislative day, about the status of pending legislation and the legislative history for each bill. LEGIS is an automated bookkeeping system for legislation and may be the single most heavily used program in Congress with the exception of the correspondence files. LEGIS, like SCORPIO, has certainly meant a more efficient process for following and understanding proposed legislation. It seems likely, however, that members have not used the new policy-related technology any more religiously than they used the labor-intensive Congressional Research Service (CRS), which has been available to Congress for decades. What members really want "is that computer building up the lists so that they can inundate voters with follow-up mail," says Dave Stockman (Republican, Michigan).[5] But even if the new system places only a little policy-relevant information into the minds, or the briefcases, of incumbents, it puts none of that information in the hands of challengers. The general pattern prevails: more help for incumbents through the wonders of modern, in-house media.

The Radio and TV Studios. As early as 1956 the Senate and House began operating separate in-house recording studios for members and leaders. The studios in both houses have always been used for the same purposes—to provide members with convenient, cheap, and sympathetic programming that can be mailed home to broadcasters and used on local channels as news or public affairs presentations. All three Senate studios and all six House studios are located in the Capitol itself or in the office buildings next-door. And

[5] James Perry, "Congressmen Discover Computer and Use It to Keep Voters in Tow," *Wall Street Journal*, March 15, 1978, p. 1.

they are subsidized by Congress to the point where prices and fees for members generally run at least several hundred percent beneath what professional news packages would cost. So, for example, videotaping a one-half-hour program on the House side in 1979 cost only $35. A fifteen-minute radio show, which would cost $100 to tape professionally, cost $3 in the studio. On the Senate side the prices are about the same. Five minutes of radio taping costs $1.50—copies are available at $0.50 each. As for sympathetic treatment, the recording studios, as always, exist to help members—not constituents—communicate their opinions and deeds.

But some things have changed for the recording studios. What has clearly changed most has been the rate of use. One official at the Capitol estimated that back in 1967, only 200 members of the House used the studios—less than 50 percent of the membership. In 1978, 352 members, over 80 percent, did so.

This increased use of in-house radio and TV can be documented in a second, more telling way. For the last two years, I have been questioning congressional press secretaries about their offices' involvement with various media, including the facilities of the House recording studios. My interviews, not yet complete, indicate that members are using the studios more and more, especially the younger members. I asked the classes of 1958, 1968, and 1978 in mail questionnaires how often they had used the radio and TV studios and found that the new classes in Congress overwhelm the most senior classes in their reliance on the studios for communicating with their districts (see figure 3–1). The newest "generation" was more than three times as likely as the oldest to have used the recording studios once a week or more. The studios, meanwhile, have kept pace with demand. On the House side, their technology is virtually the most advanced available. And between 1960 and 1980 the staff of the recording studios doubled in size.

Other In-House Press. The radio and TV studios are only part of the congressional in-house press. For over 120 years the House and Senate have maintained a network of auxiliary offices which aid the press as it covers the membership day to day. It all began in 1857 when the Senate and then the House opened their own Press Galleries. Following the establishment of the first two Press Galleries in the nineteenth century, Congress responded with five more in the twentieth—a Radio and Television Gallery and a Periodical Gallery for each house and a Photographers' Gallery for both, all of which existed by 1960. The staffs in all seven galleries work in a rather strange environment, servants of the media as well as of the Congress. While the correspondents are paid by their respective news organizations,

FIGURE 3–1

MEMBERS USING HOUSE RADIO AND TV RECORDING STUDIOS AT LEAST
ONCE A WEEK, CLASSES OF 1958, 1968, AND 1978

SOURCE: Responses from fifty-eight mail questionnaires received from congressional offices in 1979.

the gallery employees are paid by the House or Senate. The galleries are there to help both the press and the Congress.

Interestingly enough, the galleries, unlike the recording studios, have not grown or changed much in the last twenty years. Staffs have stayed about the same in number, if not scope. Again, many of the top people who run the galleries today have been there since 1960. That the studios have changed while the galleries have not may be merely a matter of luck or coincidence. But my guess is that this represents, to some degree, a meaningful pattern of congressional change that fits nicely with David Mayhew's approach to Congress. The studios help members more than the galleries, so the studios have been more likely to experience change, more likely to have been kept up.

Thus, in terms of in-house media, *Congress has expanded and adapted most in the areas that help members directly. It has done less in the areas that are general and institutional in emphasis.* Congress has adjusted to developments in the media as Mayhew's theory would predict—selectively, and "personally," with special concern for the electoral life of its individual members.

There is one final dimension, perhaps more important than the rest, which suggests how much the in-house media have grown in the last twenty years. Back in 1960 press secretaries were not an exclusive accoutrement of the executive branch. There *were* press secretaries on Capitol Hill—George Smathers was reputed to have had three of them. But press secretaries labeled as such were few in number in the Senate and practically nonexistent in the House when Congress entered the 1960s. Because definitions change and press secretaries are often called something other than "press secretary," it is almost impossible to quantify precisely the growth of the congressional press secretariat, but the information that does exist indicates that that growth has been striking.

In 1960 there were no professional associations for press secretaries; now Congress actually has three—one in the Senate (bipartisan) and two in the House (one Democratic, one Republican). Not surprisingly, the Senate secretariat organized first, back in 1961. The House, with its less intense orientation toward the media, did not get around to establishing its press secretaries' associations until 1976. As for growth in personnel, according to a past president of the Senate Association of Press Secretaries, "two or three people" in that association had the title "press secretary" back in 1961. Now there are "one hundred or so dues-paying members" (past secretaries are included). More important, as of 1979, according to the *Directory of Congressional and Federal Agency Personnel*, there were only three senators (Sarbanes, Melcher, and Exon) who did not list a press secretary on their office payroll. Many senators have two press aides, some three.

In the House, the transformation has been slower but similar. The House Democratic Association of Press Secretaries had 125 dues-paying members in 1979. Membership was going up year by year, according to Gary Caruso, president of the organization, and he expected up to 200 members in the 97th Congress.

The growth in the congressional press secretariat suggests again that the media-mix in Congress has not been so bad for the members. They hire press people, after all, to praise them, not to harm them. It is not possible to say which side started the escalation in personnel, the press or the Congress. But in either case the growth of the new journalism has probably been countered, or its effects at least diluted, by the growth in the press secretariat. Looking back over the last twenty years, one official in the congressional press corps put it this way: "While there isn't the same cozy relationship [here] anymore, a reason for that may be that everybody has a press secretary. You have to work harder to get through the barrier they put up."

Television in the House. Nothing stands more visibly for change in the relationship between Congress and the media than the national televising of House floor proceedings. But along with change has been a commitment to continuity—House TV is another case study in how Congress has adapted to the media by looking out for number one, the membership.

Congress first considered changing the rules to allow broadcasting in 1922—fifty-five years before either house got around to actually doing so. In 1944 then Senator Claude Pepper introduced the first resolution providing for telecasting and broadcasting from the Senate floor, but until 1978 the Senate allowed neither. Even then only radio was allowed—and only during the debate on the Panama Canal Treaty. Nonetheless, it was still somewhat surprising that the House acted more quickly than the Senate in providing for television. In the thirty years following World War II it was almost always the Senate that had permitted greater access for television, not to the floor, but to investigations and hearings. Indeed the Senate became almost telegenic in the 1950s, 1960s, and 1970s with the McClelland hearings, the McCarthy hearings, the Fulbright hearings, and the Ervin hearings.

The House, with the exception of the Republican Congresses in the 1940s and 1950s, had never provided for—let alone permitted—telecasting of anything other than joint sessions and ceremonial occasions. Until 1970, the House even prohibited coverage of committee hearings. Traditionally, the leadership in the House had served as the greatest pocket of resistance to televising Congress. But with the change in the House leadership in the 1970s, and with a growing number of studies indicating how little attention the House was attracting on television compared with the Senate, the House took its first tentative step toward televising in 1975. Finally in 1977 the House passed H. Res. 866.

This measure was not what the reformers in the House had had in mind. They had tried both in committee and on the floor to grant to the networks full control of the new TV system in the House, cameras included. But the leadership, still more camera-shy than the members, beat back all attempts to make the system an "unofficial" one. Under the terms of H. Res. 866, all equipment and all personnel in the system are part of the House of Representatives. Control of the system is in the hands of the Speaker, who exercises that control through a Speaker's advisory Committee on Broadcasting and an advisory team working in the House Recording Studio.

In keeping with the tradition of adapting the media to their own needs, the members and the leadership have provided for themselves quite well. H. Res. 866 provides for in-house technicians with stationary cameras (nobody can be pictured falling asleep or inadvertently acting uncongressional under this system), blackened screens during roll-call votes (members cannot be caught changing their votes at the last moment, or even voting at all for that matter), and ready access to videotape files (members can, if they wish, send "news" clips to the stations back home at very low cost). Added to all that is continuous live coverage of all proceedings, broadcast by over 850 cable TV systems across the nation on C-SPAN (Cable Satellite Public Affairs Network).[6]

Has all this helped or hurt anybody? Speaker O'Neill was convinced from the outset that the system would hurt him and the House leadership and the institution. Experience has sometimes borne him out: O'Neill received 1,000 letters from viewers, 90 percent of them critical, after he reprimanded Congressman Jim Mattox for appearing on the House floor in shirtsleeves. But most members and analysts believe that the Speaker has generally overstated the case.

Two factors confounding attempts to evaluate the impact on the public have been the lack of information on the size of the audience watching House proceedings on television and the lack of network (or station) utilization of the tapes themselves. The major audience for television would, of course, be the network audience—now estimated to be above 55 million viewers nightly. But the networks have tended not to use the tapes of floor proceedings, in part because they objected to the House's decision to keep control of the cameras and in part because the networks still regard the House as less newsworthy than the Senate.

The only other news audience comes through C-SPAN, the 850 cable systems which tie directly into the Capitol telecasts. The potential audience for C-SPAN is, at present, 18 million viewers, but nobody knows who watches, or how often. The fact that the networks and C-SPAN only provide for a limited coverage or a small audience is a major reason for assuming that House TV has caused little public response. But the members themselves provide another reason.

Although some reformers worried that members would use videotapes of themselves in their districts, few have done so, and those who have have not been pleased with the response back home. *Congressional Quarterly* reports that in the first three months of the

[6] For a thorough discussion of the history and politics of House TV, see Donald Hirsch, "Televising the Chamber of the House of Representatives: The Politics of Mass Communications in a Democratic Institution," thesis, Oxford University, 1979.

system only seven members bought tape. As of May 1979, only one member, Virginia Smith (Republican, Nebraska), had used her tape for distribution to local news outlets. The other six purchased tapes for personal use, for a library, for a constituent, and for use in high school social studies classes.[7] The conclusion seems to be that the system has been underused by both networks and members and relatively invisible to constituents.

The members themselves seem pleased with the new system. Although they resent the limited quantity and negative tone of the network coverage of the proceedings (the only time all three networks led the evening news with House videotapes of the floor was the day Michael Myers was expelled), overall the members have judged the system a success. Among members of the class of 1978, for example, 56 percent of those responding to my survey were delighted with the TV system. As on the other items in the survey, older members, recruited in a different era, were less enthusiastic: only one in seven of the class of 1958 felt that the House TV system was very beneficial to him or Congress. But on balance, the membership was as pleased with the system as O'Neill was displeased. Positive references from all respondents outnumbered negative responses by almost two to one.

Much of the argument against televising the proceedings sprang from three basic apprehensions: that it would lead to grandstanding on the floor; that it would slow down the work of Congress; that it would weaken the leadership. Perhaps all three charges can be reduced to one—television would alter the behavior of members on the floor.

Although no major studies have been published so far, the most recent evidence suggests that the behavior of the members while on the floor *has* changed, but only slightly, since the inception of House TV. This evidence for the most part comes from Congressman John Anderson, who, before his campaign for president, made televising the House one of his legislative priorities.

One of Anderson's aides, Don Wolfensberger, compared behavior on the floor in the 95th and 96th Congresses, before and after the introduction of TV. Using fifteen quantitative indicators of floor activity, Wolfensberger found that there *was* an increase in the amount of time spent in passing legislation or resolutions (up 54 percent per measure); an increase in the amount of time the House was in session each day (up 6 percent); and an increase in the number of pages in the *Record* per measure passed (up 44 percent). Although Wolfensberger refuses to construe this as an effect of TV

---

[7] *Congressional Quarterly, Weekly Report*, May 5, 1979, p. 829.

per se and says that his most recent data show no effect of TV whatever, his original findings are at least consistent with the original assumption that TV would prolong debate and lead to grandstanding.

It appears that television has had some effect on the behavior of the membership on the floor. It also appears that the effects have run toward helping the *members*—not the leaders—who are given time, on television, to question public policy, to attack the administration, or, ultimately, to circumvent the leadership. Perhaps the major institutional impact of House TV, however, has been not change in floor proceedings but something almost nobody predicted. For want of a better term this change can best be labeled the "Barnes effect."

Michael Barnes (Democrat, Maryland) was not yet elected when the House passed H. Res. 866. But he was there when the system finally began. And, having watched his colleagues on the floor in the one month following full implementation of the system, Barnes concluded that the major effect had been procedural.

> I have a feeling that history may conclude that Congress finally figured out what it was doing when TV came to the chamber. It used to be that all a representative knew about the vote he was running to cast was 'If it's Tuesday, this must be Fisheries Management. . . .' But it's not quite so superficial anymore. It's on TV. If the member is in his office . . . he can leave the television turned on . . . and follow what's going on. . . . I think the case can be made that Congress has finally found a way to keep up with itself.[8]

Barnes's colleagues seem to agree with him that the real meaning of House TV is greater minute by minute familiarity with what is happening on the floor. In my survey, when asked about the principal benefit of House TV, forty-five of the fifty members who thought there had been any benefit mentioned *first* the increased ability of members and staff to follow legislation on the floor.

But, the more the system gives members the chance to follow the floor closely, the more it weakens the power of committees, fellow members, staff, and leadership. If members themselves know what is happening, they need rely less often on the other forces which have traditionally affected their performance on the floor. So O'Neill's complaints may have some basis in fact—TV does shift power, albeit slowly, away from leaders of all sorts and toward members. Once again the new media system serves to help members—not Congress.

The House is now considering adding, as early as 1981, a much larger computerized television system—one with up to thirty-six

[8] Michael Barnes, "What the House Didn't Know About TV," *Washington Post*, April 17, 1979, p. A21.

channels for data transmission, a built-in UPI wire service, and even a bookkeeping capacity. This suggests that the in-house media will increase even more substantially over the next twenty years than they have during the last twenty and that those increases will benefit individuals more than the institution.[9]

The Campaign Media: Potential Problems for Incumbents

Campaign media are those that candidates use to get elected. The major difference between campaign media and in-house media is who pays: Congress pays for in-house media out of general office accounts; candidates pay for campaign media out of private campaign funds. Since 1960 three basic changes have occurred in the relationship between Congress and its campaign media: (1) candidates now use the media more, (2) they use them more effectively, and (3) challengers find in the campaign media a new opportunity, but one still qualified by the old reality of incumbent advantage.

1. Media use. Most of the tools used in congressional campaigns in 1980 were available in 1960. Even direct mailing existed then. The differences lie in emphasis and degree. Candidates rely substantially more on the media than they used to and substantially less on party or personal contact.

While comparable and detailed figures on media expenditures are not available for the last twenty years, we know from the work of Edie Goldenberg and Michael Traugott that by 1978 congressional candidates were spending well over half (56 percent) of their total campaign budgets on all the mass media combined.[10] These authors estimate that in the six years between 1972 and 1978 the amount spent on broadcasting alone in House elections tripled.[11] My own survey data, collected from members of the classes of 1958, 1968, and 1978, show the same pattern. I asked all three classes about the strategies and priorities each member had used in his or her first successful congressional campaign. I asked, for example, whether the member had hired a media consultant—a better indicator, perhaps, than dollars and cents. None of those responding from the class of 1958 said yes; but among the class of 1968, 43 percent said

[9] "House Studies Big Expansion of Computer, TV Facilities," *Congressional Quarterly, Weekly Report,* December 29, 1979, p. 2970.
[10] Edie Goldenberg and Michael Traugott, "Resource Allocation and Broadcast Expenditures in Congressional Campaigns" (paper presented at the annual meeting of the American Political Science Association, Washington, D.C., September 1979), p. 7.
[11] Ibid., p. 6.

yes, and for the class of 1978, the figure was 63 percent. I also asked each member's office to what degree the member had relied on half a dozen campaign techniques, some media-based, others not, to win that first election, whether in 1958, 1968, or 1978. Again the increasing reliance on campaign media came through strikingly—and very clearly at the expense of political parties. The percentage of those relying "a lot" on all of the campaign media combined (print, radio, TV) had increased by over thirty-five percentage points since 1958, while the percentage relying "a lot" on party had declined by fifteen points. Over the last twenty-five years, all the media are up. Parties are down. (It should be noted that in the 1980 campaign the Republicans did spend $8.3 million *as a party* to help defeat Democrats in Congress through a high-powered television campaign.)

2. *Effects of the campaign media.* By spending so much more than ever before, congressional candidates have both created and understood a new electoral environment. The increasing use of the media is both cause and reflection of the growing impact of campaign dollars on electoral returns.

Using figures from Senate campaigns conducted in 1956, 1970, and 1972, Gary Jacobson found that, even after he had controlled for incumbency and party status, the correlation between broadcast advertising and voter preference *quadrupled* between 1956 and 1970 and edged up again slightly in 1972.[12] For Democrats and Republicans the pattern was practically identical: the correlations were up dramatically over twenty years, with coefficients approaching absolute levels of 0.5. Jacobson's data lend considerable credence to the assumption that, as voters continue to grow less loyal to party and candidates continue to spend more money to attract votes, the campaign media become more influential. In fact, Jacobson's figures indicate that in Senate primary elections in the 1970s, media expenditures alone accounted for more than 25 percent of the variance in voter preference.

Approaching the same question in a different way, John Wanat found even stronger evidence for media-based congressional voting during the 1970s. In an investigation of seats with no incumbent running Wanat found the correlation between dollars spent on the media and votes received by primary candidates to be a surprising 0.56.[13]

---

[12] Gary Jacobson, "The Impact of Broadcast Campaigning on Electoral Outcomes," *Journal of Politics*, vol. 37 (1975), p. 781.

[13] John Wanat, "Political Broadcast Advertising and Primary Election Voting," *Journal of Broadcasting*, vol. 18, no. 4 (Fall 1974), p. 418.

The media still represent at best a share of campaign success—but as Jacobson clearly shows, that share is appreciating. In 1970 and 1972, twenty-one incumbents were defeated in House races, two-thirds of them by challengers who outbroadcast them. Part of the reason for members' greater concern about their electability is the potential threat that the campaign media pose in congressional politics.

3. *Meaning for challengers.* This growing impact of the campaign media seems to contradict the notion that the new media system helps incumbents. Clearly the campaign media do threaten those in office. But it is also true that members of the House in 1980 were more likely than ever to be reelected. Although the pattern in the Senate is more ambiguous, the fact is that the campaign media remain for most members of Congress a *potential* threat. A serious attack that relies on campaign media *can* fatally damage an incumbent. But most often no such challenge materializes. For one thing, most challengers cannot compete in dollars and cents.

While it is probably true, as Jacobson shows, that challengers get more impact per dollar than incumbents,[14] it is still true that incumbents outclass challengers in the sums they can raise. The average House incumbent spent $98,000 in seeking relection in 1978; challengers spent $49,000—exactly half as much.[15] At least in the House, a case can be made, for arguing: that the campaign media have not much redefined congressional electoral politics; that television advertising is still too expensive and too inefficient for most House campaigns, where TV dollars are largely wasted reaching people who live outside the district; that incumbents still make more use of the media than their challengers; and that, at best, the campaign media have made House campaigns a wee bit less certain than before. At least in the House, the new system has not meant more defeats for incumbents. Incumbents still have more media advantages than challengers.

The News Media: Cynicism and Symbiosis in the Two Worlds of Press

The news media are what most of us think of as *the* media. But even the news media are less than monolithic in their relations with Congress. Television news differs from print, print differs from radio, radio differs from TV; and in each medium, local coverage differs from national. In terms of impact these differences are crucial.

[14] Gary Jacobson, "The Effect of Campaign Spending in Congressional Elections," *American Political Science Review.* vol. 72, no. 2 (June 1978), p. 489.

[15] Goldenberg and Traugott, "Resource Allocation," p. 9.

National Press Coverage of Congress. The intuition that the news media are increasingly hostile to Congress fits best the reality of the *national* press. The evidence abounds. One might start with an article by Mary Russell in the *Washington Post*, filed in November 1979. Headed "Hill Wages Energy War with Pop Gun Legislation," this article epitomizes the cynicism about Congress that the members have come to hate:

> In the next six weeks, Congress is likely to pass three or four showy energy bills, and when members go home for Christmas, President Carter and the leadership will be warmly congratulating each other on their energy victories.
> But how much these bills will help in cutting U.S. energy consumption and oil imports is a subject for skepticism.
> Congress's pattern of response to the national energy problem has become fairly clear.
> It is to give money to people and sometimes create new agencies but not to take chances or inflict pain. It is all strained carrots and no sticks.[16]

Russell's conclusion was: "The chosen congressional weapon for fighting the oil cartel is—storm windows."

My own content analysis of network news coverage of Congress leads me to believe that this approach is not confined to the national print media. Back in 1976, after the Supreme Court in *Buckley* v. *Valeo* gave Congress thirty days to reconstitute the Federal Elections Commission or witness its demise, David Brinkley commented to an audience of 15 million, "It is widely believed in Washington that it would take Congress thirty days to make instant coffee."[17] The complete results of my analysis of network coverage of Congress suggest much the same thing—the national press is fairly tough on Congress. ABC, CBS, and NBC ran 263 "Congress stories" in January and February of 1976, according to my analysis, and among them I found not a single item that placed Congress or its members in a positive light. I did find 36 stories (14 percent) that tended to present Congress or its members in a negative light.[18] The fact that Congress received no good press on the evening news for a period spanning five weeks in 1976 suggests that the national press do not find much about Congress to their liking.

[16] Mary Russell, "Hill Wages Energy War with Pop Gun Legislation," *Washington Post*, November 7, 1979, p. A2.
[17] David Brinkley, NBC "Nightly News," February 3, 1976.
[18] Michael J. Robinson and Kevin R. Appel, "Network News Coverage of Congress," *Political Science Quarterly* (Fall 1979), p. 412.

But no published content research has established that the behavior of the congressional press corps has actually become more
negative since the 1960s. For the purposes of this chapter I have tried
to fill the vacuum somewhat by comparing congressional news coverage in the 1960s and in the 1970s. My method has been simply to
compare the networks' treatment of essentially similar stories in the
1960s and in the 1970s.

The Coverage of Brewster and Flood. In December 1969, Senator
Daniel Brewster (Democrat, Maryland) was indicted in federal court
on charges that included illegally accepting money for what amounted
to legislative favors—bribery. Nine years later, Congressman Daniel
Flood (Democrat, Pennsylvania) was indicted on federal charges of
much the same sort. Though the two cases are not identical, it seems
reasonable to compare the coverage given them in the press and to
take that coverage as evidence of how the behavior of the press had
changed.

Using the Vanderbilt *Television News Index and Abstracts,* I
counted the stories that network television broadcast on the Brewster
and Flood cases, including all network stories heard on the evening
news in the year of the indictment or the year following—1969 and
1970 for Brewster, 1978 and 1979 for Flood.

If readers who are old enough to remember the 1960s are per-
plexed by the fact that they remember Dan Flood perfectly well but
cannot for anything recall Dan Brewster, the reason lies not so much
in the number of years that have passed as in the press coverage the
two cases received. According to the *Index,* Flood was referred to in
fifty-nine different news stories, while Brewster was mentioned in
eight. More incredible, Flood was the principal news focus or a
secondary news focus for 4,320 seconds of network time, while stories
about Brewster amounted to only 170 seconds. Flood-related stories
received twenty-five times as much network news attention as did
Brewster-related items, even though Brewster was a senator and
Flood "only" a representative.

Some of this difference is accounted for by the fact that Brewster
stood alone in his scandal, while Flood had the misfortune of being
implicated in a much broader scandal—along with then Congressman
Joshua Eilberg and then U.S. Attorney David Marston. Marston in
particular increased the newsworthiness of the Flood case because
Marston was a Republican in a Democratic administration and was
eventually fired by President Carter for reasons having more to do
with "old politics" than incompetence. But these extraneous factors
cannot easily account for all of the difference. The Flood coverage, so
much more extensive than anything even dreamed of in the Brewster

case, serves to corroborate the idea that the national press had changed during the 1970s—had become more "cannibal" in its congressional reporting.

The networks' treatment of other scandals, too, is consistent with the view that the national press has changed—has grown more likely to practice investigative journalism and hard-nosed objectivity. In fact, this has been *especially* true of network journalism. In 1980, we find NBC, along with *Newsday*, actually breaking a full-blown congressional scandal: it used its magazine program "Prime Time" to make public a set of developments NBC had been investigating for days, if not weeks—the FBI's role in ABSCAM. This "new" network journalism made household words of Wilbur Mills, Wayne Hays, and Allen Howe in the mid-1970s, with a zeal practically unknown in the early years of TV news, before Vietnam and Watergate. So while one might make a case that the *Post* and *Times* have *not* changed much since 1960, the *overall* image coming out of the nationals—papers and networks combined—is more stark, more serious, more intrusive, and more investigative in 1980 than it has ever been.

Local Press Coverage of Congress. Conceding that the national press has become increasingly hard-bitten is easy. Making a similar case for local press coverage of Congress is much more difficult. History, logic, and the evidence all indicate that the local media have not really been overcome by the Watergate syndrome, so conspicuous in the national media.

The idea that the local press, based in the states or outside the established circles in Washington, has a more cordial relationship with Congress than the national press is an old one. Writing back in the mid-1950s Donald Matthews noticed that

> the basic tactic of the [senators] is to provide services and special favors to reporters which then may be withdrawn in the event that newsmen do not live up to their end of the bargain—i.e., render favorable coverage. . . . The seriousness of this situation, from the reporter's standpoint, *depends largely on which level of news he writes. The local-story reporter, with many fewer potential sources and less prestige on the Hill, can be hurt a great deal more than the top news reporter with a wide group of potential news sources.*[19]

From our perspective what is most interesting about this interpretation of the local press is that it remained intact throughout the 1960s

[19] Donald Matthews, *U.S. Senators and Their World* (New York: Vintage, 1960), p. 211, italics added.

and 1970s—before, during, and even after Watergate. In 1972, Mark Green, James Fallows, and David Zwick made the case again that incumbents dominate their local press. According to them,

> one 1965 study found that about a third of the members of the House said that newspapers in their districts printed their news releases verbatim, and that another third wrote their own columns for the local press. . . .
>
> The small town editor, anxious to fill his columns, and having no Washington bureau to prepare stories for him, relies on the newsmaker more than, say, reporters for the *New York Times*. In Congressman David Obey's rural Wisconsin district, all the daily newspapers and half the weeklies publish his newspaper columns.[20]

Ben Bagdikian offered similar conclusions in 1974 in "Partners in Propaganda":

> Most members still do not have to answer pertinent questions for the voters back home, and most continue to propagandize their constituents . . . with the cooperation of the local news media. This process started a long time ago, but the price of an immobilized government has now come due.[21]

At least as late as 1974, critics of the press were still complaining about what one might best call a *symbiotic* relationship between the local media and incumbents in Congress—symbiotic not only because each "partner" profited from the continued relationship, but also because each clearly understood the other's mission and needs.

Because the theory of media symbiosis in the post-Watergate era is at least as controversial as it is important, it needs to be backed up with evidence. The evidence presented here is of three types: (1) interviews with members, staff, and press people; (2) the local and national press coverage of an unusual congressional "event," namely the Flood scandal; and (3) a case study of the press coverage one member of the House received from the major paper back in the district during one of the last five years.

1. *Perceptions.* One of the more widely shared opinions on Capitol Hill is that the local media behave less "seriously," less

[20] Mark Green, James Fallows, and David Zwick, *Who Runs Congress?* (New York: Bantam Books, 1972), p. 239.

[21] Ben Bagdikian, "Congress and the Media: Partners in Propaganda," in Robert O. Blanchard, *Congress and the News Media* (New York: Hastings House, 1974), p. 298, reprinted from the *Columbia Journalism Review* (January/February 1974).

"aggressively," and less "sensationally" than the national media. Some of the congressmen and staff I interviewed rejected the premise that the local press is softer than the national press, but most saw a fairly clear split between the two worlds of news. One veteran press official interviewed at the Capitol not only saw the differences, he felt he could explain them.

> I'd say yes [the national press] are tougher. The nationals represent great powerful forces. Conversely, the regional guy, the little and small town guy is concentrating on . . . half a dozen, maybe a dozen members. And he sees them day in and day out. Consequently, he does establish . . . he has to . . . he has to be invited back in. His demeanor and his attitude is somewhat different. It's more flexible, more on a personal basis now. He knows he's there to do a reporting job and that the congressman is there to get whatever publicity he can. The [nationals] say, so he [the member] doesn't like me. He needs us. We're big. We're powerful. We can publicize him [nationally]. So if he doesn't like us—the hell with him.

Members also tend to define the nationals as "hostile" and the locals as "gentlemanly." One committee chairman in the House acknowledged the different sort of relationship he—and the Congress—have with the local press, a relationship that seems to meet our definition of symbiotic.

> The Washington media are obviously a little more high-powered compared to the [state] media. The Washington press tends to appeal to the Washington psyche—and be politically sensational or more gossipy . . . more than in [my state] or in the other parts of the country. [*My state's*] *media tends to be a little more personalized and appreciative of our problems. I always enjoy appearing before the [local] media and find that they are courteous and considerate and professional.* (Italics added.)

The Washington press sees the same thing—the local press is softer on Congress. One network correspondent who called the nationals "selectively tough" said that the locals behave even less aggressively. "The local press," he said, "is still spoon-fed." As evidence he cited his own hometown media, which, he argued, had always had cordial relations with local congressmen:

> The classic case is Dan Flood. He is God back home. I was home when it all broke open. What they were getting back home [in the media] was they're picking on our boy Dan.

> The same was true with Wilbur Mills. The papers back home said Wilbur's in trouble and we've got to rally around our boy Wilbur.

These remarks not only fit the notion of symbiosis, they also suggest a test. If the national and local press do treat members differently, the differences should show up in their coverage of a story that received attention from both.

2. The Trials of Dan Flood. In January 1978 Steven Elko accused his former boss, Congressman Daniel J. Flood, of knowing about bribes Elko had taken on Flood's behalf. Thirteen months later a federal jury in Washington failed to reach a verdict in Flood's trial for bribery, perjury, and conspiracy. Flood resigned from Congress in January 1980, and in February he agreed to plead guilty to a misdemeanor, sparing himself a second trial. This episode provides us something we do not often have—a chance to compare the press coverage of a member of Congress in the national and local media during the modern press era. As a scandal, it is, of course, unrepresentative of most news coverage, yet it offers us a rare chance to see how the two levels of press behave.

The period of analysis is twelve months, from January to December 1978, just before Flood's trial ended. For those twelve months I examined every story in the *Washington Post* and the Wilkes-Barre, Pennsylvania, *Times-Leader* (the largest daily newspaper available in Flood's hometown) in which Flood's name appeared in the headline or story heading. There were 131 such stories in the *Times-Leader*, 24 in the *Post*. This discrepancy is in no way surprising. Flood was Wilkes-Barre's member. To the *Post* he was a scandal, not a representative. What, in fact, was a little surprising was that both the *Post* and the *Times-Leader* played the story straight: *none* of the 155 stories could be considered obviously slanted toward Flood or against him; all were consistently "objective." While neither Flood nor his staff would have regarded the headline "Dan Flood Indicted" (*Times-Leader*, September 6, 1978) good press, the story below was balanced and heavily factual.

However, the *type* of coverage Flood got was different in the two dailies. First, the *Times-Leader* was much more likely to feature stories about Flood's support in the district. Twenty-six stories—20 percent of the total local coverage—dealt with the public response, and twenty-five of them were positive, focused on the support for Flood. In the *Post*, there were only two "local response" stories, and one of them was negative, conveying the message that local support was *not* as enthusiastic as most people had anticipated. The placement of the stories shows the same sort of pattern. The *Post* tended to put the scandal news about Flood up front, on page one in 42 percent of the cases. In the *Times-Leader* only nine stories, or 7 percent, made page one, and three of these stories reported tributes to Flood.

One of the few opportunities for a favorable news story about Flood was a benefit dinner given in Wilkes-Barre in December 1978 by a group calling itself the Trust Flood Committee. Both local newspapers—the *Times-Leader* and the *Scranton Times*—covered the fundraiser. And so did the *Washington Post* and the *New York Times*. The local papers, breaking with their usual pattern, put the story up front; the *Times-Leader* made it the day's major headline. Not surprisingly, the national papers put the story toward the back, on page four in the *Post*, page eight in the *New York Times*. But the most vivid difference was the contrast in the headlines.

The *Times-Leader* headed its story " 'Trust Flood' Event Draws Hundreds." The *Post* opted for "Thin Crowd at Testimonial Still Warms Flood's Heart." The *Scranton Times* and *New York Times*, coming from towns closer than Washington but farther than Wilkes-Barre, ran headlines which quite literally put them in between the *Post* and *Times-Leader* in their slant: the *Scranton Times* went with "Estimates Vary on Bash for Dan Flood," the *New York Times* with "Benefit for Flood Draws Few Benefactors." The general pattern holds—the local press was sympathetic, the national press less so. Local papers focused on attendance at the benefit, national ones on the "no-shows."

Interestingly, the no-shows were covered in the *Times-Leader*, in an analytical piece, on page one, headed, "It's Who Wasn't There . . ." and which read much more critically than the lead story. The second piece was written by a staff reporter named Nancy Kathryn Huff, a twenty-three-year-old graduate of Penn State with a degree in journalism. Huff was doing new journalism because she was a newer journalist. Her piece indicates that the new journalistic ethic has been creeping into the local media—print particularly. But as of 1978, in Wilkes-Barre, the main story was still "hundreds for Flood." The local press in Wilkes-Barre did cover the Flood case— and not badly, just differently from the national press.

3. The Case of Congressman Press. The Flood case was a major scandal, and because of that fact all the media covered the developments rather fully. But it says next to nothing about day-to-day local press coverage for the large, if admittedly shrinking, number of members who never face an indictment or trial. To examine the "normal" side of local press coverage of Congress I looked at the local coverage given recently to a mid-level member of the House who had never been involved in a political or personal scandal. By searching through this member's press releases and press clippings from the major local newspaper in his district for a period of one year, I was able to get a sense of how the local press treats a scandal-free congressman—a member more "representative" than Dan Flood.

At the outset two things should be said about "Congressman Press." He is not generally considered a big media man—at best he is press aware, not press obsessed. Second, the major newspaper in Press's district—the paper from which the clippings were taken—is neither small in circulation nor badly regarded. It is a typical American daily, not a rag.

During the year I chose to study (one of the last five), Congressman Press's office issued 144 press releases, or about three per week. (According to a survey I am conducting in the House of Representatives, Press sent out releases just slightly more often than the average member.) During the same year the major paper in Press's district published 120 stories mentioning Press or featuring him. More than half of the stories drew heavily on the press releases. Among stories in which Congressman Press was "featured" (mentioned in the headline or the first paragraph) 54 percent were essentially reworded releases. Given that there were fifty-two featured pieces in toto, on average, every other week Congressman Press was featured in a story virtually written in his own office.

Congressman Press's good relations with the press extended beyond his press releases. News not originating in Press's office was almost invariably "good news." Of the stories not constructed from press releases, half reported something favorable about Press—a political endorsement, a tribute paid to him, or a new grant made by the government benefiting his district. Adding together the news generated by press releases and "good news" from other sources, Congressman Press managed to attract forty positive stories during the year, out of a total of fifty-two featured stories—77 percent of his news coverage in his district's major daily (see table 3–1).

A member of the staff suggested that Press was an unusual case and that it would be hard to duplicate a relationship as pleasant as this one. Press's reputation was pristine; nothing had disturbed his symbiotic relationship with the media or the people in his district. Perhaps, but there is evidence to suggest that symbiosis is the rule, not the exception.

What may be the best evidence for believing that the local press is not Woodstein—let alone Evans and Novak—comes from the Center for Political Studies (CPS) at the University of Michigan. For the last two congressional elections Arthur Miller and his associates have been doing content analysis of local press coverage, of both

TABLE 3–1

CONGRESSMAN PRESS'S COVERAGE IN HIS DISTRICT'S MAJOR DAILY,
"FEATURED" STORIES ONLY

Type of Story	Number of Stories
Favorable coverage	
Press releases rewritten	28
Tributes to Press	8
Grant announcements	2
Endorsements	2
Total	40
Neutral coverage	
Features, predictions, events	7
Negative coverage	
Press is stalling on legislation	1
Opponent's criticism quoted	2
Other	5
Total	8

SOURCE: Author.

Congress and congressional campaigns. Their data suggest that the local press—the press generally—do not treat incumbents negatively, even during the last weeks of a campaign. Indeed, the press tends to treat incumbents positively, at least slightly so. Using a sample of 216 newspapers, CPS found that in the last phase of the 1978 congressional campaign the average congressman received a score of 1.9 for his coverage in the local press, on a scale ranging from 1.0 (totally positive) through 3.0 (totally negative).[22]

Incumbents fare well, getting positive attention, and lots of it. Incumbents receive twice the coverage their challengers get and, according to Miller's data, more positive coverage than challengers or Congress as an institution or the government generally.[23] The differ-

[22] Arthur Miller, "The Institutional Focus of Political Distrust" (paper prepared for the American Political Science Association, Washington, D.C., September 1979), p. 39. The idea of a symbiotic relationship between Congress and the press is spelled out in an article by Delmer Dunn, "Symbiosis: Congress and the Press," which is reprinted in Blanchard, *Congress*, pp. 240-249. For an interesting example of symbiotic cooperation between the *national* press and a member of Congress, see the account of how the *Los Angeles Times* worked with Congressman Pete Stark (Democrat, California) to investigate and publicize the problems of Americans in Mexican prisons, in Susan H. Miller, "Reporters and Congressmen: Living in Symbiosis," Journalism Monographs no. 53, January 1978.
[23] Miller, "Institutional Focus," p. 39.

ences are small, but they always favor incumbents. Obviously Miller's score for incumbents fails to approach the score enjoyed by Congressman Press—in Miller's terms, a very impressive 1.3. But, given that Miller was considering post-Watergate campaigns, and only the last five weeks of each—when one would expect the press to be at its toughest—his data support the view that the local press is cordial, not adversarial.

One other indirect indication of the symbiotic relationship comes from my own survey of members of the House in the classes of 1958, 1968, and 1978. Members or their press secretaries were asked how often "local TV," "local newspapers," "local radio," "the networks," "the wires," "the newsweeklies," "the *Post*," and "the *Times*," treated them "fairly." Fewer than 3 percent of the legislators felt that the press as a whole (all eight of these media considered together) treated them badly. And, although the figures are confounded by a large number of congressmen who said that a particular medium did not cover him "at all," the picture that emerges suggests very little resentment toward specific news sources—and *virtually none toward the local press*. Even the *Post* and *Times* were considered "rarely" or "never" fair by only 7 percent of respondents (interestingly, the *Post* scored worst). One might even conclude that the basic relationship between Congress and the press is not that different from what Matthews described twenty-five years ago when he wrote that, despite "the potential sources of conflict, the relations between [Congressmen] and reporters, are remarkably free of friction."[24]

The responses to my survey also suggest that congressmen are very much like the public they serve in a way never yet considered: the public tends to like Congress less and less but its own representatives more and more; congressmen, meanwhile, all complain about a bloodthirsty, hostile, biased press—yet they give *specific* media high marks for fairness and objectivity. This probably reveals something about the nature of human observation of broad institutions and the particulars within them, but it also reinforces our original point—that the relations between Congress and local press outlets are mostly cordial and pleasant, especially when it comes to local TV and local radio.

The New News on Capitol Hill. One of the less conspicuous changes affecting press coverage of Congress has been the steady increase in the size of the Capitol Hill press corps. Figure 3–2 shows the number of people and press organizations in Washington holding credentials to cover the Congress between 1960 and 1976. Although

---

[24] Matthews, *U.S. Senators*, p. 213.

FIGURE 3-2

GROWTH OF THE CONGRESSIONAL PRESS GALLERIES, 1960–1976

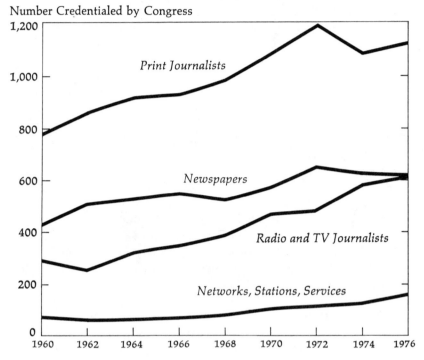

Number Credentialed by Congress

SOURCE: *Congressional Directory*, 1960-1976.

these figures badly inflate the number of working correspondents on the Hill, they indicate the relative growth among the various types of news media in Congress.

Without doubt the greatest growth has come in radio. Figure 3–2 shows an increase of 175 percent in the number of both radio and TV correspondents admitted to the congressional press corps in a sixteen-year period. During that period, the number of print journalists increased by "only" 37 percent. The rate of increase for electronic news people has been precisely five times greater than for print, and the overwhelming majority of the new media people are in radio.

Radio and electronic news coverage of Congress has rendered the Capitol Hill press corps more regional—hence, more local—in its behavior. This localizing of news through "regional" coverage of Congress has probably meant that the news about members comes out much "softer" than would have been the case without the explosion in radio. For two reasons, regional radio has probably worked to dilute the impact of the new journalism in Congress. First, regional electronic news people are, by definition, more local in outlook than the national press and, therefore, more dependent on access to members. Regional radio and local television people bring their local concerns with them to Congress, and they need to establish good relations with the few members who share those concerns.

Second, the electronic media *generally* treat Congress "better" than the print media. Virtually every congressmen and senator I interviewed personally expressed the belief that electronic journalists were objective in their news reports, more so than print. But "objectivity" really meant "niceness" in this context. Not one member in my mail survey of over 100 members of the House complained about the local radio or TV coverage he had received.

Press aides also believe that nonnetwork TV and radio news are less serious, less difficult, less hard. A committee aide who was recently quoted in a series of memos about "Congressional Press Relations" frankly admitted that "television doesn't exercise independent news judgment. Instead they learn what and who is news from the morning paper."[25] Another press secretary said that radio stations read AP and UPI wires and call for a statement from the member when they want one. "When that happens," he said, the member merely "gives them what they need over the phone."[26]

Members I interviewed recognized—even criticized—the softness of the news coverage on local or regional TV and radio. One said, "TV people need thirty seconds of sound and video at the airport when I arrive—that's all they want." Another, who had done some press work himself, said bluntly:

> I have never yet met a local TV reporter—very few of them—who seems to have much background information about the subject he or she is covering. During the interview, they don't know what question to ask. If they do know what question to ask, you give them the answer and they get an expression in their eyes so you know they don't know what they're talking about. There are notable exceptions but I'm talking about the norm.

Part of this is the "Ted Baxter" quality of local and regional TV. But beyond simple lack of sophistication, it reflects problems inherent in the medium. One regional radio reporter in the Capitol confided that having to get the member's voice on tape meant that she needed more

[25] "Congressional Press Relations: A Guide for Press Assistants," House Select Committee on Congressional Operations, reprinted from *STAFF* magazine, 0-29-837 (Washington, D.C., 1978), p. 7.
[26] Ibid.

access than a print reporter would normally require. But whatever the reasons for the softness of the electronic media, the dramatic growth in regional radio coverage (and what regional TV coverage exists) has meant that the national press and networks have been subtly confounded by a burgeoning "localized" press corps which outnumbers them and which treats Congress and congressmen with greater respect.

Given all this growth and competition in regional radio and the concomitant increase in local radio and TV news, the congressional news corps as a whole cannot be said to be increasingly hardbitten. If the eye-witness news format continues to move to Washington, as it has to some degree, only the members who get caught *in flagrante,* doing something awful, will have real problems. For most members the growth in regional, electronic news means a more favorable prognosis than either they perceive or the media themselves understand.

Explaining the Difference. The local and national press are two separate worlds, and since 1960 they have grown more distinct. Why is this so, and what are the implications?

First, a qualification. The differences between the national and local press should not be exaggerated. The nationals do not often go out of their way to be tough when toughness is unwarranted; our analysis of congressional news in 1976 showed that eight out of ten stories on network news were *not* negative.[27] And Robert Blanchard, in a survey of congressional correspondents conducted in the early 1970s, found that over 70 percent of the reporters spent "quite a bit of time" demonstrating to sources that they could be trusted; over half admitted that they worked at appearing "sympathetic" to congressional sources.[28]

Moreover, locals can be tough when they have to be. Milton Hollstein describes, for example, the treatment Congressman Allan Howe received at the hands of the Salt Lake City media. The press, he said, served as "pillory" when Howe was caught with a decoy prostitute, and its "excessive," "gratuitous," "knee-jerk," and "questionable" coverage of the incident "made it impossible for [Howe] to be re-elected" to Congress, even before the reported facts had been corroborated.[29]

[27] Robinson and Appel, "Network News."

[28] Robert Blanchard, "The Congressional Correspondents and Their World," p. 237, in Blanchard, *Congress.*

[29] Milton Hollstein, "Congressman Howe in the Salt Lake City Media: A Case Study of the Press as Pillory," *Journalism Quarterly,* vol. 54, no. 3 (Autumn 1977), p. 454.

Nonetheless, the basic differences in local and national coverage need some explanation. Most of those who have offered explanations have emphasized the variations between the local and national press in size and beat. A few others have dwelled on the economic self-interest of the local press; the theory holds that publishers urge editors to persuade journalists to treat the local congressman kindly in the hope that he may, at some point, vote for or amend legislation that will profit the newspaper. Another form of economic determinism has been used to explain the pleasant relationship between local broadcasters and congressmen. The theory here is that a contented congressman might go to bat for an FCC-licensed broadcaster if there were a licensing challenge. Both of these economic theories hinge on the owners' seeking to maximize their economic self-interest. The journalists are secondary.

But social psychology probably has as much to do with the relationship between the media and Congress as economics does, and the correspondents' behavior probably matters more than the interests of their capitalist publishers. At least half a dozen studies all make it clear that symbiosis emerges from a network of friendships and "mutual dependencies" between journalists and newsmakers.[30] But the representatives of local media are drawn in closer to the sources than the national press; mutual dependency is a larger ingredient in their friendships with the newsmakers. This brings us back to matters of size and beat.

Size. Almost by definition, national media are large, local media small. Nationals not only maintain larger resources with which to dig for news, they also have the freedom to move on from whatever they have just dug up. But locals stay where they are and continue to need access to the *same* people and places day after day. If the press were business one might think of the nationals as consultants and the locals as foremen. Consultants do their work and get out, while foremen have to stay put. For the most part, consultants are tougher than foremen; like the national press, consultants are expected to be tougher.

---

[30] There is a growing number of articles and books dealing directly with social or psychological basis for symbiotic relations. See Walter Gerber, "Two Communications of News: A Study of the Roles of Sources and Reporters," *Social Forces*, vol. 39 (October 1969), pp. 76-83; Dan Nimmo, *Newsgathering in Washington* (New York: Atherton, 1964); W. Phillips Davison, "Diplomatic Reporting: Rules of the Game," *Journal of Communication*, vol. 25 (Autumn 1975), pp. 138-146; Carolyn S. Dyer and Oguz Nayman, "Under the Capitol Dome: Relations between Legislators and Reporters," *Journalism Quarterly*, vol. 54, no. 3 (Autumn 1977), pp. 443-453; Susan Miller, "Congressional Committee Hearings and the Media: Rules of the Game," *Journalism Quarterly*, vol. 55, no. 4 (Winter 1978), pp. 657-663.

The big media—especially network television—have actually grown large enough to get by with less access than they needed not so long ago. The members have never had much need to seek out the *New York Times* for coverage: relatively few constituents read the *Times* outside New York—or even inside New York for that matter. But increasingly members need to seek out the networks, regardless of where their district or state happens to be. Networks reach every constituency, if not every constituent.

So, size—especially the size of the networks—gives the national press a real advantage in dealing with members. The local media are still imprisoned by their smallness and weakness. One regional radio reporter who had recently come to cover Congress for an independent news agency made this confession:

> My biggest surprise coming here was that I was told [in graduate school] to stay your distance. You can't do that. In graduate school I had been programmed that I am a reporter and I will cover Congress and I will not each lunch with press aides. That's baloney. You don't get any stories. The name of the game here is access. Unless you have access how can you get a story? There's a lot of ego around here. . . . To go out and be a hard-hitting [journalist] the guy's not going to come off the floor and talk to you.

This correspondent, whose agency had fewer than five reporters, made it very clear that access means everything to the reporter.

Beat. The nationals' growth in size and importance has been recent, but they have always enjoyed a different beat from the locals. Nationals for the most part focus on the institution, not on individual members. In my mail survey of the House, I asked members how fairly they had been treated by the *New York Times*, the *Washington Post*, newsweeklies, the wires, and the networks. The overwhelming majority, about 75 percent, said that the national media never seemed to cover them at all. A survey of House members in 1978 indicated that over forty percent of the legislators did not appear *once* on network news during the 95th Congress.[31]

The fact is the nationals ignore members and pick on the institution—unless there is a scandal to cover. Of the thirty-six stories coded as negative toward Congress in my one-month analysis of network news in 1976, thirty were about Congress, not congressmen. Focusing on institutions makes it easier to be tough. One does not have any particular pair of eyes to avoid when one attacks Congress. This is

[31] "Congressional Perceptions of Network Television Coverage of the United States House of Representatives," mimeographed, 1979.

one reason why, as we have seen, Congress received more negative coverage than positive in 1978 but congressional *candidates* got more positive coverage than negative.

Add to all this the very real tendency for the national media to recruit the tougher journalists coming out of the local press and you get a fairly complete explanation for the hardness of the Washington press corps and the softness of the local news. The nationals look hard at the institution. The locals exchange glances with their representatives. This pattern holds unless the local member gets into trouble: then all the press—national, regional, local—glares. Such is the nature of the press in Congress.

Consequences

Now that we have considered the changes in the in-house, campaign, and news media as each relates to Congress, we must ask, So what? What has the new media-mix done to or for Congress? Let us consider this question along three dimensions: attitudinal, electoral, and institutional.

Attitudes: News and the Paradox of Public Opinion. Because the national news media have grown apart from the local media, and because the local media have probably been expanding more rapidly than the rest, the news media help explain a most interesting paradox in American public opinion—nationwide contempt for Congress and district-wide esteem for its members. The two types of media covering it coincide with the two sides of Congress's image.

I asked members of the press and of Congress whether they thought that the media help explain the concomitant animosity toward Congress and affection for congressmen, and a majority of those taking a position agreed. One press official in the Senate, who has worked with the press since the Eisenhower administration, felt the media were at the heart of the paradox.

> I think this is all attributed to the media creating this image. Yeah, absolutely. How [do] the people get the image back home? It's only what the media give them. This is all they know. They are exposed to the local TV stations that carry a little film clip of their senator or congressman. . . . People see you.

A House press secretary and former reporter agreed even more strongly:

I think you are unquestionably right—unquestionably right. You can get eloquent testimony from the editor of [Southern newspaper] on this. I'll never forget a conversation he and I had about five years ago . . . one night over whiskey. . . . He said I just don't understand . . . I pick up the paper and I read something Congress has done and I say those silly SOBs. My son would know better than that. I say to myself what dunderheads would do something like that? Must be Congressman [name]. No, [name] is a damned intelligent guy. He'd be a credit anywhere. Must be this local Congressman to the South. . . . No [name] I know him. He's a damned sharp guy. Must be like somebody from [city]. Somebody like [name]. No it couldn't be [name]. He made a tremendous success of his [business].

Of course, there are other interpretations of the paradox of opinion in Congress. Some authorities on Congress contend that members actually do a good job as representatives but that the institution actually fails to do its job as a legislature. Others, like Fiorina, contend that members work the bureaucracy so effectively in the interests of their constituents that constituents learn to respect them but not the institution. Both of these interpretations seem ultimately too literal. Constituents simply do not deal enough with their congressmen to produce the paradox of congressional public image. Only the media are broad enough in reach and scope to account for the bulk of opinion toward Congress or its members. CPS congressional election studies in the 1970s indicate that 52 percent of all citizens read about their member in the newspapers; 14 percent had met the member personally. Fewer than one person in six ever deals with a member directly, even using a very loose definition of "direct" contact.[32]

Knowing what we do about local coverage, we may plausibly assume that the local press accounts for much of the favorable image that members enjoy. Miller provides a fairly direct confirmation of this assumption. His research finds a substantial direct correlation between the district's press coverage (favorable or unfavorable) of the member and the district's perception of him.[33] Equally relevant, Miller's correlation between local press coverage of Congress, the institution, and attitudes toward Congress in a given district is both direct and significant.[34] So, it seems that districts with more negative

[32] Miller, "Institutional Focus," p. 37.
[33] Ibid., p. 39. The correlation is 0.23, significant at the 0.001 level.
[34] Ibid. In this case, the correlation is 0.29.

press about Congress, the institution, hold more negative views of Congress—districts with more positive press go significantly in the other direction. The national media, which reach everyone with their critical coverage of the institution, and the local media, which reach constituents and accommodate members, *together* serve as the single best explanation for the paradox of public opinion toward Congress.

Elections: The Media and Electability. The fact that the nationals relinquish to the locals the job of covering individual congressmen has direct implications for the members' safety at election time. Locals keep their readers relatively happy with their representatives by giving incumbents lots of coverage, most of it favorable. The result is safer incumbency. And when one factors in the growth of the in-house media, which inevitably serve to protect incumbents, the result is ever greater safety for those holding office—precisely the pattern that has prevailed among House membership since 1960.

Gary Jacobson has argued convincingly that safety in elections corresponds to incumbents' ability to control their media coverage.[35] Incumbent presidents, for example, are not nearly as safe as House members, in part because presidents do not fully control their image in print or on TV. The news media control that image, or at least produce it. Ads can counteract, but cannot negate, the image the news creates. House members control much of their own press— much more than presidents, governors, or senators. Members control their press because they (1) make greater and more sophisticated use of in-house media, (2) attract, by and large, more money than challengers in ad campaigns, (3) maintain a closer relationship with the local press than senators, and (4) attract much less coverage from the nationals so long as they stay unindicted.

House members have grown increasingly safe electorally as they have gained greater control of all the media at their disposal. It is, in fact, another illustration of Converse's tried and true theory of information flow and partisan stability.[36] With no news about members getting through other than that which the members themselves control or influence—with no unfavorable information reaching the public—House members stay safe.

Not only do the media help account for the increasing safety of House incumbents, they also explain why in recent years new members elected out of synch with their constituency—the Toby Moffetts

[35] Jacobson, "Impact of Broadcast Campaigning," p. 774.

[36] Philip Converse, "Information Flow and the Stability of Partisan Attitudes," *Public Opinion Quarterly*, vol. 26 (Winter 1962), pp. 578-599.

and Tom Downeys—have not had trouble in their first effort at reelection. New members are not unseated after their first term in part because new members know best how to use and exploit the new media-mix. Even in the Republican landslide of 1980, "only" nine of fifty-six remaining members of the Democratic class of 1974 lost seats. Overall, only about 10 percent of the House incumbents were defeated in the landslide.

The Senate media-mix is very different. Senators' relationships with the local media are less intimate because senators deal with whole states, not with one or two papers as House members do. If propinquity explains cordiality, senators lose out because they simply cannot be as close to their press—or their constituents—as members of the House. The senator also attracts better financed challengers, who can buy TV time and who can use their resources more efficiently than practically any House member. The campaign media can hurt senators more because their challengers are more likely to be able to afford them. But most important, senators attract national coverage—a must for any potential presidential contender, but a potential disaster for an incumbent who comes out looking bad on the evening news. Given the politics of his state, Senator Frank Church was an example of a prime-time disaster. Obviously, the new media-mix in Congress does not treat senators as well as House members, in part because the Senate competes in the same arena as the national press, while the House makes its accommodation with the locals back home. Somewhat ironically, powerful senators are less able to control their images than "invisible" House members. In the Senate campaign of 1980, thirteen of twenty-nine incumbents went down to defeat, which approaches a 50 percent attrition rate. In 1980, as in the recent past, the House incumbents were four times safer than the Senate incumbents.

The Institution: Unchanging Roles. Obviously, not everything has changed. Some of the most important aspects of the relationship between the mass media in Congress continue much as they were in 1960. One of these is the news media's preoccupation with the presidency. Although the data are inconclusive, it seems that Congress as an institution is still very subordinate to the executive in news attention and news manipulation.[37] The print media have been inching

[37] My own research shows practically no change in the level of presidential news on network evening news (all networks) between 1969 and 1977. In 1969 I found on network news 3,516 stories featuring the president and 2,339 featuring the House or Senate or Congress. In 1977 I found 3,556 stories featuring the president and 2,080 featuring Congress—an even greater advantage

back toward a more equitable balance between presidency and Congress, but television has stayed with the executive. The events in Iran and Afghanistan have combined to prove that the presidency still has a unique position in national news. Congressional attempts to woo the press—House TV included—have failed to shift the media's bias from the White House to the Capitol. If anything, electronic news coverage of the House has meant a little less attention for the Senate, but not much less for the president.

The presidential hegemony that is still felt in the press means a public that "thinks presidential" and relies on presidents to get us through, make things happen, control public policy. This is not simply a quantitative advantage that the presidency enjoys. The media have consistently treated the executive less negatively than the Congress. For reasons that follow rather closely those which explain the easier coverage given the membership than Congress per se, the executive generally gets better press than the legislative branch. Even in 1974— the year of Nixon's resignation—the press treated Congress more negatively than the president: according to the Center for Political Studies at Michigan, the president received coverage that was 39 percent negative, but the Congress was saddled with negative press amounting to 42 percent of the total.[38]

The results of this continued assault on Congress have proven to be substantial. Whether the explanation is "reality" or "the media," Congress has not had a better public image than the president since 1960, except in some of the Watergate years. In fact, even in September 1979, when Jimmy Carter's public approval rating on the Associated Press/NBC poll plunged to 19 percent—the lowest level of public approval assigned to his or *any* presidency, ever—the Congress still did worse: the Congress stood at 13 percent—six points, or 30 percent, below Carter. Both the quality and quantity of national press coverage of Congress has hurt Congress in its competitive relations with the presidency. After Watergate, after Vietnam, after all of it, the media still help render us a "presidential nation"—while making us less "congressional."

There is perhaps a major lesson in all this concerning the media, our political institutions, and their respective roles. *The media,* by

---

for the president than in 1969. Susan Miller, using 1974—the year when impeachment proceedings were instituted against Nixon—reached very different results, with Congress getting slightly more print coverage than the president. See "News Coverage of Congress: The Search for the Ultimate Spokesman," *Journalism Quarterly,* vol. 54, no. 3 (Autumn 1977), p. 461.

[38] Arthur Miller, Edie Goldenberg, and Lutz Erbring, "Type-Set Politics: The Impact of Newspapers on Public Confidence," *American Political Science Review,* vol. 73 (June 1979), p. 71.

focusing so fully on the office of president and then inevitably on the inadequacies of any person holding the job, *may be producing an office that is more powerful but at the same time may be weakening the political power of each individual president.* On the other hand, *the media,* by treating Congress poorly but its incumbents relatively well, *may be strengthening incumbents but weakening their institution.* This process has probably been at work since the advent of national radio.

The Institution: Changing Membership. Institutional change probably flows less quickly from changes in Congress's media image than from changes in its personnel. Only fifteen members of the 1980 Senate were senators in 1960; only forty-one members of the 1980 House were members then. The newcomers have changed Congress more than anything else. But it is my contention that the most important institutional change to have occurred as a result of the new media-mix in Congress has been with the membership. The new media-mix, in and out of Congress, has manufactured a new kind of candidate, a new kind of nominee, and a new kind of incumbent. This is not simply a matter of looks or hair style, although clearly they are part of the change. It comes down to a question of style or legislative personality—what James David Barber might call "legislative character."

We have already seen evidence of how different the new generation in Congress is in its attitude toward the media. Compared with the class of 1958, the class of 1978 was three times more likely to make heavy use of the congressional recording studio, three times more likely to regard the House TV system as "very useful," three times more likely to have relied "a lot" on TV in the last election. Over 60 percent of the class of 1978 said "yes" when asked if they had used paid media consultants in their first successful campaign for Congress. Nobody in the class of 1958 answering my survey had used a media consultant to get elected the first time. Almost beyond doubt the media culture of the membership has changed.

Although these figures pertain to campaign style more than legislative character, one may infer that the increasingly greater reliance on the media for nomination, election, status in the Congress, and reelection is one sign of a new congressional character—one more dynamic, egocentric, immoderate, and, perhaps, intemperate. The evidence here is speculative and thin. But interviews and recent studies indicate that the media, intentionally or unintentionally, have recruited, maintained, and promoted a new legislative temperament.

One media consultant who works for Democrats and started

doing media campaigns in the early 1970s pointed out that in the old days (the 1960s) the machines sent "grey, [Richard] Daley types" to Congress, but that the media have changed the style. Another consultant who started helping Republicans with their media campaigns in the late 1960s and has recently directed a major Republican presidential campaign believes that the media (plus the decision in *Buckley* v. *Valeo,* the case outlawing limits on a congressional candidate's spending) have changed the type of congressional candidate and officeholder.

> You look through . . . and you get the guys with the blow-dried hair who read the script well. That's not the kind of guy who'd been elected to the Congress or Senate ten years ago. You've got a guy who is not concerned about issues; who isn't concerned about the mechanics of government; who doesn't attend committee meetings; who avoids taking positions at any opportunity and who yet is a master at getting his face in the newspapers and on television and all that. You get the modern media candidate which is, in a lot of ways, Senator [name], who has no objective right to be elected to public office.

The same consultant sees a new style of legislator:

> You get a lot of young guys particularly who do two things, sort of the typical young congressman these days. He gets elected, he hires a bunch of pros to run his office, sets up a sophisticated constituent contact operation through the mails and through other things and an actuality service and all that kind of thing. Then he goes out and showboats to get more press so that he gets reelected and is considered for higher office. Those become of much more importance to him than the functioning as a national legislator or part of a branch of government.
>
> And I think that you . . . get that type of person who comes out of those sort of activist ranks but they're not so much issue-oriented, they're just people, they're showboats and there are a lot of those people in any class of Congress, much more so I suspect than there were ten years ago. [Why?] Because of media, because it does attract a different kind of person or a person who adjusts to the reality of the best thing to do.

These remarks only touch on the question of character per se, and research on legislative character is extremely scarce. One of the few studies, still unpublished, was by Donald Hellman, who interviewed the personal secretaries of twenty members of the 95th Congress, asking specifically about the personality and character of their bosses. Ten of the secretaries worked for freshmen; ten for very senior members. Hellman asked directly about the way the members acted under pressure or in adversity. Checking the responses for adjectives conveying images of members, he found that older members were described as "softer," "weaker," "more open" than freshmen. Older members—despite what one might expect on the basis of aging per se—were one and a half times more likely to be described in "soft" terms.[39]

Not surprisingly, I find an explanation for this in the media. The new media-mix in congressional politics encourages and promotes people who are telegenic and possibly egocentric. The implications are straightforward enough—a Congress that is less likely to get along with itself, more likely to focus on higher office, less likely to behave as a group than as a disjointed collection of individuals.

Of course, it is also a more energized Congress. That set of outcomes is not inherently good or bad for politics, but it does work to the detriment of Congress as an institution. In fact, the changes wrought by the media on congressional character may be the most damaging consequence of all for the institution per se. But, here again, what hurts the institution has done little to hurt the individual members.

Conclusion. In the final analysis the changes in congressional media over the last twenty years have produced mixed blessings and not just a few ironies—for Congress, for its members, and for us.

For the House membership the changes have meant greater safety but, at the same time, greater anxiety about getting reelected. Not surprisingly, the members are more likely to remember the trials of Dan Flood than the case of "Congressman Press." Ironically, the media themselves have been less likely to worry about post-Watergate morality than many of the members of the House or the Senate.

For the senators, changes in the media-mix have meant less safety but, at the same time, greater opportunity for achieving national prominence. Network news coverage of the Senate can make an investigating senator a household word in a matter of days. Some senators have become nationally prominent through television almost overnight.

On both sides of the Capitol the changes in the media have given younger members and maverick members more political visibility— and consequently greater power—than ever before. But at the same

[39] Donald Hellman, "Change in the Personalities of Congressmen," master's paper, Catholic University Department of Politics, 1978, p. 19.

time, modern news media have also meant that all the members of Congress work in an institution that has ever increasing image problems. In a final irony the modern media in Congress mean that although more policy information is directly available to members than ever before, the members themselves spend no more time with that information than they ever did. Public relations, after all, has become more and more demanding on the members' time. Policy can be more efficiently handled by staff or subcommittee.

The media generally benefit public people, not public institutions. For the most part the new media-mix has rendered Congress no less safe, but a little less serviceable—the members no less important, but the Congress a little less viable. The major impact of the modern media on Congress has not been the result of post-Watergate journalism but the inevitable consequence of focusing more public attention on elected officials, all of whom owe their jobs to local constituents. The media have made congressmen somewhat more anxious, somewhat more adept at media manipulation, and somewhat more responsive to local interests. But this merely shows us that Congress and its membership have a highly democratic base. What the new media have done to Congress is what one would expect when the level of information concerning an essentially democratic institution increases—greater responsiveness to the locals and greater concern about saving oneself. In all that, there is obviously good news, and bad.

PART TWO

The Institution

4

Subcommittee Government: New Channels for Policy Making

Roger H. Davidson

On Capitol Hill, the center stage of policy making is held by the committees and subcommittees. They are the political nerve ends, the gatherers of information, the sifters of alternatives, the refiners of legislative detail. "It is not far from the truth to say," wrote Woodrow Wilson in 1885, "that Congress in session is Congress on public exhibition, whilst Congress in its committee-rooms is Congress at work."[1] Wilson characterized legislative policy making as "committee government"; today, the term "subcommittee government" is nearer the mark.

As both houses of Congress discovered within a generation after their inception, legislative assemblies that not merely ratify laws but draft them must rely on specialized subgroups to attend to legislative details. Public policy is, of course, usually the work of many hands. Oftentimes, individuals are credited with policy innovations that, if truth be told, are the products of many people working over a period of months or years. An often-asked question is, Where do policies originate? To a considerable extent, the answer is in committee and subcommittee rooms on Capitol Hill.

Subcommittee government, then, lies close to the core of the present-day Congress and has everything to do with its capacities and limitations as a policy maker. Despite its unflattering media image— as a fusty place inhabited by obdurate and senile politicians—Congress in the past two decades has become perhaps the most radically altered of all our major governmental institutions. Changes have permeated

---

The views expressed in this chapter are the author's and do not necessarily reflect those of the Congressional Research Service.
[1] Woodrow Wilson, *Congressional Government* (New York: Mentor Books, 1954), p. 79.

virtually every nook and cranny on Capitol Hill—membership, structures, procedures, folkways, and staffs. Present-day subcommittee government works very differently from the committee government system of Wilson's day, of the post-1910 era, even of the post–World War II period. Yet the present system was not built overnight, but rather developed out of its antecedents in response to pressures both outside and inside the institution. In order to comprehend subcommittee government, therefore, it is essential to understand its predecessors and the forces that shaped them.

The Mechanisms of Change

I have argued elsewhere that it is instructive to view congressional change as a form of organizational innovation.[2] Like all organizations, Congress strives for self-preservation, protecting its autonomy and influence. To maximize its survival in such terms, it must adjust successfully to external demands while coping with internal pressures. These constitute the outside and inside pressures for innovation— what one might call the demand-pull and cost-push of organizational equilibrium—which alone or in tandem can challenge the organization to reassess its traditional ways of doing things. Problems of both types impinge upon congressional workgroups.

External pressures upon congressional workgroups typically emanate from the structure of the public agenda—for example, the number and type of problems presented to Congress for resolution. No one disputes that we live in an age of massive and obtrusive government activity. In spite of much-heralded taxpayers' revolts, the range and depth of governmental involvement show no sign of waning: although people resist paying taxes, they expect governmental services to be available, and erosion of local taxing powers tends merely to shift demands to state and federal governments. As the decade of the 1970s began, the environmental movement had just come of age, generating novel legislative and oversight demands; as the decade closed, Congress made a major commitment to resuscitate the Chrysler Corporation—no doubt a precedent for other troubled industries. As the number and range of public issues have grown, workgroups have proliferated on Capitol Hill, mainly subcommittees, task forces, and special or select committees.

Substantive shifts in policy agendas also produce shifts in the Capitol Hill workgroup structure. New subjects are added; old topics

[2] See, for example, Roger H. Davidson and Walter J. Oleszek, "Adaptation and Consolidation: Structural Innovation in the U.S. House of Representatives," *Legislative Studies Quarterly*, vol. 1 (February 1976), pp. 37-65.

are pushed aside, though very rarely removed altogether. As George Galloway once observed, the history of the United States can be written in terms of the creation (and sometimes abolition) of congressional workgroups. Thus, Commerce and Manufactures panels soon appeared in the House and Senate (in 1795 and 1816, respectively); Public Lands dated from 1805 and 1816, respectively; the House Freedman's Affairs Committee appeared in 1866. The Senate's Pacific Railroads Committee appeared in 1863, and the House Roads Committee in 1913. Spurred by the Russians' Sputnik satellite, the U.S. space program was boosted by the creation of two committees in 1958—House Science and Astronautics and Senate Aeronautical and Space Sciences. Demands for policing members' behavior led to ethics panels in the Senate (1964) and the House (1967). In its 1977 reorganization, the Senate kept up with the times by adding "Energy" and "Environment" to two of its committees; as the energy crisis deepened, the House in 1980 pondered creating a new committee.

Another external factor is competition from the executive branch. The noted constitutional scholar Edward S. Corwin once characterized the Constitution as "an invitation to struggle" between Congress and the other governmental branches. Accordingly, workgroups are created to compete with executive agencies in gathering information or to oversee the implementation of policies. For example, when Congress enacted the Budget and Accounting Act of 1921 it also consolidated the scattered appropriations functions into a single committee in each house. Confrontations with the Nixon administration over the impoundment of appropriated funds hastened the enactment in 1974 of a new budgetary process, with its twin House and Senate budget panels. And while congressional committees by no means exactly mirror executive agencies, there is a rough parallelism through which given congressional workgroups develop proprietary interests in their executive-branch counterparts.

Internal pressures, on the other hand, emanate in part from individual members' goals. Realizing the relevance of committee seats to their political careers, members seek seats on committees dealing with matters of importance to their constituents or affording opportunities for public exposure and recognition. Several consequences flow from this. First, committee systems in both houses have been structured to embrace a wide range of interests, often quite narrowly defined. Moreover, norms are sufficiently permissive to allow legislators to gravitate to workgroups complementing their backgrounds or constituency needs—westerners to Interior, ocean-port representatives to Commerce or Merchant Marine and Fisheries, rural-area legislators to Agriculture, urbanites to Banking, and so forth. Second, to impress

101

voters and expand their influence, members prefer to hold seats on several workgroups, if possible serving as chairmen or ranking minority members. Hence, persistent pressures are exerted to expand the number of available workgroups and the overall number of seats and leadership posts.[3]

Another internal force for innovation was factional warfare over control of committee and subcommittee chairmanships. This was essentially an ideological and generational dispute over the seniority system, fought within the Democratic ranks and caused by a temporary mismatch between the party's senior leadership (overwhelmingly conservative and southern) and its rank and file (increasingly northern and liberal). By the early 1970s this internal contradiction had been resolved in favor of youth and liberalism.

The Triumph of Subcommittee Government

During most of the development of Congress, the basic organizational building block was the standing committee. Although in their earliest years the two chambers processed legislation with ad hoc committees and floor deliberations, the House established its first standing committee (Elections) in 1789, adding several others over the following three decades. In 1816 the Senate created its initial twelve standing committees. A large number of committees came into being—at one time, no fewer than sixty-one in the House and seventy-four in the Senate. As committees proliferated, their influence, prestige, and autonomy grew. By 1885 Wilson wrote of government by the standing committees of Congress; later, Mary Parker Follett observed that "Congress no longer exercises its lawful function of lawmaking; that has gone to the committees as completely as in England it has passed to the Cabinet."[4]

The old-style committee system, it is well to remember, accommodated pressing institutional needs, external and internal. The policy agenda demanded expertise and specialization, yet the growing size of the two chambers impaired floor decision making on detailed questions. As new executive agencies appeared, legislative workgroup specialization was a natural concomitant. There was also an internal spur to the proliferation of committees: the emergence, late in the nineteenth century, of legislative careerism. As more and more mem-

[3] Louis P. Westefield, "Majority Party Leadership and the Committee System in the House of Representatives," *American Political Science Review*, vol. 68 (March 1974), pp. 1593-1604.

[4] Mary Parker Follett, *The Speaker of the House of Representatives* (New York: Longmans, Green, 1896), p. 246.

bers made careers out of congressional service, their committee memberships and leadership posts opened routes of advancement within Congress. In order to regularize these internal career ladders, the seniority "rule" became virtually inviolable.

The system was prevented from flying apart initially by a reasonably coherent party structure, which toward the end of the nineteenth century brought both chambers close to party government.[5] By the 1920s, however, party government was no longer a viable organizing principle. Committee autonomy was buttressed when, in its 1910 "revolt" against Speaker Joseph G. Cannon, the House suspended the Speaker's power to make committee assignments and schedule floor debates. In the Senate, party coherence was undermined by the Seventeenth Amendment, which obliged senators to seek an electoral base that was often independent of partisan or patronage networks. Committee autonomy and seniority careerism became pervasive in both houses, where leadership was described by perceptive observers as "invisible" or "in commission."[6]

Needless to say, committee government was no sudden creation. The workgroups' autonomy flowed from such factors as rising workloads in the chamber, the members' careerism, rigid adherence to seniority in the selection of committee leaders, and the long-term erosion of partisan loyalties. Under such circumstances, rejection of strong centralized leadership was virtually inevitable. The Senate never institutionalized such leadership; the House explicitly rejected it in 1910 and by 1919 had abandoned the alternative of caucus control as well. Although partisan leadership was not impossible, the most successful leaders were those who, like House Speaker Sam Rayburn (1940–1946, 1949–1952, 1955–1961) and Senate Majority Leader Lyndon Johnson (1954–1961), bargained skillfully with committee leaders and represented their interests.

The Era of the Committee Chairmen. The zenith of committee government occurred between the years 1937 and 1971, when it seemed that Congress was ruled by a relatively small coterie of powerful committee chairmen. Of course, not all committee chairmen were blessed with extraordinary talent or skill, the vagaries of the seniority system being what they were. To a remarkable degree, however, the two

[5] See David W. Brady, *Congressional Voting in a Partisan Era* (Lawrence: University Press of Kansas, 1972); and David J. Rothman, *Politics and Power: The United States Senate, 1869-1901* (Cambridge: Harvard University Press, 1966).

[6] George Rothwell Brown, *The Leadership of Congress* (Indianapolis: Bobbs-Merrill, 1922), chaps. 12, 14; Robert Luce, *Congress: An Explanation* (Cambridge: Harvard University Press, 1926), p. 117.

chambers came to be dominated by the personalities and resources of these individuals. The Senate boasted such chairmen as Carl Hayden of Appropriations, Carter Glass of Banking, Richard Russell of Armed Services, Arthur Vandenberg of Foreign Relations, and Walter George and Russell Long of Finance. In the House were such figures as Clarence Cannon of Appropriations, Carl Vinson of Armed Services, Wayne Aspinall of Interior, Howard W. Smith of Rules, and Wilbur Mills of Ways and Means.

These committee barons wielded formidable powers, informal as well as formal. All the individuals mentioned above (and a number of others like them) brought to their jobs single-minded dedication, experience gained from long association with the committee's subject matter, and a mastery of technical issues matched by very few of today's members.[7] Yet talent was not the sole base of the chairman's power, and in any event not all chairmen were equally talented or forceful. The "other face of power" for even the most respected chairmen was tough-minded use of formal prerogatives and procedures. Chairmen could, and often did, control the flow of legislation, hire staff, monopolize time in hearings, dominate paperwork, and manipulate subcommittee workloads to tighten their grip upon committee policy making. Strong chairmen retained the most important issues in full committee and discouraged the development of subcommittees, either eliminating them altogether (as did Mills in Ways and Means) or keeping their jurisdictions tightly constricted (as did Vinson on Armed Services). Even when subcommittees were employed, the committee chairmen molded them by appointing their members and chairmen. Between 1937 and 1971 the workgroups in both houses were dominated by a handful of senior leaders.

Moreover, committees, especially in the House, were protected by procedures and norms from intrusions by noncommittee legislators. Bills were typically referred exclusively to a single committee, remaining under that committee's jurisdiction in perpetuity. Norms of specialization and reciprocity discouraged legislators outside the committee from meddling. In the House, the Rules Committee often granted committee leaders' requests for "rules" limiting amendments or waiving points of order against committee-reported bills—which inhibited a committee's would-be critics. In the House, too, unrecorded teller votes used for amendments in Committee of the Whole had the effect of discouraging noncommittee members from remaining on the floor and no doubt gave committee leaders countless "unearned"

[7] For a favorable portrait of one of the most effective of these seniority leaders, Wilbur Mills, see John F. Manley, *The Politics of Finance* (Boston: Little, Brown, 1970), esp. chap. 4.

floor victories. Although the Senate had no such restrictions, adhering to the principle of open (and often extended) floor debate, organizational folkways frowned upon aggressive participation by members who were junior or who were not on the relevant committee.[8] In both houses, the final stages of the legislative process were tightly controlled, for membership on conference committees was normally reserved for senior committee members.

Nor did these prerogatives flourish in a vacuum. As usual, both outside and inside pressures had forced the legislative workgroups to adapt. Post–New Deal growth in the national government, of course, placed ever greater pressure upon Congress for specialization; and the dispersion of power in the executive branch encouraged direct linkages between committees and agencies. The era of big government also legitimized interest groups' participation in decision making affecting them—a type of corporate policy making that Theodore Lowi terms "interest group liberalism." Thus congressional linkages with policy communities frequently took the form of tripartite arrangements among the committee that processed the legislation, the executive agency that implemented it, and the lobby group that benefited from it. These were the so-called iron triangles—a shorthand term that embraced a wide variety of relationships. Whatever form they took, they characterized a large number of policy arenas, especially those associated with domestic distributive policies.

The seniority leaders' power was underpinned by Congress's organizational attributes. First, careerism in both houses had reached a high plateau marked by low turnover and lengthy tenure. In the 93rd Congress (1973–1974), for example, the average House member had served 5.6 terms or more than 11 years, the average senator almost 2 terms or 11.2 years. With such extensive tenure, nearly everyone had a stake in the internal seniority ladders. Second, party committees endeavored to give members the committee assignments they preferred—a tendency that accentuated certain committees' membership biases and perpetuated their decision-making premises and norms. Once ensconced in their committees, members realized that their Washington reputations hinged upon diligent committee performance, and their chances for leadership upon longevity.

Yet another buttress for the committee system lay in factional tensions within the two houses. Although during this period the Democrats controlled Congress for all but four years (1947–1948 and

[8] For the Senate, see Donald R. Matthews, *The U.S. Senators and Their World* (Chapel Hill: University of North Carolina Press, 1960), pp. 92-97, 99-101; for the House, see Richard F. Fenno, Jr., "The Internal Distribution of Influence: The House," in David B. Truman, ed., *The Congress and America's Future* (Englewood Cliffs, N.J.: Prentice-Hall, 1965), pp. 71-73.

1953–1955), from the second Roosevelt administration well into the 1970s the party was badly divided between its liberal presidential wing and its conservative congressional wing (southerners, for example, composed the majority of Senate and House Democrats well into the 1950s). Typically lacking party competition, southern and border states were in the habit of repeatedly returning their incumbents to Washington—a habit that made those members winners in the seniority game. Even when the Democrats' conservative wing was on the wane, its leaders benefited from alliances with Republicans to prolong their dominance over policy making. Within the committees, conservative Democratic chairmen frequently enjoyed close working relationships with their minority counterparts. Some notable examples were Tom Connally and Arthur Vandenberg (Senate Foreign Relations), Clarence Cannon and John Taber (House Appropriations), Wilbur Mills and John Byrnes (House Ways and Means), and "Judge" Smith and a succession of ranking Republicans (House Rules).

In other words, the committee chairmen of this era—despite their press image as crotchety obstructionists—were successful precisely because they spoke for intracommittee majorities (not limited to the majority party) and facilitated those majorities' political or career goals. When chairmen proved unable or unwilling to facilitate these goals—whether through incompetence, laziness, or obstreperousness—they often found themselves bypassed and their powers emasculated. When finally the system itself became dysfunctional in meeting institutional or individual member needs, it was transformed into a very different set of arrangements.

The Revolt against Seniority. That transformation took place in the early 1970s, primarily within the majority Democratic party. One effect of the seniority system was to perpetuate the political triumphs of the previous generation; when the party's factional balance shifted, seniority caused a generation gap between leaders and backbenchers. Such a gap—in region, district type, ideology, and even age—lay at the heart of the Democrats' seniority struggles. Even as the Democrats became a truly national party, their earlier regional base was perpetuated by their seniority leaders: as late as 1973, southerners composed less than 30 percent of congressional Democrats, yet commanded 46 percent of House full-committee chairmanships and 53 percent of those in the Senate. As new members arrived in the late 1960s and early 1970s, the gap between them and the seniority leaders widened. In 1973, the average House committee chairman was sixty-six years old and had almost thirty years of congressional service behind him; the average Senate chairman was sixty-four years old and had twenty-one years' experience. Not only did such a situation squander talent in the mid-seniority ranks, but it eventually generated frustration and resentment.

The fires of resentment were fueled by shifts in the electoral system that heightened the value of the visibility, credit-taking, and staff resources associated with committee leadership posts. Grass-roots party organizations declined, in most localities forfeiting their historic roles as sponsors and anchors for political careers. Politicians necessarily became individual entrepreneurs, relying upon their own resources for building and nurturing supportive constituencies. Laborious cultivation of reputations within committee chambers—a hallmark of the "seniority-protégé-apprenticeship system"—counted for little in this electoral environment. What the new breed of politicians needed was the "quick fix": early acquisition of the public platform and staff associated with committee leadership, and perhaps a conspicuous role in floor deliberations. Senators, with statewide constituencies (and often White House aspirations), were the first to dilute the old committee system; and soon the House followed suit.

The mileposts on the path toward subcommittee government are too numerous to be recounted here, and in any event have been fully documented elsewhere.[9] In the Senate, the transformation occurred in the 1960s and was relatively peaceful. The process was launched by the so-called Johnson rule, whereby every Democratic senator received at least one major committee assignment, and was hastened by the open, benign leadership of Majority Leader Mike Mansfield (1961–1976).

In the House, the revolts were spasmodic and occasionally bitter. The first assaults on chairmen's prerogatives occurred within the committees, in a series of internal revolts against recalcitrant or inept leaders. Second, prodded by a growing liberal majority typified by the Democratic Study Group (DSG), the Democratic Caucus began to reassert its role in ratifying leadership choices—timidly at first but with increasing forcefulness—until in 1975 three seniority leaders were actually pushed aside by caucus votes.

Finally, and most important, committee chairmen's powers were circumscribed by the institutionalization of subcommittees. Already numerous, subcommittees were originally creatures of the full committees, dependent upon the chairmen for their membership, powers,

[9] See, for example, Norman J. Ornstein, "Causes and Consequences of Congressional Change: Subcommittee Reforms in the House of Representatives," in Ornstein, ed., *Congress in Change: Evolution and Reform* (New York: Praeger, 1975), pp. 88-114; and David W. Rohde, "Committee Reform in the House of Representatives and the Subcommittee Bill of Rights," *Annals of the American Academy of Political and Social Sciences*, vol. 411 (January 1974), pp. 39-47.

and staff. Now, as a result of a series of Democratic Caucus actions, subcommittees acquired a life of their own. In 1971 members were limited to chairing only one legislative subcommittee—a move that enlarged the ranks of seniority leaders and brought more junior members into leadership roles. In 1973 the so-called subcommittee bill of rights empowered majority-party caucuses within each standing committee (subject to Caucus regulations) to determine the subcommittees' membership, size, jurisdiction, and budget—formerly prerogatives of the committee chairmen. Two years later, most committees were required to establish a minimum number of subcommittees.[10]

For the record, similar tensions, though more generational than ideological, surfaced among Republicans. For the GOP, however, internal seniority was never a burning issue. Because of the GOP's prolonged minority status, its seniority posts were less valued than the Democrats'. Lacking the incentive of chairmanships, moreover, senior GOP members were quicker to retire, producing rapid generational turnover. Republicans thus focused their attention on floor reforms that would give them greater leverage over debate and voting.

The changes that took place in the 1970s were adaptations of a specialized workgroup structure that emerged in the nineteenth century and reached its maturity in the World War II era. The new system of subcommittee government is very different from its predecessor, which has been so convincingly described by researchers of the 1950s and 1960s. The new system is not mature, in that not all of the details of its operations have been institutionalized. Yet it is a highly complex and articulated system. It has profound implications for present and future policy making. And, it has brought a new generation of problems which, although widely acknowledged by members, are unlikely to be resolved in the foreseeable future. To understand these implications and problems, we must probe more deeply into the character of the new order.

Members' Roles in Subcommittee Government

From the individual legislator's point of view, congressional workgroups are useful because they assist in attaining personal and career goals. Not only can workgroup assignments enhance a legislator's reelection chances, but they enable him to shape public policy, or to influence fellow members, or to lay the groundwork for a subsequent career. No wonder, then, that newly elected members concentrate on gaining attractive assignments and that leaders are under intense pressures to maximize the number of attractive options.

[10] House Democratic Caucus, *Manual* (revised May 2, 1979), Sections M II–M V.

Multiplicity of Assignments. Of all the characteristics of subcommittee diffusion, the most striking is the huge number of workgroups and assignments. In the 96th Congress (1979–1980), there were 113 *standing* workgroups (committees and subcommittees) in the Senate and 170 in the House. These units represented 965 available seats or positions in the Senate and nearly 2,500 in the House. Accordingly, the average senator held nearly 10 seats on standing workgroups, while the average representative had 5.5 assignments. Leadership posts were also numerous: in the 96th Congress, all but two Democratic senators and nearly half of all Democratic representatives chaired a committee or subcommittee. On the Republican side of the aisle, all of the senators and 80 percent of the representatives were ranking members of these units.

When all workgroup positions are included—not only seats on standing committees and subcommittees, but also seats on select, special, and joint committees and statutory boards or commissions— the full weight of members' commitments becomes evident. A House study completed in 1979 found that there were 210 jurisdictional units and the average representative boasted 6.2 assignments. Many members had far heavier commitments: no fewer than 223 representatives (159 Democrats and 64 Republicans) had 7 or more assignments, and one member had 13.[11] Figure 4–1 graphs the number of assignments in both parties, with the figures for majority-party members tending to be higher.

Recent decades have witnessed a seemingly inexorable proliferation of congressional workgroups and workgroup seats and a steady rise in the average member's number of assignments.[12] The only significant reversal of these trends took place in 1977, when the Senate consolidated a few of its committees and imposed stricter limits on the number of assignments an individual could have. Thus committees (standing, special, joint) were reduced by nearly a quarter, from 31 to 24; subcommittees were cut by one-third, from 174 to 117. Average assignments dropped from 18 (committees and subcommittees) in the 94th Congress to 11 in the 95th.[13]

If sustained personal participation in workgroup deliberations is a valid standard, then the typical senator or representative falls

[11] U.S. House of Representatives, Select Committee on Committees, *Final Report*, H. Rept. 96-866, 96th Congress, 2nd session, 1980, p. 303. Unless otherwise indicated, House figures are drawn from this document.

[12] Ibid., p. 302. Senate data through 1976 are summarized in U.S. Senate, Temporary Select Committee to Study the Senate Committee System, *The Senate Committee System*, 94th Congress, 2nd session, 1976, pp. 6–7.

[13] Judith H. Parris, "The Senate Reorganizes Its Committees, 1977," *Political Science Quarterly*, vol. 94 (Summer 1979), p. 332.

FIGURE 4–1

HOUSE MEMBERS' COMMITTEE AND SUBCOMMITTEE ASSIGNMENTS, 1979

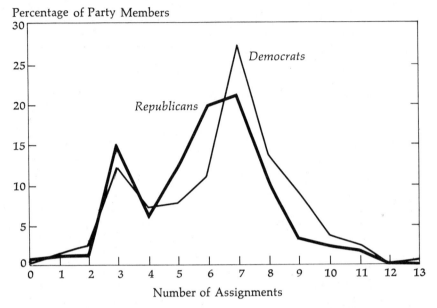

Percentage of Party Members

Number of Assignments

NOTE: Assignments include memberships on 210 panels, including standing, select, and joint committees and subcommittees, or subunits thereof.

SOURCE: U.S. House of Representatives, Select Committee on Committees, *Final Report*, H. Rept. 96-866, 96th Congress, 2nd session, 1980, p. 322.

short. With so many assignments, members are overextended and hard pressed to manage their crowded schedules. Scheduling problems, in fact, are endemic, with committee quorums difficult to achieve and members' attention often focused elsewhere. On peak days— midweek (Tuesdays through Thursdays) and midsession (April through July)—members commonly face scheduling conflicts between two, three, or more of their committees.[14] Even within given committees, scheduling is often haphazard—which means that subcommittees with overlapping memberships have the most conflicts. All too often, consideration of policy issues is limited to the chairman, perhaps one or two colleagues, and staff aides—a situation that im-

[14] U.S. House of Representatives, Commission on Administrative Review, *Administrative Reorganization and Legislative Management*, H. Doc. 95-232, 95th Congress, 2nd session, 1977, pp. 27-31; U.S. Senate, Commission on the Operation of the Senate, *Toward a Modern Senate*, S. Doc. 94-278, 94th Congress, 2nd session, 1977, pp. 35-38.

pairs the responsiveness, if not the expertise, of legislative workgroups.

In many cases, especially in the House, workgroups would be unwieldy if all the members showed up. Most House standing committees have become too large for viable deliberations. Appropriations has fifty-four members; most other major committees have more than forty members, followed closely at thirty-nine by such popular interest-based committees as Small Business and Merchant Marine. Subcommittees, too, are sometimes very large: two Merchant Marine and Fisheries subcommittees have twenty-eight members, and one on Banking, Housing, and Urban Affairs has twenty-seven. In the Senate, committees and subcommittees are markedly smaller, although one full committee, Appropriations, has twenty-eight members and two others twenty.

Under pressure from members and factions desiring representation, party leaders not only have allowed assignments to proliferate but have tended to accede to members' preferences for assignments. Inevitably, this means that legislators gravitate to those committees with which they, or their constituents, have the greatest affinity. Thus, many congressional workgroups are not microcosms of the parent houses, but are biased in one way or another. Overrepresentation of farm areas on agriculture panels, westerners on House Interior or Senate Energy, those representing major military installations on Armed Services, and seacoast interests on House Merchant Marine are familiar cases of demographic bias. From a painstaking compilation of committee rosters, one student concluded that more than half of all House committees were "plainly unrepresentative" of the parent chamber as the decade of the 1970s began.[15] Some of the most influential committees—Appropriations, Finance/Ways and Means, and House Rules—have become more representative, mainly because of pressures upon party leaders for balance. But on many other committees and subcommittees, biased memberships prevail.

Biased recruitment patterns, reinforced by long-term associations with clienteles outside the workgroups, yield decisions heavily predisposed toward the very interests under the workgroups' purview. As one representative observed in 1973 during the hearings of the Select Committee on Committees (Bolling committee), "It has generally been regarded . . . that the members of the committees should

---

[15] Carol F. Goss, "House Committee Characteristics and the Distributive Politics" (paper delivered at the annual meeting of the American Political Science Association, September 1975); Roger H. Davidson, "Representative and Congressional Committees," *Annals of the American Academy of Political and Social Science,* vol. 411 (January 1974), pp. 48-62.

almost be partisans for the legislation that goes through the committee and for the special interest groups that are affected by it."[16] To the extent that workgroups are boosters for the programs they sponsor, vigorous questioning of those programs may be frowned on by members and outside clienteles. Raising questions, it is argued, will only weaken a program's support and hamper the implementing agencies. Oversight is often shunned not only because it is regarded as unglamorous and unrewarding, but because it threatens workgroup norms and interpersonal comity.

Roles and Time Budgets. Proliferating workgroup responsibilities are only one aspect of the job of today's legislators. Legislative activities necessarily compete with other demands—constituency relations, most notably—for members' attention and time. The constituency service role has grown both quantitatively and qualitatively, as any Capitol Hill observer whose memory stretches back to the early 1960s can attest. Explanations for this phenomenon are not lacking: the growing size, educational attainment, and awareness of constituencies; technological innovations in communication and transportation (for example, the jet plane, WATS lines, and computerized mailings); the decline of parties, which has forced incumbents to devise alternative strategies of self-promotion; and the public's expectations, which have kept pace with the members' increasing willingness to run errands for their constituents. Whatever the causes, legislators are more and more attentive to their constituents—traveling home frequently, making personal appearances, and working on mailings, newsletters, and other forms of communication.[17]

Escalating expectations on all sides have forced subtle changes in the ways legislators spend their time. Senators were the first to surrender the bulk of their legislative work to staff aides. In the House, the transformation is more recent. Well into the 1960s, representatives typically did their own research and preparation for committee meetings and floor debates. According to a study completed in 1965, the average House member devoted virtually one day a week to "legislative research and reading"; he devoted another 3.5 hours

---

[16] U.S. House of Representatives, Select Committee on Committees, *Committee Organization in the House*, 93rd Congress, 1st session, 1973, vol. 1, p. 38.

[17] On district attentiveness, see Richard F. Fenno, Jr., *Home Style: House Members in their Districts* (Boston: Little, Brown, 1978), pp. 206-210; and Glenn R. Parker, "Sources of Change in Congressional District Attentiveness," *American Journal of Political Science*, vol. 24 (February 1980), pp. 115-124. Suggestive findings concerning legislators' activities are reported in: U.S. House of Representatives, Commission on Administrative Review, *Final Report*, H. Doc. 95-272, 95th Congress, 1st session, 1977, vol. 2, pp. 876-882.

a week to committee work outside of committee meetings, and spent 2.7 hours writing speeches and articles.[18]

If legislators have curtailed their personal legislative research, their involvement in the mechanics of the legislative process remains very high. Indeed, if we are to trust the available figures, representatives today spend virtually the same proportion of their time (about 38 percent) in committee meetings and floor sessions as they did in the mid-1960s.[19] That this commitment of time has remained constant in the face of escalating constituency demands is no doubt due to dramatic rises in both workgroup sessions and floor votes. Nonetheless, it is difficult to imagine that qualitative changes have not occurred: committee-hopping has become a habit, as has casual or symbolic floor voting—suggesting that the lawmakers' time may not be efficiently spent. Moreover, their scanty preparation often leaves members dependent on cues from staff and others: the average representative in 1977 reported spending only 12 minutes a day preparing legislation or speeches and another 11 minutes reading.

Many legislators express the desire to spend more time on legislation. In the 1977 survey, 154 House members were asked to identify those activities that should be very important and those to which they actually devoted a great deal of time.[20] The greatest gaps occurred in such activities as studying and legislative research; overseeing executive agencies, either personally or through formal subunits; debating and voting on legislation; negotiating with other members to build support for legislation; and working in committees to develop legislation. The respondents were also asked about the differences between what others expected them to do and what they thought they should be doing. The most commonly cited problem, mentioned by fully half of the members, was that "constituent demands detract from other functions." A second complaint, cited by 36 percent of the legislators, was that "scheduling problems and time pressures detract from the work of the House."

The dilemma faced by members who wish to concentrate on policy making is more than a matter of "scheduling"—though that is part of the situation. It is also a case of conflicting role expectations, of demands from various quarters that threaten to outrun legislators'

18 John S. Saloma in Donald G. Tacheron and Morris K. Udall, *The Job of the Congressman*, 2nd ed. (Indianapolis: Bobbs-Merrill, 1970), pp. 303-304.

19 U.S. House of Representatives, Commission on Administrative Review, *Administrative Reorganization and Legislative Management*, pp. 18-19.

20 House Commission on Administrative Review, *Final Report*, vol. 2, pp. 875 ff. See also Thomas E. Cavanagh, "The Two Arenas of Congress: Electoral and Institutional Incentives for Performance" (paper presented to the annual meeting of the American Political Science Association, 1978), esp. table 10.

schedules and energies. The prime institutional stratagem for coping with this dilemma is to rely on staff assistants—in members' offices, in committees and subcommittees, and in supporting agencies.

To a large degree, subcommittee government is staff government. The modern Capitol Hill bureaucracy betrays the character of Congress as a decentralized, nonhierarchical institution. It is not one bureaucracy but many, clustered about centers of power and in some sense defining those centers. Efforts to impose a common framework on the staff—in terms of, say, recruitment, screening, job definitions, salary schedules, equal opportunity, or grievance procedures—have thus far been stoutly resisted by legislators but will unquestionably resurface in the future.

The Policy-Making System

Within each chamber, policy making is now more than ever a multistage, multilayered process. Subcommittees are the leading initiators and drafters of legislative measures and reports. Full committees may play one of several different roles: they may deliberate *de novo* on legislation, they may review their subcommittees' decisions, or they may simply pass the subcommittees' products along to the full chamber. The chambers are the ratifiers or modifiers of proposals emanating from subcommittees and committees.

As a general proposition, the influence of full committees has declined in comparison with other elements in the process. Within the committees, initiative has tended to pass to the subcommittees. Beyond the committees, barriers erected to discourage involvement by interested members outside the originating panel—whether in information monopolies, voting arrangements, limitations upon debate or amendments, or informal norms—are less formidable today than they were a generation ago. At all stages, formal sessions are typically open rather than closed.

While the overall shifts, as reflected in gross workload indicators, are fairly evident, it would be mistaken to assume that *all* policy making adheres to these prescriptions. If there is any lesson to be gleaned from the rich and varied committee studies of the 1960s and 1970s, it is that, in Fenno's words, "congressional committees differ from one another."[21] Varying mixtures of members—who differ in personal goals and commitments—yield very different decision-making practices. Environmental factors—the issues and institutions

[21] Richard F. Fenno, Jr., *Congressmen in Committees* (Boston: Little, Brown, 1973), p. 280.

114

with which workgroups must deal—also have an impact on decision making.[22] House committees differ from Senate committees, the former being traditionally more autonomous and less permeable than the latter. What was true of committees in the 1960s is doubtless true of subcommittees in the 1980s.

The recentness of the shifts means, moreover, that numerous details have yet to be filled in. As yet there is no survey of subcommittees as broad in scope as Fenno's classic work on full committees. Not nearly enough is known, for example, about relationships between subcommittees and full committees, between subcommittees and chamber leaders, or among subcommittees themselves. Do today's subcommittee chairmen really compare to committee chairmen of an earlier era? To what extent are they masters of their own jurisdictions? To what extent do they control legislative outcomes? Answering such questions ought to have high priority on the research agenda of the next few years.

Given these caveats (which are by no means trivial), it is nonetheless useful to specify the broad outlines of what I have called subcommittee government. For this picture I draw upon available workload data, as well as particular cases of legislative policy making. Because the cases that are familiar tend to deal with highly salient and controversial issues, they may exaggerate somewhat the leading features of the decision-making system. Precisely because they are such high-priority matters, however, such issues are sensitive tests of congressional performance.

Committee and Subcommittee Work Patterns. The vitality of congressional workgroups is attested by the data presented in figure 4–2. The number of meetings has risen steadily in the Senate, dramatically in the House—equaling or exceeding the growth in the number of work units. In many cases the increased activity flowed directly from dispersion of subcommittee leadership posts, as younger, activist legislators assumed the newly available positions and proceeded to schedule hearings and sponsor legislation.[23]

[22] For some intriguing hypotheses concerning the impact of environmental factors, see David E. Price, "Policy Making in Congressional Committees: The Impact of 'Environmental' Factors," *American Political Science Review*, vol. 72 (June 1978), p. 568 et passim.

[23] For example, U.S. House of Representatives, Select Committee on Committees, *Monographs on the Committees of the House of Representatives*, committee print, 93rd Congress, 2nd session, 1974, pp. 51-52; and Norman J. Ornstein and David W. Rohde, "Revolt from Within: Congressional Change, Legislative Policy, and the House Commerce Committee," in Susan Welch and John G. Peters, eds., *Legislative Reform and Public Policy* (New York: Praeger, 1977), pp. 61-67.

FIGURE 4–2

CHANGING COMMITTEE AND SUBCOMMITTEE WORK PATTERNS,
84TH–95TH CONGRESS, 1955–1978

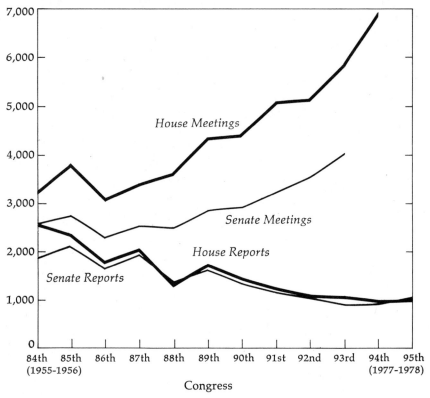

NOTE: Meetings include committee and subcommittee meetings; reports include
bills and joint resolutions.

SOURCE: U.S. House of Representatives, Commission on Administrative Review,
Administrative Organization and Legislative Management, H. Doc. 95-232,
95th Congress, 1st session, 1977, pt. 1, p. 4; U.S. Senate, Commission on the
Operation of the Senate, *Policy Analysis on Major Issues*, committee print,
94th Congress, 2nd session, 1977, p. 6; *Congressional Record*, vol. 124 (November
15, 1978), p. D 1583.

Subcommittee government came to the Senate in the wake of
the 1946 Legislative Reorganization Act and spread to the House a
decade or so later. In the early post–World War II years, according
to figures compiled by Lawrence C. Dodd and George Shipley, nearly
two-thirds of all Senate hearings were held in subcommittees.[24] In

[24] In Lawrence C. Dodd and Richard L. Schott, *Congress and the Administrative
State* (New York: John Wiley, 1979), pp. 190-210.

those same years, House subcommittees accounted for only about 20 to 25 percent of that chamber's hearings. In the mid-1950s, the proportion of House subcommittee meetings jumped to more than half, climbing steadily to 70 percent. This dramatic shift in meeting activity in the House occurred prior to the much-publicized subcommittee reforms of the early 1970s, which apparently served to ratify and legitimize a revolution that was already well advanced. Subcommittees now dominate legislative schedules in both houses, accounting for approximately 80 percent of all workgroup meetings in the 95th Congress (1977–1978).

Although this implies that subcommittees are now "where the action is," it does not mean that subcommittees are autonomous. True, investigative and oversight activity centers on the subcommittees—of which a dozen in the House and two in the Senate are explicitly designated for those purposes. It is also true that subcommittees tend to frame the issues and do the initial specifying of details. However, the scope and autonomy of a subcommittee's activities hinge upon a variety of intra- and extracommittee variables. Subcommittees normally lack separate appropriations and must depend on the full committee's sufferance for personnel, expenditures, hiring authority, scheduling, and even jurisdiction. On salient issues, moreover, subcommittees find many other members eager and able to get in on the action.

Subcommittees have long dominated the work of the Appropriations Committees, but they have lost much of their autonomy. One impetus for the new congressional budget process, in fact, was the charge that neither chamber brought together the thirteen regular appropriations bills to consider their relationship to one another. Budget committees were supposed to provide this overall scrutiny of budgetary and fiscal priorities. Although both panels have eschewed subcommittees, they have experimented with "task forces" specializing in specific budgetary categories. In the revenue committees, textbook examples of autonomous committees ("corporate" committees, in Fenno's term), the impact of the shift toward subcommittees has been mixed. The Senate Finance Committee retains a strong corporate identity, while the House Ways and Means Committee is markedly weakened. Reforms aimed at the post–Wilbur Mills panel, according to one student, left it "with a membership less willing to make tough tax decisions, without the strength to sustain tough tax decisions on floor votes, and without the ability to protect House members from having to cast votes on unpopular provisions."[25]

[25] Bruce I. Oppenheimer, "Policy Effects of U.S. House Reform: Decentralization and the Capacity to Resolve Energy Issues," *Legislative Studies Quarterly*, vol. 5 (February 1980), pp. 15-16.

In other issue areas, workgroup patterns are quite varied. Issues with low public salience and arousing little conflict are typically handled in subcommittee with little interference at the committee or floor stages. In the absence of incentives for widespread member involvement, legislators and staff members from the panel with original jurisdiction are the primary, and perhaps the only, cue-givers. As in the past, such issues probably account for a large portion of the legislation processed by Congress. Issues that are salient and conflictual are quite a different story, as we shall see.

Workgroups range widely in workload and productivity. Figures compiled by the House Select Committee on Committees indicate that during the 95th Congress two Commerce subcommittees (Energy and Power; Health and the Environment) held 169 and 177 meetings respectively, consuming nearly 500 hours apiece. This was more than four times as much time as was required by *all* subcommittees of the House District or Administration committees. Busier subcommittees resemble full committees in their workloads; not surprisingly, the Energy and Power Subcommittee was a prime candidate in 1980 for elevation to full-committee status. At the other end of the scale are subunits that rarely meet, either because their duties are limited (the Subcommittee on Printing, for example, met six times for a total of 2.3 hours during 1977–1978) or because their subject matter has diminished in importance (the Cotton Subcommittee, for example, held five meetings in 1977–1978, for 3.7 hours).[26]

More workgroup activity does not necessarily mean more laws. As figure 4–2 indicates, the number of reports to the full chambers has actually declined over the past twenty-five years, as has the number of laws passed. However, these figures are deceptive. It is true that, although more bills are introduced than previously, fewer are reported, receive floor consideration, or attain final passage. However, those measures that are passed tend to be longer, more complex, and subject to more floor amendments than their predecessors.[27] Moreover, the volume of oversight activity—which does not inevitably lead to formal reports or statutory revisions—has grown significantly. In both houses, the number of hearings has grown overall.[28]

Jurisdictional Politics. Jurisdictional politics is a ubiquitous feature of present-day congressional policy making. To hold jurisdiction means

[26] U.S. House of Representatives, Select Committee on Committees, *Final Report*, H. Rept. 96-866, 96th Congress, 2nd session, 1980, pp. 303-304.

[27] Allen Schick, "Complex Policy Making in the United States Senate," in U.S. Senate, Commission on the Operation of the Senate, *Policy Analysis on Major Issues*, committee print, 94th Congress, 2nd session, 1977, pp. 4-7.

[28] Dodd and Schott, *Congress*, pp. 168-169.

to claim a piece of the action. Therefore, jurisdiction is as central to the life of a member or a congressional subunit as votes or the ability to hire staff. It is assiduously cultivated by aggressive committee and subcommittee leaders and in many instances is the subject of bitter contests or elaborate negotiations. It is also commonly subject to overlaps and duplication—given the multiplicity of congressional workgroups and the complexity of contemporary issues. Everyone seems to be getting in on the policy-making act; or, some might say, everyone is getting in every one else's way.

One of the commonest forms of overlap occurs simply because the same policy objectives may be approached through authorizations, appropriations, or revenue measures—by no means separate processes, as textbooks sometimes imply. A leading student of the appropriations process writes:

> The real world of the legislative process differs considerably from the idealized model of the two-step authorization-appropriation procedure. Authorization bills contain appropriations, appropriation bills contain authorization, and the order of their enactment is sometimes reversed. . . . Moreover, the enactment of the Congressional Budget Act of 1974 further compounds the problem of distinguishing between the two stages.[29]

In a word, appropriations subcommittees can and do deal with policy matters; authorizations bodies can and do force the hand of appropriations panels, and in some cases even dabble at appropriating themselves. What is more, policies that can be promoted by government spending can usually be promoted by tax incentives, and vice versa.

Following the constitutional provision (Article I, Section 5) that "each house may determine the rules of its proceedings," the respective chambers specify the jurisdictions of their committees. These were first codified in the 1946 Legislative Reorganization Act but by the early 1970s were so obsolete they only approximated the legislation actually handled by the committees. Committee reform efforts in the House (Bolling committee, 1973–1974) and the Senate (Stevenson committee, 1976–1977) were aimed at modernizing and realigning committee jurisdictions. Although neither effort resulted in jurisdictional shifts, both produced jurisdictional definitions that were far more detailed and precise than they had been before.

[29] Louis Fisher, "The Authorization-Appropriation Process in Congress: Formal Rules and Informal Practices," *Catholic University Law Review*, vol. 29 (Fall 1979), pp. 52-105.

119

Today subcommittees, too, claim jurisdictional territories of their own. Under the old committee system, subcommittee jurisdictions were determined by committee chairmen—sometimes capriciously, sometimes with an even hand. Nowadays, these jurisdictions are supposed to be agreed upon by a majority of the full committee's majority-party members, although committee chairmen or their staff in practice refer the measures. In the Senate these jurisdictions are rarely embodied in the rules, resting instead upon internal committee precedent or negotiation. As part of the "subcommittee bill of rights," House subcommittees are guaranteed jurisdictions and prompt referrals of bills. Some House committees, like Foreign Affairs or Science and Technology, have rules spelling out subcommittee jurisdictions in detail; in other cases subcommittees are not listed at all or are merely listed by name. Certain key policies are dealt with in full committee—for example, the internal revenue code (Finance; Ways and Means) and foreign assistance bills (Foreign Affairs). A very few committees, like Rules, still give their chairmen considerable discretion, and most provide for discharging subcommittees from considering measures after a given period of time. Because jurisdictional overlap among these units is inevitable, they frequently meet together to conduct hearings or to mark up legislation.

Throughout most of their history, the two chambers referred legislation to single committees, which then accrued by precedent jurisdiction not only over that measure but also over any subsequent measures that were amended to or flowed from it. However, activist legislators learned to draft bills artfully so that they would be referred to their own committees, sometimes by framing them as amendments to existing statutes already within their committees' jurisdiction. The rush for new jurisdictional territory stretched out of shape the traditional jurisdictional metes and bounds, as embodied in the rules.

The Senate, with its courtesy norms and its informal modes of doing business, easily achieved multiple referrals of legislation through unanimous consent motions resting upon private negotiations among the interested parties. During the 95th Congress (1977–1978), 236 multiple referrals were recorded in the Senate—most shared by two committees though some involving as many as four.[30] Joint referrals are most common in such areas as energy or transportation (Energy and Natural Resources; Environment and Public Works; Commerce, Science, and Transportation); health and welfare (Finance; Labor and Human Resources); and federal legal policies (Governmental Affairs; Judiciary). Unanimous consent agreements represent only a portion of

[30] *Congressional Record*, vol. 125 (February 7, 1979), p. S1126-7.

committees' cooperative efforts, which often take the form of off-the-record agreements for sharing meetings or personnel.

Joint reference of legislation came to the House in 1975. Before then, precedents forbade referral of measures to more than a single committee, although the same effect could be achieved by clever legislative drafting. In 1973, for example, three committees—Interior, Merchant Marine, and Public Works—were considering bills pertaining to deep-water port terminals. Following a recommendation of its Select Committee on Committees (the Bolling committee), the House authorized the Speaker to refer bills, or parts of bills, to more than a single committee. Three types of multiple referrals are employed: in a *joint referral,* a measure is referred to two or more committees simultaneously. To date the record for joint referrals is held by the Health Services Act of 1979 (H.R. 2969), which went to nine standing committees and seven subcommittees. In a *sequential referral,* a measure is referred first to one committee and then another, usually with time limits. In a *split referral,* various titles or sections are sent to different committees. For example, President Carter's 1977 omnibus energy bill (H.R. 6831) was divided and referred to five panels: Banking, Commerce, Government Operations, Public Works, and Ways and Means.

The Speaker also has the authority to create ad hoc committees or make other arrangements for referring legislation. In 1975 Speaker Carl Albert created such a panel to deal with the outer-continental shelf, with members drawn from Commerce, Merchant Marine, and Foreign Affairs. Two years later Speaker O'Neill created an ad hoc energy committee to expedite processing of President Carter's energy package (H. R. 6831). That same year a special committee to consider the president's welfare reform proposals was created by enlarging Representative James Corman's (Democrat, California) Ways and Means Subcommittee on Public Assistance and Unemployment Compensation to include the chairmen and six members each from Agriculture and Education and Labor.

Multiple referrals are now commonplace in the House. Of the more than 4,000 joint referrals occurring during 1977–1978, many involved the energy-environment-transportation nexus (Commerce, especially) or tradeoffs between taxing policies (Ways and Means) and a host of programmatic approaches aimed at the same problems.[31] During the same period, multiply referred energy bills found their way to no less than seventeen standing committees and the Ad Hoc

[31] See House Select Committee on Committees, *Final Report,* pp. 441-481. Figures are based on referrals, not measures, so that a bill referred to three committees is counted three times.

Energy Committee. Similarly, health bills involved nineteen standing and two special committes, while transportation bills involved eighteen standing and two special committees. These are the leading zones of overlap, but are by no means unique in current policy making.

Multiple referrals are advantageous because, as the Bolling committee argued in proposing them in 1974, they "facilitate intercommittee cooperation and infuse flexibility into the committee system."[32] They open the doors of policy making to a wide range of actors at the crucial point of subcommittee and committee deliberations. They open up the system at other points as well. Once a measure has been reported, there are several sets of legislators and their staffs—not just one—familiar with the issues and the legislative history. And when the measure reaches conference, managers from the relevant committees are appointed, enlarging the expertise and viewpoints represented on the conference committee. In short, multiple referrals can broaden participation in the two chambers by breaking up the monopolistic control committees and subcommittees once exerted over legislation in "their" jurisdiction.

At the same time, multiple referrals accentuate the decentralized, unwieldy character of congressional policy making. On both sides of Capitol Hill, legislators complain that, by increasing the number of actors with delaying or vetoing powers, multiple referrals erect new obstacles to policy making. Multiply referred measures are in fact less likely to be reported or passed than singly referred bills, according to 1977–1978 figures compiled for the House (see table 4–1). In that period only fifty-five multiply referred bills passed the House. This represented less than 3 percent of all such bills introduced, compared with the nearly 10 percent of all singly referred bills that reached final passage. What is more, multiply referred bills require more time, money, and energy to process. According to data from the House's computerized information base, 25.7 hours of hearing and markup time were required to report the average multiply referred bill, compared with 5 hours for the average singly referred bill.[33]

The organizational costs of the new procedures inevitably led to proposals for curbing or limiting them. The 1979–1980 Select Committee on Committees (the Patterson committee) proposed an amendment to the rules designed to prevent delay by any single committee. However, it is hard to tell how many of the delays are due to organiza-

[32] U.S. House of Representatives, Select Committee on Committees, *Committee Reform Amendments of 1974*, H. Rept. 93-916, 93rd Congress, 2nd session, 1974, p. 59.
[33] House Select Committee on Committees, *Final Report*, p. 474.

TABLE 4–1
SUCCESS RATES OF BILLS IN THE HOUSE, 95TH CONGRESS

	Intro- duced	Reported	Reported vs. Intro- duced	Passed	Passed vs. Intro- duced
All bills	18,065	1,490	8.2%	1,615	8.9%
Singly referred bills	16,232	1,410	8.7	1,560	9.6
Multiply referred bills	1,833	80	4.3	55	3.0
Multiply referred as a percentage of all bills	10.1	5.4	—	3.4	—

SOURCE: U.S. House of Representatives, Select Committee on Committees, *Final Report*, H. Rept. 96-866, 96th Congress, 2nd session, 1980, p. 474.

tional overlays and how many flow from the character of the legislation. After all, multiply referred bills are inevitably more complex —technically, not to mention politically—than measures that fit neatly into jurisdictional pigeonholes.

Subcommittee policy making is characterized not merely by the large number of individuals and subunits that are, or can be, involved at the deliberative stage. It is distinguished also by the multiplicity of interests that can be brought into play. When the airline industry sought subsidies for a new generation of quieter, more energy-efficient planes, the proposal went to the Senate Finance Committee, which showed little enthusiasm, but then acquired new life in the Senate Commerce Committee, whose members were more favorably inclined toward the industry. Senator Edward Kennedy (Democrat, Massachusetts) used his Judiciary Antitrust and Monopoly Subcommittee as a lever to promote the airline and trucking deregulation issue when industry-oriented Commerce dragged its feet. Energy, environment, health, or welfare issues are contested not only for jurisdictional turf, but also for review and veto powers on behalf of interests that have gained beachheads on various panels. Deliberation on multiply referred energy bills, for example, involves a cacophony of voices representing various producers, consumers, environmentalists, and regional concerns. This is a key reason why the energy crisis, described by President Carter as "the moral equivalent of war," has failed to stimulate a coherent legislative response.

In the case of salient, conflictual issues like energy, subcommittee government accentuates Congress's natural deliberateness and decentralization, leading to renewed criticisms of legislative *immobilisme* as well as to demands for expediting certain measures—in current argot, placing them in the "fast track." Congressional leaders are under pressure from the White House, editorialists, and interested parties to push and cajole the cumbersome subcommittee structure into processing measures more speedily. In 1975, for example, House Democrats appointed a special caucus task force headed by then-Majority Whip Jim Wright (Democrat, Texas) to develop energy proposals to counter those of President Ford. As a party task force, the Wright group merely "commended" its proposals to the consideration of various standing committees; even so, the task force was an attempt to fill an organizational vacuum. Two years later Speaker O'Neill, anticipating an energy package from the new Carter administration, arranged for creation of a forty-member Ad Hoc Energy Committee, composed largely of members from the standing committees with jurisdiction, to hold general hearings, to make sure that the standing committees met their deadlines in processing their respective portions of the package, and to assemble the committee reports into a "clean" bill (H. R. 8444) for deliberation by the full House. Though chosen to reflect the leadership's wishes, this body was representative of the House in terms of region, ideology, and standing committee memberships. Given the difficulty of reshaping workgroup jurisdictions, the Ad Hoc Energy Committee was probably the most effective instrument available at the time.[34]

Yet the ad hoc committee option, as its name implies, is a temporary expedient, cumbersome and not to be invoked every time coordination is required. In the case of energy, a more permanent solution (or partial solution, inasmuch as only a portion of the relevant jurisdiction was affected) was subsequently proposed by the Patterson committee in the form of a new energy committee—a proposal summarily rejected by the House. Even if successful, it would of course have had no impact on other areas of committee overlap such as health, transportation, welfare, or international economics. And even if a system of watertight committees were possible, which it is not, it would hardly negate the openness of present policy making on Capitol Hill. For beyond the committees and subcommittees, altered floor procedures, not to mention a new infrastructure of member cue-giving and cue-taking, have opened up congressional policy making still further.

Multiparty Politics. Today's congressional policy making is permeable not only at the early deliberative stages but also at later stages to

[34] Oppenheimer, "Policy Effects," pp. 22-24.

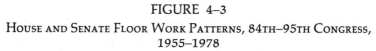

FIGURE 4–3

House and Senate Floor Work Patterns, 84th–95th Congress,
1955–1978

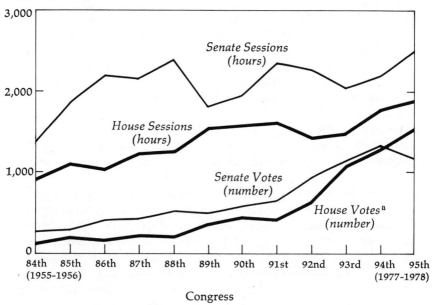

Congress

[a] Includes recorded teller votes, instituted in 1971.

Source: U.S. House of Representatives, Commission on Administrative Review, *Administrative Organization and Legislative Management*, H. Doc. 95-232, 95th Congress, 1st session, 1977, pt. 1, p. 4; U.S. Senate, Commission on the Operation of the Senate, *Policy Analyses on Major Issues*, committee print, 94th Congress, 2nd session, 1977, p. 6; *Congressional Record*, vol. 124 (November 15, 1978), p. D 1583.

participation on the part of a variety of members, whether or not they serve on workgroups holding jurisdiction over the legislation at hand. According to every measure, floor participation is at an all-time high: sessions require more hours and are scheduled virtually year-round; more and more pages of the *Congressional Record* are required (33,517 in 1977–1978) to record the debates; and more recorded votes than ever occur in each chamber—over 1,100 in the Senate and 1,500 in the House in 1977–1978 (see figure 4–3). In 1977–1978 the House was in session three times as long and the Senate twice as long as in 1955–1956. During the same period, the number of recorded votes rose fourfold in the Senate and tenfold in the House.

Patterns of floor activity have followed somewhat different

courses in the two chambers. As a smaller body, the Senate has always valued its tradition of leisurely debate and has, by the same token, looked more tolerantly on floor votes. Exerting tight control over time limits and floor amendments, the House traditionally ran its business more briskly than did the Senate. Pressure for more freedom in floor voting led the House in 1971 to institute the recorded teller vote, followed two years later by electronic voting. Thus the House today has as many or more votes than the Senate.

Like workgroup deliberation, floor deliberation can be prolonged or perfunctory, meticulous or trivial. Large numbers of routine or noncontroversial measures slip through the chambers virtually unnoticed, as they always have—although these days the votes are more likely to be recorded.[35] But on a large number of issues, a wide spectrum of members are found speaking or offering amendments in both chambers. Debate no longer need be dominated by a handful of committee elders while other members are discouraged by procedural limitations or informal norms. Nowadays subcommittee leaders freely shepherd legislation on the floor, with or without the assistance of full-committee elders. In the first year and a half of the 96th Congress (1979–1980), a sample of House subcommittee chairmen reported having managed an average of three bills on the floor.[36] In reporting the debates, the press refers democratically to "panel chairmen"—regardless of which committee is involved or whether it is a committee or subcommittee.

Leadership involvement in subcommittee activities typically revolves around scheduling legislation once it has cleared the full committee. In their preliminary examination of House Democratic leaders' communications with subcommittees, Deering and Smith found wide variation in subcommittee-leader linkages. "The majority leadership," as they put it, "has yet to establish a systematic relationship with these new power centers in Congress."[37] In the first eighteen months of the 96th Congress (1979–1980), the average subcommittee chairman interacted with the leadership less than once a month regarding subcommittee business. Some chairmen dealt with the leadership on a weekly basis; others had never done so. Interaction was influenced by such factors as the issue's significance, par-

[35] See Elizabeth Drew, "A Tendency to Legislate," *New Yorker* (June 26, 1978), pp. 80-89.
[36] Christopher J. Deering and Steven S. Smith, "Majority Party Leadership and the New House Subcommittee System" (paper presented at a conference on "Understanding Congressional Leadership: The State of the Art," cosponsored by the Everett McKinley Dirksen Center and the Sam Rayburn Library, Washington, D.C., June 10-11, 1980), p. 11.
[37] Ibid., p. 39.

tisan and ideological considerations, and the personal and policy relationships between the individuals involved. Leadership intervention typically occurred late in the measure's history, and at the subcommittee chairman's initiation.

Aside from those who help manage the floor debates, there are junior and minority-party legislators whose views might not otherwise be exposed. Not a few junior legislators have recently achieved their reputations through vigorous debate, adroit floor maneuvering, and sponsorship of key amendments. Republicans, too, find floor debate a useful opportunity to air potentially popular views that may be quashed in committee. It is no accident that, according to time budgets gathered by the Obey Commission (1977), Democrats tend to spend more time in subcommittee and committee sessions, while Republicans tend to devote more time on the floor.[38] In other words, those not in control at the committee stage find in floor debate a chance to appeal to the court of public opinion.

Amendments are the chief currency of those who seek to influence legislation through floor deliberations. Oftentimes the amendments are designed to counteract the biases of the workgroups that drafted the legislation in the first place. Just as often the amendments are symbolic, designed to force members to declare themselves on broad issues that attract outside groups. Amendments on abortion and budget-balancing are prime examples. For example, when the Education Department authorization was debated in mid-1979, it was soon burdened with dozens of amendments, many having little to do with the new agency's structure or charter—on such matters as abortion, busing, school prayers, and racial quotas. Although the amendments were widely publicized and passed by substantial margins, they were unceremoniously dropped by conferees and the measure was subsequently approved.

One irresistible form of floor legislation is the appropriation rider, usually in the form of the so-called limitation amendment—an amendment that prohibits the use of money for certain purposes. Such amendments were the vehicle for terminating funding for the supersonic transport and the Vietnam war. Amendments have also been offered to bar the use of funds for such purposes as water projects, military aid to foreign countries, promulgation of OSHA regulations, school busing, destabilization of foreign governments by the CIA, food stamps for strikers, and maintenance of FBI files. Many limitation amendments are offered by appropriations subcommittees

---

[38] Thomas J. O'Donnell, "Controlling Legislative Time," in Joseph Cooper and G. Calvin Mackenzie, eds., *Congress at Work* (Austin: University of Texas Press, forthcoming).

at the request of authorizing committees. Floor amendments have increased markedly in recent years, however, according to a 1978 study by the House Democratic Study Group.[39] The increase is attributed to the assertiveness of Congress in exercising control over federal expenditures and to the House's 1971 teller vote reform. Sponsorship of such amendments depends on which political party controls the White House. During the Nixon-Ford years, Democrats offered nearly 60 percent of the limitation amendments, whereas Republicans offered nearly 80 percent of them during the Kennedy-Johnson years. More recently, members of both parties have been equally apt to offer such amendments—evidence of their increasing popularity.

In the Senate, floor participation is open to everyone. The Senate deeply cherishes its tradition of full and leisurely debate. During the past generation, the Senate's sharpest procedural controversies were over the question of cloture rules for shutting down filibusters, and by 1975 the number of votes needed for cloture had been whittled down from two-thirds to three-fifths. No sooner was the new rule in place than senators devised ways of getting around it—by introducing delaying amendments after cloture had been invoked. Although some of these loopholes were closed—by precedent-shattering rulings in 1978 and by rules changes the following year—floor participation in the Senate remains high. Rules are generous, and very little is heard of earlier folkways hostile to participation by younger members or those not on the relevant committee.

Broader floor participation, facilitated by relaxed procedures and permissive norms of behavior, is at the same time an outgrowth of complex, pluralistic networks of information sharing and mobilization. Members and their staffs are more hard pressed than ever to assemble and digest information on the vast number of measures and amendments to be decided upon. Thus they seek out information—at the very least, cues on how to vote—from expert sources, knowledgeable members of the workgroup with jurisdiction, party leaders, executive specialists, or lobbyists.

Increasingly significant as sources of voting cues are the informal voting-bloc groups. Prior to 1970 there were only a handful of them—most notably, the liberal Democratic Study Group (DSG, 1959), the liberal Republicans' Wednesday Group (1964), the bipartisan and bicameral Members of Congress for Peace through Law (1966), and several informal GOP clubs. Now there are more than fifty

---

[39] Democratic Study Group, "The Appropriation Rider Controversy," Special Report 95-12, February 14, 1978.

groups, most of them dating from 1975 or later.[40] The Northeast-Midwest Coalition, known as the Frostbelt Caucus, looks after regional interests in such matters as tax burdens and fuel allocations and claims 200 members from eighteen states. The 140-member Textile Caucus is a largely southern group dedicated to protecting the industry against regulation and foreign competition. Other groups bear such names as the Rural Caucus, the High Altitude Coalition, the Senate Steel Caucus, the Forum on Regulation, the Black Caucus, and the Environmental Study Group. A majority are limited to members of a single chamber, but some embrace both chambers. A few are partisan, but the overwhelming majority are bipartisan. Although neither recognized by House or Senate rules nor eligible for direct appropriations, many of these groups (though not all) boast such resources as separate staffs or offices, newsletters or reports that are circulated, regularized funding, established subunits, regularly scheduled meetings, and whip systems.

Informal groups have grown and prospered because they perform functions that individual members find useful—in particular, assistance with legislative, political, and electoral goals. For many members, such groups offer an alternative source of information and voting cues on specific issues—information and cues that reflect legislators' own values as members of regional, ethnic, issue, or ideological blocs. Oftentimes these groups also perform legislative leadership functions, linking members to outside groups, forming legislative proposals, planning strategy, and mobilizing like-minded members for floor debates, amendments, or votes. Membership in such groups can prove an electoral aid: they are cited to prove members' fidelity to certain interests, and they frequently channel campaign assistance in the form of advice, money, or literature. Many groups model themselves after the highly successful Democratic Study Group, which prepares weekly guides to upcoming floor decisions that are widely consulted and far more detailed than anything produced by party whips. The DSG has also coordinated liberals' strategy for reforming House procedures and gives campaign assistance to liberal candidates.

These voting-bloc groups constitute a new sort of multiparty system on Capitol Hill. To be sure, some are little more than paper organizations whose main purpose seems to be to help members claim credit for promoting particular causes. Yet many of these groups perform party-like functions: they provide a label that

[40] Daniel P. Mulhollan and Arthur G. Stevens, "Congressional Liaison and the Rise of Informal Groups in Congress" (paper presented at the 1979 annual meeting of the Western Political Science Association).

members find useful, and they focus attention on particular issues or interests. Most significantly for policy making, such groups provide alternative channels of information and mobilization on issues—channels that often work independently of party or committee-based groupings.

These Capitol Hill groups, needless to say, mirror the present state of interest articulation and aggregation in the political system at large. That is to say, policy concerns are effectively articulated by a multiplicity of groups, but little aggregation takes place. Few developments have been more repeatedly announced, in fact, than the long-term decline of the traditional political parties and the expansion of interest groups. To the traditional producer-oriented federations —labor, professional, business, and agricultural—have been added a plethora of groups, some with quite specific concerns (the famous "single-interest groups"), some with an ideological cast. Lobbyists represent such diverse interests as individual business firms, cities, counties, states, beneficiaries of hundreds of government programs, antiabortionists, born-again Christians, nuclear power advocates and opponents, and all sorts of consumer and environmental interests. It is not the narrowness of these groups that is novel, but rather their number and range, and their unwillingness to accept brokerage by political parties. Faced with such a confusion of voices, it is little wonder that legislators seek not one party label but many, shaping their images in terms of their factional allegiances. In turn, these groupings provide multiple access to information and voting cues, permitting members to participate, however superficially, in floor decisions that once would have been controlled by party leaders or committee experts.

The diffusion of congressional policy making confronts outside agencies and groups with a bewildering array of access points. Not that access is difficult to achieve; far from it. What is difficult is deciding which access points are worth exploiting. Formerly, an executive agency or lobby group forged alliances with the handful of legislators who served on the relevant committee or who shared the interest in question. These members could be counted upon in turn to carry the gospel to their colleagues. In contrast, large numbers of legislators must now be contacted. Liaison officers from executive agencies, for example, work with voting-bloc groups and frequently canvass large numbers of members, not excluding the most junior members. As one State Department liaison officer observed, "It used to be that all one had to do was to contact the chairman and a few ranking members of a committee; now all 435 members and 100 senators have to be contacted."[41]

[41] Ibid., p. 5.

Because of its permeability, congressional policy making defies easy characterization. For more than a generation, students have tagged policy-making arrangements with the metaphor of the "iron triangles"—more or less closed networks of communications among congressional subcommittes, executive agencies, and the outside clientele groups. The concept symbolized a great variety of subsystem relationships—many of which were neither ironclad nor triangular. Today these relationships are, in fact, so complex and fluid that the metaphor may be altogether misleading; Heclo, for one, proposes to substitute the vaguer term "issue networks."[42] The present open system may be a transitory result of the coming of age of a new set of interests—especially environmental, consumer, and "public-interest" groups. More likely, it is a long-range shift in our politics, rooted in demographic and institutional changes. Whatever its ultimate meaning, the essential characteristics of the new system are openness and complexity.

Conclusions

Congress is inevitably a reactive institution. For better or worse, it mirrors the nation's political life—its values, standards, and organizing principles. Thus, today's Congress is open, egalitarian, and fragmented. It lacks leadership or consensus, and its ideological or partisan commitments are uncertain.

In the 1960s, critics worried about the representative character of congressional decision making. Long careers and low turnover seemed to heighten the insular, small-town atmosphere of the Hill; newly active political groupings, like blacks or consumers, were ill represented; the seniority system isolated committee leaders; legislative norms discouraged outsiders from participating; decision making all too often took place in closed circles and behind closed doors. Today few commentators would fault Congress on these counts. Capitol Hill is a far more open, democratic place than it was a decade or so ago. The transformation is not unlike that which has affected the political parties during the same period.

Now the chief impression is of buzzing confusion. The two houses of Congress lack organizing issues or lines of battle. In place of party labels there are individual politicians in business for themselves, and a series of shifting coalitions around specific issues. Instead of a few leaders or checkpoints for legislation, there are many. It is as if we are witnessing a reincarnation, on an enlarged scale, of

[42] Hugh Heclo, "Issue Networks and the Executive Establishment," in Anthony King, ed., *The New American Political System* (Washington, D.C.: American Enterprise Institute, 1978), p. 102.

the one-party factionalism that the late V. O. Key, Jr., identified in the southern states of an earlier day: "multifaceted, discontinuous, kaleidoscopic, fluid, transient."[43]

Legislators themselves profess to be dissatisfied with subcommittee government. In a survey of 101 House and Senate members in 1973, a foreign policy study commission discovered that 80 percent were dissatisfied with "committee jurisdictions and the way they are defined in Congress."[44] Only 1 percent of the legislators were "very satisfied" with the jurisdictional situation, while 13 percent were "very dissatisfied." Four years later, a survey of 153 House members identified committee structure as the most frequently mentioned "obstacle" preventing the House from doing its job.[45] "Scheduling" and "institutional inertia" were next in line. Reforming the committee structure was by far the most frequently mentioned suggestion for improving Congress: 41 percent of the representatives interviewed mentioned it.

Members' uneasiness about policy-making arrangements is eloquently revealed in the frequency of institutional soul-searchings. Since 1970 the House has authorized two intensive studies of its committee system (the Bolling committee, 1973–1974, and the Patterson committee, 1979–1980); the Senate has had one (the Stevenson committee, 1976–1977). At the same time two broad management studies were undertaken: the Commission on the Organization of the Senate (1976–1977) and the House's Commission on Administrative Review (1976–1977). None of the efforts resulted in fundamental alterations of committee procedures, though there were incremental alterations. No matter how dissatisfied members may be with subcommittee government, they shrink from making radical changes. According to a 1979 survey by the Patterson committee, more than 70 percent of the 184 responding members agreed both that the committee system badly needed major repair and that their colleagues were likely to reject such remedies in favor of more modest changes.[46] Major alterations are no doubt resisted because they threaten to upset Congress's internal balance, threatening not only legislators' workgroup careers but also their mutually advantageous linkages with outside clientele groups.

[43] V. O. Key, Jr., *Southern Politics in State and Nation* (New York: Alfred A. Knopf, 1949), p. 302

[44] Commission on the Organization of the Government for the Conduct of Foreign Policy, *Report*, Washington, D.C., 1975, appendix vol. 5 (appendix M).

[45] House Commission on Administrative Review, *Final Report*, vol. 2, pp. 868-869, 871-873.

[46] House Select Committee on Committees, *Final Report*, p. 284.

Subcommittee government mirrors the atomization of political life in the country at large. This era may well prevail until the pressure of systemic challenges becomes too strong to resist, or the galvanizing force of an issue or a political movement once again alters the face of the political landscape. For the moment, discontent is widespread, but a palpable sense of crisis is lacking.

5

Delegation, Deliberation, and the New Role of Congressional Staff

Michael J. Malbin

Roger Davidson's chapter has documented the proliferation and growing importance of congressional subcommittees and their effect on Congress's workload. Every aspect of the new Congress detailed by him has been marked by a growth in congressional staff: more subcommittees mean more subcommittee staff; more workload means more delegation; and the heightened susceptibility of committee decisions to floor reversal relates to the increased legislative staff resources available to minority party and junior members of Congress. However, the importance of the staff explosion of recent decades goes well beyond these matters. To be sure, Congress today is more decentralized and does more work than in the past. But, even more important, Congress does its work in a different way, and this in turn is both reflected and reinforced by the growth and use of congressional staffs.

Congress has been pursuing at least four somewhat conflicting aims as it has increased the size of its staff over the past few decades. Its aims have included: (1) a desire to be less dependent on the executive branch and outside interest groups for information, (2) a desire, especially among Republicans and junior Democrats to put their own imprint on issues of national importance, (3) a desire on the part of an increasing number of members to devote their time and resources to gaining credit in the media for putting new issues on the legislative agenda instead of working quietly to impress their colleagues through committee specialization, and (4) a desire on the part of almost everyone in Congress to gain some control over their expanding workloads and over the increasingly fragmented nature

---

This essay has been adapted from Michael J. Malbin, *Unelected Representatives: Congressional Staff and the Future of Representative Government* (New York: Basic Books, 1980). Copyright 1980 by Michael J. Malbin.

of their work. Of these different goals, the first suggests an increase in the size of Congress's professional staff but says nothing about the way the staff should be used or how it should be controlled, the second suggests that the staff should not only grow but that resources should be dispersed, and the third suggests giving the enlarged staff new kinds of things to do. All three of these objectives have more or less been attained in the years since World War II. However, the first three objectives are incompatible with the fourth.

Congress has failed utterly to cope with its workload. If anything, the growth of staff has made the situation worse. First, on the level of sheer numbers, more staff means more information coming in to each member's office, with more management problems as different staff aides compete for the member's time to present their own nuggets in a timely fashion. The member under these conditions is becoming more of a chief executive officer in charge of a medium-sized business than a person who weighs, debates, and deliberates public policy.[1] Second, the problems created by large numbers are exacerbated by the staff's new roles. Increasingly, the members want aides who will dream up new bills and amendments bearing their bosses' names instead of helping the bosses understand what is already on the agenda. The result is that the new staff bureaucracy and the workload it helps create threaten to bury Congress under its own paperwork, just as surely as if the staff never existed. Before we can assess the impact of the staff's new roles, however, we should spell out in more detail the connections between staff growth and the issues raised by Davidson's essay.

Staff Growth

The United States Congress in 1979 was an institution made up of 539 senators, representatives, and nonvoting delegates and 23,528 staff (see table 5–1). By way of comparison, the second most heavily staffed legislature in the world is the Canadian Parliament, with a staff of approximately 3,300.

[1] Former Representative Abner Mikva (Democrat, Illinois) told me his way of dealing with this problem was to go to a hideaway office where the staff could not find him. He said he needed a place where he could read and think without being interrupted by staff aides who constantly wanted to add to his pile of papers, but said that he was reluctant to close the door to his own office because it would discourage the aides from coming up with the new ideas and information that he wanted from them.

For two eloquent public statements reflecting the concern of members with staff growth, see "Additional Views of Senator Daniel P. Moynihan, Democrat, New York," in U.S. Senate, Committee on the Budget, *Report on the First Concurrent Resolution on the Budget, FY 1980,* S. Rept. 96-98, 96th Cong., 1st sess., April 12, 1979, pp. 330-333, and James L. Buckley, *If Men Were Angels: A View from the Senate* (New York: G.P. Putnam's Sons, 1975), pp. 117-149.

TABLE 5–1

CONGRESSIONAL STAFFS, 1979

Branch	Employees
House	
Committee staff[a]	2,073
Personal staff	7,067
Leadership staff[b]	160
Officers of the House, staff[c]	1,487
Subtotal, House	10,787
Senate	
Committee staff[a]	1,217
Personal staff	3,612
Leadership staff[b]	170
Officers of the Senate, staff[c]	1,351
Subtotal, Senate	6,350
Joint Committee Staffs	138
Support Agencies	
General Accounting Office	5,303
(30 percent of total GAO staff)	(1,591)
Library of Congress	5,390
(Congressional Research Service only)	(847)
Congressional Budget Office	207
Office of Technology Assessment	145
Subtotal, Support Agencies	11,045
(Subtotal, including only CRS in Library of Congress and 30 percent of GAO)	(2,790)
Miscellaneous	
Architect	2,296
Capitol Police Force	1,167
Subtotal	3,463
Total	31,783
(Total, including only CRS in Library of Congress and 30 percent of GAO)	(23,528)

[a] Includes select and special committee staff.

[b] Includes legislative counsels' offices, House Republican Conference, Democratic Steering Committee, Majority and Minority Policy Committees, Office of the Vice-President.

[c] Doorkeepers, parliamentarians, sergeants at arms, clerk of the House, Senate majority and minority secretaries, and postmasters.

SOURCE: *Report of the Clerk of the House*, July 1, 1979, to September 30, 1979; *Report of the Secretary of the Senate*, April 1, 1979, to September 30, 1979; Workforce Analysis and Statistics Branch, U.S. Office of Personnel Management, *Federal Civilian Workforce Statistics, Monthly Release*, October 31, 1979, p. 6.

It was not always this way. Until only a few decades ago, most congressional committees did not have permanent professional staffs, personal staffs were minuscule, and support agency staffs were not much larger. The elected representatives of the people debated, compromised, and reached decisions about the nation's legislative business on their own. The new era began, roughly, with the Legislative Reorganization Act of 1946. At that time, Congress was housed comfortably in six buildings, members worked directly with their colleagues, and people had reason to believe that their opinions, expressed in letters, would be read by the people they voted to put in office. This has all changed. Congress is now a vast enterprise crowded into fifteen buildings, with one more under construction and others in the planning stages.[2]

Of course, many of the 23,528 people do not work directly on legislation. Most of the 10,000 or so on personal staffs work on press releases and constituency related casework, while many in the Library of Congress, General Accounting Office, and various service staffs do work that relates even less directly to the legislative process. The four kinds of staff with the greatest influence over legislation are committee staffs, legislative aides on personal staffs, some support agency staffs, and the staffs serving the leadership and ad hoc groups. All have grown over recent decades. Just as important, all have been hiring a different type of person than the Capitol Hill staffer of decades past, and all have tended to increase the workload while strengthening the forces of institutional decentralization in Congress.

Senate Republican leaders announced shortly after it became clear that they would control the Senate in 1981 that they would cut the cost of running the Senate by 10 percent. If they can live up to that pledge, it could mean some reduction in the numbers that have been mentioned. Still, this would do little to reverse the basic changes of the past three decades. Senate committee staffs would remain twice as large as they were in 1965, while personal staffs would be rolled back only to the levels of 1978. Moreover, the Republicans are likely to have their staffs doing many of the same kinds of things Democratic staffs did when they were in the majority, if their behavior follows the patterns established by Senate Republicans in the examples cited below.

Committee Staffs. Congressional committees began hiring part-time, temporary clerks in the 1840s. In 1856, the Senate Finance and House Ways and Means committees started receiving regular appropriations

[2] Richard E. Cohen, "The Hill's Building Boom," *National Journal* (August 12, 1978), pp. 1294-1295.

for full-time clerks,[3] and the remaining committees all had full-time clerks by the end of the century.[4] According to one count, committee staff in 1891 numbered sixty-two in the House and forty-one in the Senate.[5] But until well into the twentieth century these positions were treated as patronage appointments for political cronies. Personal and committee staffs were thoroughly intermingled in practice in the House and by law in the Senate. For example, legislation during the 1920s specified that the three top clerks from a new Senate chairman's personal staff were to become clerks of the committee and that committee staff was to help the chairman with the work of his personal office.[6]

Nonpartisan professional committee staffs began to be developed at about this time on the House and Senate appropriations committees and on the newly formed (1926) Joint Committee on Internal Revenue Taxation. It was the money committees' successful experience with professional staffs that led Congress to institutionalize the practice in the Legislative Reorganization Act of 1946.[7] As part of a general realignment and reduction in the number of congressional committees, the act permitted all committees to hire up to four professional and six clerical workers each. (Exceptions were made for the two appropriations committees, which were allowed to determine their own staffing needs.) The permanent professionals authorized by this act (who have since been designated as "statutory staff") were expected to be nonpartisan. Additional people for specific investigations were to be hired as needed, supposedly on a temporary basis. But as early as the act's first years, committees began to hire such additional people on a quasi-permanent basis, so that ultimately the distinction between statutory and investigative staffs has become one that is honored rather in technical job descriptions than in on-the-job responsibilities.

The aim of nonpartisan professionalism apparently was maintained during the first six years after reorganization. Kenneth Kofmehl's *Professional Staffs of Congress*, the first book-length treatment

[3] Harrison W. Fox, Jr., and Susan W. Hammond, *Congressional Staffs: The Invisible Force in American Lawmaking* (New York: Free Press, 1977), p. 15.

[4] Judy Schneider, "Congressional Staffing, 1947-78," a study prepared for the Congressional Research Service of the Library of Congress, August 24, 1979, reprinted in U.S. House of Representatives, Select Committee on Committees, *Final Report*, 96th Cong., 2d sess., April 1, 1980, pp. 531-532.

[5] Fox and Hammond, *Congressional Staffs*, p. 171.

[6] Kenneth Kofmehl, *Professional Staffs of Congress* (West Lafayette, Ind.: Purdue University Press, 1962), p. 4. My thanks to Andrew Linehan (of the Carnegie Endowment for International Peace's Project on Executive-Congressional Relations) for drawing my attention to the importance of this passage in Kofmehl's book.

[7] P.L. 79-601; 60 Stat. 812.

of staffs, was based on research done in the three Congresses between 1947 and 1952 (eightieth through eighty-second). It described "the prevailing nonpartisan operation of most committees"[8] with minority party subcommittee chairmen on many committees and the whole staff accessible to every committee member on two-thirds of the committees Kofmehl studied. However, even as Kofmehl did his research, the system was already beginning to break down. By the end of his six years, several committees were beginning to designate some staff members as majority and others as minority.[9] Still, the prevailing conception of staff permitted Kofmehl to describe such party designation as "erroneous":

> It is not the function of the committee aides to promote particular policies but rather to facilitate the work of the entire committee by procuring information, by arranging for the services of other elements of the legislative and executive branch staffs, by pointing up relevant factors the committee should take into account when considering certain problems, by incorporating the committee's decisions in bills and reports and by discharging the manifold other staff duties that conserve the committee members' time and render less difficult the performance of their vital office. The members of a committee themselves, not the staff, should take care of the majority and minority interests and presumably, as politicians, should be well-qualified to do so.[10]

Today, very few committee staffs even try to meet Kofmehl's standard. Most had already moved decisively away from the nonpartisan even-handedness by the time the first edition of Kofmehl's book came out in 1962. By then, Congressman Clem Miller's published letters to his constituents described committee staffs in terms that showed that he for one regarded them as employees of the chairmen of the full committees and, through them, of the committees' majorities.[11] In the Senate, Randall Ripley's 1965 research led him to conclude:

> On most of the committees, most of the professional staff members are directly responsible only to the chairman. He appoints them and they retain their jobs only so long as they please him with their efforts. They tend to share his political coloration as well as his formal party affiliation. A few of the staff members may not have this special rela-

[8] Kofmehl, *Professional Staffs of Congress*, p. 52.

[9] Ibid., p. 58.

[10] Ibid., p. 67.

[11] Clem Miller, *Member of the House: Letters of a Congressman* (New York: Charles Scribner's Sons, 1962), p. 13.

tionship with the chairman; but they are likely to have a similar relationship with the ranking minority member or, in a few cases, another senior member of the committee, probably a member of the majority party.[12]

This control of staff by chairmen led Republicans in the late 1960s to agitate for professional minority staff on every committee. The Legislative Reorganization Act of 1970[13] appeared to give the Republicans what they wanted. It increased each committee's statutory professional staff from four to six, required that two of the six professionals and one of the six statutory clerical staff be selected by the minority, and said that no less than one-third of each committee's remaining funds should be used for minority staff.

But Democrats in both the Senate and House decided to ignore the one-third minority staff requirement in 1971 and in subsequent years. The provision was revived in House committee reforms adopted in 1974 (H. Res. 988), but the House Democratic Caucus trimmed the proposal back again in 1975 by dropping the one-third guarantee for investigative staff while granting the minority one-third of each committee's increased allotment of eighteen statutory professionals and twelve clerical staff. However, as part of its 1977 reform resolution (S. Res. 4), the Senate required committees to give the minority a full one-third of all statutory and investigative staff within four years, and it is well on its way toward achieving this goal.

At the time the Legislative Reorganization Act of 1970 was passed, House committee staffs were about four times as large as they had been in 1947 (702 versus 167), and Senate committee staffs were about three times as large (635 versus 232). These numbers kept going up during the 1970s. Senate committee staffs nearly doubled again between 1970 and 1979 (to 1,098) while those in the House increased more than two and a half times (to 1,959; see table 5-2).

The growth of Senate committee staffs between the 1950s and mid-1970s was a direct result of the dispersal of power to junior senators, a process that began under the majority leadership of Lyndon B. Johnson. The so-called Johnson Rule of the 1950s assured every Democratic senator of at least one good committee assignment. Over the years, as this worked itself out, most Democratic senators were able to become chairmen of subcommittees, each with its own staff.

In the House, too, staff growth and internal democratization have gone hand in hand. The staff increases on House committees in

[12] Randall B. Ripley, *Power in the Senate* (New York: St. Martin's Press, 1969), pp. 201-202.
[13] P.L. 91-510, 84 Stat. 1140.

TABLE 5–2
Committee Staffs, Selected Years, 1891–1979

Year	House	Senate
1891	62	41
1914	105	198
1930	112	163
1935	122	172
1947	167	232
1950	246	300
1955	329	386
1960	440	470
1965	571	509
1970	702	635
1971	729	711
1972	817	844
1973	878	873
1974	1,107	948
1975	1,433	1,277
1976	1,680	1,201
1977	1,776	1,028
1978	1,844	1,151
1979	1,959	1,098

SOURCE: 1891-1935: Harrison W. Fox, Jr., and Susan Hammond, *Congressional Staffs: The Invisible Force in American Lawmaking* (New York: Free Press, 1977), p. 171. 1947-1978: Judy Schneider, "Congressional Staffing, 1947-78," Congressional Research Service, August 24, 1979, reprinted in U.S. House of Representatives, Select Committee on Committees, *Final Report*, 96th Congress, 2d session, April 1, 1980, p. 539. Schneider's figures are only for the statutory and investigative staffs of standing committees. They do not include select committee staffs, which have varied between 31 and 238 in the House and 62 and 172 in the Senate during the 1970s. 1979: *Report of the Clerk of the House*, July 1, 1979, to September 30, 1979; *Report of the Secretary of the Senate*, April 1, 1979, to September 30, 1979.

the 1970s resulted largely from the 1973 House Democratic Caucus's "Subcommittee Bill of Rights" that liberated subcommittee chairmen from the control of the chairmen of full committees.[14] As a result, most of the committee staff increases in the House during the 1970s have been at the subcommittee level, and many subcommittee staffs of the late 1970s were as large as full committee staffs of the 1960s.

[14] See Norman J. Ornstein, "Causes and Consequences of Congressional Change: Subcommittee Reforms in the House of Representatives, 1970-73," in *Congress in Change*, Norman J. Ornstein, ed. (New York: Praeger, 1975), pp. 88-114, especially p. 106.

TABLE 5–3
Personal Staffs, Selected Years, 1891–1979

Year	House	Senate
1891		39
1914		72
1930	870	280
1935	870	•424
1947	1,440	590
1957	2,441	1,115
1967	4,055	1,749
1972	5,280	2,426
1976	6,939	3,251
1977	6,942	3,554
1978	6,944	3,268
1979	7,067	3,612

Source: Through 1976: Fox and Hammond, *Congressional Staffs*, p. 171. For 1977 and 1978, Senate: Schneider, "Congressional Staffing, 1947-78," p. 540. For 1977, 1978, and 1979, House: *Report of the Clerk of the House*. For 1979, Senate: *Report of the Secretary of the Senate*, April 1, 1979, to September 30, 1979.

Thus, in both the House and the Senate, the increases in staffing of the 1950s and early 1960s were accompanied by a shift away from nonpartisan professional staffs serving whole committees to a system of staffs working primarily for individual members, generally chairmen. Since then, the principle of individual control has not changed, but the distribution of staff resources has become more widespread. This broader distribution both results from and reinforces internal democratization as more members have the staff resources to pursue their own legislative ends.

Personal Staffs. Other forms of staff growth also have tended to support the growing decentralization of Congress. In this connection the increased number of legislative aides on personal staffs is an obvious case in point.

Although members who were not chairmen were first allowed to hire staffs of their own in 1893,[15] most of the growth has taken place since 1947 (see table 5–3). Since 1947, personal staffs have increased from 1,440 to 7,067 in the House and from 590 to 3,612 in the Senate.

[15] Fox and Hammond, *Congressional Staffs*, p. 15-16.

TABLE 5–4

MEAN NUMBER OF PERSONAL STAFF WITH LEGISLATIVE DESIGNATIONS,
BY MEMBER'S PARTY AND REGION, 1972–1979

Year	Sample Size	All Members	Southern Democrats	Other Democrats	Republicans
House of Representatives					
1972	100	1.3	1.1	1.7	1.2
1979	435	2.2	1.8	2.4	2.1
Senate					
1973	98	3.9	3.1	4.4	3.7
1979	100	5.5	4.9	5.4	5.8

SOURCE: House in 1972 and Senate in 1973, Norman J. Ornstein, "Legislative Behavior and Legislative Structures," in James J. Heaphey and Alan P. Balutis, *Legislative Staffing: A Comparative Perspective* (New York: John Wiley and Sons, 1975), p. 169. House and Senate, 1979, calculated by the author after consultation with Ornstein to make sure the same criteria were used to decide who should and who should not be counted; from U.S. House of Representatives, *Report of the Clerk of the House from Jan. 1, 1979 to March 31, 1979*, 96th Congress, 1st session, H. Doc. 96-136, and U.S. Senate, *Report of the Secretary of the Senate from Oct. 1, 1978 to March 31, 1979*, 96th Congress, 1st session, S. Doc. 96-21, Parts 1 and 2. Staff titles derived from these sources were cross-checked with Charles Brownson, ed., *1979 Congressional Staff Directory* and Congressional Monitor's *Bimonthly Directory of Key Congressional Aides.*

Since most personal staff aides do not work on legislation, the growth in personal staff does not by itself say anything about the growth of legislative assistance. Unfortunately, it is impossible to know how many legislative aides there were in the House and Senate before 1970, when the Legislative Reorganization Act introduced formal professional titles for people on personal staffs. But it is possible to talk about growth in the 1970s. The increase in the number of legislative aides in both the House and the Senate has been fairly modest, going up from an average of 1.3 per House member in 1972 to 2.2 in 1979 and from an average of 3.9 per senator in 1973 to 5.5 in 1979 (see table 5–4).

From the numbers, it seems obvious that most of the members' new personal staff aides do constituency-related work that may help an incumbent win reelection[16] but has little to do with the legislative process. Still, an increase of even one legislative aide per member is

[16] See Morris P. Fiorina, *Congress: Keystone of the Washington Establishment* (New Haven: Yale University Press, 1977), pp. 56-60.

enough to produce a large number of amendments for the floor—particularly since the increase in both chambers is greatest among Republicans and Southern Democrats, who are most likely to be opposed to the thrust of committee reported legislation. (Thus, for example, we saw junior Republicans such as David Stockman of Michigan and Richard Cheney of Wyoming having the resources to lead the unsuccessful 1979 floor fight against federal loan guarantees for the Chrysler Corporation even though neither was on the committee that reported the bill.) The increases in personal legislative aides among Republicans and Southern Democrats in turn reflects changing conservative attitudes toward the use of staff. Liberal Northern Democrats were far more likely than Republicans or Southern Democrats to rely heavily on staff during the early 1970s, but the situation was evening up in the late 1970s as some media-conscious, new-style conservatives began using staffs to develop national issues in a manner similar to that pioneered by the liberal Democrats of previous years.

Support Agencies. The support agencies have also grown in the 1970s (see table 5–5). Although the connection between this and internal democratization may not be clear at first glance, the link comes through the growth of policy analysis and the way analysis is used by the members.

In 1970, the 332 people who worked for the Library of Congress's Legislative Reference Service performed largely bibliographic, speechwriting, and factual research chores. The role of the service was expanded significantly by the Legislative Reorganization Act of 1970 (Sec. 321), which changed its name to the Congressional Research Service (CRS) and gave it the job of analyzing and evaluating legislative proposals upon request from a committee. Between 1970 and 1976, CRS's staff grew rapidly—from 332 to 806. With the increased staff has come more policy analysis and research. By the end of fiscal 1975, one study estimated that 63 percent of CRS's staff and 71 percent of its budget were devoted to these activities,[17] although "quick and dirty" research done on a fast deadline still seems to outweigh more thoughtful analysis.[18]

[17] James D. Carroll, "Policy Analysis for Congress: A Review of the Congressional Research Service," in U.S. Senate, Commission on the Operation of the Senate, *Congressional Support Agencies: A Compilation of Papers, Committee Print*, 94th Congress, 2d session, Washington, D.C., 1976, p. 6.

[18] See, for example, Michael J. Malbin, "CRS—The Congressional Agency That Just Can't Say No," *National Journal* (February 19, 1977), pp. 284-289; and Richard E. Cohen, "The Watchdogs for Congress Often Bark the Same Tune," *National Journal* (September 8, 1979), pp. 1484-1488.

TABLE 5–5

DEVELOPMENT OF THE SUPPORT AGENCIES, SELECTED YEARS, 1946–1979

Year	Library of Congress	(Congressional Research Service only[a])	General Accounting Office[b]	Congressional Budget Office	Office of Technology Assessment
1946			14,219		
1947	1,898	(160)	10,695		
1950	1,973	(161)	7,876		
1955	2,459	(166)	5,776		
1960	2,779	(183)	5,074		
1965	3,390	(231)	4,278		
1970	3,848	(332)	4,704		
1971	3,963	(386)	4,718		
1972	4,135	(479)	4,742		
1973	4,375	(596)	4,908		
1974	4,504	(687)	5,270		10
1975	4,649	(741)	4,905	193	54
1976	4,880	(806)	5,391	203	103
1977	5,075	(789)	5,315	201	139
1978	5,231	(818)	5,476	203	164
1979	5,390	(847)	5,303	207	145

[a] Legislative Reference Service through 1970.

[b] The GAO's job changed after World War II. Before 1950, the GAO was responsible for auditing all individual federal transactions and keeping record of them; 1950 legislation transferred these responsibilities to the executive branch. The staff reductions through 1965 result from this change. See Frederich C. Mosher, *The GAO: The Quest for Accountability in American Government* (Boulder, Colo.: Westview Press, 1979), p. 124.

SOURCE: Library of Congress, *Annual Reports of the Librarian of Congress.* GAO 1946-1965, *Annual Reports of the Comptroller General of the United States.* OTA 1974-1976, *Appendixes of the Budget of the United States,* for fiscal 1976 (p. 18), 1977 (p. 18), and 1978 (p. 40). CBO 1975, Joel Havemann, *Congress and the Budget* (Bloomington, Ind.: Indiana University Press, 1978), p. 109 (figure is as of October 1975; the CBO's director took office on February 24, 1975). GAO 1970-1978, CBO 1976-1978, and OTA 1977-1978, Judy Schneider, "Congressional Staffing, 1947-78," Congressional Research Service, August 24, 1979. For 1979: U.S. Office of Personnel Management, *Federal Civilian Workforce Statistics,* Monthly Release, October 1, 1979, p. 6.

The General Accounting Office (GAO), established by the Budget and Accounting Act of 1921, is seven years younger than CRS's forebear, the Legislative Reference Service. During the 1960s it began expanding its traditional auditing functions to include reviews designed to "measure the effectiveness of a wide variety of government programs."[19] Congress affirmed its support of this new emphasis in the 1970 Legislative Reorganization Act, which explicitly directed the GAO to do "cost benefit studies of government programs" (Sec. 204). In response to this mandate, the GAO began hiring a more diverse group of professionals. True, the GAO still considers itself the watchdog of the federal treasury and stations accountants and auditors in every executive branch agency. However, by 1975, only 2,701 of its 4,142 professionals (or 65 percent) were members of the two traditionally dominant professions,[20] accountants and auditors. And, a study of the GAO in 1976 reported that 35 percent of the GAO's workload and more than half of its self-initiated work can be described as program evaluation.[21] Most of these are retrospective analyses of programs already in existence, but a fair number are prospective evaluations of legislation under consideration.

The two small remaining support agencies, the Office of Technology Assessment (OTA) and Congressional Budget Office (CBO), were created by statutes passed in 1972 and 1974, respectively, and began operations in 1974 and 1975.[22] Staff levels at the CBO have been around 200 since its first year, while OTA has grown steadily to a complement of 145 staff in 1979. About one-third of the staff at CBO and all at OTA directly or indirectly analyze and evaluate the implications of policy choices for Congress. (The rest of the staff at CBO works on budget estimating and scorekeeping.)

All four support agencies are organized along bureaucratic lines and are much more akin to the traditional nonpartisan staffs than the recently ascendant individualistic staffs of most committees.[23] Despite

---

[19] Martin J. Fitzgerald, "The Expanded Role of the General Accounting Office," part of a "Public Policy Forum on the New Congressional Bureaucracy," *The Bureaucrat*, vol. 3, no. 4 (January 1975), p. 385. For two recent book length treatments of the GAO, see Frederich C. Mosher's history, *The GAO: The Quest for Accountability in American Government* (Boulder, Colo.: Westview Press, 1969), and a companion book by Erasmus Kloman, *Cases in Accountability* (Boulder, Colo.: Westview Press, 1979).

[20] U.S. General Accounting Office, *1976 Annual Report of the Comptroller General of the United States*, Washington, D.C., 1977, p. 221.

[21] Joseph Pois, "The General Accounting Office as a Congressional Resource," in Commission on the Operation of the Senate, *Congressional Support Agencies*, p. 40.

[22] Technology Assessment Act of 1972, P.L. 92-484, 86 Stat. 797; Congressional Budget and Impoundment Control Act of 1974, P.L. 93-344, 88 Stat. 297.

[23] OTA has had difficulties defining a distinct mission for itself and for a time was in danger of becoming almost like personalized professional committee staff for OTA's congressional board members. The latter problem may have eased somewhat, but not the former. See Dick Kirschten, in "The Misplaced Mission of OTA." He said the OTA's staff had been "divided for the most part into political fiefdoms.... Now in its fourth year, OTA never has been able to shake the

this, the growth in support agency policy analysis helps reinforce the same internal decentralizing forces that were responsible for the growth of personalized subcommittee staffs. While most support agency analysis is produced at the request of chairmen or ranking minority members, overlaps in subcommittee jurisdiction as well as the virtual autonomy of most subcommittee chairmen mean that requests for analysis can be placed on just about any controversial issue. Since support agency reports become available to all senators and representatives upon release, the net result is to destroy the monopoly of information once enjoyed by committee chairmen. Anyone willing to let a subcommittee staff member or legislative aide take the time to study these reports is in a position to challenge the judgments of commitee chairmen, and often will.

Leadership Staffs and Ad Hoc Groups. The 1970s have seen increases not only in the staffs that introduce, negotiate, and analyze bills and amendments for committee members and other specialists, but also in the staffs that process information so as to help build coalitions among nonspecialists in the last stages before floor votes. These staffs generally do little more than react to materials developed elsewhere.

We already have encountered two other kinds of reactive staff that intervene between committees and the floor: legislative aides and support agency staff. Most legislative assistants in the House and Senate spend their time preparing their members for floor votes on issues that do not vitally concern them. They ride the elevators with their boss before the vote and, in the rush, their nuanced phrases may, unintentionally or intentionally, influence how a member votes. These quick briefings, always important in the Senate, have lately become a factor in the House as well, as the introduction of electronic voting in 1975 has cut the time allowed per roll call from thirty to fifteen minutes, thereby reducing the time available for conversation among members. CRS also helps inform nonspecialist members by nonpartisan "issue briefs" prepared for the House and Senate computer system. However, these briefs tend to be read not by the members but by legislative assistants who then brief the members verbally.

---

reputation—whether wholly deserved or not—of functioning as little more than a joint committee, serving the whims of its 12-member congressional board." *National Journal* (November 12, 1977), p. 1777. See also, D. Kirschten, "After the Bash, the Crash," *National Journal* (February 4, 1978), p. 202, and "OTA Patronage—At a Reduced Price," *National Journal* (March 11, 1978), p. 404, and Richard E. Cohen, "Taking Control of the Troubled OTA," in "The Watchdogs of Congress," *National Journal* (September 8, 1979), p. 1485.

Two remaining kinds of staffs are important at this stage of the process: leadership staffs and the staffs of ad hoc issue and regional caucuses. In general, they are in competition with each other, and their role is very different in the House and in the Senate. As has often been observed, the Senate, with only 100 members, has much less need than the House for formal coordination and a highly structured leadership. The staffs reflect this. Thus, in 1978 the Senate majority leader and majority whip had a combined total staff of only nine while the role of formal issue groups and regional caucuses was virtually nil. In the House, the leadership and caucus staffs are both more significant. In 1978, the Democratic leadership had a staff of forty-six and the Republicans forty-three. Most of these aides help with whip counts, scheduling, press relations, and other tasks related to the leaders' verbal communications with members, but a few in each party add to the written information flow with whip notices and (on the Republican side only) summaries of major bills and amendments.

The Republicans got the idea for doing bill summaries from the oldest of the ad hoc groups in the House, the liberal Democratic Study Group (DSG), which was founded in 1959 and had a staff of fifteen in 1978. Although best known outside Congress for its work on congressional reform, the DSG's summaries of bills and amendments—generally presenting arguments for and against divisive proposals—are probably read more widely than any other single collection of congressionally produced written material about pending legislation. The small Democratic Research Organization (with a staff of three) and the Republican Study Committee (with a staff of ten) both were formed in the early 1970s to provide conservative alternatives to the written material produced by the DSG and Republican Conference.[24]

The 1970s was a period of explosive growth for ad hoc groups. DSG was the only such group in existence before 1960. Two others were formed during the 1960s, seven between 1970 and 1974, and thirty from 1975 to 1979.[25] While several of the new groups are little more than excuses for occasional press releases (such as the Congressional Roller and Ball Bearing Coalition), most permit a pooling of personal staff resources to create alternative sources of information for members. As such, they compete with committees and with the leadership. Their growth, in other words, has fed the same decentralizing forces that produced the personalization of committee staffs.

[24] See Michael J. Malbin, "Where There's a Cause There's a Caucus," *National Journal* (January 8, 1977), pp. 56-58.
[25] U.S. House of Representatives, Select Committee on Committees, Task Force to Review Congressional Changes in the 1970s, *Final Report*, pp. 70-71.

Career Goals and the Staffer's Life. As we suggested earlier, the shift toward personalized control of committee staff has gone hand in hand with a shift in the type of person hired for the job. Once a sinecure for patronage appointments and later a professional job for mid-career bureaucrats, congressional staffs increasingly have become filled with people who see their jobs in Congress as stepping stones to something else. Legislative aides on personal staffs and research staffs who work for ad hoc issue groups try to move to committee staffs. These staffs, in turn, seem to be positioning themselves for jobs elsewhere in the Washington political community.

Recent research on staffs has highlighted the new career pattern. Harrison Fox and Susan Hammond have found that legislative assistants in the House tend to be in their twenties, while Senate personal staff professionals and committee professionals in both chambers are generally in their thirties and forties.[26] Perhaps more important, they found that 50 percent of their sample of 302 committee staff aides had been on the job four years or less, another 33 percent for four to ten years, and only 17 percent for eleven years or more.[27]

Clearly, most personal and committee staff aides are not settling in as career civil servants working toward their retirements. There are important exceptions, of course, and a few committees still hire people who view their jobs much the same way as do their counterparts in executive agencies.[28]

Nevertheless, young professionals on the move seem now, after three decades of staff growth, to dominate the positions from which staffs influence policy. The members seem to want it that way. Several have said in interviews that they "hire them young, burn them out, and send them on."

[26] Fox and Hammond, *Congressional Staffs*, p. 173.

[27] Ibid., p. 178; Robert H. Salisbury and Kenneth A. Shepsle argue that Fox and Hammond overstate the degree of turnover, some of which may be due to such factors as the creation of new committees. Nevertheless, even their more modest numbers suggest a career pattern that is quite different for most committees from the pattern that seems to have prevailed from the 1940s through early 1960s. See "Congressional Staff Turnover: Its Causes and Consequences" (paper presented at the annual meeting of the Southern Political Science Association, November 1-4, 1979, and available through the Center for the Study of American Business, Washington University, St. Louis).

[28] Interestingly, the support agencies also seem to be peopled with another sort of "new style," young professionals—the policy analysts. While the future ambitions of the policy analysts may not affect policy as directly as the ambitions of the committee staff members, they are clearly part of the same set of Washington "issue networks" as the committee staffs, and their training, if not their ambition, does affect policy. These analysts may not affect the legislative agenda as directly as new style committee staff lawyers, but they do affect the way members think about and debate issues.

Moreover, the working conditions on Capitol Hill and the Washington setting in which they occur all contribute toward producing staffs who have these same perspectives. The young lawyers on the staffs tend disproportionately to be highly sought after people from top-ranked schools. They are paid well (salaries of $40,000 and above are common for committee professionals), and they are allowed to exercise a great deal of power at a relatively young age. The experience is exhilarating for a while. Washington lawyer-lobbyist Harry McPherson described the feeling in a book about his years working for Lyndon Johnson in the Senate and White House. Explaining his decision to go straight from law school to Johnson's staff, McPherson wrote:

> Why did I choose this "experience" instead of beginning a law practice and finding a responsible place in a small community? Partly because I wanted to find out what goes on in the councils of power—very much as a subway straphanger wants to know about scandals among the famous. Partly because I wanted to "do good", and a decade after Roosevelt it still seems as if Washington is the grand arena for doing good. Partly—perhaps chiefly—because I wanted to cast a shadow, to feel, however vicariously, that I have affected significant events and therefore exist.[29]

But for most of the professionals the exhilaration does not last forever. For one thing, they quickly reach a salary level not far below the legal maximum and then stay put. Another factor may be the overcrowded and noisy offices and the unpredictable and sometimes incredibly long working hours, many of which are spent doing nothing, or dreaming up new things to do, while waiting for five minutes of the member's time at the end of the day. But the most basic factor, the one that ultimately starts to grate on so many staff people, is the knowledge that however powerful they may appear, or however often they may have turned their own opinions into laws, they will never be anything other than surrogates for someone else. One successful young staffer who was in the middle of looking for another job captured this in a comment that could have been echoed by hundreds of his colleagues: "I just don't want to spend the rest of my life carrying someone else's water."

Working for someone else does not bother most people, of course. But members of Congress go out of their way to hire people who are both bright and ambitious, and let them exercise power in an environment in which they are constantly made aware of their lack

[29] Harry McPherson, *A Political Education* (Boston: Little, Brown, 1972), p. 8.

of independence. If many of the aides appear arrogant to the outside world—and many do—these same people may be as deferential as the most humble of junior executives when it comes to dealing with the person they refer to as "The Senator," "The Congressman" or "The Chairman." (The capital letters are there, even in speech.) As committee staffs have become more like personal staffs, with each staff aide directly under the control of a single member, the precariousness of the job becomes self-evident. Staff members all have friends whose chairman retired, switched committees, or was beaten, leaving them with a new chairman wanting to "clean house." They all know competent people who were fired without warning because the boss sensed a slight, or just felt it was time for a change.

This uncertainty is undoubtedly valuable from the members' point of view: it is their best lever for keeping some control over the situation. The members delegate enormous authority to their staffs and cannot possibly keep track of all or even most of what goes on in their name. But one thing they can do is to react instantly when they hear of something they do not like. "The rule that applies here," one staff director said, "is that you can exceed your authority only once. Then you'll either be fired or you won't have much authority."

The relationship of dependence between staff and member (Fox and Hammond called it "feudal" and likened the scene to a royal court) may not bother those who get McPherson's existential thrill out of casting a shadow. But it does get to others, who are told periodically by former classmates that sooner or later they ought to think about finding a "real job" if they do not want to be left "behind." They fear their friends may be right.

One staff director talked about his attempts to get into a law firm. He was in his early thirties and wanted to go back home to the Midwest. It was not easy. The firms in his home town wanted to start him out at the bottom. Sure, he had six years of high powered, legislative experience, but what did that have to do with family or local corporate law? He had never even drawn up a pleading or drafted a contract, they pointed out. Neither were the local corporations much more open-armed to the returning native. They all knew he was bright and would love to have him come back—at two-thirds his congressional salary. About the only firms that would talk about a raise wanted him to lobby. But the young staff director thought that if he had to lobby he might as well stay put in Congress. His friends back home would not consider lobbying a "real job" either, and he still enjoyed what he was doing.

When the joy starts to fade, however, the difficulty of returning home and the potential rewards of the nation's capital lead many of them to think about jobs in the Washington community. Committee staffs are expected, as part of their job, to get to know the people who work in their policy areas.[30] These are the people to whom the staffers turn when they want to, or have to, change jobs. By cultivating and becoming part of their policy networks, they insulate themselves from the insecurities of feudal dependence on their bosses.

Of all the possible kinds of "network" jobs in Washington, two seem clearly to be preferred: political appointments in the executive branch and lawyer-lobbying. An article in *National Journal* which traced what happened to twenty-one professional majority staff members who left the Senate Commerce Committee from November 1976 to May 1978 found that three got other jobs on Capitol Hill (all with Warren Magnuson [Democrat, Washington] the former chairman of the committee), twelve got political appointments elsewhere in the federal government (eight as commissioners, administrators, or political staff on agencies or regulatory commissions within the committee's jurisdiction), four became Washington lawyer-lobbyists, and two went back home to Seattle to work on issues they had handled in committee.[31]

Nor is the Commerce Committee's experience unusual. As of mid-1979, the chairmen of the Federal Communications Commission (Charles Ferris), Federal Deposit Insurance Corporation (Irvine H. Sprague), Federal Energy Regulatory Commission (Charles Curtis), Federal Maritime Commission (Richard J. Daschbach), Federal Trade Commission (Michael Pertschuk), Interstate Commerce Commission (A. Daniel O'Neal, Jr.), National Endowment for the Arts (Livingston L. Biddle, Jr.), Tennessee Valley Authority (S. David Freeman), the administrator of the Veteran's Administration (Max Cleland), and two of six commissioners on the Federal Election Commission (John W. McGarry and Max L. Friedersdorf) all came directly or almost directly from jobs on congressional staffs. (Pertschuk, Daschbach, and O'Neal all worked for the Senate Commerce Committee.) Scores of others fill the middle-level ranks of the cabinet level agencies.

Staff members who do not go to the executive branch are per-

[30] Hugh Heclo has referred to these clusters of people in public and private interest groups, congressional staffs, think tanks, and the executive branch as "issue networks." See his "Issue Networks and the Executive Establishment," in Anthony King, ed., *The New American Political System* (Washington, D.C.: American Enterprise Institute, 1978), pp. 87-124. See also Laurence Leamer, "Networks," *The Washingtonian* (November 1979), pp. 158-160 and 202-218. Nicholas Lemann, thinking more in terms of careers than policies, called them "survival networks" in "Survival Networks: Staying in Washington," *The Washington Monthly* (June 1978), pp. 23-32.

[31] Linda E. Demkovich, "The Cautious Approach of Cannon's Commerce Committee," *National Journal* (May 27, 1978), p. 849.

fectly content to make handsome livings as lawyer-lobbyists. Harry McPherson took what many would consider the ideal path: from congressional staffer to White House aide to one of Washington's most sought after lawyers and perennial presidential advisers. But, just as there are those who skip the legislative branch before fitting into the Washington community,[32] so are there plenty of congressional aides who skip the executive branch and still do very well. Michael Lemov failed to get an appointment to the Federal Trade or Consumer Product Safety Commission and went to a law firm where he handles consumer protection issues for private clients affected by the bill he drafted as a House Commerce Committee aide. S. Lynn Sutcliffe (Senate Commerce Committee), William Van Ness (Senate Interior Committee), Howard Feldman (Senate Government Operations Committee), and Charles Curtis (House Commerce Committee) formed a law firm in 1976 that has been thriving. (Curtis left the firm in 1977 to become chairman of the Federal Energy Regulatory Commission.) Also thriving is Blum, Parker and Nash, a new firm active on energy issues that has seven former staff members as partners or associates.[33]

All of these successful young lawyers trade directly on the fact that they know the laws and regulations concerning their clients because they helped write them, and they know the senators, representatives, and agency personnel who can affect these laws and regulations. They rarely get involved in direct conflicts of interest, and they rarely go out and blatantly advertise the obvious. (One new consulting firm did precisely that in a memo advertising its services to prospective clients for a $200,000 retainer,[34] but the incident was unusual.) Successful former aides generally know they do not have to do this.

What happens to congressional staffs after they leave Capitol Hill is only of indirect relevance to the influence of staff in the legis-

[32] Nicholas Lemann, "Protege Power: The Wonderful World of Special Assistants," *New Republic* (April 7, 1979), pp. 10-13.

[33] James W. Singer, "Practicing Law in Washington—An American Growth Industry," *National Journal* (April 7, 1979), pp. 10-13.

[34] Malmgren, Inc. sent a five-page memorandum to prospective clients in 1978 pointing out that two of its top people, Harald B. Malmgren (the president) and Jeffrey Salzman, used to work for Senator Abraham A. Ribicoff (Democrat, Connecticut), a member of the Finance Committee. The memo was sent specifically to firms likely to be hurt by the controversial increase of U.S. taxes on income earned abroad. "It is well known," the memo said, "that the likely pattern of compromise, or the best basis for a new solution, is the proposal introduced by Senator Ribicoff, and Salzman has been the principle [sic] drafter of all the variations of the approach. (He was, of course, formerly Legislative Assistant to the Senator.)" The memo also advertised Malmgren's credentials in similar terms. See George Lardner Jr., "Hill Expertise for Sale: $200,000" *Washington Post*, April 10, 1973, A1 and A14.

lative process. The real issue is whether people's behavior *while they are on* congressional staffs is affected by the Washington career models constantly before them. Given their need to protect themselves against the uncertainties of their jobs, staff members would have to be inhuman not to be affected in some way; the question is how.

Congressional Staff and the Legislative Process

New Legislative Ideas. The staff's influence pervades the legislative process. No stage in that process is more important than the first: determining Congress's agenda. And at no stage have the newer style staffs had a greater impact on the way Congress works. It is the one point in the process where the interests of the members, the goals of the staff, and the position of the staff members in the Washington issue networks come together to influence what Congress does.

The importance of this stage to Congress as an institution cannot be overemphasized. Despite the popular misperceptions about executive branch domination of Congress's agenda, the fact is that much important legislation gets its start in Congress.[35] Given its workload, Congress is able to retain control over its agenda only through the medium of congressional staff. However, the manner and scope of legislative initiatives depends more on the way members use their staffs than on sheer numbers. Some members hold their staffs under tight rein. They like their staffs to limit themselves to sifting other people's ideas, explaining the options to the member, and perhaps coming up with some original, but closely related alternatives. The staff of the Joint Committee on Taxation works this way. Other members loosen the reins somewhat, letting staffs use their technical expertise aggressively to criticize the approaches before the committee and suggest better ways to do the job. The House Armed Services Committee uses its staff in this way to rewrite the annual military procurement authorization bill almost line by line. But the loosest reins are held by those members who in effect let their staffs take the lead, while they "backstop" what the staff is doing.

These last have been called "entrepreneurial" staffs by David Price.[36] The term is illuminating. It draws our attention to staffs who

[35] See Ronald C. Moe and Steven C. Teel, "Congress as Policy-Maker: A Necessary Reappraisal," *Political Science Quarterly*, vol. 85 (September 1970), pp. 443-470, and Nelson W. Polsby, "Strengthening Congress in National Policymaking," *Yale Review* (Summer 1970) reprinted in N. Polsby, ed., *Congressional Behavior* (New York: Random House, 1971), pp. 3-13.

[36] David E. Price, "Professionals and 'Entrepreneurs': Staff Orientations and Policy Making on Three Senate Committees," *Journal of Politics*, vol. 33 (May 1971), pp. 316-336.

act as if they were merchants, buying "products" wholesale, sifting through them, and then selling a few of the choicer items to favored retail "buyers"—the staff aides' bosses.

The connection between the interests of members, the goals of staff entrepreneurs, and the legislative agenda is direct. Senators and representatives believe their interests with the electorate are advanced if they can claim credit for authoring important bills or amendments or instigating well publicized hearings. At the same time, their reputations inside Congress are advanced by their being identified with well-chosen issues they can make "their own." Thus, out of concern for their internal and external reputations, the members are led to tell their staffs to look for "new ideas" for hearings, bills, or amendments. The staffers improve their positions with the boss if they come up with ideas that have a chance of going somewhere in Congress and in the press. This same activity simultaneously enhances the position of the staff person in the Washington community. The aide becomes known to insiders as the person "really" responsible for such and such a program. Furthermore, as the aide becomes accepted and trusted by the member, he becomes known in Washington as someone worth cultivating as a "middle man": a person with an institutional stake in listening to new ideas from friendly interest groups and then selling the members on the ideas the aide finds most promising.

Senator Warren G. Magnuson's twenty-three-year tenure as chairman of the Senate Commerce Committee (1955–1978) is an almost letter-perfect illustration of the relationship between members' interests, staff goals, and committee agendas on a committee with entrepreneurial staff,[37] while the Senate Select Committee on Small Business would have little reason for being if its staff did not behave in this manner.[38] In fact, in the years since Price wrote, the entrepreneurial style has become dominant in the Senate, while growing more common in the House.

The impact of entrepreneurial staffs has been both procedural and substantive. Substantively, the interests of these staffs and their members lead them constantly to be looking for "new ideas." In effect, this means the staff is expected to look for "problems" amenable to legislative fixes. If a "problem" cannot be found, a "crisis" might do; but the last thing the staff needs is a set of intractable "conditions." At one time, the institutional incentives leading staffs toward these new issues resulted in an unmistakable partisan bias, as

[37] David E. Price, *Who Makes the Laws: Creativity and Power in Senate Committees* (Cambridge, Mass.: Schenkman Publishing Co., 1972), pp. 28-29.

[38] Michael J. Malbin, *Unelected Representatives: Congressional Staff and the Future of Representative Government* (New York: Basic Books, 1980), chap. 3.

the problems discovered tended to be social ones to be remedied by governmental action. Now, as the government has gotten more active, the problem might just as easily be governmental, and the remedy a corrective amendment instead of a new program. In both cases, however, the approach tends to lead staff—with their own time frameworks already shortened by their desire to gain credit in the Washington job network—to exaggerate the members' politically natural but nevertheless unfortunate tendency to avoid thinking of the long-range impacts of the policies before them.

The atmosphere in which staff entrepreneurialism flourishes also creates a bias in favor of issues that look good in the press. There is a two-way relationship here: publicity may move an issue forward; issues are put forward for the sake of publicity. Senator Magnuson's new staff and legislative style grew directly out of his desire for publicity that would help him get reelected in 1968. Other senators may react less abruptly, but no less directly. Thus, the staff looks not only for issues the press will like, but a good entrepreneurial staffer is expected to know how to "package" what he has in a way the press will find interesting.

The self-interest of members and their entrepreneurial staffs may motivate a great deal of what the staffs are asked to do, but the institutional consequences extend beyond the electoral aims that set the activities in motion. By creating incentives for finding new legislative issues, the Congress enhances its role as an independent body able to influence the national agenda in broad terms. However, as more and more of Congress's 250-plus committees and subcommittees adopt this staff style, the effect will be—indeed, to a large extent already has been—to turn staff into a mechanism for generating more work for Congress instead of helping it manage the work it already must do. In addition, the same incentives that lead chairmen to use staff entrepreneurs to drum up new issues, lead other members to look for amendments for which they too may claim credit. The result, therefore, is not only more work but increased decentralization, as non-chairmen have the resources to pursue their interest in not letting committee or party leaders set the terms of floor debate.

Staff Negotiations: Sunset. What is the staff's role once an idea makes it to a member's personal legislative agenda? Part of the staffer's job is to drum up publicity, both for the legislation itself and for his senator or representative. If a member has adopted an idea solely for its symbolic value, as they often do,[39] publicity may be

---

[39] See David R. Mayhew, *Congress: The Electoral Connection* (New Haven: Yale University Press, 1974), passim.

the end of it. But if a member is serious about getting a bill passed, he will have to start thinking about building a majority coalition.

First, the staff and member line up the initial sponsors. Then, as the leading sponsors try to gain more supporters in committee, before floor action or during a conference, they may be forced to modify their original proposal—either by adding new ideas or by softening the impact of something another member may find troublesome. In the Senate, this process of "massaging" a bill's language almost always takes place at the staff level, with direct negotiations between senators limited to a few rare instances in which items are too politically sensitive to be handled solely by staff. In the House, the members still tend to talk to each other directly about detailed legislative language, but less than they used to. Two examples can be used to make this point clearly: the staff negotiations over "sunset" legislation during 1975–1978 in the Senate and the late-1977 phantom conference on the differing House and Senate Veterans' Education Benefits bills.

"Sunset" is the popular description for a bill sponsored by former Senator Edmund S. Muskie (Democrat, Maine) that would have required all federal programs to go through a process of periodic review and reauthorization. From its initial stages in late 1975 until Senate adoption in 1978, the sunset bill went through a succession of detailed staff negotiations to which the senators paid little direct attention. Yet, in the end, the senators retained clear control over those aspects of the process that affected them politically—even while paying scant attention to the substance—by the way they chose the participants and set the ground rules for the staff negotiations. (The House did virtually nothing on sunset during this period.)

The process through which the sunset bill went may be outlined as follows:

First, the staff of Senator Muskie's Subcommittee on Intergovernmental Relations (IGR) of the Committee on Government Operations picked up an idea Muskie had tried unsuccessfully in earlier bills because it fit in with a general political theme he was developing. The staff decided the time was ripe for a major legislative push and convinced Muskie to let them work on it.

Second, the IGR staff worked on getting the general ideas into detailed legislative language. They *informed* Muskie of what they had done, and, hearing no objection, they went ahead.

Third, the staff got together with the staffs of other people on Government Operations to get their support and incorporated their ideas into the bill.

Fourth, rather than wait for groups to come to them, the staff *took the initiative* in trying to build coalitions with outside interest groups.

Fifth, when the bill failed to get to the floor in 1976, the staff redrafted the bill on their own to try to meet objections that had surfaced in the Senate Committee on Rules and Administration, which had successfully asserted its right to share jurisdiction over the bill. Again, the staff informed Muskie *after* the redrafting, not before, and again got no objections.

Sixth, when the main cosponsors on the renamed Governmental Affairs Committee could not come to an agreement with Senator Charles Percy (Republican, Illinois), the committee's ranking minority member, over the timing of sunset and Percy's own regulatory reform bill, the staffs were told to "work it out" in staff meetings. When they did, most of the amended bill sailed through the committee without public discussion.

Seventh, to save the bill from certain death before the Rules Committee, Muskie urged Chairman Howard Cannon (Democrat, Nevada) to create a staff working group. The group (consisting of representatives from each of the standing committees as well as IGR) completely redrafted the bill in a way that Muskie found unsatisfactory. After some five months of hard work, the staff group gave its draft to Senator Claiborne Pell (Democrat, Rhode Island) who succeeded Cannon as chairman at the start of 1978 after a shuffle of seats caused by the death of the chairman of another committee. Pell was up for reelection in 1978 and the last thing he wanted was a lengthy public battle with Muskie.

Eighth, to get himself out of the political hole into which the working group's resolution might have put him, Pell asked first the GAO and then the GAO together with the IGR staff to come up with another compromise set of proposals.

Ninth, when Robert Byrd, the Senate majority leader, felt a similar sense of unease with the bill Pell reported, he asked yet another group of staff people to give the bill one more massaging. This was the fourth and final staff "committee" to "mark up" the bill before it reached the floor and was passed by the Senate in the closing days of the 95th Congress.

Through all the steps, the staffs were shaping the bill, taking account of their senators' interests, reporting back to their senators on the agreements they had reached, and arguing the political case for their decisions to their bosses. The senators seemed little in evidence through this whole process, but they clearly were not absent. If one were to ask, Who was in charge? the answer in this case seems to be: the senators, but with significant qualifications. Only a few senators seemed to follow or care about the details of this bill, but they all seemed to know exactly how it might affect them politically. On issues of political importance to the members, the staffs may have become wedded to their own points of view, but they were pulled back more than once by their bosses. What the senators did *not* seem to know or care about, however, were the different options the staff was considering, each of which might equally satisfy the senators' political needs while having a very different substantive impact. (Muskie and Cannon seem to have followed the issues down to this level, but the other senators did not.)

While the senators did seem to be well enough in charge of their staffs to control the political effects of their work, the process this bill went through did not look even remotely like a civics textbook picture of legislative deliberation. There was a lot of deliberation, to be sure, but it all seemed to be going on between staffs. The senators talked to (or received memos from) their staffs, but they did not seem to talk much to each other. Moreover, while senators may have known roughly what the staffs negotiated in their own names, it seems clear that only Muskie and his staff—and not even the other cosponsors or many of their staffs—knew why each major item was in the bill in the form it had taken.

Staff Negotiations: GI Bill. While the preparation of the sunset bill covered a three-year period, the phantom conference on veterans' educational benefits involved only one week of intensive staff negotiations. The House and Senate had passed very different bills extending and increasing educational benefits for veterans in 1977. The House acted first, passing a straightforward bill on September 12 that increased veterans' benefits by 6.6 percent. The bill passed under a suspension of the rules by a vote of 397–0. The Senate bill, containing a number of significantly different provisions, was adopted on October 14 by a vote of 91–0. The Senate vote came about three weeks before the first session of the 95th Congress was expected to adjourn. The timing was par for the course for a veterans' bill. For several years in a row the two veterans' committees seemed to have a talent for bringing major bills to the floor toward the end of a session—a time of the year when the crush of business makes it impossible for most members to focus on the issues, demand regular procedures, or contemplate the thought of endangering cost-of-living increases for veterans.

Because of the timing, conferees never were formally appointed to work on the bills, and the members themselves met only once over an informal breakfast. Instead, the leaders of the two veterans' committees used the calendar as their excuse for letting the staff do the work of a conference committee. Key staff people simply sat down for three days in late October and early November and worked out the differences among themselves. These differences went well beyond monetary questions to what the committee members saw as issues of principle.[40] As a result, the staff level compromise was no simple split-the-difference affair. The staffs had to come up with imaginative new formulations significantly changing existing law.

The new formulations were presented individually to the half dozen most important committee members as they were worked out. These members ratified the decisions, which were then put into legislative language in a marathon staff session that listed until 4:00 A.M., November 3. Written copies were not even available later that morning, when the bill was brought up on the House floor under unanimous consent procedures. It was adopted without a dissenting vote in a debate that showed clearly that no one, including the committee and subcommittee chairmen, could answer basic factual questions on the floor. The Senate debate the next day was slightly better informed because the written language at least was in hand, but, like the House, the Senate cleared the argument unanimously with only a limited discussion.

Except for one brief breakfast meeting of the House and Senate chairmen held before the staff began its work, conversations among the members about the matters being negotiated simply were not part of the negotiating process. While the lack of a conference is far from normal—there was some protest about this in the House[41]—the delegation to staff was not extraordinary, and the lack of a formal conference was far from unprecedented. The chief counsel for the House Veterans' Affairs Committee said in an interview, "I can't remember but one formal conference being held since 1973, when I came here." Olin Teague (Democrat, Texas), since retired but then chairman of the education subcommittee and a long-time champion of GI benefits, said: "It's just quicker and easier without a whole lot of people."[42]

More Information, But Better Informed? The examples described so far show that the staff explosion of recent decades both adds to Con-

[40] The three major issues were (1) whether the amount of benefits should vary with average tuition costs in a state, (2) whether the length of time during which a veteran may use benefits should be extended, and (3) whether Women's Auxiliary Service Pilots from World War II should be considered veterans entitled to benefits.

[41] *Congressional Record*, daily ed., November 3, 1977, pp. H 12149 (Congressman Edgar) and pp. H 12158-H 12159 (Congresswoman Heckler).

[42] Quoted in Colman McCarthy, " 'Tiger' Teague and the Veterans Compromise," *Washington Post*, November 19, 1977, p. A19.

gress's agenda and helps members cope with it. Members who delegate clearly are able to keep their fingers in more pies than they could otherwise. Still, more is not necessarily better. Later, we will explicitly consider some of the costs of excessive delegation. First, however, let us consider one of the presumed benefits.

Members of Congress freely acknowledge that the main reasons for the growth of staff have to do with the distribution of power *within* Congress more than the functioning of Congress as a whole. Nevertheless, the public justification for the growth of legislative staff had to do primarily with Congress's need to have its own sources of information independent of the executive branch and outside interest groups. There can be no doubt that larger committee and support agency staffs have meant more information coming into Congress. Yet more information may not automatically mean better informed members of Congress. Three examples relating to Congress's consideration of energy policy in the 94th (1975–1976) and 95th (1977–1978) Congress show why this is so: staff oversight on the House Commerce Subcommittee on Energy and Power, chaired by Congressman John Dingell (Democrat, Michigan); energy oversight on the House Commerce Subcommittee on Oversight and Investigations, then chaired by former Congressman John Moss (Democrat, California); and the use of policy analysis in the natural gas debate of 1977–1978.

The Dingell and Moss subcommittees each conducted a great deal of energy oversight during the four years studied. Moss gained a reputation during his career as one of Congress's most active investigative chairmen from a consumer advocate point of view, while Dingell was a Moss protégé who said that effective legislation could not be separated from effective oversight. Each of their subcommittees had a staff large enough for many a full committee of only a few years ago, and each gave the staff considerable leeway to develop investigative topics for later action. Each staff was productive, and its productivity in each case created management problems. Both Dingell and (for three of the four years) Moss relied on a single staff person to coordinate and to some extent funnel the information generated by staff investigators on its way to the chairman. (Staff director Frank Potter performed this task for Dingell while the chief counsel Michael Lemov did the job of energy investigation for Moss.) The need to depend on staff produced predictable distortions in the flow of information, as both Potter and Lemov used their independent judgment to implement their bosses' natural tendencies in a manner that seemed to exaggerate their effect.[43] For Dingell, investigations were important, but secondary to legislation. Hence, there

[43] See Malbin, *Unelected Representatives*, chaps. 6 and 7.

161

was a tendency to downplay or delay the presentation of material learned by the staff if it might endanger the process of legislative compromise. Potter, taking his cues from his boss, acted on his own on several occasions to softpedal, delay, and in at least one case scuttle an investigation the public presentation of which might have proven legislatively or politically embarrassing. Lemov, in contrast, tended to overplay the information developed by the investigative staff. Sometimes acting on his own in light of his boss's cues and sometimes on direct instruction, Lemov regularly had the staff present isolated and sometimes unproven allegations of deliberate natural gas withholding by major drillers as if they proved a pattern pervasive in the industry. In at least one case, they stifled the results of one investigation (on the American Gas Association's data about gas reserves) that failed to prove allegations Moss made about the industry that could not be substantiated.

We should be very clear about what these examples show. There is no suggestion here that Lemov or Potter was an independent agent or that they were acting contrary to their chairmen's readily apparent wishes. Rather, the point is to dislodge the easy assumption that more information developed by the staff means more information of use to Congress as a whole. The transmission belt between staff member, staff director, chairman, subcommittee, and the full chamber includes many stopping points where information can be turned back or distorted before it moves on, often in ways that cannot possibly be checked by other members, given the system of personalized committee staffing in which staff members owe their loyalty and hence their information only to the person who hires them.

The use of policy analysis in the natural gas debate raises another point entirely. The problem there was not that information was withheld or otherwise unavailable—there was a surplus of information. Countless "analyses" of the consumer costs and supply benefits of price deregulation were produced by committee staffs and support agencies and then cited in committee and on the floor. Each was based on its own mathematical model. The quantitative conclusions about costs and benefits were tossed around by members with great authority and were suitably headlined in the press. Whatever their rhetorical utility, however, the studies in fact were of little intellectual benefit. Every one of them had to assume answers to questions that were really ones of geology, international relations, antitrust law, and political philosophy. If the members had understood, debated, and at least tentatively answered all of those questions, they would have had all they needed to decide how to vote—without the models. The models added nothing new to this debate, largely because their quantitative conclusions followed directly from the more important non-quantitative premises. Unfortunately, the members never got beyond the numbers to do the work needed to expose the assumptions. Hence, they were in no position to use the models properly, let alone choose among them. That should hardly be a surprise: the quantitative conclusions do seem authoritative, after all, and exposing assumptions takes more time than a member can possibly put in. Failing to do that work, however, simply means delegating more to a staff whose activities help create the information overload in the first place.

An Alternative Model. The examples given so far represent fairly typical staff activities and problems. Moreover, the staffing changes of recent years have all tended to work in the direction indicated by the examples. Despite this, it would be a mistake to think of committee and subcommittee staffs as if they were all the same. The variations among staffs are every bit as great as the ones among sub-committees indicated by Davidson. In terms of the effect of staff on the legislative process, however, the biggest difference seems to be the difference between *personalized* and *corporate* staffs. Corporate committee staffs are ones that see themselves working for their committee as a whole; personalized staffs see themselves owing their primary loyalty to a particular senator or representative. The purest form of corporate staffing may be found on the few committees that retain the ideal of professional nonpartisanship envisioned in the Legislative Reorganization Act of 1946, such as the staffs of the House and Senate Appropriations committees and the Joint Committee on Taxation. Entrepreneurial committee staffs, whether investigative or legislative, tend to be the most highly personalized and least corporate of all. Yet, while it would be fair to say that all entrepreneurial staffs are personalized and most personalized staffs are becoming more or less entrepreneurial, it would be wrong to equate the two ideas: several partisan staffs retain some corporate features, and a few have become identified with individual chairmen without becoming entrepreneurial.

In general, corporate staff aides are more likely than personalized ones to see themselves working for Congress for a long time. As a result, they tend to see themselves as handmaidens and facilitators rather than as innovative, behind-the-scenes leaders climbing the first rungs on the Washington career ladder. This can be seen immediately from the careers of a few of the senior professionals on corporate committees. To start with an example from a partisan staff, the Bronx born Richard J. Sullivan was hired as chief counsel of the House Public Works Committee in 1957 by Charles Buckley, who chaired the committee from 1955 to 1965 and who also came from the Bronx. But Sullivan has far outlasted Buckley, staying on as chief counsel during the chairmanships of George H. Fallon (1965–1971), John A. Blatnik (1971–1975), Robert Jones (1975–1977), and Harold T. Johnson (1977–). In the process, he has developed a reputation among insiders as an indispensable person to know if you are interested in a pork barrel project. The people serving with Sullivan on the full-committee staff's top positions also have long terms of service; most have worked for at least four chairmen. More interesting is the way the majority and minority staff work together. On other committees, the majority accepts the responsibility for doing the administrative work and writing committee reports while the minority limits itself to writing additional views on points of disagreement. On Public Works (and on Senate Armed Services at least through 1978 and a few other committees), the minority staff shares the workload with the majority on all points except those on which the members specifically disagree with each other. (In the Senate, the Environment and Public Works Committee staff does not share its workload in the same way, but Bailey Guard has been the minority staff director under four different ranking minority members with different political perspectives.)

Although Sullivan and Guard have long records of service when compared with most other partisan committee staff aides, the two appropriations committees outdo all others in staff longevity. Their nonpartisan staffs try to hire people in mid-career with specialized executive branch experience. They emphatically are not looking for, and do not attract, young people who are out to make reputations before they move on. As one Senate Appropriations staff member said:

> People who are looking for "some hill experience" are not going to come to Appropriations. They just would not have the latitude or the legislative vehicle to show off their creative work. All you get to show for your work here is a change in a number in a bill that otherwise looks the same year in and year out.

A House Appropriations staff member seconded this, saying that "there is a tradition of people staying for quite a while and retiring from this staff."

Longevity is usually a clear indication that a professional staff is able to serve different committee and subcommittee chairmen (or ranking minority members) with different political outlooks. On the two appropriations committees, most of the staff work for the subcommittees, where almost all of these two committees' work is done.

Continuity of staff service is made easier in the House by the fact that House Appropriations is the only committee on either side to base its nominations for subcommittee chairmanships on subcommittee seniority. Thus, Joseph P. Addabbo's accession in 1979 to the Defense Subcommittee chair long held by George H. Mahon may lead to significant changes in defense policy, but it did not mean a change in subcommittee staff. Addabbo had been well served by Ralph Preston during his years on the subcommittee. There was no reason for him to think that would not continue.

The more remarkable story about institutional continuity has to do with the Senate Appropriations Committee. Until the early 1970s the House and Senate Appropriations staffs almost mirrored each other. Then the Senate staff was hit with a rash of retirements at precisely the time when the ethos of professionalism seemed no longer to carry weight with the senators. Twelve of the thirteen new subcommittee "senior clerks" were promoted from within, as befits a "professional" staff, but the newer subcommittee chairmen began trying to place people loyal to them in the entry level professional staff slots. By the second half of the decade the committee was going along with the other Senate committees that were hiring designated minority staffs and personal committee aides for the junior members.

As if this were not enough to produce a change, Warren Magnuson became chairman of the Senate Appropriations Committee in 1978. Magnuson, we recall, was the senator who made entrepreneurial staff activity famous with the latitude he gave Commerce Committee staff in the 1960s. Magnuson even imported some of this style to his appropriations subcommittees when—to the consternation of his committee colleagues—he put Harley Dirks on the staff. Dirks had worked for Magnuson for a year on the Democratic Senatorial Campaign Committee when Magnuson had him hired for appropriations in 1966. Perhaps the first person on the staff hired with no previous budgeting experience, Dirks was considered a "Magnuson person" for all of his eleven years on the Senate Appropriations Committee staff.

Thus, there was every reason to believe Magnuson would try to make the committee staff more personalized and partisan when he became chairman in 1978. Moreover, the new chairman immediately hired two of his leading aides from the Commerce Committee, Thomas Allison and Edward Merlis, for the full committee's central staff. Speculation ran high that similar appointments would soon follow. However, it did not work out that way. Within a year, the two activists had moved on: Allison to the executive branch and Merlis to the Judiciary Committee. Magnuson neither expanded the central committee staff nor hired political people to replace these two. He thus seemed to confirm a thesis proposed in an interview by the now retired Congressional Research Service senior specialist Walter Kravitz: "My feeling is that staffs, like all organizations, take on lives of their own," Kravitz said. "The kind of a tradition that is established on the staff is very important. Then even the chairman and the members have to face up to it, and even if they don't go along entirely, they will be influenced." Kravitz had this thesis very much in mind when he built up the nonpartisan core staff of the House Budget Committee in his service as that committee's staff director. But the staff he used as his model was that of the Joint Committee on Taxation.

The Joint Committee on Internal Revenue Taxation (as it was called until 1977) was set up in 1926 as an investigative committee but quickly became a holding operation for the professional non-partisan staff that served as the principal staff for both the House Ways and Means and Senate Finance committees on tax legislation.[44] Although the staff's role has declined from its 1964–1976 peak under staff director Laurence N. Woodworth, it still serves as an example of the important role nonpartisan staffs can play on highly partisan issues.

Woodworth, his successor Bernard M. (Bob) Shapiro, and their staffs have seen themselves almost as teachers. The staff puts in an extraordinary amount of effort before the committees start to work on a major tax bill, preparing voluminous material that lays out the arguments and political interests on each side of the major issues to be considered. While all staffs do this to some extent, the joint tax committee goes beyond normal partisan staff briefings to publish the material in advance of the committee's deliberation. In that way, members on and off the committee can know the issues before the committee closes off any options. While members not on the committee rarely read the material themselves, the staff spends hours explaining the issues to reporters so that, through the press, the other members and the general public will know the political implications of the technical debate going on in the committee.

This educational posture has had important political benefits for the Ways and Means Committee. The House expected the committee,

[44] For previous studies of the staff of the Joint Committee on Taxation, see John F. Manley, "Congressional Staff and Public Policy-Making: The Joint Committee on Internal Revenue Taxation," *Journal of Politics*, vol. 30 (November 1968), pp. 1046-1067, and *The Politics of Finance: The House Committee on Ways and Means* (Boston: Little, Brown, 1970), pp. 307-319, David Price, *Who Makes the Laws: Creativity and Power in Senate Committees* (Cambridge, Mass.: Schenkman Publishing Co., 1972), pp. 194-198, and "Professionals and Entrepreneurs: Staff Orientations and Policy Making on Three Senate Committees," *Journal of Politics*, vol. 33 (May 1971), pp. 316-336.

when it was chaired by Wilbur Mills (1958–1974), to be a "responsible" body whose judgment would end up more or less a carefully compromised reflection of the will of the whole House. The geographically balanced membership came from politically "safe" districts. While the Democratic members through 1974 were nominated by their state or area delegations, the leadership of the committee and the party always looked for people who believed in compromise and whose political security let them withstand interest group pressure. The House's "closed rule" policy for tax bills, whereby the House had to accept or reject committee bills without amendment, was a tribute both to the House's faith in the committee and to its unwillingness to face the results of public debates over interest group sponsored tax amendments on the floor.[45] By giving the press a balanced education early, the staff helped make the system work. Members across the political spectrum would be alerted that something of interest was going on before the committee locked itself in and a closed rule made it too late to change.

Woodworth was an educator of a different sort for the members of the committee: less a lecturer and more a counsel helping the members see the implications of the choices before them. "I always felt he was trying to bring out the best in me, rather than explaining himself," Barber Conable (Republican, New York) once told the *Wall Street Journal*.[46] But Woodworth's role in committee went well beyond this. Because he had won the members' trust, they let him take the lead in developing compromises, and they held him out to lobbyists as a filter through which their amendments had to pass before the members would consider them. In both of these roles, Woodworth's technical skills were what the outsider was likely to notice first. However, in both, the members knew that what they were getting grew as much out of his knowledge of the member's politics as out of his familiarity with the details of the Internal Revenue Code.

Two facts are crucial to an understanding of the role the nonpartisan staff played when it was asked to help the committee reach a compromise. First, the staff was encouraged to function in a nonpartisan manner because both the chairman (Wilbur Mills) and the ranking minority member (John Byrnes) thought bipartisanship best

---

[45] For two accounts of the connections between how members were appointed, the committee's compromising "restrained partisanship," and the closed rule, see Manley, *The Politics of Finance*, and Richard F. Fenno, Jr., *Congressmen in Committees* (Boston: Little, Brown, 1973), pp. 1-138.

[46] John Pierson, "Larry Woodworth: Dulce et Decorum," *Wall Street Journal*, December 9, 1977, inserted in the *Congressional Record*, daily ed., December 12, 1977, E7372.

fit their own and their committee's interests. Second, the staff was able to remain in the background largely because Mills and Byrnes knew enough about both the code and the interests of the members on their respective sides of the table to make the choices among the options themselves.

Nevertheless, the staff's nonpartisan professionalism should not be confused with apolitical neutrality. It did not advocate one policy over another, but it did work to move the legislative process forward. In effect, therefore, even though Woodworth was not the "chairman's man," he naturally ended up devoting more of his time to the House and Senate committee chairmen's needs than to others'. When things got busy at the end of a session, this more than occasionally led other committee members to feel shortchanged. No one ever criticized Woodworth for this. He and his staff often worked through the night, and members realized that one person can only do so much. But they did want some staff of their own to supplement the joint committees.

The Senate rules changes of 1975 and 1977 required the Finance Committee to create a minority staff and distributed personal legislative staff to the committee's junior members. (House Republicans on Ways and Means have had their own professional tax experts since the early 1970s.) The distribution of resources helped take some pressure off the joint committee staff, but it also allowed the junior and particularly the minority members to develop and push amendments of their own, much as the policy entrepreneurs on other committees did.

It is no accident that minority staff entrepreneurs on Senate Finance became more important when Robert Dole (Republican, Kansas) succeeded Carl Curtis (Republican, Nebraska) in 1979 as the committee's ranking Republican. Dole sees tax policy as the cutting political issue of the 1980s. To dramatize the differences between Democrats and Republicans for political purposes, he considers it vital to present policy alternatives on the Senate floor instead of working toward a bipartisan consensus and simply voting "no" where agreement cannot be reached. While the nonpartisan staff of the Joint Committee on Taxation has been helpful to Dole technically, his political decision clearly limits the staff's ability to act as mediator.

The way committee partisanship affects the utility of staff nonpartisanship was even more evident with the House Ways and Means Committee during 1975–1976, the first two years of Al Ullman's chairmanship. Ullman (Democrat, Oregon) was thrust into the lead when Mills stepped down suddenly at the end of 1974 to concentrate on his ultimately successful battle against alcoholism. He found himself in charge of a committee that was markedly different from the one on which he had been serving. The House Democratic Caucus first stripped away the power committee Democrats had held for more than fifty years of serving as their party's Committee on Committees. Then, the caucus expanded the committee's size from twenty-five to thirty-seven and selected new members primarily with an eye toward their views on policy and not at all with the old concern for finding people with a proven willingness to compromise. The net result was that a committee once made up of knowledgeable members who restrained their partisanship and were willing to follow the lead of their strong chairman became a hydra-headed collection of people who had little concern for the committee's corporate power on the floor, chaired by a man who had neither the skills nor the resources to assert his leadership. The situation placed severe pressures on the nonpartisan Woodworth and his staff. Ullman found himself depending on Woodworth not simply for advice but for solutions. As a result, Republicans began questioning how long the staff could retain its nonpartisan credit.

Interestingly, the situation changed again in 1977. Woodworth left the staff to join the administration. Shapiro, while certainly a capable person, was not in a position to serve Ullman as Woodworth had, nor did he want to. At the same time, Ullman—more confident now in his role as chairman—beefed up his own tax staff on the Ways and Means Committee, thus reducing his need to create partisan pressures on the joint committee staff. The sequence of events demonstrated a simple truth about nonpartisan staffs: to be useful, they must work for a committee that either does not need personalized partisan staff help or is able to get that help without compromising the nonpartisan staff itself.

What benefits do the members gain from having a nonpartisan professional staff available to help them on tax legislation? These are considerable, as the members on both Ways and Means and Finance universally testify. The staff gives them much more help understanding complex tax issues than they could possibly get from ever-changing cadres of legislative assistants. The staff may have to give *more* time to the chairman than other members, but the other members know that the information they do get has not been distorted to meet the chairman's or anyone else's political needs. Moreover, since the members believe they can rely on the staff to keep sensitive points confidential—even from the chairman if necessary—they have no qualms about getting the staff's expert advice as they work on their own amendments. This advice is more than technically expert. The joint tax committee gives the members a neutral institutional memory of the sort political appointees in the executive branch get from better career civil servants. When an idea is floated, the joint tax staff is likely to remember whether a similar idea came up in the past and to what political effect. But the staff does not substitute its judgment for the members', press for its own point of view, or even negotiate on the members' behalf. As a result, the members of the Finance and Ways and Means committees may not "process" quite as much legislation or do as many investigations as some other committees, but what they do can truly be called the members' own work.

Conclusion

What can we conclude from all this? Has the staff explosion of the past three decades helped or hurt Congress? We grant without question that senators and representatives are better able to do their own jobs as individuals by having professional legislative staffs accountable directly to them. But our question really is an institutional one: How well does the system that helps the members as individuals serve the legislative branch as a whole?

The answer to this question is not the same at every point of the legislative process. If we take Congress's workload as given and focus on negotiations, we see that the staffs, acting as surrogates for their "bosses," do as creditable a job of representing their interests as any attorney would for a client in a parallel situation outside Congress. With loyal surrogate-lawyers carrying out their wishes, the members are able to follow more issues than they could if they had to attend all meetings personally. Institutionally, this means that both the members as individuals and Congress as a whole are able to manage a heavier workload with the staffs than would be possible without them. To some extent, therefore, the staffs do seem to help Congress do its work.

But, as we have seen, the surrogate-lawyers are generally expected to be more than just passive representatives of their clients: they are also expected to go out and drum up new business. The increased use of personalized, entrepreneurial staffs has helped Congress retain its position as key initiator of federal policy, despite the growing power of the executive branch. The relationship between this use of entrepreneurial staff and Congress's power seems almost obvious. Most other national legislatures do not give individual members similar staff resources; most legislatures depend on their cabinets for almost all policy initiatives. Congress is not so passive today, thanks largely to its staff.

The system of individualized staff control seems also to be responsible for much of the oversight that gets accomplished outside of the General Accounting Office. Having a substantial number of staff people with appropriate investigative authority seems a necessary condition for congressional oversight of the executive branch and the independent regulatory commissions. But it is not a sufficient condition. Oversight also depends on chairmen and staffs who consider the effort worthwhile. For some reasons, collegial nonpartisan committee staffs have not provided much oversight. Perhaps it is because their accessibility to all members of a committee leaves them with little time for anything else; perhaps because committees that are willing to retain nonpartisan staffs try to restrain their partisanship and maintain close relationships with their counterparts in the executive branch. Thus, the movement away from a system of collegial nonpartisan committee staffing to a more personalized one has been associated with an increase in congressional oversight activity, largely because a personalized system lets chairmen have activist staff entrepreneurs, and chairmen who use entrepreneurial staffs tend to be more interested in maintaining their independence from the executive branch.

Yet, while the growth and use of staff has produced these beneficial results, there is a gloomier side: the effect of staffs on Congress's ability to act as a deliberative body. To see the importance of this issue, we need to consider some of the basic functions Congress was meant to perform in our constitutional scheme of government. Congress, we learn from *Federalist* No. 52, was meant to serve as a substitute for direct meetings of the citizens.[47] Representation was likely to produce not only a more manageable process than direct democracy, but better results. A representative system would require elected members from one district, with one set of needs and interests, to talk to members from districts with different needs and interests, if the members hoped to achieve anything.[48] Indirect communication, such as we see today, was not what was envisioned: direct communication among elected members was considered essential to informed deliberation.

Why are direct conversations important? Why is it not adequate for members to rely on staff mediation and communication by memorandum? The reason is that while indirect communication can convey a great deal of information, it cannot help a member *feel* or *sense* his colleagues' reactions to his own or each other's arguments. To go back to an example mentioned earlier, information about who would

[47] Alexander Hamilton, John Jay, and James Madison, *Federalist* No. 52 (New York: Modern Library, 1937), p. 343.
[48] Ibid., No. 63, pp. 411-413.

171

bear the cost of natural gas deregulation is something staff perhaps can convey in principle, but only the members can decide who *ought* to bear what cost.

Direct conversations among the members are so important to the legislative process that facilitating them was, until recent years, a primary objective behind many of Congress's otherwise incomprehensible procedures. Most people are inclined to avoid conversing or debating with those with whom they disagree. One of the most important strengths of Congress over the years has been the way its structure has encouraged people to engage in a process that most people naturally prefer to avoid. While party discipline has tended to stifle this process in other countries, Congress's procedures have been designed to encourage, inform, and structure communication among the members in ways that would both promote deliberation and discourage longstanding resentments. That was the real reason for allowing closed committee meetings[49] and for the elaborate rules of personal courtesy governing debate.[50] In recent years, however, the members have weakened the procedures designed to protect their ability to debate and deliberate freely. Debate and discussion have lost their central place in the legislative process, and that loss has had serious consequences. The growing importance of staff is but one reflection of the new situation.

For a process of legislative deliberation to function reasonably well, at least three distinct requirements must be satisfied. The members need accurate information, they need time to think about that information, and they need to talk to each other about the factual, political, and moral implications of the policies they are considering. The new use of staff undercuts each of these requirements. The first, and simplest, relates to the flow of information. We saw from our examples that the growing dominance of large "chairmen's staffs" has produced management problems that result in uncertainties in the flow of information from staffs to chairmen and from chairmen to others in the Senate or House. Most of the information reaching members may well be reliable, but it would take an expert to sort out the reliable from the unreliable, and even an expert cannot know

[49] For two articles that connect recent reforms to a decline in the deliberative processes on revenue issues, see Catherine E. Rudder, "Committee Reform and the Revenue Process," in Lawrence C. Dodd and Bruce L. Oppenheimer, eds., *Congress Reconsidered* (New York: Praeger, 1977), pp. 117-139, and I. M. Destler, "'Reforming' Trade Politics: The Weakness of Ways and Means," *Washington Post*, November 28, 1978, A19.

[50] U.S. House of Representatives, *Constitution, Jefferson's Manual and Rules of the House of Representatives of the United States, 96th Congress* by William Holmes Brown, Parliamentarian, House Doc. 95-403, 95th Congress, 2d session, 1979, secs. 359-373 and 749-752.

about material that has been stifled to serve a staff's or chairman's own interests.

This problem is probably the easiest of the three major problems associated with the growing role of staff to resolve in principle. If every committee had a nonpartisan staff core, there would be fewer occasions on which Congress would receive intentionally partial or distorted information from its staff. To the extent that nonpartisan professional staffs are inadequate in providing all the Congress asks of its staff, Representative Ullman's solution on the House Ways and Means Committee would seem to have much to recommend it. Let every committee have a dual staff: a nonpartisan professional core to do the kind of work done by the staff of the Joint Committee on Taxation and a personalized chairman's (or ranking minority member's or junior member's) staff to be more entrepreneurial, investigative, or political.

Still, this does not seem to get at the heart of the issue. Improving the accuracy of the information flow would not, for example, have created more time for the members to wade through the kind of complex material they were given on natural gas deregulation. The reason members rely on staffs to do their negotiating, and the reason they are not able to be critical consumers of the information they receive, is that they have more to do than time in which to do it. The second problem with the use of staff, therefore, is that it has not left the members with more time to concentrate on their legislative work. If anything, the use of entrepreneurial staffs has meant an increase in the numbers of hearings and amendments considered every year. About the only way Congress could improve this part of its present condition would be to reduce its agenda systematically and substantially. However, this solution raises further problems. While it is true that reducing the legislative agenda would probably improve deliberations on the items that remain, it hardly would improve the representative character of the government as a whole. If one accepts the present role of government, reducing Congress's agenda would simply let more of what happens in the other branches go without congressional review. As an answer to a problem of democratic representation, that cure seems worse than the disease. But whether desirable or not, it may not even be possible to reduce Congress's agenda substantially, given the present role of government. The bureaucracy finds itself compelled repeatedly to come back to Congress to clarify vague delegations of authority from the legislative branch—delegations that generally are vague because specificity might have endangered the chances for getting anything through Congress. But even if Congress managed to delegate with perfect clarity, the bureaucracy would have an interest in coming back repeatedly to protect or expand its role.

Congress, in other words, would have a hard time ducking out of much of its workload without taking the unlikely step of dealing with that workload's root sources. About the only way to reduce Congress's workload without vastly increasing the discretionary power of the less representative branches of the government would seem to be to reduce the size and complexity of government as a whole. However, the size of the bureaucracy is itself only an intermediate reason for the size of Congress's agenda. The growth of government has come about partly because the nation has become more complex, but even more, as James Q. Wilson has pointed out, because people have changed their ideas about what government should do.[51] People in government have *chosen* to respond to more of the demands being made upon them, and these responses in turn have generated more demands. In fact, elected officials, their staffs, and bureaucrats often do not even wait for someone to articulate a demand before they get to work on the response: given the chance, they look for problems to solve, encouraging demand as much as responding to it.

Thus, there is a connection between the world of ideas, the size of the government's agenda, and the way Congress does its work. That connection helps us understand the third, and most basic, problem with the new role of congressional staff—the use of staff negotiations as a substitute for direct conversation and deliberation among the members. Direct conversations and deliberation still do take place, of course.[52] But there can be no question that in recent decades there has been an increase in indirect negotiation and decrease in direct deliberation.[53] That should come as no surprise. After all, negotiating is precisely what members expect most of the committee

[51] James Q. Wilson, "American Politics, Then & Now," *Commentary* (February 1979), pp. 39-46.

[52] See Joseph M. Bessette, "Deliberation in Congress" (paper presented at the 1979 Annual Meeting of the American Political Science Association, Washington, D.C., August 31-September 3, 1979), for a discussion of this theme. The paper is based on Bessette's "Deliberation in Congress: A Preliminary Investigation" (Ph.D. diss., University of Chicago, 1978).

[53] For an analysis of a parallel decline in the role of deliberation in party politics see Nelson Polsby, "The News Media as An Alternative To Party in the Presidential Selection Process," in Robert A. Goldwin, ed., *Political Parties in the Eighties* (Washington, D.C.: American Enterprise Institute, 1980), p. 60, where Polsby talks about recent changes in the nominating process as involving a "transformation of a set of decisions from deliberative to nondeliberative modes." Congress would still be a deliberative body, according to the definition of deliberation in Polsby's essay; nonetheless it is interesting that the decline of deliberation in Congress to which I refer and its decline in the nominating process, mentioned by Polsby, have occurred at roughly the same time.

staffs and legislative aides to be doing. The staff of the Joint Committee on Taxation does mediate and supply information without negotiating, but few others still limit themselves in this way. That is precisely why Congress would be better off if more committees looked to this staff as a model.

We have been talking so far about the ways in which the use of staff has affected Congress procedurally. Has there also been a discernible effect on the substance of public policy? Staffs clearly do influence policy in thousands of little ways in any given year, but has the dependence on staff had any *systematic* impacts on policy? Our answers here must be more tentative than they were for procedural matters, but at least two kinds of effects suggest themselves—one relating to the role of the Washington issue networks and a second relating to the naturally narrow focus and inertia of staff negotiations.

The most direct impact of the role of staff has to do with the reception Congress gives the ideas put forward by groups or individuals that have no identifiable constituency, such as some of the smaller issue groups on the right and left, academicians, and issue specialists in think tanks and consulting firms. Senators and representatives are too busy to see every lobbyist who comes their way and must depend on their staffs to screen them. Organizations and individuals with real political or economic power have little difficulty getting in the door to make their case, but people who have nothing to offer but their ideas have a tougher time. However, since the staff's future careers in the Washington community often depend on their gaining reputations as innovators, it is in their interest to spend time listening to people whose ideas may help them put something new on the oversight or legislative agenda, even if those people have no political constituencies of their own. The interwoven interests of the participants in the various issue networks leads them to work together to identify problems they can then use their expertise to solve. The future interests of the staff flow directly from the changes in career patterns that we discussed earlier, in which staff jobs are stepping stones for ambitious young lawyers instead of places where mid-level bureaucrats and political cronies end their careers.

The tendency of the staffs' career interests to enhance the power of experts without constituencies is reinforced by the staffers' backgrounds. The new staffs tend to be young lawyers who came to Washington because they had been political activists and wanted to "make a mark" on "the system." In addition, their undergraduate and law school training has tended to make them more sympathetic to arguments based on general ideological principles (from the left for Democratic aides and from the right for Republicans) than either

175

their classmates with "real jobs" or the elected members. The technocratic and ideological staffers may be different people, or the same staff person may embrace both attitudes. Moreover, both may work side by side with other staff people whose legal specialization and ambitions, experience, and background lead them to act as interest group advocates. But major corporate, trade association, and labor union interests would have little difficulty being heard in a Washington that had no staffs, nor would an issue-based organization that had developed a deliverable political constituency. Where the staffs make a difference, therefore, is in their openness to, career interest in, and institutional need for ideas and slogans whose political power initially lies only in the fact that staff people and journalists are willing to listen to them.

While the first systematic substantive impact of staff on policy comes out of its entrepreneurial role, the second comes from its role in negotiations. Both have the net effect of increasing the amount of legislation that gets passed and broadening the range of interests served by that legislation. The job of a staff negotiator is to help move the process toward a resolution. While a member may pull him back, it almost always is in the interest of the staff negotiator to see a set of negotiations through to a successful conclusion. This is particularly true if the program contains some section that the staff member can think of as his own. The program—or the planned hearing, if the person is an investigator—may represent a major investment of time for a staff person whose future may depend on gaining recognition in Washington for having made a difference. As a result, the process of staff negotiation tends to lend practical weight to the view that the purpose of the legislative process is to fashion agreements behind which the greatest number of self-appointed interested parties can unite.[54] The impetus of staff, in other words, is to build coalitions by having programs respond, at least symbolically, to more demands, rather than let them die their natural death. The result is increasingly inclusive, increasingly complex legislation that can only be understood by an expert. Needless to say, this increases the power of permanent Washingtonians with the necessary expertise, such as former staffers.

In the course of building the coalitions described above, staffs consider programs in isolation from each other. It is not normally in their interest to question how a program affects the budget, the overall structure of government, or the ability of citizens to understand

[54] Theodore Lowi refers to this as "interest group liberalism" in *The End of Liberalism: Ideology, Policy, and the Crisis of Public Authority* (New York: W.W. Norton & Co., 1969), pp. 68-97.

what their government is doing. Of course, members themselves have the same inclination to see programs in isolation from each other. If they did not, they would scarcely tolerate the way staffs negotiate in their name. But a member who serves on several different committees, directly communicates with constituents, and sits down with other members to share the results of their composite experiences, is far more likely than an aide to have some basis for getting beyond this narrow focus to think about the relationships between policies in ways that cross lines of issue specialization.

It should be obvious by now that one cannot fully discuss the growth and use of congressional staff without confronting fundamental questions about the nature of representation in an era of governmental complexity. On the one hand, dependence on congressional staff has, as we have seen, increased the relative power of technocratic issue specialists and of groups with no economic or political constituency. This both reflects and reinforces the complexity of government. On the other hand, Congress has reacted to the governmental complexity it has created by building up its staffs defensively to preserve an important role for itself. But the size of those staffs and the way they are used has reinforced the situation in which the deliberative aspect of representation gets short shrift on all but the broad outlines of a few issues.

The weakening of deliberation is serious for a Congress that works best when it responds to constituents' needs and interests in a setting that encourages the members to think more broadly. The process no longer forces members to talk to each other to resolve the tough issues; the agenda keeps them busy with other things. The trouble Congress had in leading the country toward a national consensus on energy policy during the 1970s was but one side effect of this, and the complexifying role of staff must bear part of the blame. If Congress is to play its crucial representative role on whatever replaces energy as the key issue of coming decades, it must find some way to limit its agenda and reinforce the role of direct deliberation. While it is hard to imagine what that might be, the future of representative government may depend on it.

6

Coping with Uncertainty: Building Coalitions in the House and the Senate

Barbara Sinclair

"Moses would have difficulty getting the Ten Commandments through [Congress] today," claims Stuart Eizenstat.[1] Anthony King characterizes American politics in the 1970s as "building coalitions in the sand."[2] And according to Anne Wexler the Carter administration, in building a winning coalition in Congress, had to start from scratch on each new piece of legislation.[3]

Is this hyperbole or has the process of building congressional coalitions become much more difficult than it used to be? Would John Kennedy agree that Carter faced a more difficult task persuading the 95th and 96th Congresses to pass his legislation than he himself did with the 87th and 88th? Would Sam Rayburn pity Tip O'Neill?

Party Strength and Party Cohesion

The most important factors influencing the difficulty of forming winning coalitions are the size of the majority party and the cohesion of the majority and of the minority. In terms of party size in the House, Carter and the current congressional leaders were considerably better off in 1979 than their counterparts in the early 1960s. In the Senate, party ratios were only slightly less favorable than they were during Kennedy's first two Congresses. As table 6–1 shows, the 1958 election destroyed the very close party balance that had characterized most of the 1950s. Since then the Democrats have never held a majority of less than 55 percent in either chamber, and the margin

---

[1] Quoted in *Congressional Quarterly, Weekly Report*, October 6, 1979, p. 2199.

[2] Anthony King, "The American Polity in the Late 1970s: Building Coalitions in the Sand," in Anthony King, ed., *The New American Political System* (Washington, D.C.: American Enterprise Institute, 1978).

[3] Talk before Congressional Fellows, November 1978.

TABLE 6–1

PARTY SIZE IN THE HOUSE OF REPRESENTATIVES AND SENATE, 1953–1980
(in percentages of the appropriate chamber's membership)

Years	Northern Democrats[a]	Southern Democrats	Democrats	Republicans
House of Representatives				
1953–58	30.9	21.1	52.0	47.9
1959–60	43.9	21.1	65.0	35.1
1961–64	38.9	20.8	59.7	40.4
1965–66	48.5	19.3	67.8	32.1
1967–74	39.9	17.1	57.0	43.1
1975–78	49.4	17.5	66.9	33.3
1979–80	46.9	16.6	63.5	36.6
Senate				
1953–58	29.2	20.8	50.0	49.3
1959–60	44.9	20.4	65.3	34.7
1961–64	47.0	19.0	66.0	34.0
1965–66	50.0	18.0	68.0	32.0
1967–74	42.0	16.3	58.3	41.8
1975–78	46.0	16.0	62.0	38.0
1979–80	44.0	15.0	59.0	41.0

NOTE: For the regional categorization, see note 4.
[a] Border state Democrats are included in the northern Democratic grouping here.
SOURCE: *Congressional Quarterly Almanac,* various dates.

has usually been considerably greater. Thus Kennedy himself had substantial majorities; but, in the House, Jimmy Carter had an even more favorable situation. In 1974, a House in which Democrats outnumbered Republicans by two to one was elected, and the 1976 election brought no significant change in the ratio. House Democrats lost a few seats in 1978 but still controlled over 60 percent of the seats. The Senate figures were only a little less lopsided. There, too, the gains made in 1974 were maintained in 1976, and the losses of 1978 were not severe; in the 96th Congress, Democrats held 59 of the 100 Senate seats.

Not only were the Democratic majorities in both chambers large in the late 1970s, these majorities were also much more northern than were Kennedy's majorities. Democrats from the South, who have traditionally been less supportive of Democratic presidents' programs than their northern colleagues, had declined as a proportion

TABLE 6–2

PARTY UNITY IN THE HOUSE AND SENATE, 1953–1978

(in party unity scores)

		House		Senate	
Years	Congresses	Democrats	Republicans	Democrats	Republicans
1953–60[a]	83–86	77.9	79.0	78.9	78.4
1961–68	87–90	79.3	80.5	75.5	77.2
1969–76	91–94	71.8	73.9	74.3	71.8
1977–78	95	72.4	77.0	72.7	70.6

NOTE: An individual's party unity score is the percentage of roll calls pitting a majority of Democrats against a majority of Republicans on which he voted with a majority of his party. The figures given here are averages for the stated groups.

[a] 1955–60, for the Senate, data for the 83rd Congress were not available in usable form.

SOURCE: House scores calculated by the author; Senate scores from *Congressional Quarterly Almanac*, various dates.

of the Democratic party and as a proportion of the total membership in both chambers.[4]

These large majorities would be of little solace to Carter and the congressional leadership if a sharp decline in party-line voting accompanied the increase in size. Table 6–2 shows that House Democrats' party unity was, in fact, lower in the 1970s than it was in the 1950s or 1960s.[5] Furthermore, Republican party unity, which had also dropped in the early 1970s, rose in the 95th Congress. The decline in Democratic unity is interesting since, during the period when it occurred, the Democratic party was becoming less southern. Still, the decline was hardly precipitous, and its effects on coalition building

[4] The regional categorization used throughout the study is: New England—Connecticut, Maine, Massachusetts, New Hampshire, Rhode Island, Vermont; Middle Atlantic—Delaware, New Jersey, New York, Pennsylvania; East North Central—Illinois, Indiana, Michigan, Ohio, Wisconsin; West North Central—Iowa, Kansas, Minnesota, Missouri, Nebraska, North Dakota, South Dakota; South—Alabama, Arkansas, Florida, Georgia, Louisiana, Mississippi, North Carolina, South Carolina, Texas, Virginia; Border—Kentucky, Maryland, Oklahoma, Tennessee, West Virginia; Mountain—Arizona, Colorado, Idaho, Nevada, New Mexico, Utah, Wyoming; Pacific—California, Oregon, Washington, Alaska, Hawaii; Northeast includes the New England and the Middle Atlantic states.

[5] An individual's party unity score is the percentage of roll calls pitting a majority of Democrats against a majority or Republicans on which a member voted with a majority of his party. House scores were calculated by the author; Senate scores were taken from *Congressional Quarterly Almanac*, various dates. Absences do not affect the scores.

were counteracted by the increased size of the House Democratic majority.

Democratic senators' party unity was also lower in the 95th Congress than it was in the 1960s. The summary figures given in table 6–2 to a certain extent obscure the amount of change, as the mean Democratic party unity score was considerably higher in the 87th and 88th than in the 89th and 90th Congresses (77.4 versus 73.7). Even taking this into account, the decrease in Democratic party unity in the Senate was marginal; furthermore, in the Senate, Republican party unity had declined considerably more sharply than Democratic unity.

Although simple summary measures present problems,[6] they constitute evidence that party cohesion has declined. Still, the data presented to this point certainly do not justify the apocalyptic statements of members of the Carter administration.

The Changing Shape of Coalitions in the 1970s

One particular feature of the measures used up to this point may help account for the discrepancy between data and rhetoric. The party unity score and the proportion of party votes lump together the trivial and the crucial. A vote on a minor bill of no concern to the congressional party leadership or to the administration is given equal weight with a roll call on a central element of the president's program. A more refined way of determining whether coalition building is more difficult now than it was in the 1960s is to examine voting behavior within specific issue areas. To do so requires a schema which will allow us to classify most of the roll calls by issue category.

Aage Clausen developed a useful issue categorization in his work on the Congresses of the 1950s and early 1960s, and others have shown it to be applicable for a much longer period.[7] The four policy categories of Clausen's to be used here are government management of the economy, social welfare, civil liberties, and international involvement. The government management category centers on legis-

[6] The most obvious is that the score does not reflect variations in the base—the number of roll calls on which a majority of Democrats voted against a majority of Republicans. The proportion of all roll calls producing such a party split declined from an average of 46.8 percent for the 87th through the 89th Congress to an average of 35.6 percent for the 90th through the 93rd Congress. In the 94th Congress, however, it rose to 42 percent, and it stood at 40 percent during the 95th, Carter's first Congress.

[7] Aage Clausen, *How Congressmen Decide* (New York: St. Martin's Press, 1973). Barbara Sinclair, "Party Realignment and the Transformation of the Political Agenda: The House of Representatives, 1925-1938," *American Political Science Review*, vol. 71 (September 1977), pp. 940-953.

lation dealing with the economy and the nation's resources. Examples are business regulation, public works, conservation and environmental legislation, energy legislation, monetary and fiscal policy, and the overall level of governmental spending. In contrast, the social welfare domain includes legislation designed to aid the individual more directly, such as aid to education, public housing, and labor legislation. The civil liberties category includes black civil rights and such issues as subversive activities regulation and federal criminal justice procedures. International involvement includes all nondomestic policy questions.

For an issue classification to be useful, not only must it make substantive sense but the votes included in a given category must elicit similar voting alignments. After House roll calls were classified into the issue domains, a procedure to select those that evoked similar alignments was employed.[8] Usually a large proportion of the roll calls met the test for inclusion in the resulting issue scale or dimension. Each congressman was then given a "support score" on each issue dimension for each of the Congresses in which he served. The support score can simply be interpreted as the percentage of the roll calls included in the dimension on which he took a position that would popularly be called liberal. For example, a high score on the social welfare dimension indicates that the congressman voted in favor of establishing and expanding various social welfare programs. A support score for a group—say, House Democrats or Northeastern Republicans —is the average of its members' scores.

Government Management of the Economy. During the 1950s and most of the 1960s controversy in the government management area centered on questions such as private versus public power, the overall level of government spending, the shape of the tax code, and public works, especially their use as an antirecession measure. As table 6–3 shows, Democrats were much more supportive of an active governmental role in this area than were Republicans. From 1953 through 1968, northern Democrats were highly supportive and highly cohesive. During the Eisenhower years, Democrats from the South were appreciably less supportive than their northern party colleagues; their support dropped slightly during the first two Congresses of the 1960s and then declined more sharply between 1965 and 1968.

During the Eisenhower years, House Republicans were quite cohesive in their opposition to an activist governmental role in managing the economy. The 1960s saw the Republicans split along

[8] For a description of the methodology, see Sinclair, "Party Realignment."

TABLE 6–3

GOVERNMENT MANAGEMENT OF THE ECONOMY SUPPORT SCORES,
BY PARTY AND REGION, HOUSE, 1953–1978

Years	Democrats[a]			Republicans		
	All	Northern	Southern	All	Northeastern	Other
1953–60	85.3	91.7	77.1	13.2	13.0	12.9
1961–64	85.5	92.1	73.5	19.3	25.5	16.0
1965–68	84.2	92.0	65.3	15.3	25.6	11.7
1969–76	70.5	83.1	45.3	24.6	39.2	19.5
1977–78	72.3	83.9	47.2	24.1	41.0	19.4

NOTE: Support scores are averages of the support scores of the congressmen in the stated group; their individual scores can be interpreted as percentages of the roll calls being considered on which they took positions that would popularly be called liberal. See references in footnote 7.

[a] Democrats from the border states are not included with either northern or southern Democrats.

SOURCE: Author's calculations from roll call data made available by the Inter-University Consortium for Political and Social Research.

regional lines, with northeastern Republicans considerably more supportive than their party colleagues from other areas. The development of a regional split within the Republican party and the deepening of the North-South split within the Democratic party can be traced both to the change in administration and to a change in the climate of politics. Although the issues at the center of controversy did not fundamentally change, the measures which got to the voting stage during the Kennedy and Johnson years were more clearly aimed at active government management of the economy than was the bulk of the legislation during the Eisenhower administration.

Public opinion polls show that during the 1960s, the Northeast became the most liberal section of the country across the whole range of issues, while the South became the most conservative.[9] Given the high intensity politics of the 1960s, it seems likely that the change in southern Democrats' and northeastern Republicans' voting behavior in Congress was a response to signals from home.

Despite the regional split within each party, in the late 1960s, voting coalitions on government management issues were party-based. The first year of the Nixon administration, 1969, marked an abrupt change in voting alignments—one that persisted throughout the 1970s.

[9] Everett Ladd with Charles Hadley, *Transformations of the American Party System* (New York: W. W. Norton, 1975), especially pp. 166–177.

The regional split within each party deepened; the support of Democrats from the South fell sharply and that of northeastern Republicans increased. During the 1970s, southern Democrats were barely more supportive than northeastern Republicans. Democrats from the border states, who during the 1950s and 1960s tended to be almost as supportive as northern Democrats, were now significantly less supportive, although they still scored considerably above southern Democrats. Furthermore, the support of northern Democrats, on average, decreased; northern Democrats were no longer as cohesive as they had been in the 1950s and 1960s. A small but significant part of this decline in cohesion was due to a drop in the support of Democrats from the mountain states. A kind of snowbelt versus sunbelt coalition structure developed (though the sunbelt bloc did not include Democrats from the Pacific states).

What caused these changes in party alignments? Largely, a shift in the issues at the center of controversy. During the 1970s, environmental and consumer protection legislation became increasingly central to the government management agenda. Meanwhile, the unprecedented peacetime inflation that plagued the economy during the 1970s altered the debate on spending policy—a change accentuated by the new congressional budget process, which provided a forum for such debate. And the Arab oil embargo thrust energy policy to the center of controversy. This new agenda led to a change in voting alignments. Environmental and consumer protection legislation had its greatest appeal to the affluent in the industrialized areas.[10] In industrializing areas, elites and often the general population as well regarded such regulation as a barrier. When the debate was phrased in terms of "environmental protection versus jobs," labor also found itself in opposition. Energy policy pitted producer against consumer interests.

Thus, northeastern Republicans representing affluent constituents in a heavily industrialized and non-oil-producing area moved toward the Democratic pole on the government management dimension. Southern Democrats representing an oil-producing and a still-industrializing area moved to the Republican pole. Northern Democrats found their usual unity on the government management dimension strained as some environmental legislation divided their constituents.[11]

---

[10] Louis Harris, *The Anguish of Change* (New York: W. W. Norton, 1973), pp. 99-118.

[11] During the 95th Congress, two different government management scales appear. In content, one is dominated by roll calls on environmental and energy legislation. Alignments on this scale show strong continuity with those in the 91st through 94th Congress and are discussed in the text. The second scale emphasizes more

TABLE 6–4

Social Welfare Support Scores, by Party and Region, House, 1953–1978

Years	Democrats[a]			Republicans		
	All	Northern	Southern	All	Northeastern	Other
1953–60	71.5	93.5	42.2	32.7	43.4	27.1
1961–68	76.6	94.4	33.6[b]	33.3	55.0	22.6
1969–72	79.4	94.8	46.7	33.3	50.0	28.3
1973–76	79.6	91.0	55.0	32.4	52.2	26.0
1977–78	78.3	89.4	52.1	27.2	46.9	21.7

NOTE: For the definition of support scores, see note to table 6-3.
[a] Border Democrats are not included with either northern or southern Democrats.
[b] The 88th Congress score is excluded. It is abnormally high and thus obscures the pattern.
SOURCE: See table 6-3.

Social Welfare. During the 1950s, both parties were more deeply split along regional lines on social welfare legislation than on legislation in the government management area. The questions at issue— labor law, minimum wage increases, public housing, aid to education —were perceived very differently in the rural but industrializing South and in the urban industrialized Northeast. The support of southern Democrats was, on the average, slightly below that of northeastern Republicans (see table 6–4).

The highly charged politics of the 1960s deepened the split in both parties. The mid-1960s saw the first major policy change in the social welfare area since the New Deal. The first general aid-to-education bill, Medicare, and major housing and mass transit legislation were passed. The passage of the Economic Opportunity Act of 1964 marked a basic expansion of the social welfare agenda. Its intent and that of later legislation such as the rent subsidy program

traditional economic questions, such as economic stimulus programs, debt limit increases, the budget resolution, and Humphrey-Hawkins. This scale elicits more partisan voting alignments than do the other government management scales in the 1970s. The heavier party component to voting alignments on this scale is probably due to the Democrats' recapture of the presidency. Democrats from all regions seem to be more willing to follow party lines on those issues, especially broad economic ones, considered by the congressional leadership and the president to be crucial to the party program, so long as their constituency interests are not fundamentally compromised. Unfortunately for the president and the leadership, the latter condition excluded many of the most crucial issues such as energy.

185

was specifically to aid the poor minority. The thrust of previous social welfare legislation had been to help the nonrich majority.

The new agenda put intense strains upon parties already divided on social welfare legislation. The result was a Democratic party deeply split between a highly supportive and cohesive northern contingent and an unsupportive southern bloc. Although the split within the Republican party was less severe, northeastern Republicans were more enthusiastic about social welfare legislation than were southern Democrats, while Republicans from other areas remained basically opposed. The 1970s saw no fundamental change in the social welfare agenda. Controversy centered on the issues that had come to the fore in the 1960s as well as the hardy perennials dating from the New Deal. The Nixon and Ford administrations were characterized by a series of confrontations between an increasingly conservative presidency and an inconsistent but frequently activist Congress.

In the 1970s the split within both parties lessened. The regional divisions which had characterized voting alignments on social welfare legislation since the 1950s were still clearly evident; but, particularly within the Democratic party, so also was a softening of the division. Although the high support of northern Democrats dropped marginally after 1972, the narrowing of the regional split was primarily due to a trend toward increased support by Democrats from the South. With the return of a Democrat to the White House, the relationship between the president and the congressional majority party changed, but both the social welfare agenda and voting alignments remained basically stable. This did not mean major advances in social welfare policy. Carter proposed few bold departures in the social welfare area; his major innovation—a basic revamping of the welfare system—did not get out of committee. Carter and some traditional Democratic constituencies found the Congress surprisingly recalcitrant in passing legislation which had been on the agenda during the Nixon-Ford years—some of which had, in fact, passed only to be killed by a presidential veto. Thus, the House defeated common situs picketing legislation and the bill establishing a Consumer Protection Agency and watered down the minimum wage bill; the Senate killed the Labor Law Reform bill.

But these setbacks were not due to any precipitous decline in congressional support on the social welfare dimension. As table 6–5 shows, the mean support scores of all groupings declined; but among Democrats the drop was marginal, and even among Republicans it was not large. On social welfare legislation generally, Carter and the Democratic House leadership could count on high support from northern Democrats. Southern Democrats provided appreciably more support than they had during the Kennedy-Johnson years. The marginal shifts were just enough, though, to stop the few key bills mentioned above.

Civil Liberties. During the mid-1950s, civil liberties legislation pitted North against South. Northerners, both Republicans and Democrats, were highly supportive, southern Democrats, unalterably opposed (see table 6–5). But between 1957 and 1964 a rather dramatic change in alignments occurred. Republican support plummeted, and a regional split lining up more supportive northeastern Republicans against less supportive members from other areas developed. This drop in Republican support was not due to a change of heart on civil rights legislation (which Republicans continued to back). Rather, during the late 1950s, a number of votes on curbing the powers of the Supreme Court were taken, and many Republicans, angered by court decisions in the subversive activities and criminal justice areas, joined southern Democrats in voting for such restraints. In the early 1960s, questions about the status of and funding for the House Un-American Activities Committee (HUAAC) reentered the voting agenda. Republicans' strong support of the committee also contributed to the decline in their civil liberties support scores. The HUAAC roll calls split northern Democrats, which accounts for the decline in their mean support.

TABLE 6–5
CIVIL LIBERTIES SUPPORT SCORES, BY PARTY AND REGION, HOUSE, 1955–1978

Years	Democrats[a]			Republicans		
	All	Northern	Southern	All	Northeastern	Other[b]
1955–56	53.1	98.1	0.7	89.0	94.4	91.0
1957–64	54.8	86.3	9.2	50.9	62.5	46.4
1965–68	51.9	73.1	10.5	33.9	50.6	32.1
1969–72	54.6	75.5	15.3	27.2	39.2	26.9
1973–76	63.6	78.1	33.3	31.3	45.3	32.9
1977–78	64.7	77.4	36.5	21.4	35.9	20.8

NOTE: For the definition of support scores, see note to table 6-3.
[a] Border Democrats are not included with either northern or southern Democrats.
[b] Southern Republicans are excluded.
SOURCE: See table 6-3.

Between 1965 and 1968, the Congress passed a number of major civil rights bills. The civil liberties agenda, in addition, included numerous proposals aimed at antiwar protestors and ghetto rioters. The 90th House began what was to become an annual ritual—the passage of measures intended to limit federal school desegregation enforcement. The antiwar protestor legislation split northern Democrats, causing a significant decline in their support. The further decline in the Republicans' score was only partly accounted for by votes on such measures. After the passage of the Voting Rights Act in 1965, the civil rights bills at issue began to change, and the Republican voting response also changed. A strong open-housing bill, for example, would directly affect Republicans' white middle-class constituents, and in both 1966 and 1968 a majority of Republicans opposed open housing.

In the civil liberties area, as in the social welfare area, the agenda and policies of the 1960s set the agenda for the 1970s. Measures aimed at antiwar protestors continued to produce roll calls. During the 92nd and 93rd Congresses, the civil liberties domain was dominated by the controversy over busing, with the House passing, by wide margins, a series of antibusing provisions. The 91st and 94th Congresses saw major but successful battles over extension of the Voting Rights Act; in the 92nd, a proposal to give the Equal Employment Opportunities Commission cease and desist powers failed.

Republican support for civil liberties proposals, already low in the mid and late 1960s, dropped further in the 1970s. Neither black civil rights nor the non–civil rights aspects of the civil liberties agenda elicited much support from Republicans. During the 1970s, as during the late 1950s and the 1960s, northeastern Republicans were significantly more supportive on the civil liberties dimension than their party colleagues from other areas. Opinion polls consistently showed the Northeast to be more liberal on civil rights and more tolerant on civil liberties issues than other areas of the country, and these differences were reflected in Republican voting behavior.[12] Nevertheless, during the 1970s, even northeastern Republicans' support was quite low. Busing and legislation aimed at antiwar protestors continued to split northern Democrats as it had in the mid and late 1960s. Although northern Democrats provided much higher support than any other regional party grouping, their support remained well below its high levels of the pre-1965 period.

The most interesting change in the 1970s was southern Demo-

[12] Samuel Stouffer, *Communism, Conformity, and Civil Liberties* (Gloucester, Mass.: Peter Smith, 1963), pp. 109-113, and Ladd, *Transformations*.

crats' increasing support on the civil liberties dimension. Their support increased marginally in the first part of the decade and then much more dramatically after the 1972 election. Although southern Democrats as a group were still far from supportive on this general civil liberties dimension, the decline in the saliency of the race issue in the South in the mid-1970s combined with the increase in black voting as a result of the Voting Rights Act clearly had an impact on how southern Democrats voted. By the mid-1970s, southern Democrats were more supportive on the civil liberties dimension than were Republicans.

As was the case in the social welfare area, the change in administrations in 1977 did not significantly change either the agenda or the voting alignments in the civil liberties area. No major civil rights legislation was up for renewal during the 95th Congress, and no measure which would fit into the civil liberties domain was high on Carter's priority list. As table 6–5 shows, the trends already evident simply continued to unfold during the 95th Congress. Southern Democratic support increased marginally while Republican support declined significantly. Quite clearly, by the late 1970s, no president could count on much support from Republicans for civil liberties legislation, but he could expect some from southern Democrats.

International Involvement. In the area of international involvement, foreign aid dominated the agenda in the House from 1952 through 1968. The foreign policy consensus which had kept other issues off the voting agenda began to break down in the mid-1960s, but during the Johnson presidency the House leadership kept most anti–Vietnam war measures from coming to the floor. By 1969, the war had transformed the question of international involvement. Assumptions that had been widely accepted were challenged, and previously noncontroversial decisions provoked heated conflict. Opposition to the Vietnam war led many to reappraise the direction of U.S. foreign and defense policy more generally. The size of the military budget, the need for a wide variety of expensive and deadly new weapons systems, and U.S. aid to repressive regimes were brought into question.

From 1969 to 1976, two distinct clusters of votes related to international involvement appeared in each Congress. One set was, in content, very similar to the international involvement dimension found in earlier Congresses. It consisted mostly of roll calls on foreign aid bills—primarily votes on across the board cuts and on passage. The other included numerous votes directly related to the Vietnam war but also roll calls on cutting Department of Defense

TABLE 6–6

INTERNATIONAL INVOLVEMENT SUPPORT SCORES, BY PARTY AND REGION, HOUSE, 1953–1978

Years	Democrats[a]			Republicans		
	All	Northern	Southern	All	Northeastern	Interior[b]
1953–60	69.0	88.3	41.2	60.8	87.3	41.0
1961–68	77.1	92.2	47.2	39.6	63.5	27.9
1969–76	63.9	78.9	36.2	51.8	73.4	43.5
1977–78	70.1	82.8	44.3	39.8	62.2	33.7

NOTE: For the definition of support scores, see note to table 6-3.
[a] Border Democrats are not included with either northern or southern Democrats.
[b] Pacific Republicans are excluded; see footnote 14.
SOURCE: See table 6-3.

appropriations, on cutting funds for a wide variety of weapons systems (the antiballistic missile, nerve gas, and the B-1 bomber, for example), on barring aid to Chile and other dictatorships, on overseas troop cuts, on prohibiting the importation of Rhodesian chrome, and on barring the Ford administration from becoming involved in Angola. This dimension will be labeled foreign and defense policy reorientation.[13] Certainly those members who supported these departures were challenging basic precepts of American foreign and defense policy.

As table 6–6 shows, voting alignments on the traditional international involvement dimension, which consisted almost exclusively of roll calls on foreign aid, did change in the 1970s. A closer look, however, indicates that the change was primarily due to the change in partisan control of the presidency. The international involvement dimension split both parties along regional lines, but all segments were more responsive to presidents of their own party than to opposition presidents.[14] In the 95th Congress, the first of the Carter presidency, this pattern continued. Northeastern Republicans and those

[13] See Aage Clausen and Carl Van Horn, "The Congressional Response to a Decade of Change: 1963-1972," *Journal of Politics*, vol. 39 (August 1977), pp. 624-666.

[14] The voting response of Pacific Republicans, largely Californians, underwent a secular change during the period under discussion. At the beginning of the period, they voted very much like northeasterners; by the end of the period, they were as unsupportive as "other" Republicans. Because this secular trend tends to obscure the administration-related pattern, Pacific Republicans have been excluded from table 6-6.

from the interior dropped in support to about their levels during the Kennedy-Johnson years. Both northern and southern Democrats increased their support, but, ominously for the president, northern Democratic support remained well below the high level of the Kennedy-Johnson years.

Throughout this period, the House displayed rather limited enthusiasm for a thorough reorientation of U.S. foreign and defense policy. As table 6–7 shows, no segment of the Republican party offered much support, although northeasterners were somewhat less opposed than members from other areas. Southern Democrats were also firmly opposed, and northern Democrats were split. Given the overwhelming Republican opposition and the divisions within the Democratic party, many of the proposals aimed at a basic reorientation of foreign and defense policy failed. The defeat of many of the more drastic proposals does not, however, mean that policy remained unchanged. Funds for the war in Indochina were eventually cut off, some cuts in defense spending were made, and Congress refused to let the Ford administration get involved in Angola.

As the reorientation dimension represented a challenge from the left to the hardline foreign and defense policy of Republican presidents, some change in the debate could be anticipated with the advent of the Carter presidency. Carter attempted to incorporate some elements of the new perspective into his foreign policy. His human rights policy, in selected instances, led him to cut off or diminish aid to right-wing dictatorships. A somewhat tougher stance on requiring the military to justify expensive new weapons systems led to the decision not to produce the B-1 bomber. Carter's foreign policy infuriated hardliners in the Congress while not going far enough to

TABLE 6–7

FOREIGN AND DEFENSE POLICY REORIENTATION SUPPORT SCORES,
BY PARTY AND REGION, HOUSE, 1969–1978

Years	All Members of House	Democrats[a]			Republicans		
		All	Northern	Southern	All	Northeastern	Other
1969–76	36.7	49.3	66.3	18.1	18.4	29.0	15.0
1977–78	42.1	54.1	67.9	24.9	18.7	32.0	15.0

NOTE: For the definition of support scores, see note to table 6-3.
[a] Border Democrats are not included with either northern or southern Democrats.
SOURCE: See table 6-3.

satisfy those committed to a true reorientation of U.S. foreign and defense policy.

In the 95th Congress, in addition to the foreign aid scale, two other major scales appeared. One represented a challenge from the right to Carter's foreign policy. Prominent were votes on a number of amendments placing restrictions on the countries to which U.S. aid might go; the countries singled out for restrictions were mostly communist or left-leaning ones, and the aim was to restrict the president's discretion. Thus, there were attempts to limit the president's discretion with respect to the Panama Canal Treaty and the pullout of U.S. troops from Korea, roll calls on the bill reimposing an embargo on Rhodesian chrome, several votes on the neutron bomb and on restoring money for the nuclear aircraft carrier, and several attempts to increase defense spending above the level Carter had requested.

The other scale included a large number of roll calls on defense spending, a number on amendments which would cut it below the level requested by the president. Votes on weapons systems, the B-1 for example, on restricting aid to right-wing regimes, on reducing overseas troop strength, and on the Turkish arms embargo were also included. The scores on this scale are not easily characterized in terms of support of or opposition to the president's policies. Members who scored high on the scale supported the president on the B-1 bomber and on the prohibition of military aid to Nicaragua; on the other hand, they opposed the president on lifting the Turkish arms embargo and on some defense spending votes.

In terms of content and ideological thrust, this scale appears to be a continuation of the reorientation dimension of the Nixon-Ford years. Voting alignments indicate that this was, in fact, the case (see table 6–7). Thus, those members committed to a reorientation of foreign and defense policy, almost all of whom were northern Democrats, did not cease their attempts to make such changes when a Democratic president was elected. Carter's policy was not in total conflict with these members' views, as had been the Nixon-Ford policy; and when they agreed with Carter, these members supported him. But when their views and administration policy were in conflict, they felt free to oppose the president. Quite clearly, the vigorous debate on a whole series of questions that, before the Vietnam war, were considered matters of consensus, represented a fundamental change in the centers of controversy—one with which relatively softline Democratic presidents as well as hardline Republican presidents will have to contend, regardless of a "shift to the right" in the wake of Iran and Afghanistan.

TABLE 6–8

Support for Carter's Position on Foreign Aid and on the "Threat from the Right" Scale, House

	Democrats			Republicans		
	All	Northern	Southern	All	Northeastern	Other
Aid	70.1	82.8	44.3	39.8	62.2	33.4
"Threat from the right"	62.4	74.9	35.7	23.4	38.1	19.1

NOTE: For the definition of support scores, see note to table 6-3.
SOURCE: See table 6-3.

Even before these events, and unlike his Republican predecessors, Carter also faced a concerted attack on his foreign and defense policies from the congressional right. In the 95th Congress, tactics developed by doves during the Nixon-Ford years were used, often very effectively, by hardline congressmen. Events in 1979 and 1980, especially Iran and Afghanistan, no doubt intensified this movement.

Table 6–8 compares voting alignments on the scale which incorporates this rightward threat to the Carter policy with those on foreign aid. The regional splits within the parties are similar on the two scales; levels of support, however, are very different. Northeastern Republicans as a group were part of the right-wing attack on Carter's foreign policy. Northern Democrats were split; their support of Carter's overall policies against attack from the right was considerably lower than their support for foreign aid, which itself was significantly below the support northern Democrats gave Kennedy and Johnson on foreign aid. Thus, when Carter and the Democratic leadership complained about the difficulty of building majority coalitions in the foreign and defense policy areas, their complaints were grounded in reality. Foreign and defense policy was no longer beyond debate, and presidential dominance had been much reduced. Because he faced challenges from both the left and the right, Carter truly was in a difficult position.

Changing Coalitions in the Senate. One would expect the changes which occurred in the issue agenda during the 1970s to affect Senate coalitions in much the same way as they influenced House coalitions. Although the sort of detailed analysis of voting alignments presented for the House is not available for the Senate, published studies make certain inferences possible. There is strong evidence, for example,

TABLE 6–9

SENATE PARTY UNITY, BY REGION, 1957–1978

(in party unity scores)

Years	Con-gress	Democrats			Republicans		
		Southern	Border and moun-tain	Other	North-eastern	Southern and mountain	Other
1957–58	85	74.7	88.4	81.6	73.4	82.2	76.9
1961–62	87	56.1	88.7	87.9	20.9	94.6	82.9
1965–66	89	46.5	84.1	84.8	62.0	91.9	79.8
1969–70	91	47.4	77.1	87.2	54.7	90.1	71.4
1973–74	93	45.5	78.8	88.3	50.4	90.3	69.7
1977–78	95	48.4	70.8	85.2	42.0	92.1	69.2

NOTE: For the definition of party unity scores, see note to table 6-2.

SOURCE: Author's calculations for party unity scores from *Congressional Quarterly Almanac*, various dates.

that the dimensional structure of voting is highly similar in both chambers and that voting alignments, at least if characterized in gross regional terms, are also quite similar.[15]

To examine change in the Senate, I looked at party unity in that chamber from 1957 to 1978, examining in detail every other Congress from the 85th through the 95th (see table 6–9). Within the Democratic party overall, the most massive change in the Senate was the severe drop in southern party unity. In the 85th Congress, southerners' average party unity was lower than that of their party colleagues from other areas, but the difference was relatively small. Southern Democratic party loyalty dropped precipitously in the 87th and declined again in the 89th. From the 89th Congress on, it never again reached the 50 percent mark. That is, from 1965 on, Democrats from the South more frequently voted with Republicans than with their party colleagues on those roll calls pitting a majority of Democrats against a majority of Republicans.

The 1970s saw the development of another but more minor regional split within the Democratic party. Border and mountain Democrats who, during the 1960s, had voted much like other non-southern Democrats, began to defect from the party position. By the 95th Congress, the difference in the means of these two groupings was

[15] See Clausen, *How Congressmen Decide* and Clausen and Van Horn, "Congressional Response."

almost fifteen percentage points. A kind of sunbelt versus snow-belt alignment may have been developing, although, as in the House, the sunbelt did not include members from the Pacific states.

Since the late 1950s, the Senate Republican party, too, has developed deep regional splits. Northeasterners' party unity has declined continuously over the period under study; by the 95th Congress they more frequently voted with the Democrats than with their party colleagues from other areas on party roll calls. Southern and mountain Republicans, in contrast, have become the loyal main-stays of their party since the late 1950s. As the remaining Republicans were a relatively heterogeneous bunch, mean scores should not be given too much weight. Nevertheless, these members as a group were considerably less loyal to party in the 1970s than they were in the 1960s.

From the point of view of a Democratic president attempting to get his program through the Senate, the implications of these changes in voting alignments were mixed. John Kennedy faced a Senate Democratic party already badly split along North-South lines. Carter faced a party in which this split, on party votes, has deepened and one in which other regional blocks—mountain and border Democrats —were considerably less reliable than in the 1960s. The split in the Republican party, however, may have provided Carter with oppor-tunities Kennedy did not have.

Implications for Presidential and Congressional Party Leadership

As the 1980s began, the policy areas which presented the greatest problems for Carter and the congressional party leadership were government management of the economy and foreign and defense policy. On government management, the House Democratic party was much more deeply split along North-South lines than it was in the early 1960s. Furthermore, northern Democratic cohesion had declined; Carter, unlike Kennedy, could not count on an almost solid bloc of northern Democrats to support his policies in the government management area. The Republican party was also less united than it was in the early 1960s; the Democratic leadership could expect to pick up some Republican votes, especially from the northeastern segment of the party. But this regional grouping was decreasing in size, and its increasing rate of defection was of only minor help to the Democratic leadership.

In the 1970s, a preponderance of the domestic issues at the center of controversy fell within the government management domain. During Carter's term, his top domestic priority was developing an effective energy policy. The fragmentation of the House Democratic party in the government management area plagued Carter, and the Senate was even more recalcitrant. Border and mountain Democrats —who, other than southerners, were most likely to defect on such issues—were a considerably larger proportion of the Democratic membership in the Senate than in the House (21 percent versus 12 percent).

On foreign and defense policy, Carter also faced considerably greater problems than Kennedy did. The questioning of a great many policies previously considered beyond debate was perhaps the greatest legacy of the Vietnam war. Carter had considerably less latitude in foreign and defense policy making than Kennedy did. Congress had successfully asserted its right to scrutinize publicly a wide variety of decisions concerning defense spending generally, the procurement of new weapons systems, and the recipients of foreign aid. This public debate itself changed the president's decision-making environment and limited his discretion.

In getting foreign aid bills through the House, Carter and the Democratic leadership had to deal with a party that was not only split along North-South lines but within which a segment of the traditionally very supportive northern contingent seemed more and more disillusioned with the foreign aid program. Furthermore, Carter faced attacks from both the right and the left on a wide variety of aspects of his foreign and defense policy. In the House, particularly, the attacks from the right presented an especially worrisome problem to the party leadership. Hardline congressmen had learned to fashion amendments that sounded extremely appealing, which many Democrats, northern as well as southern, found difficult to oppose. In 1979, for example, during debate on the Panama Canal Treaty implementation legislation, a series of amendments were proposed which, if adopted, would have scuttled the treaty. Both the administration and the Democratic leadership worked very hard on the bill, yet several of these amendments were beaten by the slimmest of margins. Many members who personally supported the treaty felt that a "no" vote on such amendments would be too difficult to explain to the folks back home.

Carter's foreign and defense policy problems clearly were not confined to the House of Representatives. The disillusionment with the foreign aid program on the part of some liberals was evident in the Senate also. In the early 1970s, Senate Democrats were more enthusiastic than their counterparts in the House about a true reorientation of foreign and defense policy—as the passage of various end-the-war amendments showed. Although in 1980 the Senate seemed less inclined than the House to attach right-wing amendments to foreign aid bills, even before Afghanistan it had shown much more enthusiasm for increasing defense spending above the levels requested by the administration.

In the government management and foreign and defense policy areas, Carter faced a more recalcitrant Congress than Kennedy. For social welfare certainly, and more debatably for civil liberties, the situation was reversed, at least in the House. On social welfare legislation, northern Democrats were about as cohesive and supportive as they were in the 1960s, and Democrats from the South provided more support than they did during the Kennedy-Johnson years. Given the considerably more northern complexion of the House Democratic party in the mid-1970s, overall support on the social welfare dimension was higher than it was during the 1960s.

In the civil liberties area, too, the support of Democrats from the South had increased; on the other hand, that of northern Democrats had declined, and Republican support had plummeted. The probability of party leadership success depended very much on the specific measure at hand. On civil rights, excluding only the question of busing, the leadership could count on nearly united northern Democratic support and a not insignificant level of support from southern Democrats. Even on the highly emotional issue of busing, the leadership could command a majority. The school busing constitutional amendment which came to the House floor in 1979 not only failed to win the necessary two-thirds vote, it did not even receive 50 percent. Republicans split 114 to 40 in favor of the amendment; Democrats 95 to 176 against. Of the 71 southern Democrats voting, 31 voted against the amendment.

On the non–civil rights components of the civil liberties dimension, a problem similar to that in the foreign policy area was evident. Conservatives had become very adept at writing amendments designed primarily to embarrass their opponents. For many members, voting against an amendment that would, for example, bar the Legal Services Corporation from getting involved in suits concerning homosexual rights was very difficult politically. Nevertheless, when it really considered a roll call on such an amendment crucial, the party leadership could defeat it. Often a major effort was not considered necessary because the conference committee could be relied upon to delete the measure.

On balance, then, the Democratic congressional leadership and President Carter were more favorably situated on civil liberties issues than were their counterparts in the early 1960s. On civil rights—the most crucial component for the Democratic party—they could command majorities. More important, the Senate filibuster was no longer used as a weapon against civil rights legislation.

Across all issues, then, should Jimmy Carter envy John Kennedy, or vice versa? Carter could argue that he clearly faced a more difficult Congress in the areas of government management of the economy and foreign and defense policy—precisely where the action was in the 1970s. In rebuttal, Kennedy could reply that, during his years in office, controversy centered on issues in the social welfare and civil liberties domains and that, in *those* areas, Congress was just as recalcitrant then as it was on Carter's priority legislation twenty years later.

It may be that a Democratic president's probability of winning majorities in the Congress has not changed very much. In the areas where they attempted to innovate, both Carter and Kennedy had trouble with Congress. In terms of the internal distribution of influence, however, the House and Senate of the 1970s were very different from the Congress of the early 1960s. Dispersion of influence, high membership turnover, and the rise to centrality of issues that not only split northern from southern Democrats but also divided the formerly cohesive northern Democrats, among themselves, have increased uncertainty. It was much more difficult in 1980 to judge whether a given proposal could pass than it had been in 1960. Consequently, making rational decisions as to what should be included in the president's legislative program was more difficult. Furthermore, if voting behavior was harder to predict and coalitions more fluid, the process of building coalitions was that much more time consuming and the allocation of time and resources that much more complicated.

Building Coalitions in the Sand?

To determine whether the coalition-building process was indeed a more uncertain enterprise in 1980 than in 1960, we will concentrate upon selected roll calls which the president, the congressional party leadership, and/or key Democratic constituencies themselves considered crucial.[16] The issue dimensions discussed earlier reveal the general shape of coalitions and thus the context within which the president and the party leadership work. But they lump together roll calls of widely varying importance.

We will attempt to determine how fluid coalitions really were at a time of high membership turnover in both the House and the Senate in the 1970s. Almost half the members of the 95th Senate

[16] Selection was based primarily upon interviews with House leaders and their staff.

were first elected in 1970 or later; sixty-one members of the 96th Senate entered that body during the 1970s, and 48 were first elected in 1974 or later. The House figures are even more striking: 58 percent of the 95th House membership and 67 percent of the 96th were first elected in the 1970s; about half of the members of the 96th House began their service in 1975 or later. On Capitol Hill, the House freshmen of the 1970s—particularly the large Democratic freshman class elected in 1974—were reputed to be an extremely independent (if not ornery) lot. It was even claimed that those northern Democrats elected in 1974 from previously Republican districts frequently voted like Republicans.

We will also take a look at the Republicans. One frequently heard that House Republicans had become a highly cohesive voting bloc. Examining the issue dimensions provided little evidence of a major increase in Republican cohesion. But cohesion might manifest itself only on selected roll calls and thus not show on the broad dimension scores. Of course, if those particular roll calls were ones considered crucial by the president and the Democratic leadership, such Republican cohesion could have a major impact on outcomes.

Coalition Building in the House. Carter's top domestic priority was passage of a comprehensive energy program. Seven roll calls on the energy bill (H.R. 8444) in the 95th House are used to assess voting behavior in this area. Included are roll calls on key amendments which, if adopted, would gut the bill (the amendments on natural gas pricing, a plowback for energy exploration, elimination of the crude oil equalization tax, and so on) as well as the crucial vote on the rule for considering the conference report. The rule provided that the energy package, which the Senate had broken down into a number of separate bills, would be considered as a whole in the House and thus that a separate vote on the unpopular gas pricing section would not be possible. The House Democratic leadership gave top priority to passing Carter's energy program, and their position prevailed on each of the seven key votes.

To assess Carter's success in foreign and defense policy we will look at eight roll calls: a vote on the bill reimposing an embargo on Rhodesian chrome, two on upholding the president's decision on the B-1 bomber, one on lifting the Turkish arms embargo as Carter had requested, a roll call on an amendment expressing congressional opposition to Carter's plan to reduce ground troops in Korea, the veto-override attempt on a weapons procurement bill, and two roll calls on amendments restricting the nations eligible for foreign aid. On all but one, Carter's position prevailed. A restrictive foreign aid amendment was adopted in 1977, but in 1978 an identical amendment was defeated. Generally, the party leadership supported and worked hard for the president's position; the exception was the Turkish arms embargo, which split the leadership. Majority Leader Jim Wright led the successful repeal effort; Chief Whip John Brademas was a major figure opposing repeal.

The reputation of the House Democratic leadership rests, in part, on its success in gaining passage of presidential priorities. It also depends upon the leadership's ability to uphold the reputation of the House as a functioning legislature on less highly visible matters. Two areas that were especially problematical for the leadership were the biannual conflicts over the budget resolution and the recurrent fight to raise the federal debt ceiling.

The eighteen budget resolution roll calls chosen include votes on key amendments and on final passage. The leadership lost four votes. During consideration of the first budget resolution in 1977, an amendment to increase defense spending passed—with the help of some covert lobbying from the administration. Liberals retaliated by voting against passage of the resolution, which failed by a large margin. When a slightly revised resolution was brought to the floor, the defense spending amendment was defeated and the resolution itself passed. In 1978, a Republican amendment cutting HEW funds passed, but the vote was reversed before the first resolution was ratified. During consideration of the second resolution in 1978, one amendment—which cut CETA and countercyclical aid—was adopted over the objections of the party leadership and the committee majority. The leadership, then, was successful in passing budget resolutions that were basically majority party documents, but it was not easy.

The recurrent fight over raising the debt limit was even more of a problem. Every member knows the ceiling must be raised periodically, yet, especially in a time of high inflation, few like to vote for increases. During the 95th Congress, the need to increase the debt ceiling arose three times; in each case, the bill failed the first time it came to the floor, then, after heavy lobbying by the leadership, passed on the second attempt.

With the return of Democratic control of the White House, labor expected to accomplish some goals stymied by the Nixon-Ford administration. Common situs picketing legislation, labor law reform, and an increase in the minimum wage were the top priorities. Despite the full support of the party leadership, common situs picketing lost on the House floor, and the House adopted a weakening amendment to the minimum wage bill. The establishment of a subminimum wage for youth was, however, narrowly defeated, and the labor law reform bill was passed after a crucial amendment on equal access was beaten (it later died in the Senate).

Both the president and the party leadership considered legislation to place the social security system on a sound financial footing among the top priority items of the 95th Congress. Four important roll calls on this bill—all of which were won—are included in the following analysis.

Finally, under the rubric of economic policy I include three roll calls that stand out as among the most important of the session. A vote on an amendment cutting the economic stimulus appropriation early in 1977 was a direct challenge to Democratic party policy and the effectiveness of the leadership in sustaining that policy in the House. The Kemp amendment to the tax bill would have drastically cut taxes and, if it had won, would have meant Republicans were setting economic policy. The Humphrey-Hawkins Full Employment Bill was a top priority of both labor and black groups, and its passage without further weakening on the floor was considered imperative by the House leadership. The key vote came on a floor amendment setting stringent inflation goals. On each of these three roll calls, the party leadership was successful.

A total of fifty-one key roll calls have been identified. Of these, the leadership lost eleven or 21.6 percent. A majority of the losses, however, were quickly reversed and thus did not actually affect policy. Only in the labor area did the leadership sustain major and permanent floor defeats.[17] But the leadership's win-loss record provides only minimal information on the difficulty of coalition formation and none on the fluidity of coalitions. An index of support for the party leadership and/or the president was constructed in each of the seven areas discussed above. An examination of support scores should provide the basis for answering the questions posed earlier: How fluid are coalitions? What has been the effect of membership turnover? How cohesive is the minority?

If by fluidity of coalitions one means the appearance of completely different voting alignments across issue areas, then clearly voting on these key roll calls cannot be characterized as fluid (see table 6–10). On each of the indexes, northern Democrats were most supportive and Republicans from areas other than the northeast most opposed. Within the Democratic party, members from the South

---

[17] This is an assessment purely of success at the floor stage; there were a number of cases—notably the 1978 tax bill—where the bill which came out of committee was not to the leadership's liking. In addition, there were some other floor defeats which are not included in the analysis because the issue, while important, did not seem quite as central as those analyzed here.

TABLE 6–10

SUPPORT SCORES ON HOUSE KEY-VOTE INDEXES, BY PARTY AND REGION

Index	Democrats				Republicans		
	All	Northern	Border	Southern	All	North-eastern	Other
Energy	74.8	84.9	62.7	53.2	10.9	22.0	7.7
Foreign & defense	64.0	74.3	49.6	42.8	26.4	41.4	22.0
Budget	72.9	81.7	66.5	52.8	8.4	16.7	5.9
Debt limit	68.4	77.0	57.1	50.2	10.7	14.1	9.7
Labor	72.2	90.2	62.9	30.3	16.4	45.2	8.3
Social security	77.2	88.0	72.9	51.7	14.8	23.2	15.4
Economic policy	81.4	89.8	78.5	61.0	4.5	11.1	2.6

NOTE: For the definition of support scores, see note to table 6-3.
SOURCE: See table 6-3.

were least supportive; on four of the seven indexes, their mean support hovered around the 50 percent mark, and, on the labor and foreign and defense policy indexes, southern Democrats were more likely to vote against than in favor of the leadership position. Within the Republican party, northeasterners in every case provided higher mean support than their party colleagues from other areas, and on labor and foreign and defense policy their support was above the 40 percent mark. In their general contours, then, coalitions were quite similar across the seven issue areas.

A close examination of the levels of support among Democrats, however, suggests the possibility of considerable fluidity. Clearly, from the leadership's point of view, southern Democrats as a group were a highly unreliable source of support, and border Democrats also frequently defected. More important, however, are the support levels of northern Democrats, the largest regional grouping and the one which had traditionally provided the greatest support. On two of the seven indexes, the leadership lost, on the average, more than one-fifth of the northern Democrats, and on another, it lost almost that much. The northern Democrats' mean support score over the seven indexes was 82.3 percent.

A rough comparison with John Kennedy's first Congress can be obtained by examining northern Democratic defections on twelve key

87th Congress votes identified by *Congressional Quarterly.* Kennedy's average loss among northern Democrats was 8.5 members—roughly 6 percent of the total. The maximum number defecting was sixteen. Kennedy was defeated on five of the twelve votes. These losses, however, were not a result of defections among northern Democrats.

For the party leadership in the late 1970s, the higher defection rate of northern Democrats was, of course, an unwelcome development; but since the number of northern Democrats in the 95th and 96th Congresses considerably exceeded that during the 87th, a higher defection rate by itself does not indicate a more difficult coalition formation process. If, however, the higher defection rate was due not to a few consistently nonsupportive members but to more fluid voting patterns, then voting behavior would be less predictable and coalition formation more uncertain.

Using the support scores on all seven indexes, we can classify members by support reliability. I divided the membership into seven categories, ranging from consistently high support to consistently high opposition, with middle categories indicating unreliability or erratic support and opposition.[18] Table 6–11 shows the relationship between this support categorization and party-regional group membership. Only seventeen Democrats fall into the three unsupportive groupings, and of these, twelve are southerners. Thus the number of Democrats consistently opposed to the leadership is small. Half of the border Democrats and close to two-thirds of southern Democrats, however, fall into the middle, relatively unsupportive and unpredictable category; more surprising, so do one-fifth of northern Democrats. The group of highly reliable supporters consists almost entirely of northern Democrats; only two non-northerners—Bob Eckhardt of Texas and Carl Perkins of Kentucky—are included. More important than the composition of the group is its size; only thirty-four House

[18] Those members with support scores of 80 percent or more on all seven indexes are classified as highly reliable supporters. On the other end of the scale are those who scored below 20 percent on all seven. Members who scored 50 percent or higher on all seven indexes and 80 percent on at least five of the seven are the next most supportive group. Again, a comparable group at the opposition end of the scale are those who scored below 50 percent on all and below 20 percent on at least five of the seven. Toward the supportive end of the continuum but clearly less reliable than the previously defined groupings are the members who scored 50 percent or greater on all but one index and 80 percent or greater on at least three of the seven. The comparable group of relatively unreliable opponents are those who scored below 50 percent on all but one index and below 20 percent on at least three of the seven. Those members whose pattern of support fit into none of these categories constitute a middle group whose voting behavior is even more unpredictable.

TABLE 6–11

Support Reliability, by Party and Region, 95th House
(in percentages of group in support category)

Party and Region	Support Level						
	High						Low
Northern							
Democrats	17.7	42.0	18.8	19.9	0.6	—	1.1
Number	(32)	(76)	(34)	(36)	(1)	(0)	(2)
Border							
Democrats	4.2	8.3	29.2	50.0	4.2	4.2	—
Number	(1)	(2)	(7)	(12)	(1)	(1)	(0)
Southern							
Democrats	1.4	8.2	9.6	64.4	8.2	5.5	2.7
Number	(1)	(6)	(7)	(47)	(6)	(4)	(2)
Northeastern							
Republicans	—	—	—	48.4	16.1	16.1	19.4
Number	(0)	(0)	(0)	(15)	(5)	(5)	(6)
Other							
Republicans	—	—	—	6.7	25.7	27.6	40.0
Number	(0)	(0)	(0)	(7)	(27)	(29)	(42)
All	8.2	20.3	11.6	28.3	9.7	9.4	12.6
Number	(34)	(84)	(48)	(117)	(40)	(39)	(52)

NOTE: For method, see text.
SOURCE: See table 6-3.

Democrats supported the leadership on 80 percent or more of the roll calls included in each of the seven key vote indexes. Less than *one-fifth* of the northern Democrats were highly reliable supporters over the whole range of issues under study.

In building majority coalitions, then, the Democratic House leadership operated in an environment characterized by considerable uncertainty in the late 1970s. Both the number of highly reliable supporters who did not have to be persuaded and the number of confirmed opponents who could be written off were small. Majorities had to be constructed from the mass of less predictable Democrats who fell between these extremes. A closer examination of northern Democratic support will allow us to draw some conclusions concerning the locus of the increased unpredictability. Democrats from the mountain and west-north-central states were more likely to fall toward the less supportive

TABLE 6-12

SUPPORT RELIABILITY AND SENIORITY FOR NORTHERN DEMOCRATS
IN THE HOUSE

(in percentages of group in support category)

Northern Democrats First Elected in:	Support Level			
	High			Low[a]
1950s or earlier	29.2	45.8	20.8	4.2
Number	(7)	(11)	(5)	(1)
1960s	22.7	52.3	11.4	13.7
Number	(10)	(23)	(5)	(6)
1970 and 1972	17.4	56.5	17.4	8.6
Number	(4)	(13)	(4)	(2)
1974	15.5	31.0	24.1	29.3
Number	(9)	(18)	(14)	(17)
1976	6.3	34.4	18.8	40.6
Number	(2)	(11)	(6)	(13)

NOTE: For method, see text.

[a] The lowest category combines the four lowest support categories in table 6-11.

SOURCE: See table 6-3.

end of the continuum than were their party colleagues from other areas.[19]

More interesting is the relationship between seniority and support. As table 6–12 shows, the proportion of members who were highly supportive increases directly with seniority; almost 30 percent of northern Democrats first elected in the 1940s and 1950s fell into the highly supportive group, while only 6.3 percent of the 95th Congress freshmen did. On the other end of the continuum, there was a clear difference between those first elected before 1974 and the 94th and 95th freshmen classes; a much larger proportion of the latter fell into the middle, relatively unpredictable, support category.

What about junior Democrats elected from districts previously held by Republicans? Table 6–13 provides some confirmation for the contention that they were particularly problematic for the leadership.

[19] Thus 40 percent of mountain Democrats and 38.9 percent of west-north-central Democrats fall at the midpoint of the support scale or below. The comparable figures for the other regional groupings vary from a low of 13.3 percent for New England members to a high of 20.8 percent for those from the east-north-central states.

TABLE 6–13

SUPPORT RELIABILITY OF NORTHERN HOUSE DEMOCRATS
FIRST ELECTED IN 1970 OR LATER, BY PREDECESSOR'S PARTY
(in percentages of group in support category)

Predecessor's Party	Support Level			
	High			Low[a]
Democrat	14.3	51.8	17.9	16.1
Number	(8)	(29)	(10)	(9)
Republican	12.3	22.8	24.6	40.0
Number	(7)	(13)	(14)	(23)

NOTE: For method, see text.
[a] The lowest category combines the four lowest support categories in table 6-11.
SOURCE: See table 6-3.

When we divide northern Democrats first elected in 1970 or later into those who won previously Republican seats and those who succeeded Democrats, quite strong differences in support patterns appear: switched-seat Democrats were much more likely to fall into the middle, more unpredictable categories. In contrast, the distribution of junior Democrats who succeeded Democrats was much more similar to that of their senior party colleagues, except that a considerably smaller share fell into the highly reliable support category.

A large proportion of the switched-seat Democrats were first elected in 1974. These members were reputed to be especially troublesome for the leadership; in fact, it was claimed that they voted like Republicans. A comparison of switched-seat and non-switched-seat members of the 94th class shows that, although the former certainly did not "vote like Republicans," as a group they were considerably less supportive than either their non-switched-seat classmates or northern Democrats as a whole. On the seven indexes, the mean scores of non-switched-seat members of the 94th class were very close to the means of northern Democrats as a whole. Switched-seat members averaged significantly lower support than their classmates on five of the seven; only on the energy and the foreign and defense policy indexes was there little difference between the two groups. On the other five, the average difference was 12.1 percentage points; on the debt limit index, it was 20.8 points. For these switched-seat members, many of whom perceived their constituencies as basically conservative, the debt limit roll calls provided an opportunity of catering to the district. They knew the leadership would eventually find the votes to pass the debt limit increase. Thus, switched-seat members could make their point for the home folks without adversely affecting policy.

Among southern Democrats, also, support is related to seniority. If we compare those first elected in 1970 or before with those who entered the House in 1972 or later, we find that the preponderance of both groups fell into the middle, unpredictable category (65.8 percent of the former, 62.5 percent of the latter). However, slightly over one-fifth of the more senior group fell into the regularly non-supportive categories in contrast to only a little more than one-tenth of the less senior group. A quarter of the less senior members qualified for the three most supportive categories; only 13.1 percent of the more senior did.

In its coalition building efforts, the Democratic House leadership confronted a relatively unpredictable party membership. Northern Democrats could no longer be relied upon to provide a solid bloc of support. Junior members, especially those elected from previously Republican districts, defected from the party position fairly frequently. To win, the leadership had to pick up a large proportion of northern Democrats, whose support was far from automatic.

The changes in the southern components of the Democratic House membership presented opportunities for the leadership but also contributed to the uncertainty of the coalition building process. On no issue could a large proportion of southern Democrats be written off as unpersuadable. Junior members particularly were a potential source of leadership support. The increase in southern support on social welfare and civil liberties issues, which was discussed earlier, was largely due to the election of more supportive members from 1972 on. Yet even the most supportive of the new members did not fall into the highly reliable category. The leadership, then, could get a fair number of southern votes on most high priority roll calls, but it had to work for each of those votes. There were precious few it could count on.

The cohesion of the minority as well as that of the majority party affects the difficulty of coalition building. Has Republican cohesiveness increased and thus compounded the Democratic leadership's problems? As table 6–10 showed, Republicans, particularly those from areas other than the northeast, were quite cohesive in opposing the Democratic leadership's positions. As one would expect, northeasterners tended to defect more frequently than those from other areas, but, except on the labor and foreign and defense policy scales, they took a clear opposition stance, and, in any case, they constituted a small minority of the party.

The actual number of Republican votes for the Democratic position varied from an average of 6.7 on the economic policy roll calls to 35.3 on the foreign and defense policy votes. The mean over all seven indexes was 17.8. On most high priority roll calls, the Democratic leadership could not expect much help from the Republican party.

The party leadership during the 87th Congress faced much the same situation. On the twelve key roll calls, an average of 24 Republicans took the Democratic position. This figure, which is somewhat higher than the comparable 95th Congress figure of 17.8, hides a good deal of variation across issues. Specifically, on the three foreign aid and trade votes, an average of 60.3 Republicans supported Kennedy's position—a much higher number than supported Carter on foreign and defense policy in the 95th Congress. On the remaining domestic policy roll calls, however, an average of only 11.9 Republicans defected—a figure even lower than the 14.9 average for domestic areas in the 95th Congress. These figures, then, indicate little change in overall terms.

The impression that junior Republicans are more ideological than their senior party colleagues, which persists on Capitol Hill, justifies a closer look at Republican support. If Republicans are divided into those first elected before 1970 and those first elected during the 1970s and we compare mean support for Democratic positions, we find that, with one exception—the energy index—in all areas the junior grouping scored lower than the senior one. Only on the debt limit index, however, was the difference substantial; in that case, junior Republicans averaged 9.3 percentage points lower than their senior party colleagues. On the other five, the average difference was only 2.6 percentage points.

The support categorization presented earlier provides another perspective on the difference between junior and senior Republicans. As table 6–14 shows, a considerably larger proportion of junior than of senior members fell into the lowest support group. Thus 40.2 percent of junior as opposed to 27.8 percent of senior Republicans provided less than 20 percent support for the Democratic position in all seven areas. Two-thirds of the junior but only half the senior Republicans fell into the two lowest support categories.

Republicans who first entered the House in the 1970s, then, were more likely than members first elected before 1970 to express strong opposition to the Democratic position across the whole range of issues. If this trend continues, the Democratic House leadership will increasingly have to rely solely upon its own party members for majorities.

TABLE 6–14

SUPPORT AND SENIORITY FOR HOUSE REPUBLICANS

(in percentages of seniority group in support category)

Republicans First Elected in:	Support Level			
	Moderate[a]			Low
1960s or earlier	18.5	31.5	22.2	27.8
Number	(10)	(17)	(12)	(15)
1970 or later	14.6	18.3	26.8	40.2
Number	(12)	(15)	(22)	(33)

NOTE: For method, see text.

[a] The moderate category is equivalent to the middle category in table 6-11.

SOURCE: See table 6-3.

Coalition Building in the Senate. To assess the difficulty of coalition formation in the Senate, a parallel set of key vote indexes was constructed. Although the roll calls included were not identical, the Senate economic policy, social security, energy, labor, and foreign and defense policy indexes were, in content, very similar to their House counterparts. Because budget resolutions and debt ceiling increases are less controversial in the Senate than in the House, votes on both were included in a single index.

Two additional indexes, in the areas of environmental policy and civil liberties, were constructed. The first included two votes each on the strip mining bill, the Clean Air Act, and the Water Pollution Control Act; the latter, a roll call concerning the president's program of amnesty for Vietnam draft evaders, one on the D.C. Voting Rights Constitutional Amendment, one on extension of the deadline for ratification of the Equal Rights Amendment, and two on busing. Most of the measures included in these indexes were on the president's priority list. Furthermore, the earlier examination of House voting alignments over time indicated that these are issue areas worthy of examination.

Democratic support, as table 6–15 shows, was highest on economic policy and lowest on the energy index. Southern Democrats were clearly the least reliable element of the party; on only three of the indexes was their support above the 50 percent mark; they provided almost no support on labor issues and little on energy, environment, and civil liberties. The scores for border and mountain Democrats were combined as, in the aggregate, their mean support was quite

TABLE 6–15

SUPPORT SCORES ON KEY-VOTE INDEXES, BY PARTY AND REGION, 95TH SENATE

Index	Democrats				Republicans			
	All	South-ern	Border and moun-tain	Other	All	North-eastern	Southern and moun-tain	Other
Energy	62.2	32.7	63.6	75.4	29.9	64.7	5.5	30.2
Foreign & defense	71.8	58.6	69.7	79.1	46.9	67.3	26.3	52.2
Budget & debt	77.2	53.9	80.0	88.1	49.4	82.0	12.5	62.6
Labor	70.8	14.0	86.4	91.6	30.6	77.8	2.5	26.7
Social security	75.2	43.9	82.0	87.3	22.0	50.0	6.5	17.1
Economic policy	80.0	65.0	91.7	82.6	18.2	38.0	6.3	16.1
Environ-ment	64.9	30.7	56.2	84.0	33.5	81.5	10.3	24.8
Civil liberties	67.4	30.7	55.4	87.3	37.0	73.3	5.0	42.5

NOTE: For the definition of support scores, see note to table 6-3.
SOURCE: See table 6-3.

similar.[20] Except on the economic policy index, both groupings were less supportive than the remaining Democrats. Although clearly the most supportive segment, these "other" Democrats nevertheless could not be considered highly reliable across the whole range of issues. Both the energy and the foreign and defense policy indexes show considerable defections from the leadership's and president's position. On energy policy, the relatively low mean score was primarily due to defections from the left; the ideological rationale for the defections, of course, does not lessen their effect—in fact, it was a liberal fili-buster that delayed action on Carter's energy bill.

On each of these indexes, the Senate Republican party was split. Northeasterners consistently provided the highest support; in six of the eight areas, their mean support was well above the 50 percent

[20] Mountain Democrats were somewhat more supportive than border Democrats on civil liberties and environmental issues, while border Democrats were more supportive on the budget and debt ceiling index.

mark, and on another it was 50 percent. Except on economic policy, northeastern Republicans supported the Democratic position at a significantly higher rate than southern Democrats, and on civil liberties and environmental issues they scored appreciably higher than mountain and border Democrats. In contrast, Republicans from the South and from the mountain states scored low across the whole range of issues. The remainder of the Republicans fell between these two extremes.

If the parallel House and Senate indexes are compared, one finds that regional voting alignments were roughly similar. Some of the apparent difference was due to the fact that mountain state members constituted a much larger percentage of the Senate than of the House. The distance between the parties, however, was much greater in the House than in the Senate; the average difference between mean Democratic and Republican scores over the seven House indexes was 59.8 percentage points; the comparable figure over the six parallel Senate indexes was 40.1 percentage points. The higher support scores of Senate Republicans account for this difference between the chambers. Compared with their House party colleagues, Senate Republicans were much less cohesive and, in aggregate, much more inclined to support the Democratic position.

What implications concerning coalition building in the Senate can be drawn from these findings? As in the House, alignment patterns did not vary radically across issues, but support levels did show considerable variation. In the Senate, but not in the House, Republicans frequently contributed significantly to victories for Democratic programs. Coalitions on high priority leadership and presidential measures were more likely to be bipartisan.

An examination of Congressional Quarterly's twelve key votes for the 87th Congress will allow us to make a rough comparison between Kennedy's and Carter's first Congresses. Over the twelve roll calls, an average of 32.1 percent of Republican senators supported the administration. But if we exclude the roll call on invoking cloture on the Communications Satellite Act ("Comsat") of 1962—on which almost 95 percent of Republicans supported the administration—the mean Republican support score falls to 26.4 percent. This is a considerably lower figure than the 33.4 percent Republican support over the eight 95th Congress indexes.

While Republican support increased, that of northern Democrats slipped. Kennedy received an average of 88.1 percent support from northern Democrats; 89.6 percent if the Comsat vote is excluded. The comparable figure for the 95th Congress is 82.7 percent. This decline was partly offset by an increase in southern support. Southern

211

Democrats' mean support on the twelve key votes in the 87th Congress was 37.3 percent (39.4 if Comsat is excluded); their mean on the 95th Congress indexes was 41.2 percent.[21]

Although this comparison is very rough, it suggests that in the early 1960s Senate alignments were not as rigidly defined in party and regional terms as were alignments in the House. It further suggests that Senate coalitions have become still more fluid in the 1970s.

Another perspective upon the fluidity of Senate voting alignments is provided by a support categorization similar to that employed for the House (see table 6–16).[22] As one would expect, there was much more overlap between the parties in the Senate than in the House. Six of the nine northeastern Republicans and two of the sixteen "other" Republicans actually fell on the Democratic end of the scale. In contrast, all the southern and mountain Republicans fell below the midpoint. The bulk of southern Democrats fell into the relatively unsupportive and unpredictable middle category. Only two fell into lower support categories—Allen of Alabama and Byrd of Virginia—and *none* were on the supportive end of the scale. Unlike the House, the Senate did not include any moderately liberal southern Democrats.

Border and mountain Democrats, although generally more supportive than southerners, were a relatively unreliable source of support for the president and the leadership. Half fell into the middle unpredictable category and only one into the two most supportive categories. The remaining group of Democrats were clearly the mainstay of leadership and presidential support. But even this grouping was far from totally reliable over the whole range of issues. Slightly over half fell into the next most supportive category, but a little more than a fifth fell into the middle unpredictable category.

This analysis, then, indicates considerable fluidity in Senate coalitions. Although comparisons between the chambers are somewhat risky, Senate coalitions seem to have been even more fluid than those in the House. Half the House members fell into the two highest or the two lowest support categories, while only 38.2 percent of senators did. If this can be taken as a measure of the predicta-

[21] This finding combined with the fact that the mean southern party unity score was lower in the 95th Congress than it was in the 87th indicates that party unity scores and similar gross measures must be interpreted very cautiously.

[22] Voting participation on the roll calls included in the social security index was relatively low. As a member was assigned an index score only if he voted on at least half the roll calls included in the index, the amount of missing data on the social security index precluded its use in this analysis. Thus the Senate support categorization is based upon the seven remaining indexes.

TABLE 6–16

SUPPORT RELIABILITY, BY PARTY AND REGION, 95TH SENATE
(in percentages of group in support category)

Party and Region	Support Level						
	High						Low
Other							
Democrats	6.3	53.1	18.8	21.9	—	—	—
Number	(2)	(17)	(6)	(7)	(0)	(0)	(0)
Mountain & Border							
Democrats	—	8.3	41.7	50.0	—	—	—
Number	(0)	(1)	(5)	(6)	(0)	(0)	(0)
Southern							
Democrats	—	—	—	86.7	6.7	—	6.7
Number	(0)	(0)	(0)	(13)	(1)	(0)	(1)
Northeastern							
Republicans	—	33.3	33.3	33.3	—	—	—
Number	(0)	(3)	(3)	(3)	(0)	(0)	(0)
Other							
Republicans	—	6.3	6.3	43.8	25.0	18.8	—
Number	(0)	(1)	(1)	(7)	(4)	(3)	(0)
Mountain & Southern							
Republicans	—	—	—	—	30.8	53.8	15.4
Number	(0)	(0)	(0)	(0)	(4)	(7)	(2)
All	2.1	22.7	15.5	37.1	9.3	10.3	3.1
Number	(2)	(22)	(15)	(36)	(9)	(10)	(3)

NOTE: For method, see text.
SOURCE: See table 6-3.

bility of voting behavior on presidential and congressional leadership priorities, then half the House and almost two-thirds of the Senate was unpredictable.

In the analysis of House coalitions, we found that membership turnover influenced voting alignments. The Senate also experienced high turnover in the 1970s; thus, an examination of the effects of turnover seems warranted. The only clear turnover effect found among Democrats was in the southern membership. With the exception of Nunn of Georgia and Johnston of Louisiana, both of whom were first elected in 1972, southern Democrats first elected in the

1970s were more supportive than their more senior colleagues. If southern Democrats are divided into those who began their tenure before 1970 plus the two elected in 1972 and those elected later in the 1970s, one finds that, except on the social security index, the junior members were more supportive than their senior colleagues. The difference in mean scores ranged from 2.8 percentage points on the economic policy index to 49 percentage points on the environmental policy scale; the average difference over the seven indexes was 21.1 percentage points.

These differences are not the result of one deviant member. If the mean score over the seven indexes is used as the criterion, Bumpers of Arkansas, with a mean of 65.7 percent, was the most supportive, and Morgan of North Carolina, with a mean of 43.6 percent, was least supportive. However, even Morgan's mean was considerably above the 33.3 percent mean of the more senior group. Only two of the more senior group had mean scores higher than the least supportive of the more junior group. Quite clearly these junior southern Democrats were neither highly reliable supporters of Democratic positions nor flaming liberals. But they were significantly and consistently more supportive than their senior colleagues.

Neither southern and mountain Republicans nor those from the northeast showed any consistent splits along seniority lines.[23] Among the remaining Republicans a clear difference between those who began their tenure before 1970 and those elected during the 1970s is evident. The junior group was consistently less supportive; the difference in means ranged from 4.9 percentage points on the social security index to 50.1 points on the budget and debt ceiling index; the average difference over the eight scales was 25.4. Because the numbers are small one should not overinterpret these findings. Nevertheless, they suggest that, outside the northeast, fewer moderate Republicans were winning election to the Senate.

The relatively low Republican unity on these key-vote indexes offers a Democratic president and party leadership considerable aid and comfort in building their majority coalitions. If, however, the seniority differences we have discovered actually represent a trend, future Democratic leaders in the Senate may increasingly be forced, as their counterparts in the House have been, to rely almost exclusively upon their own party members.

---

[23] Northeastern Republicans elected during the 1970s were less supportive than their senior colleagues on three of the indexes—economic policy, budget and debt ceiling, and social security. This may be the beginning of a trend, but these members were still voting more like their senior regional colleagues than like Republicans from other areas, in the late 1970s.

The Sources of Unpredictability

In building congressional coalition, did the Carter administration, as Anne Wexler claims, have to start from scratch on each new piece of legislation? My analysis shows that Wexler's statement is hyperbole. In both chambers, voting followed discernible patterns. The president and the Democratic congressional leadership could expect support from a large proportion of northern Democrats; southern Democrats remained the major problem.

The analysis, however, also shows that coalitions were quite fluid; few Democrats were highly reliable across all issue areas; few could be written off. As a result, coalition building was more complex. The number of members the leadership had to contact and persuade had grown. Gauging the probability of winning was more difficult, and so was deciding how to spend scarce time and resources. The frequency with which the House leadership lost votes which it subsequently turned around is indicative. The list for 1979 includes the debt limit increase bill, an amendment cutting the State Department authorization by 10 percent, a "killer" amendment to the stand-by gas rationing bill, the second Budget Resolution, an amendment immediately terminating oil price controls, and the Panama Canal Treaty implementation bill conference report. In each case, the leadership's position prevailed on the second attempt—clear proof that a winning coalition *could* be fashioned. That a skillful and active leadership lost the first time shows how difficult it is to gauge what, and how much, needs to be done to win.

In part, the increased fluidity of alignments is the result of the issues at the center of controversy in the 1970s. Energy, environmental and consumer issues, and foreign and defense policy questions split not just North from South in the Democratic party; they also divided northern Democrats. Continued high inflation began to affect debate on a wide variety of social welfare and economic policy questions, with the potential for deepening intraparty splits.

Changes in rules and norms during the 1970s also decreased predictability. In the House, the institution of the recorded teller vote drastically affected the dynamics of the floor stage. Forcing a recorded vote on an amendment is extremely easy. Because the vote is recorded, members cannot simply follow the party or committee leadership, even if they wish to. The visibility of the vote requires careful political calculation. Given the skill of the right in fashioning politically embarassing amendments with considerable constituency appeal, the "safe" course for many members was to vote against the leadership's position. A series of other rules changes spread influence more equally in the House and severely reduced the power of committee chairmen. High turnover had changed the complexion of the membership. Socialized to politics during the turbulent 1960s, entering the House in a period of challenge to the power structure, and, in the case of many of the large 1974 Democratic class, elected from previously Republican districts, the freshmen of the 1970s were unwilling to wait to make their mark. Both personal inclination and political necessity dictated a high level of activity and full participation at the committee and floor stage as soon as they began their terms. The result of these changes was a severe decline in intercommittee reciprocity. The premise that one should "go with the committee" no longer held. Consequently, the number of amendments offered on the floor rose astronomically. During the 87th Congress, 240 recorded votes were taken; during the 95th, 1,540.

Senate floor procedures have always allowed recorded votes on amendments, and the norm of committee reciprocity seems never to have been as strong as it was in the House. The further decentralization of the Senate in the 1970s, high membership turnover, and the types of issues at the center of controversy do seem to have led to a further decline in committee reciprocity and a consequent increase in the number of recorded votes. The 87th Senate took 428; the 95th, 1,152.

The willingness of members, Democrats as well as Republicans, to offer amendments and the ease with which a recorded vote can be had dramatically increased unpredictability. The House leadership's probability of getting ambushed on the floor was much higher in 1980 than it once was. Frequently the leadership did not know in advance about all the potentially disastrous amendments that would be offered; and, in any case, it was impossible to conduct whip polls on all. Furthermore, the leadership's time and resources were limited; the great increase in floor activity stretched both to the limit. Ignorance of the meaning of a complex amendment, fear of political consequences, or the erratic behavior of some members during late night sessions could easily lead to the adoption of disastrous amendments.

Coping with Uncertainty. As the 1980s begin, the House Democratic leadership is in the process of evolving a variety of strategies for coping with the new House. Freshmen members are vigorously courted; they are wined, dined, and given orientation briefings. The leadership, of course, hopes that the new members will be grateful, but, in addition, the contact provides the leadership information about the new members which will make persuasion more effective. The very extensive traveling the leadership undertakes to help reelect

Democratic members serves the same dual function.

The expansion of the whip system during the 1970s is another response to the changing House. The addition of ten at-large whips who are appointed by the leadership and thus can be counted on to be loyal increases the leadership's capabilities to some extent.

The appointment of task forces charged with the passage of major bills is an O'Neill innovation. Usually chaired by a junior congressman and with a large proportion of its membership drawn from the junior ranks, the task force increases the number of people working, in an organized way, to pass the bill at issue. The leadership's choice of junior members for many task force positions is, in part, due to the belief that junior members are more effective at persuading their peers than are senior members. In addition, work on a task force gives junior members a piece of the action, provides them with an understanding of the problems of the leadership and, it is hoped, identification with the leadership. "Give me a frustrated guy," Speaker O'Neill has said, "and I'll give him a job to do, and he becomes a 'Tip O'Neill man.' "[24]

In addition to these strategies aimed at coping with unpredictability, there has been considerable discussion of using the Rules Committee to reduce unpredictability on the floor. The more frequent employment of modified closed rules which restrict the number and type of amendments that may be offered has been proposed, and the growing dissatisfaction with present floor procedures may result in moves in that direction.

A comparable move in the Senate is not feasible, given that chamber's rules. Furthermore, it is exceedingly unlikely that either chamber will revert to the relatively placid and predictable state which characterized Congress during the 1950s. The issues are different, the rules are different, and the membership is different. In time, all three are likely to change again, but not in such a way as to bring back the Congress of a bygone era.

Ideology, Constituency, and Party

Some observers of Congress contend that members are more ideological than they used to be and that this has increased the problems of the party leadership. Certainly if we compare the 1970s with the 1950s, the political spectrum has widened; positions considered beyond the pale by the vast majority in the 1950s now find significant numbers of adherents, and this is reflected in the congressional mem-

24 Quoted in the *New York Times*, June 4, 1979.

217

bership. The number of hot issues has also increased and politics is more intense. These changes have complicated the coalition formation process. The more heterogeneous membership and the large number of divisive issues are problems.

Some claim that congressional voting is increasingly based upon the members' ideology rather than upon constituency. This argument has been made most forcefully with respect to voting on energy questions, but the studies that support it suffer from both methodological and conceptual problems.[25] In particular, they tend to conceptualize the constituency as an undifferentiated mass. Yet on most controversial questions, there will be differences of opinion within a member's constituency, and he will have to decide which segment, if any, he will attend to. For reelection, the key elements of the constituency are the reelection constituency—those people who have supported the member with their votes in past elections—and the supportive elite—that part of the politically active electorate that has provided more than just voting support.

Most members' views on most issues are very similar to those of their supportive elite. The congressman, after all, has been recruited from among them—he is one of them. Consequently, by reflecting the opinions of his supportive elite in his votes, he is voting his own ideology, and vice versa.

Elites generally have a pretty clear view of their own economic interests and of the policies congruent with those interests. As a result, voting on energy policy generally follows producer versus consumer lines. Republicans from predominantly consuming areas are less supportive of proconsumer policies than Democrats from the same areas because their business-based supportive elites do not see energy price controls as being in their interest.

Although the congressman's own views and those of his supportive elite are likely to be highly similar, this is not necessarily the case for the congressman's views and those of the broader reelection constituency. If, on an issue highly salient to the reelection constituency, the supportive elite and the reelection constituency hold conflicting views, the congressman does face a dilemma. For northern Democrats, sociocultural issues—busing, abortion, school prayer, law and order—are most likely to produce such a conflict. For those northern Democrats who represent predominantly middle-class dis-

[25] For an example, see Edward J. Mitchell, "The Basis of Congressional Energy Policy," *Texas Law Review*, vol. 57 (March 1979), pp. 591-613. These studies show that energy roll calls correlate highly with the scores assigned congressmen by one or more of the rating groups, such as ADA and ACA. Thus, they assume that the rating group scores are pure measures of the member's personal ideology, unaffected by constituency pressures—an obviously untenable assumption.

tricts, constituent concern over continued high inflation is leading to similar problems on economic and social welfare policies. In at least nine out of ten cases, the challenge the Democratic leadership faces when their members are confronted with such a dilemma is to persuade the members to vote their own views rather than those of their reelection constituency.

Northern House Democrats of the 1970s certainly seem to have stronger personal ideological convictions than their counterparts of the mid-1950s. That they have stronger convictions than northern Democrats first elected in 1958 or in the 1960s is doubtful. Furthermore, there is no evidence indicating that they regularly vote their ideology when it conflicts with the views of key elements in their constituency. Common wisdom among old Hill hands is just the opposite: that junior members are not committed to anything, that, far from being too rigid, they are too flexible and inclined to follow every whim of their constituencies. One senior staffer long associated with liberal causes, after complaining about junior Democrats' lack of commitment, added, "Of course, it's not clear what in the hell there is to be committed to now." Therein lies the crux of the problem.

The extent of party voting at a given time is basically a function of the extent to which party members receive conflicting or congruent signals from their constituencies. Because the party leadership and the president have so little influence upon members' reelection chances, they can affect voting behavior only marginally. The marginal influence is important because it may make the difference between passage and defeat of major legislation. But the leadership works within the constraints set by the relationship between congressmen and their constituencies.

The current leadership has been skillful in using its limited resources to cope with the problems created by rule and norm changes and by heavy membership turnover. The growing Democratic ideological malaise could become an insurmountable problem for the leadership and the president. The sociocultural issues of the late 1960s and early 1970s split the Democratic party but did not endanger the consensus among northern members on core elements of Democratic party ideology in the economic and social welfare areas. The prominent issues of the late 1970s and 1980s—especially inflation—threaten to do exactly that.

The majority party leadership does not have now and never has had the resources necessary to lead successfully an utterly fragmented party. Without agreement among a substantial proportion of the Democratic membership on at least some basic tenets, the most skillful leadership is doomed to failure. Alternatively if, under the impetus of a strong, clear public demand for action and the leadership of a creative Democratic president, a new consensus emerges, the House leadership will appear very potent indeed. Both the extensiveness of leadership resources and the skill with which they are used affect legislative success. But much more important to the success of party and presidential leadership are the character and intensity of the dominant issues and whether they cut along or across party lines; over this, the leadership has no control.

The Policy Implications of Change. The unpredictability of the coalition formation process, particularly the tendency to rewrite bills on the floor, probably does result in more sloppily drafted and inconsistent legislation. The distorted allocation of floor time results in an increasing end-of-the-session rush during which some bills may not receive the scrutiny they deserve. Others may have to be watered down because of the inordinate bargaining power minorities possess when the chambers are working under severe time constraints. Unpredictability also increases the chances of misjudgment. The president, fearing defeat, may not propose a measure, even though it would actually have passed. Conversely, measures that look like sure bets may, even after the investment of considerable time and resources, go down to defeat.

But can we make the sweeping judgment that, because of internal reforms and high membership turnover, Congress is less capable than it was in the 1950s and 1960s of dealing with the major problems which confront the country? I very much doubt it. The institution's problems are simply different—not worse. Instead of a policy process dominated by powerful, conservative committee chairmen, one in which crucial decisions were made in secret and thus were relatively insulated from public influence, we now see a process characterized by extreme individualism, one in which open, public decision making often hinders compromise.

The "solution" is likely to be the same as the solution throughout this century. In part because centrifugal, constituency related forces are so strong, Congress is a reactive institution; it cannot anticipate. It is not, however, impervious to strong stimuli from its environment. A crisis, a strong clear demand from the public for action, will produce a congressional response, as it has throughout this century. A Congress in which veto points have been weakened, in which the process is open to public scrutiny, may, in fact, react more quickly and adequately than the more insulated Congress of the past. How Congress performs its legislative role depends much more upon the character of the environmental forces impinging upon its members than upon its internal organization.

PART THREE
The Policy Process

7

Congress and the Presidency

Charles O. Jones

In his classic work comparing forms of government, Woodrow Wilson stressed the absence of organic connections between the legislature and the executive in the United States. "In all other modern governments," he wrote,

> the heads of the administrative departments are given the right to sit in the legislative body and to take part in its proceedings. The legislature and executive are thus associated in such a way that the ministers of state can lead the houses without dictating to them, and the ministers themselves be controlled without being misunderstood—in such a way that the two parts of the government which should be most closely coordinated, the part, namely, by which the laws are made and the part by which the laws are executed, may be kept in close harmony and intimate cooperation, with the result of giving coherence to the action of the one and energy to the action of the other.[1]

The large majority of governments continue to foster executive-legislative relations by the constitutional connections referred to by Wilson. Not so the United States, which severed the executive from the legislature in its Constitution.

The principal purpose of this essay is to explore recent developments in congressional-presidential relations. William J. Keefe concludes that: "presidential-congressional relations . . . are often unpredictable, sometimes unfathomable, and always complex."[2] "It

---

I am most appreciative to Bert A. Rockman, Samuel C. Patterson, and the editors of this volume for their helpful comments.

[1] Woodrow Wilson, *The State*, rev. ed. (Boston: D.C. Heath, 1904), p. 546.

[2] William J. Keefe, *Congress and the American People* (Englewood Cliffs, N.J.: Prentice-Hall, 1980), p. 120.

all depends" appears to be the principal generalization one is led to by an attempt at fathoming these institutional associations. But on what does it all depend? It is argued here that relations between Congress and the presidency depend substantially on how each judges the legitimacy and competency of the other.

This chapter is organized to treat the following questions: What appear to be the principal determinants of relations between the two branches? What difference does it make when each challenges the legitimacy or competency of the other? What happens when a Richard M. Nixon becomes president? What happens when a Jimmy Carter becomes president? Can we expect conditions to change? But before we examine these questions it is useful to set the stage with a brief discussion of constitutional structures and contemporary events.

One President and Two Legislative Bodies in an Age of Disrespect

One cannot begin an analysis of the connections between Congress and presidents without acknowledging their context. First, the constitutional setting. The investment of executive power in a single, independently elected individual tends to focus public and media attention on that person as representing all government. There he is—a Franklin D. Roosevelt or Dwight D. Eisenhower or Lyndon B. Johnson or James Earl Carter. We study his intentions and goals, watch for his reactions to events, discuss his appointments, critically analyze his statements and initiatives. Students of the American system argue that our balance of powers among the three branches surely demands more balanced reporting than a Washington press corps preoccupied with the White House seems ready to provide. But let's face it, Congresses are known by the presidents they keep, not the leaders they select, the constituents they serve, or the reforms they enact.[3] Madison interpreted Article II as restraining the executive "within a narrower compass." In an active government, however, the presidency "being more simple in its nature . . ."[4] was bound to receive a degree of public attention that, itself, guaranteed active participation by the president in decision making. As Keefe observes: "The president's advantages begin with the expectations that others have about his leadership role in the nation's political life."[5] At no

[3] This attention to the president has advantages and disadvantages. As Bert A. Rockman observed in comments on this paper, presidents pay a particularly high price for the decline in institutional respect. "Presidents are seen as the institution, i.e., the presidency is far less disengaged from the president than Congress is from its members."

[4] Both quotations from *The Federalist* (New York: Modern Library, 1937), p. 323.

[5] Keefe, *Congress*, p. 108.

time is this more obvious than when a crisis develops, as with the taking of hostages in Iran and the invasion of Afghanistan by the Soviet Union.

The two legislative bodies called Congress, separated from each other and from the executive, also must be comprehended as constitutional structures in this exercise. At the most basic level, Article I reminds us that presidential-congressional relations are not relations between one person (and his appointed aides) and one body of persons organized hierarchically. Rather the president acting through aides must negotiate with a variable set of congressional actors through time, through legislative stages, across issues, and for two legislative bodies. To be sure, patterns emerge that provide continuity and stability to the connections. But the complexity of the relationship has often been dealt with by oversimplification.

Another basic contextual matter is that of the disruptive issues of the last fifteen years. The list is impressive: the struggle for civil and political rights, Vietnam and its many domestic implications, the Great Society programs with their problems of funding and implementation, President Nixon's challenges to the organizational and programmatic directions of past decades, Watergate and its ripple effects throughout government, and the recent set of energy and environmental problems which have come to dominate the governmental agenda. These issues have been described and analyzed in many works and do not require special review here. Our interest is in their effects on the political context of presidential-congressional contact. Among these effects are the following:

- a decline in trust and respect for governmental institutions and political leaders
- a demand for reform of governmental structures and political (including policy) processes
- a melding of what were formerly distinctive issue types—foreign and domestic; national, state, and local; the three "E's," energy, environment, economy; and so on
- a shift from the more expansive to the more consolidative programs—from new thrusts to more effective means to achieve existing goals

This brief review reminds us of the importance and difficulty of understanding Congress and the presidency. It also urges us to form a simple model which will aid in understanding.

What Determines Congressional-Presidential Relations? President Carter offered this candid self-appraisal to a news conference following a speech to the American Society of Newspaper Editors:

225

> I think I have found it is much easier for me in my own administration to evolve a very complex proposal for resolving a difficult issue than it is for Congress to pass legislation and to make that same decision.
>
> The energy legislation is one example. I never dreamed a year ago in April when I proposed this matter to the Congress that a year later it still would not be resolved. I think I have got a growing understanding of the Congress, its limitations, and its capabilities and also its leadership, which was a new experience for me altogether, never having lived or served in the federal government in Washington.[6]

I will treat the details of this interesting statement later. For now, I simply want to stress the importance of how the president views Congress and how the members, in turn, view the president. It is clear that President Carter has a conception of what Congress is and what it ought to do—a picture he admits may originally have been distorted. We may find that each branch's notions about the other help to explain policy and the political relationships between them.

Legitimacy and *competency* are two of the most important standards by which actors in each branch judge each other. Legitimacy refers to whether persons have the right to be involved in decision making. Judgments about this right may be based on such factors as an interpretation of proper constitutional authority, the means by which a person assumes an office, and personal conduct in the office. Competency refers to whether persons have the capabilities required to be effective in decision making. Judgments about competency may rely on such factors as experience, training, expertise, commitments, and availability of staff.

Judgments are made about whole institutions or about parts thereof. For example, the president and his aides may question the legitimacy of the House Committee on Rules without doubting the right of the House itself to act (as seemed to be the case during the Kennedy administration when the coalition of southern Democrats and Republicans on the Rules Committee threatened to kill important domestic legislation). Similarly, questions of legitimacy or competency may be raised about a particular action (such as the impoundment of funds in the Nixon administration) or about action within a particular issue-area (such as a highly technical or sensitive foreign policy issue being dealt with by Congress)—without implying doubt about the legitimacy or competency of the presidency or Congress.

[6] Reprinted in *President Carter—1978* (Washington, D.C.: Congressional Quarterly, Inc., 1979), p. 92A.

Many of the traditional determinants of congressional-presidential relations—constitutional prerogatives, political party, personality, electoral margins, media expectations—influence how congressional and presidential actors view each other. Accordingly, changes in these factors may alter interbranch evaluations. But the argument here simply is that the assessments themselves provide a useful entry point for explaining, perhaps even predicting, how the two branches get along.

If they react positively toward the other branch, members of Congress or the president and his aides will also have opinions about the policy activities proper for that branch. For example, assuming that a congressional committee chairman pictures the president and his aides as legitimately and competently involved in an issue area, he or she may have in mind specific types of activities which they can perform properly. Should the president engage in activities other than those deemed proper, the committee chairman may reevaluate the president's legitimacy or competency in dealing with the issue at hand. Members of one branch may be expected to have opinions about the legitimacy and competency of the other branch to perform each of the following policy activities:

- agenda setting (including problem identification and definition)
- program development (including planning, choice among alternatives, building support, funding)
- program implementation (including interpretation and application)
- program evaluation (including specification of goals, measurement, and recommendation for change)
- program coordination (including comparative analysis)

To summarize, I have argued that it is useful for understanding relationships between the branches to explore how actors in Congress and the presidency view each other's legitimacy and competency to cope generally and to cope with specific issues. These estimates of institutional and individual capabilities are influenced by political and personal factors and, when positive, lead to judgments about the specific policy role to be played by each branch.

What about Negative Evaluations? When a presidential-congressional partnership is successful, presidential and congressional actors respect one another's position, talent, and specialized capacities. Their partnership is defined and circumscribed by estimates of what each does well. This situation by no means eliminates conflict, but disagreements tend to focus on substance rather than process, structure, or constitutional position.

What happens when those in one branch challenge the legitimacy and competency of those in the other? Negative evaluations set the stage for the encroachments that so concerned Madison. *The really significant effect of one institution's disparaging view of the other is its effect on the behavior of the viewer.* If one branch sees the other as neither trustworthy nor dependable, it will see itself as called upon to assume full responsibility. Ernest Barker worried that such encroachments sprang from the very nature of institutions:

> Every human institution tends naturally to institutionalism. It exaggerates itself. Not content with discharging its specific function, it readily seeks to encroach. . . . Instead of seeing itself as a part, which must play its function as such, and claim no more than that, each institution is prone to see itself as a whole, *to regard itself as a rounded O,* and to claim a total sovereignty. That is an aberration. . . .[7]

What I suggest is that proneness to "rounded O's" is directly related to negative interbranch evaluations. Rounding the "O" is more than a pleasant little redundancy. It means creating a total policy process within one branch of government.

A basic challenge to the integrity of either branch naturally elicits a response. With the partnership dissolved, one may expect the challenged branch to react like the challenger—by expanding its activities. The encroachments of the challenging branch will be the basis for expansion by the challenged branch. Ironically the same rationale will be used—loss of legitimacy and competency by the other branch.

Negative evaluations of legitimacy and competency can have important consequences in the national policy process. Stalemate is one of the more immediate effects. But other, potentially more serious, results may occur. Public apathy, even alienation, may follow stalemate, with low turnout in elections casting doubt on the legitimacy of those elected. Under these circumstances negative interbranch evaluations result in a self-fulfilling illegitimacy. Meanwhile, where complex social, economic, and defense-related programs are already in place, the bureaucracy may be expected to assume the tasks of governing—essentially through rational increments to existing policy. This outcome is not a result of some devious bureaucratic design. Rather, it stems from the decline of trust between separated partners.

[7] Ernest Barker, *Essays on Government,* 2nd ed. (Oxford: Clarendon Press, 1951), pp. 70, 71. Emphasis added.

The Nixon Presidency

Presidents, Congresses, and their various components, can be rated by applying the tests of legitimacy and competency—both as an impressionistic exercise and as a much more particular scientific endeavor. Accomplishing the latter requires elaborate explication of criteria, specification of sources, collection of data for several administrations, and careful analysis of findings and is, therefore, beyond the scope of this chapter. At the level of educated impressions, however, one can do quite well with this scheme in explaining the relations with Congress of Presidents Franklin Roosevelt, Harry Truman, Dwight Eisenhower, John Kennedy, or Lyndon Johnson, both in general and on various issues. Each of these administrations was characterized by both branches' doubts about each other's legitimacy and competency to deal with particular issues. One only need mention Roosevelt's court-packing plan, the Taft-Hartley Act of the 80th Congress, the many budgetary and domestic policy conflicts during the Eisenhower administrations, the Bay of Pigs disaster of the Kennedy administration, and, of course, Vietnam. Further, it has been characteristic of all administrations that relations deteriorate over time. President Roosevelt's relations with Congress were going from bad to worse before World War II. Truman's conflicts with Congress were legendary throughout his presidency and became extremely trying toward the end of his elected term. Eisenhower had to deal with a Democratic Congress for six of his eight years in office, and his successes on Capitol Hill showed a steady decline. Neither Kennedy nor Johnson served a second term, and the former was in office less than three years. In Johnson's case, an initial period of harmony between the branches on domestic issues was followed by intense conflict over the proper course of action in Vietnam.

It is not surprising to find conflict and competition between the two major policy-making branches of the national government. In general, however, these challenges have tended to be program-directed; that is, those in one branch have doubted the legitimacy or competency of those in the other branch to cope with *an issue*. Occasionally challenges were made to the whole institution—the legitimacy of third and fourth terms for Roosevelt was questioned, as was the competency of the "do-nothing" 80th Congress. But in most cases judgments have been policy specific and, as composite evaluations, more positive than negative.

The case of the Nixon administrations, particularly the second administration, appears to be quite different. Here is an instance of interbranch evaluations that were more negative than positive and applied to a whole institution, not just parts thereof. With all that has been written on the Nixon administration, one finds relatively little systematic analysis of congressional relations—particularly those of the president's staff.[8] But what analysis there is confirms the negative valence of congressional-presidential evaluations. I have selected two particularly cogent accounts to illustrate this tendency. The first, by Nelson W. Polsby, describes the conditions leading to the executive's negative evaluations of Congress. The second, by Ralph K. Huitt, goes more directly to Nixon's dealings with Congress. Here is how Polsby describes the Nixon terms:

> It was a strong presidency, strong in the sense of setting and achieving goals. Yet it achieved its ends principally through the device of attacking, crippling, neutralizing, and diminishing the powers of other legitimate power centers in the political system. Underpinning this approach to presidential government were two articles of belief, frequently stated by Mr. Nixon or one or another of his spokesmen. The first held that the accountability of the President ran solely to his electoral majority. Politics for Mr. Nixon was electoral politics, campaign politics. Election conferred a mandate, an entitlement for him to act in office as his predecessors had acted—in small ways as well as large ways.[9]

The second article of belief, according to Polsby, followed logically from the first and directly supports the argument here. As a Republican with a Democratic Congress and a New Deal bureaucracy, Nixon was, in his view, mandated to fight the good fight, against overwhelming odds. He believed that:

> The elite political stratum in this country . . . was out of step with the dominant mood of conservatism in the country at large. Thus, in his view, his election conferred not only an extraordinary measure of legitimacy upon him, but also a kind of illegitimacy upon many of the very people with

[8] See John H. Kessel, *The Domestic Presidency: Decision-Making in the White House* (North Scituate, Mass.: Duxbury Press, 1975), where he analyzes the internal workings of the Domestic Council, including some material on how the staff members viewed Congress. "[The members] were seen as advocates for constituency interests, and while they were respected in that capacity, this very advocacy limited their ability to determine overall priorities" (p. 69). There are many journalistic accounts of Nixon's White House staff.

[9] Nelson W. Polsby, *Congress and the Presidency*, 3rd ed. (Englewood Cliffs, N.J.: Prentice-Hall, 1976), p. 51. I must acknowledge a larger debt to Professor Polsby. We often discussed the Nixon presidency during the period 1971-1974. I learned a great deal from him and have no doubt that some of the ideas expressed here are traceable to that education.

whom a President ordinarily does business—the bureaucrats, interest group leaders, and journalists, Congressmen and party leaders of official Washington. These after all, had for the most part been elected neither in the close election of 1968 nor in his landslide of 1972 [or, if they had, they came from constituencies made safe from the ebb and flow of American politics].[10]

In a most interesting practical review of "White House Channels to the Hill," Huitt uses an analogy to marriage to analyze successful presidential-congressional relations. He identifies two elements as indispensable to the partnership between the president and Congress: "that both parties want it to succeed and . . . that workable arrangements be established which make the crucial day-to-day lives flow together easily without letting every chore or responsibility become a possible confrontation."[11] Workable arrangements are the natural means of accommodation once good will and intentions exist. "But what if a president does not want a marriage with Congress?" With this question Huitt turns to the extraordinary Nixon years.

> The Constitution does not say that he must [marry Congress]. Nixon did not seem titillated by the prospect. In fact, he seemed to balk Congress by turning the relationship upside down. Historically, the principal checks Congress has had on the president came from maintaining control of the negatives—that is, the president asks for what he wants, and congressional power comes from the liberty to decide how much of it to let him have or what to give him in its place. But Nixon did not seem to want anything from Congress. To be sure, he initiated domestic programs and proclaimed priorities, but he seemed to lose interest in them quickly. . . .
>
> Trying to oppose Nixon on domestic programs was, as some Congressmen put it, like "pushing on a string." There was no resistance. Instead, *Nixon tried to run things without Congress.* Impounding funds, deferring the spending of them, shifting money from one purpose to another—these gave him control of what really mattered, the allocation of government resources. He had effectively got control of the negatives, a role reversal that seemed for a time to bemuse Congress.[12]

---

[10] Ibid.

[11] Ralph K. Huitt, "White House Channels to the Hill," in Harvey C. Mansfield, Sr., ed., *Congress Against the President* (New York: Praeger, 1975), p. 71.

[12] Ibid., p. 76. Emphasis added.

We see in these statements precisely the developments described earlier as associated with negative evaluations. If a competing institution—Congress in this case—is of dubious legitimacy, then the country must be run without it. This conclusion of Nixon's was facilitated by his priorities—foreign policy and the reduction of domestic programs. Had Nixon wished to enact an elaborate domestic program, he would have been less free to exlude Congress.

So far the discussion of the Nixon presidency has proceeded without mention of Watergate. Negative evaluations of Congress by the president and his aides preceded Watergate and surely would have been present had Watergate not occurred. Counterevaluations of President Nixon by members of Congress would have challenged his legitimacy anyway—on the basis of Nixon's excesses.[13] Watergate simply speeded up the process, as the president's unlawful acts provided the ultimate evidence for illegitimacy—the symbolic "smoking gun."

The Congress Reacts. Speaking to a *Time* magazine forum on the state of Congress in 1975, Senator Edmund S. Muskie (Democrat, Maine) reminded his colleagues and others in attendance that Congress was, after all, the legislature, not the executive.

> Let me say this about Congress . . . a Congress is not a President . . . a Congress should not be a President . . . a Congress should be nothing more, nothing less than what it is: a reflection of the will of our people and the problems that disturb them and the actions they want taken. The Congress ought to improve its ability to serve that function.[14]

Senator Muskie showed himself to be unusually perceptive about recent developments in Congress. He was, in essence, advising Congress not to develop a total policy process on Capitol Hill.

What was the basis of Muskie's concern? I have argued that an institution which has been challenged on so basic a matter as its legitimacy to make decisions will respond with a challenge of its own. The challenge to Congress came from Nixon, and the "new Congress" we hear about might well be labeled the "Nixon Congress."

[13] It is relevant in this connection that a conference on "The Constitutional Crisis: Congress vs. the Executive" was held on Capitol Hill, March 7-8, 1973, after the Watergate event but before the Watergate revelations. Many members of Congress were in attendance. The discussion topics included: impoundment, war powers, executive agreements and treaties, executive privilege, and impeachment. See *New Priorities*, vol. 2, no. 1 (Fall 1973). The whole issue is devoted to a summary of the conference.

[14] The speech is reprinted in John L. Steele, ed., *The Role of Congress II: A Study of the Legislative Branch* (New York: Time, Inc., 1975).

Certainly Nixon's actions and attitudes stimulated many of the changes that have taken place on Capitol Hill.

Elsewhere I have identified three roles for Congress in the policy process—as an *initiator* of comprehensive policies, as a *reserved partner* to the executive, and as a *facilitator* of interests.[15] That Congress should assume any of these roles may be the view of the whole membership, of the members of each house, or of the leadership. The most pretentious role is that of initiator since it is based on the belief that the House, the Senate, or both working together, can define problems, set priorities, identify options, and analyze effects. In other words, Congress can govern.

> Presumably this need for independent analysis results from executive incapacity to analyze the problem and develop proposals and/or the production of "wrong results" by the executive. . . . Thus, the Congress-as-initiator model may be said to assume an organizational contretemps between the two branches, resulting from substantive or partisan considerations or both.[16]

The reserved partner role does not require elaborate discussion since it is traditionally well understood as acknowledging presidential leadership in policy. When, during the first two years of the Johnson administration, Congress almost automatically enacted presidential proposals, it was functioning in the classic reserved partner mode.

The facilitator role favors the political over the planning process.

> A plan is the beginning, not the end, of policy making. All voices must be heard—not just those of the expert, technician, and planner. Those holding this view do not believe for a moment that the analysts will have adequately accounted for the diversity of interests in the pre-legislative stage. The public interest, therefore, emerges from representing all viewpoints. . . .[17]

Normally, one may expect a combination of these roles to characterize congressional structure and behavior. But at any one time a particular congressional role may dominate. Stimulated in large measure by Nixon's negative evaluations, many important members of Congress assumed the pretentious role of initiators of comprehensive policies.

[15] Charles O. Jones, "Congress and the Making of Energy Policy," in Robert Lawrence, ed., *New Dimensions to Energy Policy* (Lexington, Mass.: Lexington Books, 1979), pp. 162-165.

[16] Ibid., pp. 163-164.

[17] Ibid., p. 163.

Substantial reform was needed in order for Congress to acquire the full capacity for comprehensive policy initiation. And so we witnessed a period of unprecedented reform on Capitol Hill during the 1970s. Three definite phases of the reform decade can be identified:

Phase 1: before the Nixon challenge. The principal reform in this phase was the Legislative Reorganization Act of 1970. This act had its roots in the work of the Joint Committee on the Organization of Congress created in 1965. Most of the changes were minor organizational and administrative ones. Though enacted in the first Nixon administration, this act presumably would have been passed even if Hubert Humphrey had been elected president in 1968.

Phase 2: response to the Nixon challenge. This group of reforms is by far the most extensive and is associated with Nixon's stated and implied challenges to the legitimacy and competency of Congress. These reforms followed the bolstering of Nixon's self-image as a result of the 1972 election. Among the most important were the War Powers Act of 1973, the Budget and Impoundment Control Act of 1974, the several changes in the party and committee systems (particularly in the House), and the expansion of congressional staff.

Phase 3: after Watergate. This last set of reforms grew out of the excesses of the Committee to Re-elect the President in handling campaign funds and, of course, the focus on ethics in government following the Watergate revelations and the president's resignation. The Federal Election Campaign Act of 1974, ethics codes, more streamlining of the committee systems, and the demands for sunset legislation and greater use of the congressional veto are all included.

In table 7–1 the many reforms of the 1970s are classified on the basis of whether they were intended to move Congress toward or away from the three roles identified earlier. Though hardly a refined exercise, this classification provides a gross impression that is useful. All of the reforms were consistent with enabling Congress to challenge the president and assume the initiator role. Several moved one house or the other away from the other two roles.

I have used the word "pretentious" to characterize the initiator role because I believe it is inordinately ambitious for Congress to prepare itself to initiate comprehensive policy programs. Having undertaken such a complex assignment, a legislature may not know where to stop imitating the executive. Thus, one may expect to witness an escalation of congressional involvement in more policy activities for more issues, which, in turn, demands more staff, greater organizational articulation, and an expansion in the number of congressional partici-

TABLE 7–1

EFFECTS OF THE NIXON-ERA REFORMS ON THE ROLE OF CONGRESS

| Type of Reform | Contributes to Congress's Role as: | | |
	Initiator	Reserved partner	Facilitator
Electoral— Regulating campaign finance	yes	yes	no
Procedural— Increasing subcommittee autonomy, changing committee jurisdiction, introducing multiple referral of bills	yes	no	yes
Political— Increasing the Speaker's power, changing committee appointments and seniority system[a]	yes	yes	yes
Analytical— Creating support agencies, OTA, CBO, CRS; increasing committee and personal staffs	yes	no	no
Jurisdictional— Checking presidential war powers, developing budget process	yes	no	no
Ethical— Disclosing and limiting outside income	yes	yes	no

[a] These reforms can be and have been used to support all three roles.
SOURCE: Author.

pants for any one issue. Given the fragmented and representative nature of Congress, as Senator Muskie warned, it demands a generous degree of pretension to pursue the initiator role.

These are interesting developments, but ambition is not sufficient to ensure effective and efficient policy dominance by Congress. Increased policy involvement by an expanding legislative population by no means implies integrated law making. In fact, without leadership, quite the reverse result may occur. In short, reactive efforts by a challenged institution to expand its functions—to "round its O"— may produce a highly diversified, even chaotic policy system.

One other piece of business must be attended to before we turn from the Nixon Congress to the Carter presidency. Gerald R. Ford became the president after Nixon's resignation. But Ford was a product of Congress, having served in the House for twenty-five years. More important, his legitimacy as president was traceable to his selection by a vote in Congress, not by a vote among the people. As Ford himself observed at his swearing-in:

> I am acutely aware that you, the voters, have not elected me as your President by your ballots . . . I have not sought this enormous responsibility, but I will not shirk it. Those who nominated and confirmed me as Vice President were my friends and are my friends. They were of both parties, elected by all the people, and acting under the Constitution in their name. It is only fitting, then, that I should pledge to them and to you that I will be President of all the people.[18]

What an extraordinary turnabout! The new president drew his approval from the very institution whose legitimacy had been challenged by his predecessor. Moreover, the Republican Ford was dependent on a Democratic Congress.

To summarize: President Nixon's challenge to the legitimacy and competency of Congress appears to have encouraged him to expand his policy organization and activities, and the Congress to do the same. With Nixon's resignation, a new president assumed office whose legitimacy was traceable to a majority vote in each house of Congress, further encouraging the legislature's ambition and growth. When Jimmy Carter came to Washington in 1977 he found a Congress in which many members had altered expectations about themselves and the presidency. As Samuel C. Patterson concludes in his recent review of Congress:

> Congress has great political power and an enormous capacity to frustrate the legislative ambitions of the President. . . . It tasted sovereignty during the exhilarating days of 1973 when it nearly removed a President, Richard Nixon, from office, and surely would have had he not resigned. We do not have congressional government in the United States in the sense that an omnipotent Congress makes all the laws, which the President and the executive branch merely enforce. Such a

[18] *Congressional Quarterly, Weekly Report*, August 17, 1975, p. 2211.

simplistic system never existed. But Congress is far more formidable as a political body today than it was in the more quiescent days of the 1950s and early 1960s. Congress is semi-sovereign.[19]

The Carter Presidency

In his most interesting paper on the political and institutional context of the Carter presidency, Bert A. Rockman identifies three cyclical phenomena of importance in analyzing a particular president—congressional activism or passivity, centralization or diffusion of presidential management, and "yearning for and disillusionment with leadership" among the public.[20] Rockman's views and the present analysis are complementary. His cycles are explained, in part, by interbranch evaluations and the reactions thereto.

How does Rockman see the Carter case? "It was Jimmy Carter's fate (and in some respects his initial appeal) to step into the presidency at a point during which the constraining elements of these cycles were at high tide."[21] In Rockman's terms, an activist Congress, a demand for more "openness" in presidential management, and public disillusionment with leadership combined to limit Carter's ability to maneuver.

These conclusions are consistent with the analysis provided in this essay. The activist Congress has been explained as a reaction to Nixon's challenges. The demand for a more diffused and open presidency follows congressional challenges to that office. The subsequent public disillusionment with national leadership can be understood in the light of these negative interbranch evaluations of legitimacy and competency during the 1970s.

What was required in 1977 for amicable and effective presidential-congressional relations? Having gotten ourselves into the situation described by Rockman, can we spot a way of getting back out again? In the abstract, it seems that the following conditions would improve the chances for reestablishing reliable connections between the separated partners:

[19] Samuel C. Patterson, "The Semi-Sovereign Congress," in Anthony King, ed., *The New American Political System* (Washington, D.C.: American Enterprise Institute, 1978), pp. 176-177.

[20] Bert A. Rockman, "Constants, Cycles, Trends, and Persona in Presidential Governance: Carter's Troubles Reviewed" (Paper delivered at the 1979 annual meeting of the American Political Science Association, Washington, D.C., August 31-September 3, 1979), p. 21.

[21] Ibid., p. 45.

Conditions in the Executive Branch

1. A president from the party that holds a majority in Congress.
2. A president familiar with and attuned to the changes in national politics and policies of the last decade.
3. A president appreciative of the inner workings of Congress—the important differences between the chambers, for example, or the operations of committees and subcommittees and their connections with the political party structure.
4. A White House staff equally sensitive to and appreciative of Congress and how it has changed.
5. Coherent presidential programs that are developed in cooperation or communication with appropriate congressional leaders.

Conditions in Congress

1. Party leadership familiar with and attuned to changes in national politics and policies of the last decade.
2. Party leadership willing to cooperate or communicate with the president and his staff in the development and promotion of programs.
3. Consolidation of the many reforms of the last decade so as to achieve the traditional functions of representation and law making.
4. Growth of electoral connections between the president and his party's members in Congress (such as perception by the members that the president's electoral success and theirs bear some relationship to each other).

While by no means exhaustive, this list offers useful general tests to apply to President Carter and the 95th Congress. On the presidential side it is apparent that the election of Jimmy Carter satisfied the first condition—he is a Democrat. He has also shown himself to be aware of the shifts in public mood over the last decade. His capabilities as a campaigner are considerable, as demonstrated in his winning the nomination and election. He has had less luck in building grass-roots support for his programs, but in general it can be said that Carter's election satisfies the second presidential condition too, a president who understands national change.

But President Carter came to Washington with a limited knowledge of the inner workings of Congress, "never having lived or served in the federal government in Washington." Moreover, the politics of accommodation and compromise so characteristic of the operations on the Hill somehow are unsatisfying to this engineer. What was second nature to Lyndon B. Johnson seems neither natural nor right to Jimmy Carter.

Substantial failure to meet the third condition need not be fatal to effective congressional-presidential relations. In fact, one might expect a president who admits his own unfamiliarity with Congress to surround himself with experts in legislative liaison. Not wishing to succumb to the Washington establishment, however, Carter chose instead to rely on those who had worked with him in the campaign and earlier when he had served as governor of Georgia.[22] As a consequence, congressional liaison from the White House was viewed by many on Capitol Hill with skepticism and even ridicule.

Meeting the fifth condition is highly unlikely if neither the third nor the fourth condition is satisfied. In recent years Carter and his aides have acknowledged the necessity of congressional contact in program development. Individuals with Hill savvy, such as William H. Cable, were added to the staff. But the communication and clearance with Congress so characteristic of other Democratic administrations have emerged slowly in the Carter administration.

On the congressional side, the change of party leaders in 1977 provided an unusual opportunity for the president. The new Speaker, Thomas P. "Tip" O'Neill (Democrat, Massachusetts) and the new majority leader in the Senate, Robert C. Byrd (Democrat, West Virginia) announced their willingness to cooperate with the new president. Both had served in congressional party positions previously—O'Neill as whip and majority leader, Byrd as caucus secretary and whip. Both had been involved in the turbulent issues and politics of the 1960s and 1970s. Thus, the first two congressional conditions for effective congressional-presidential relations, cooperative and aware party leaders, were satisfied as fully as at any time in recent history.

President Carter had it within his power to make the two leaders look good in Congress by consulting them, providing them with favors and support in their dealings with the membership, and relying on them as principal sources of information about the mood and interests of the membership. As new leaders themselves, they were naturally anxious to look good before their own party colleagues. And, of course, their effectiveness with the House and Senate Democrats was important to the success of the president's program. Unquestionably, a new partnership could have been forged in the 95th Congress between the president and the party leaders in Congress.

---

22 It is not unusual for a president to appoint his closest advisers from among those who have worked with him in campaigns or previous public positions. However, since most presidents have previously served in Washington, they can draw from a cadre of persons familiar with Congress.

Far from making them look good, President Carter and his staff seemed intent at first on making congressional leaders look bad. The president pressed for decisions like the reduction of water projects that were bound to cause problems for Democratic leaders. He sometimes ignored the courtesy of informing members about appointments within their states or districts. He formulated a major energy program with little or no consultation with the party and committee leaders who would have to manage it through Congress—and then announced it to the people first, the Congress second. He altered proposals, or dropped them altogether (the fifty-dollar rebate, for example)—sometimes after leaders had already committed themselves and their resources to enactment. Byrd and O'Neill consolidated their leadership positions during the first year of the Carter administration. But essentially they did it on their own, often in spite of the problems created for them by the president. Thus, they owed no particular allegiance to the president. It was, in fact, quite remarkable that they remained as outwardly loyal to the president as they did during this first troubled year.[23]

The third and fourth congressional conditions, consolidation of reforms and growth of electoral connections, were not met to any substantial degree. Congress is, even now, in the process of consolidating the reforms of the last decade. It is still not altogether clear what the full range of their effects will be. Subcommittees have more staff and have increased their functions in the policy process. Members too have more staff, and many have expanded their legislative activities. In some cases, committee chairmen play a different role than before—perhaps a more managerial or brokerage role. The reforms seem to have embroiled members in comprehensive budget games. And party leaders have increased responsibilities—particularly in the House. The reforms appear to have expanded, but not shaped, congressional participation in the policy process. In a recent essay, Samuel H. Beer speaks of "equilibrium without purpose" in discussing our lack of a public philosophy in the post–New Deal era.[24] Up to

---

[23] For a review of this first year see *Congressional Quarterly, Weekly Report,* December 24, 1977, pp. 2637-2642. President Carter's presidential support scores in Congress for the first three years of his administration were closer to those of Nixon than to those of either Kennedy or Johnson. The average presidential support scores for the first three years after election were: Eisenhower, 82 percent; Kennedy, 84.5 percent; Johnson, 84 percent; Nixon, 75 percent; and Carter, 77 percent. *Congressional Quarterly, Weekly Report,* January 12, 1980, p. 91. See the analysis by George Edwards on what presidential support scores reveal and hide: *Presidential Influence in Congress* (San Francisco: Freeman, 1980), chap. 7.

[24] Samuel H. Beer, "In Search of a New Public Philosophy," in King, *New American Political System,* p. 44.

now, congressional reforms appear to have dispersed policy influence and leadership without a clearly defined purpose in doing so.

The fourth condition assumes that a vital link is necessary between the processes by which the president and Congress come to be in Washington. This connection has never been strong. The framers of the Constitution did not intend it to be—indeed they rejected the direct link of having the president selected by Congress. But there have been times in the recent past when members of Congress had reason to believe that their electoral fate was positively connected to that of the president. The Johnson landslide of 1964 is the principal case in point. The first two years of the Johnson administration were among the most productive of domestic legislation in history.

In the 1976 election, Jimmy Carter won the presidency by a very narrow margin (50.1 percent of the total vote). Meanwhile, Democratic candidates for the House polled 56.2 percent of the total vote. They led the president in every region—by 5.3 percentage points in the East, 8.3 points in the South, 4 points in the Midwest, and 9 points in the West. Senate Democratic candidates also outpolled the president (54.4 percent to 50.1 percent). In two cases Carter ran behind Senate Democratic incumbents who were defeated, and he lost all five of the states in which Senate Democratic incumbents were defeated.[25] Small wonder that, in the words of a Washington journalist, "the members think that what happens to the president doesn't happen to them as members of Congress."[26] A member of Congress put it this way: "The relationship between the President and Congress is partly a result of how well the President is doing politically. Congress is better behaved when he does well. . . . Right now, it's almost as if Congress is not paying attention to him."[27]

One does not get a very encouraging picture of the prospects for productive congressional-presidential relationships from this brief review. It should be noted, however, that the conditions I have described are demanding. They reflect the changes in both institutions—a more dependent presidency and a more independent Congress—and taken together they allow, perhaps, less room for miscalculation than there was in the past. As Eric L. Davis rightly observes: "If Carter and

[25] Data taken from Congressional Quarterly, Weekly Report, March 10, 1977, pp. 488-489.

[26] Taken from an interview for the author's paper entitled, "Can Our Parties Survive Our Politics?" prepared for a conference on "The Role of the Legislature in Western Democracies," Selsdon Park, England, April 20-22, 1979.

[27] Statement by Representative Richard B. Cheney (Republican, Wyoming), a former White House staff aide, in Richard E. Cohen, "The President's Problems," in Thomas E. Cronin, ed., The Carter Presidency Under Pressure (Washington, D.C.: National Journal Reprint Series, 1979), p. 35.

his associates were to attempt to replicate their predecessors' approaches to legislative relations, they would be using an entirely inappropriate set of strategies and tactics."[28] So the challenge to any new president in 1977 was considerable; for Jimmy Carter it was monumental.

In summary, in 1977 the occupant of the White House was an intelligent and socially aware Democrat without either Washington experience or any apparent interest in acquiring it. At the other end of Pennsylvania Avenue was a Congress with able but uncertain leadership seeking to consolidate a plethora of democratizing internal reforms. More bluntly, a dependent president, demonstrating artless policy behavior, faced an independent Congress, anxious to assume a pretentious policy-making role.

How does each evaluate the other? Again, only the most general review will be attempted here. Neither set of actors—presidential or congressional—seriously questions the institutional legitimacy of the other set. To be sure, there are individual cases where both are charged with having exceeded their authority, but no more perhaps than in other administrations before Nixon. For the most part the evaluations are positive on the legitimacy test.

The same cannot be said for the competency test, however. The president seems to have had to learn about the capabilities of individual members, the committees and subcommittees, and the institution as a whole. By his own admission, he has "got a growing understanding of Congress." Carter appeared to rely on his experience in Georgia in evaluating congressional competence, and generalizing from this experience did not help him establish workable relationships with Congress.

Meanwhile, many members of Congress believe that the reforms of the past decade have increased their competence—not only to perform the traditional functions of representing constituents and participating actively in law making, but to expand their involvement to program development and evaluation, foreign and domestic. Thus, it was particularly unfortunate that this Congress faced a president less able than most to appreciate the increased self-confidence on Capitol Hill. No doubt we all have experienced similar deflations—failing to have an accomplishment applauded, understood, appreciated,

---

[28] Quoted in Dom Bonafede, "The Tough Job of Normalizing Relations with Capitol Hill," in Cronin, *Carter Presidency*, p. 37. Amitai Etzioni agrees with this point, noting that "all the talk about a return to a LBJ-mastery of Congress disregards both the unconstitutional nature of a domination by the executive, and that forces in Congress, more than in the White House, make such a return quite impossible." "The Lack of Leadership: We Found It In Us," *National Journal*, vol. 12 (February 23, 1980), p. 335.

or even acknowledged by a person who counts. It should not be difficult for one who has had such an experience to understand how disappointed some members of Congress were with the new president.

Negative evaluations of competency, like negative assessments of legitimacy, prompt the challenged institution to return the insult. Further, each appraisal has its most important effect on those who do the evaluating. Carter's hesitancy about the capabilities of Congress led him to formulate programs within his own family of advisers, and then to assume they would be enacted because they were intelligently or logically drafted (assigning to Congress the reserved partner role).[29] However, this very approach confirmed for many members of Congress that Carter himself lacked the capacity to lead. The president's failure to acknowledge the growth of Congress's ambitions and capabilities in the area of policy formation showed a lack of political judgment on his part, according to some. Lack of political judgment is as serious an indictment as can be made of a politician's competence. How should one expect members of Congress to react under these circumstances? It was predictable that many would seek to outdo the president. This solution is not a very firm foundation for amicable presidential-congressional relations. Thus, one found commentators making assessments like these:

> In the battery of attacks President Carter has received recently from Congress, one conclusion stands out: There is a massive gap in communication and coordination between the White House and Congress and nothing short of a Carter reelection is likely to heal the breach.[30]

> With the 96th Congress scheduled to convene January 15, President Carter may find it easier to normalize relations with 900 million Chinese than to establish harmonious operations on Capitol Hill.[31]

The Carter administration may prove to have been an interesting interregnum between what the presidency was before the thunderbolt of the Nixon challenges and what it will become in the future. Perhaps a Carter was inevitable after the events of the mid-1970s. It does seem apparent that a weakened presidency was desired by many.

---

[29] Another view might be that Carter's engineering background led him to be cautious about consulting members of Congress since their politics would upset his carefully developed (engineered) plans. I am indebted to Bert A. Rockman for this observation.

[30] Cohen, "The President's Problems," p. 35.

[31] Bonafede, "The Tough Job of Normalizing Relations with Capitol Hill," p. 36. For a more sympathetic evaluation of the Carter administration from one who worked in it, see Etzioni, *National Journal* (February 23, 1980), pp. 334-337.

Carter was attractive to those desiring a weak presidency in large part because of his unfamiliarity with the Washington scene. But Carter's narrow victory at the polls in 1976 was by no means inevitable. What if Gerald Ford had won? He, too, would have been constrained in his exercise of the office. But the checks would have been more political, less personal. Ford would have had to cope with large Democratic majorities in both houses of Congress, and a quite different congressional-presidential relationship could have been expected.

What about the Future?

In his eloquent essay on the parliamentary system of government, Ernest Barker specified the conditions he regarded as essential to effective government in a free society. He said:

> How do men act—or rather, how do they plan and determine their action . . . ? The answer is that they "get together." They pool their minds: each puts forward his point of view, and all discuss and compare their different points of view. That . . . is what happens everywhere, in any living, reasoning, free society. It happened in tribal gatherings and folkmoots, thousands of years ago; and it happens still today. That is parliament, or "parley": that is the use of "the Word", which, as the Evangelist tells us, "was in the beginning," and which . . . will be with us to all eternity. But no parley or use of the Word, stops short at mere parley or words. . . . We seek by all our talk, and by all our comparison of points of view, to discover a common point of view which will satisfy us all, and on which we can all agree to act. . . . Our search is a search for the common—for a *modus convivendi*—for what the politicians call a "compromise". . . . It is not an easy thing to do. Individual reason, partial views, and sectional interests, are all very obstinate things. The common reason which is the common freedom of the whole society may be a fine elixir and a precious concord of minds: but it is not easily distilled, or readily crystallized. Yet the common reason has to be found, however difficult the finding may be, and it has to be found by a process of common thought. Either that—or you submit yourself, passive and unreasoning, to the dominion of a single section of the dictatorship of a single man. There is no other way. And if you submit yourself, passive and unreasoning, your society ceases to be a free society. . . . Any society, to be worthy of the name, must consist of *partners*, who enjoy a say in the affairs of the society. When a society ceases to be that, it

ceases to be a society! It becomes a mere heap of the leader and his followers—followers strung together, like so many dead birds on a string, by the compulsion of leadership.[32]

This statement serves the dual purposes of reminding us of what must be preserved and warning us of the consequences of failing to preserve it. The Nixon-Watergate interlude did not exactly produce "a mere heap of the leader and his followers," but it is fair to say that it contributed to conditions that directed us away from, not toward, partnership in governing.

"Congress is supposed to represent the voters, and if our assembly does not work with the chief executive, the battle for democracy is lost before a shot is fired."[33] The constitutional structure creates special demands on the American partnership. Any union or "search for the common" will be influenced by structure. In Britain, the process is facilitated by the party system, particularly when one party can command a majority in the House of Commons. In the United States, however, separate elections create special requirements if a partnership between executive and legislature is to develop and be maintained. The most severe test comes when the voters select a president, like Nixon, of one party to serve with a Congress in which the other party has a majority; at the opposite extreme, conditions are most propitious for partnership when a majority party leader in Congress—a Lyndon Johnson—is elected president. Party has the potential to facilitate the partnership between the branches in the United States. Its decline, therefore, takes on special significance for the topic under discussion.

Barker acknowledges that finding the "common reason" is "not an easy thing to do" under the best of circumstances, and it requires special patience and talent in the American constitutional setting. Because of the lack of formal or structural ties between the branches, the mutual evaluations discussed in this chapter take on added significance. What appears to have happened in the 1970s is that both the presidency and the Congress have lost any clear or realistic picture of how each can or should participate in the national policy process. Creating a new partnership will not be possible until the two groups share common expectations about what each can do well. If, to paraphrase Senator Muskie, Congress tries to do the work of the president and the president tries to do Congress's work, both will fail.

[32] Barker, *Essays in Government*, pp. 67-68.
[33] E. Pendleton Herring, *Presidential Leadership* (New York: Rinehart, 1940), p. 45.

So a first order of business is for the leadership on both sides to recognize the attitudinal and structural effects of these turbulent times and to reevaluate the strengths and weaknesses of their present circumstances. What do we want a president to do? What do we want a Congress to be? Until these questions are treated in a serious and comprehensive manner, the kind of active, vibrant, and productive partnership Barker describes will be far off.

The debate on these questions cannot proceed as though the last fifteen years had never happened. Changes have occurred which must influence the analysis and expectations of each branch. For example, the expansion of congressional and presidential staffs, much of it designed to counter the perceived inadequacies of other institutions, is now an integral part of each institution. The faces will change but the positions will not disappear. The question is not, Will these staffs continue to be there? They most assuredly will. It is rather, What will they be doing? Even more important is the question, How will the president and members of Congress use or relate to these new bureaucracies?

James S. Young describes our traditional accommodation between presidential and constitutional government as follows:

> We kept alive our constitutional system and the slow-moving pluralistic politics that go along with it, while building a contingency system around the Presidency, able to act alone and fast to provide disaster prevention and relief. We sustained these two different kinds of government while avoiding a head-on collision between them.[34]

According to Young, "the Nixon Administration witnessed an historic confrontation" between presidentialism and constitutionalism. I have argued that the Nixon administration directly challenged the legitimacy of other, constitutionally ordered institutions on the way to consolidating policy activities in the White House. Fred Greenstein believes that "today's presidency is an institution in search of new role definitions."[35] Young agrees. He recommends "retrenching presidential power in order to preserve it . . . winding down presidential government in order to save the presidency, for the things only it can do."[36] I am taken with this idea as applicable both to the presidency and to Congress. Both institutional populations have expanded the scope and concept of their functions in the policy process. As a

[34] James S. Young, "The Troubled Presidency: II," *New York Times,* December 7, 1978, p. 23.

[35] Fred I. Greenstein, "Change and Continuity in the Modern Presidency," in King, *New American Political System,* p. 83.

[36] Young, "The Troubled Presidency: II," p. 23.

consequence, the elected officials in charge of each institution are in danger of playing a reduced role in the political system. Their efforts to do it all have resulted in an expanded technical staff that now threatens to overshadow, perhaps overwhelm, the president and the members of Congress. Young argues that "White House efforts to presidentialize the bureaucracy . . . only end up bureaucratizing the presidency."[37] Very much the same thing can be said about Congress, though the two bureaucracies—administrative and legislative—are quite different in structure, style, and outlook.

But the deed is done—the expansions of the White House and Capitol Hill staffs have taken place. I do not believe that they now can simply be reduced. Presidential and congressional staff positions are more than jobs. They come to be the connecting tissue among elected public officials, between them and the bureaucracy, and between them and private interests. These staffs also serve as an institutional memory for the many commitments made in the name of public officials. Let us, therefore, accept their existence, and the likelihood that they will continue to exist and grow.

The more important matter is finding what it is that the president and members of Congress can do effectively in this new environment. Each must decide what it can do well, so that this vast new technical staff apparatus can be shaped accordingly. Each branch's attempts to do everything probably hasten the day when elected officials will be no more than honorary resident managers of an ever-expanding group of technicians.

Young believes that "to recapture that tenuous harmony between constitutionalism and presidentialism" the president must assume a special, very public, leadership role.

> It means getting the Presidency substantially out of the business of managing the executive branch: ceding large parts of that domain to Congress, courts, and Cabinet, but not ceding the President's power to pre-empt or intervene when reasons of state require. It means putting distance between the Presidency and the permanent government in Washington—distance enough to enable a President to watch the Government as the outsider he really is, to know when it is getting the country into serious trouble and when it isn't, to know when to step in and when to stay out.
>
> It also means regaining the ability, within the Presidency at least, to distinguish between true and pseudo crises, real alarms and false ones, threats to the Republic and mere problems for the Administration. . . .[38]

[37] Ibid.
[38] Ibid.

According to Young, this "statecraft" requires "reconstituting the institutionalized Presidency" to curb its tendency to expand the scope of the president's activities. Young does not submit to the temptation of recommending a reduction in the institutional paraphernalia of the presidency. Rather, he is interested in more clearly specifying the president's responsibilities—as he puts it, "retrenching Presidential power in order to preserve it." In this spirit, Young proposes that the president make the rest of the government—Congress and the bureaucracy—"come up with solutions to pressing public problems."

Of course, this reversal of aggrandizement, or encroachment, is easier prescribed than realized. It obviously depends to a considerable extent on how the incumbent views the job. What is called for is a president who respects the legitimacy and competency of the national government in Washington. This simple requirement must be met, it would seem, before the president can expect to make the system work for him and the nation.

I have started with the president because he remains so vital for directing and influencing the work of Congress and the bureaucracy. Just as both resonated to the vibrations of disdain and distrust in the Nixon and Carter administrations, so we may expect them to react positively to an administration supportive of their capabilities. The president can stimulate, if not totally manage, the rest of the policy system.

But just as the government is "too big, too complex, and too pervasive in its influence" for the president "to direct the details of its important and critical programming,"[39] it is also too big for the members of Congress to command fully. It seems clear, to paraphrase Greenstein, that today's Congress is an institution in search of new role definitions. Much of Young's analysis of the president applies as well to members of Congress. They may have to retrench in order to preserve, to wind down (or at least redefine) in order to save themselves for what they can do well.

The traditional functions of Congress in the policy process have been representing interests, serving constituents, and finding bases for compromise, albeit with notable differences in style and organization between the House and Senate. Staff increases have made Congress better able to accomplish the first two functions, not the third. But, as table 8–1 suggests, the really important development is that the reforms of the last decade, including staff increases, have encouraged the members of Congress to expand their functions to those less suited to legislative organization, such as program development, coordination, and evaluation, all of which are associated with the initi-

[39] Statement by Dwight D. Eisenhower, quoted in Greenstein, "Change and Continuity in the Modern Presidency," p. 84.

ator role. However justifiable the changes were as a counterforce to Nixon's presidential performance, their consequence is an over-extended Congress.

A change of presidents can accomplish the kind of transformation Young speaks of. It is not so simple for Congress to reorient itself. Bicameralism, limited leadership, complex committee organization, and a high return of incumbents constrain its capacity to adjust quickly. It seems apparent, however, that members must reevaluate what it is they want Congress to do. I argue that party and committee leaders in each house must develop means for taking charge of their own organization and processes. It is particularly important that leaders direct the work of the committee and research support staffs (such as the Congressional Budget Office, the Office of Technology Assessment, and the Congressional Research Service).

I am not proposing the reduction or elimination of staff. Rather, I am stressing the need for congressional leaders to emulate Young's revitalized president by reducing the policy functions of the staff so that Congress can recapture its proper political role. How can that happen in our Congress? It probably will not happen unless the presidency changes along the lines suggested by Young. Congress probably will try to broaden its policy-making role as long as the president fails to command the presidency.

"Any society, to be worthy of the name, must consist of *partners....*" The framers of our Constitution created a structure that tests our capacity to form a partnership between the legislature and the executive. In the Nixon period each branch sought to go it alone. So extensive were the consequences that a return to former times is not realistic. Nixon did give us a new kind of government in Washington! But partnership still is possible—if it is adapted to the important structural changes of the last decade. The way to start may well be to reestablish trust and respect between the president and Congress. A change in attitudes, not further organizational reform, is what is now required.

8

The Local Roots of Domestic Policy

R. Douglas Arnold

Congress and Local Politics

Members of Congress are inevitably caught in a crossfire of competing expectations. They are national legislators, charged with such exalted goals as furthering the national interest, providing for the common defense, and promoting the general welfare. They are also local representatives, elected by and accountable to narrow geographic constituencies, and held responsible for protecting and advancing myriad local interests. Most policy debates in Congress reflect both forces. They are simultaneously battles between legislators with conflicting conceptions of the national interest, and struggles among the defenders of divergent local interests.

Nowhere is this duality more evident than when Congress decides how to spend the government's nearly one-quarter share of the national output. Spending decisions represent fundamental political choices about the ends government should serve, and legislators debate them with the seriousness such fundamental choices demand, examining not only the propriety of government's pursuing particular ends but also their relative priority, given competing ends and scarce resources. But spending decisions are also choices about means toward various ends, and legislators devote enormous energy to examining these alternative means. Here the question is not only which solution will best contribute to a particular end, but also how various alternatives might affect each legislator's constituency. When spending is on the agenda, so is the question of *where* all those dollars will be spent.

I am indebted to Martha Derthick, Fred Greenstein, Stanley Kelley, and Richard Nathan for their careful critiques of an earlier draft of this essay.

Congressmen are presumed to have an intense interest in how federal funds are allocated—and in how much flows into their districts. What effect does this quest for local benefits have on the way Congress makes public policy? Does it distort policy choices from the very beginning, forcing Congress to pursue aberrant or inconsistent ends or to adopt inappropriate means? Or do congressmen succeed in separating their wish for a share of the spending from their evaluation of programs and policies? In this chapter I attempt to determine just what imprint the congressional quest for local benefits leaves on national policy.

Congressmen are perfectly capable of putting aside their interest in local benefits and focusing exclusively on a program's national benefits. Examples abound. Sometimes, however, their preoccupation with local benefits becomes so great that it overpowers any serious consideration of a program's more general costs and benefits. What determines whether and, if so, how extensively the quest for local benefits affects the shape of public policy? I argue in this chapter that it depends on (1) the nature of the policy alternatives, (2) how they are presented to Congress for decision, and (3) the composition of the constituency and interest group forces pushing congressmen in various directions. Finally, I explain how the impact of the quest for local benefits has changed during the past two decades and how these changes can be traced to variations in the three factors just mentioned.

The Quest for Local Benefits. It is easy to understand why congressmen crave shares of federal spending for their districts. Most communities enjoy having outside money spent in their midst, whether by corporations, universities, or governments, because it stimulates the local economy and generates employment. Granted, not all forms of spending are equally attractive; some impose considerable local costs. Oil refineries, chemical plants, and nuclear reactors, for example, are sometimes unwelcome. Most forms of federal spending, however, are relatively "clean" and do not belong in this class.

Many congressmen would support their communities' claims for shares of federal spending simply because they believe this is what good representatives should do. But this belief hardly explains the intensity of their commitment to procuring local benefits or their willingness to devote so much of their time and resources to this end. Probably the best explanation is that obtaining benefits produces electoral payoffs, or so it is thought.[1] The causal links between local

[1] David R. Mayhew, *Congress: The Electoral Connection* (New Haven: Yale University Press, 1974), pp. 52-61.

251

benefits and elections are two. First, the direct beneficiaries of federal spending may reward a congressman for his help with their votes, campaign contributions, and organizational support. These last two are particularly likely to come from corporate and union leaders, both because they are in a position to know precisely what a legislator has done for them and because they have the means to show their gratitude lavishly. Second, a skilled congressman can use local benefits to generate favorable publicity for himself, reaching the less attentive public. The expectation is that voters will appreciate his good deeds even if they enjoy no direct benefits themselves.

How does an assembly of legislators, all craving local benefits, make public policy? This question has sparked much debate among those interested in public choice.[2] If acquiring local benefits were their *only* goal, the legislature would surely be in trouble, for the members' interests would be in direct opposition, and intense conflict would almost be inevitable. A majority might divide up the benefits among themselves, denying any to the minority, or an endless succession of majorities might form and dissolve as benefit packages were introduced, overthrown, and replaced. But the reality of congressional politics is more complex. Congressmen are not single-minded seekers of local benefits, struggling feverishly to win every last dollar for their districts. However important the quest for local benefits may be, it is always tempered by other, competing concerns.

Evaluating Spending Programs. When congressmen evaluate programs they consider how funds will be distributed among their districts. But what else do they consider? What other attributes of programs affect their judgments? In general, one would expect them to evaluate the costs and benefits. Spending programs provide a whole series of benefits: to the direct beneficiaries, to the bureaucrats, corporations, and workers who help deliver services, to the localities where beneficiaries and service-deliverers reside, and (perhaps) to citizens generally. The same programs also impose costs: on those who pay taxes to support government spending, on those who would be better off without government involvement in certain spheres of activity, and (perhaps) on society at large. Here, for simplicity, I assume that congressmen evaluate three classes of costs and benefits.

[2] James M. Buchanan and Gordon Tullock, *The Calculus of Consent* (Ann Arbor: University of Michigan Press, 1962), pp. 135-145; Brian Barry, *Political Argument* (London: Routledge and Kegan Paul, 1965), pp. 250-256; Morris P. Fiorina, "Legislative Facilitation of Government Growth" (Paper presented at the conference on the causes and consequences of public sector growth, Dorado Beach, Puerto Rico, November 1978).

First, they evaluate a program's *general* costs and benefits. Such benefits include national security, economic growth, increased literacy, improved public health, and other collective goods that people value because they believe everyone profits, including themselves. Although many people value these public ends, they do not necessarily agree on their relative priority, on what costs should be incurred in their pursuit, or even on which are the federal government's responsibility. Congressmen usually divide on these issues. When they divide systematically we speak of their divergent philosophies of government or ideologies.

Second, congressmen evaluate the costs and benefits for *groups*. No matter how well a program serves the national interest, it also affects the interests of readily identifiable groups—teachers, airplane manufacturers, construction workers, oil companies, consultants, bankers, and so on. Some groups receive sizable benefits (as service-providers), others bear disproportionate costs. All have an important stake not only in the ends of government spending but also in the means. With the well-being of such groups dependent on government decisions, congressmen naturally consider *who* benefits (both directly and indirectly) when they evaluate alternative spending programs.

Third, congressmen evaluate the costs and benefits for *localities*. The eventual impact of local benefits on congressional policy making depends crucially on how congressmen evaluate both the general and group costs and benefits associated with particular programs. Local benefits become paramount when congressmen believe that a program would have few general or group benefits, or considerable costs of either type. In contrast, the impact of local benefits is minimal when congressmen value highly a program's general or group benefits.

A few examples make the distinctions clear. Most congressmen support enthusiastically the vast federal programs for medical research. The question of where medical research funds will be spent seldom enters the debate, presumably because congressmen and their constituents value the general benefits that flow from medical advances. Similarly, congressmen support the national park system or national defense, regardless of whether money is spent in their districts. For other programs, such as public works projects, that provide few general benefits, the question of where funds will be spent predominates. Still other programs survive neither on their general benefits nor on their local benefits, but rather on the benefits provided to organized groups. Congressmen vigorously support the veterans' hospital program, whether or not they have hospitals in their districts. The existence of large, well-organized veterans' groups encourages such support and makes unnecessary the strategic allocation of the hospitals themselves. The general point is clear. The importance of local benefits in congressional consideration of a spending program depends on what other types of benefits the program provides and on how congressmen perceive them.

Organized interest groups have long represented some of the recipients of group benefits. More recently, however, public interest groups championing a wide range of causes with general benefits have proliferated, as have groups with a primary interest in how local benefits are allocated. The latter include organizations of mayors, governors, and county officials, as well as various regional federations that heighten competition between frostbelt and sunbelt. The activities of these three types of groups affect how congressmen evaluate the various benefits associated with a program and, as I will show, affect the importance of local benefits in congressional decision making.

The Allocational Process. How deep an imprint the quest for local benefits leaves on public policy also depends on the *process* by which local benefits are allocated. The likelihood that it will be deep is greatest when Congress itself allocates the benefits to localities and does so concurrently with the basic policy choices that shape the program. The likelihood is less when allocational and policy decisions are separated in time or made by different institutions, as when Congress outlines the policy and bureaucrats allocate the benefits.

Congress itself decides when, where, and how allocational decisions are to be made. But its options are limited both by tradition and by the simple fact that no legislature could possibly make all such decisions itself. The options available to Congress are three: congressional allocation on a project basis, allocation by formula, and allocation by delegation of authority to bureaucrats. All three methods are currently used.

In the following sections I examine how Congress handles actual spending programs, searching always for the local roots of national policy. I trace explanations for basic policy choices back to congressmen's local political needs, with variations in their impact accounted for by the combined effects of interest groups, allocational processes, and the relative attractiveness of other programmatic benefits. The analysis is organized according to how allocational decisions are made because these differences in process affect powerfully the way other factors influence policy choice.

A federal system allows the national government to attack problems by two routes. It can design and implement programs completely at the national level, or it can provide state and local governments with financial assistance for specific purposes. Since direct federal spending and intergovernmental assistance require very different means for allocating local benefits, I examine them separately.

Nowhere do I examine the vast programs of transfer payments to individuals. Some of these involve direct federal spending (social security, Medicare), and some are administered as grant programs (public assistance, Medicaid). I steer clear of these programs because their political logic is fundamentally different. Competition for local benefits does not dominate the stage, for there are no geographically specific benefits to be assigned. The central political questions revolve around the scope of benefits, eligibility criteria, and program administration. As entitlement programs, they provide benefits to individuals without regard to where they are located. Thus, there are no local benefits for which congressmen can claim credit.

Direct Federal Spending

Allocational decisions for direct federal spending include choices about where federal employees will work, where to build such federal facilities as military installations, office buildings, dams, and laboratories, and where to award procurement and other contracts. Although such decisions can be made either by Congress or by the bureaucracy, it should come as no surprise that Congress has retained for itself the fun of dispensing benefits with exceptional local payoffs and has granted to bureaucrats the task of allocating less valuable commodities.

Congress and Water Projects. Nowhere has Congress's hold on allocational decisions endured longer than in the area of federal water projects—the dredging of harbors and taming of streams.[3] If recent battles between Congress and President Carter are any indication, the system is unlikely to change. Federal funding began innocently enough, for there were obvious general benefits in most early water projects. Relatively small investments in the development of harbors and navigable rivers promised (and delivered) dramatic benefits, as decreased transportation costs stimulated foreign and domestic trade and encouraged economic expansion and national growth.

Looking back it is easy to see that the total general benefits of many early projects exceeded their total general costs by a wide margin. This happy result owed much to chance, for the allocational system itself was not designed to measure and compare in any systematic fashion the general costs and benefits of water projects. The

[3] Arthur Maass, *Muddy Waters* (Cambridge: Harvard University Press, 1951); John Ferejohn, *Pork Barrel Politics* (Stanford, Calif.: Stanford University Press, 1974).

system ran on local initiative. The impetus was local benefits. Civic boosters and those with a direct, sizable interest in inexpensive water transportation agitated for federal projects in their localities. Individual congressmen then championed these local projects and worked to obtain congressional approval and funds. Individual projects clearly served the interests of both constituents and representatives. Local advocates prospered because rich Uncle Sam paid all the bills for projects that concentrated local benefits on them, and congressmen could bask in the glory that grateful beneficiaries bestowed upon them. In the beginning, the general benefits usually exceeded costs because most areas proposed relatively simple projects—removing a sand bar here, straightening a channel there—for which small investments could return immense dividends in improved transportation.

Later, when most simple projects had already been undertaken, local advocates proposed ever more complex schemes: moving mountains, connecting rivers that had always chosen separate paths to the sea, and transforming simple streams into major waterways. The logic at the local level was unchanged, for as long as the federal government was paying the tab, the local advantage was clear. The logic at the national level, however, was not as compelling, for the total general costs of many projects exceeded their projected general benefits, at least as calculated by today's accepted methods of cost-benefit analysis.

Why would Congress continue to approve projects of dubious worth? One possibility is that representatives were ignorant of the true costs and benefits. Evaluating the flow of costs and benefits over time is no easy task, particularly since local advocates had every incentive to emphasize the benefits and minimize the costs. Although this explanation may once have been valid, it is less persuasive today when presidents, economists, and others have done everything possible to make the case against projects with little merit. Yet Congress continues to approve them with undiminished enthusiasm.

It is easy to see why. Each project provides both sizable group benefits (to waterway users and to industries favored with lower transportation costs) and abundant local benefits (economic stimuli and employment). These benefits are visible, concentrated, and easily traceable to a congressman's actions, so that voters and group beneficiaries know precisely whom to reward. The costs, on the other hand, are borne by millions of anonymous taxpayers, who have little incentive to organize in opposition because each pays but a few dollars for all water projects. The costs are dispersed among the many, and not easily traceable to actions for which individual congressmen could be blamed. Except in wartime, congressmen have long been spared having to vote for tax increases, thanks to an elastic tax system and their willingness to accept persistent deficits.

The whole system is glued together with all-inclusive allocational criteria, so that over time practically every congressman can receive a share of the action. Districts for which navigation projects are unsuitable often find happiness with projects that control floods. Only the most arid districts are ineligible for either, and they profit from yet another program, administered by the Bureau of Reclamation, whose goal is to rearrange water supplies and make deserts bloom. When it comes to water, there is truly something for everyone. Allocational decision making is concentrated in the Public Works and Appropriations committees. This perpetuates the policy of inclusiveness. Although there is some evidence that committee members are especially generous with their own districts, their generosity is not boundless, and it deprives others of little.[4] Actually the committees *must* treat others fairly if they seek to maintain those huge congressional majorities that allow them to overpower presidents who occasionally veto public works bills. Since all are included, the system survives and continues to create enormous local political capital for congressmen at surprisingly low political cost.

Congress has long been vigilant in protecting this system from those who are blind to its virtues. In 1877 the House responded to the "excessive economy mindedness" of its own Appropriations Committee by stripping it of any authority over water projects and giving a more sympathetic legislative committee (Rivers and Harbors) the right to handle both authorizations and appropriations.[5] (Jurisdiction over water projects was returned to Appropriations in 1920; the committee has since looked elsewhere for economies.) More recently, since 1936, Congress has required a favorable cost-benefit analysis of all water projects before congressional funding. Although this change may appear fiscally conservative, its implementation suggests the opposite. Congress gave the job of performing the cost-benefit analysis to the same agency, the Army Corps of Engineers, that administers the program—hardly a disinterested party! Furthermore, both Congress and the corps have sanctioned methods that allow creative accounting of benefits, conservative estimates of costs, and a discount rate that pretends (through grandfather clauses) that money can be borrowed as cheaply today as a few decades ago.[6] These deviations from accepted methods of analysis can dramatically affect

4 Ferejohn, *Pork Barrel Politics*, pp. 129-232.
5 Richard F. Fenno, Jr., *The Power of the Purse* (Boston: Little, Brown, 1966), pp. 43-44.
6 Ferejohn, *Pork Barrel Politics*, pp. 42-46.

the results. The corps argues that the $1.7 billion attempt to connect the Tennessee River to the Gulf of Mexico via Alabama (providing an alternative to the centuries old, natural route down the Mississippi) will yield $1.20 for every $1.00 invested. But two economists with no obvious interest at stake estimate a return of only thirty-nine cents on the dollar.[7] The corps's analyses are equally suspect in many other cases. Their value to Congress, however, is to legitimate the illegitimate, and at that they are superb.

National policy on waterways and flood control does not emerge from any debate about how extensive a water transportation system the nation should build or how much we should spend protecting those who chose to settle on known flood plains. Questions about general costs and benefits are seldom raised. Instead policy bubbles up from the bottom. It is principally an amalgamation of what groups and localities request, and thus it serves waterway users and entrepreneurial localities more than the national interest. Although one can imagine good national policy emerging from such a process, in the case of water projects it clearly does not.

Three consequences devolve from this system. First, as I have already argued, the nation invests billions in projects for which the benefits are unlikely to equal the costs. Second, the federal government probably overspends on water projects relative to competing needs for which the political logic is less compelling. Third, although the nation has developed one of the finest water transportation systems in the world, this accomplishment has contributed to the deterioration of its rail system. Taxpaying railroads that must find credit at market rates cannot compete with waterways built and maintained at public expense and for which no taxes are paid—any more than they can compete with federally subsidized highways.

The prospects for reforming the way Congress formulates national policy on waterways development are not encouraging. The system endures because so many congressmen value highly the benefits it produces. When anyone attacks either the system or the projects it selects, congressmen stand united to defend it, as if some fundamental congressional right were threatened. The basic problem is that few individuals see profit for themselves in leading opposing coalitions. Presidents occasionally lash out against it with a veto (cheerily overridden by Congress), but they seldom invest much in sustained battles. No doubt they prefer conserving their political capital and good will for more important issues. (The whole program expends less than $3 billion annually.) President Carter, who declared war on

[7] Alvin M. Josephy, Jr., "The South's Unstoppable Waterway," *Fortune* (August 27, 1979), p. 81.

some of the most outrageous projects in his first year, is the exception. Although he scored a few hits, the initiative poisoned congressional relations for a considerable period, and it is unlikely that Carter or his successors will try again soon. Within Congress, those opposed to the system are expected to remain quiet. Recently Robert Edgar (Democrat, Pennsylvania) proposed an amendment to delete funding for the Stonewall Jackson dam in neighboring West Virginia. Not only was his amendment shouted down, but the incident prompted a colleague to propose a "Pinocchio Award" for those who could not keep their noses out of other people's business.[8] The system frowns menacingly at those who think federal tax money wasted in other districts is of common concern.

The allocation of rivers and harbors projects is not typical. The closest parallel is the companion program, administered by the Bureau of Reclamation, that spends just under a billion dollars annually creating water supply systems for the arid West.[9] But precisely because they are an extreme case, these water programs make very clear the consequences of certain forces. First, these programs provide sizable, concentrated benefits to both groups and localities, but little in the way of general benefits. Naturally, the direct beneficiaries, who have much at stake, fight diligently for their cause. Second, most of the costs are diffuse and general; few are local or specific to any group, and no individual suffers much. As a result, those who suffer are not highly motivated to mobilize opposition. (Railroads have endured substantial costs, but they have not resisted very effectively.) Third, the underlying patterns of costs and benefits, and particularly the concentration of local benefits and scarcity of local costs, stimulate congressmen to champion projects for their districts. Congress has naturally retained control of such programs because they offer such immense opportunities for taking credit and so few for receiving blame.

Bureaucrats and Direct Federal Spending. Congress has shared with bureaucrats authority over most other direct federal spending. Actually it had little choice. It would be inconceivable for Congress itself to make the thousands of allocational decisions associated with spending a few hundred billion dollars annually. Exactly how authority is shared varies widely, again depending crucially on the composition of general, group, and local costs and benefits. Of course, by granting bureaucrats the authority to make certain decisions, Congress does not

[8] Charles M. Tidmarch, "A Brief Excursion in the Land of Pork" (unpublished paper, Union College, 1979), p. 7.
[9] This and subsequent budgetary estimates refer to the 1980 budget.

necessarily lose the ability to shape them. As long as Congress retains control over funds, it can manipulate those dependent on them.

Research and development. Representative of those programs in which local benefits play a relatively minor role are the vast federal programs for research and development. Concentrated in the National Aeronautics and Space Administration (NASA) and the Departments of Defense, Energy, Education, and Health and Human Services, these programs disburse over $30 billion annually to universities, private companies, federal laboratories, and other research facilities. These programs remain relatively detached from the mad scramble for local benefits because they provide (or promise) general benefits for which there is widespread political support. Few doubt the wisdom of medical, energy, or defense oriented research, even where conflict abounds over priorities within these classes. Given this consensus on general benefits, careful allocation of local benefits is not crucial to the survival of a program. Furthermore, any tendency Congress may have to meddle when bureaucrats allocate benefits is minimized when the issues at stake are highly complex and the responsible bureaucrats are technical specialists.

The impulse to meddle is probably greatest when the government builds completely new research facilities, as opposed to distributing grants and contracts to universities or corporations that are already fixed geographically. For most new facilities, one can argue that the eventual quality of their research is independent of their location, whereas that argument is easily dismissed when allocations are made among existing units that already differ enormously in quality and capabilities. Bureaucratic decisions about the location of new federal facilities are made infrequently and on a case-by-case basis. But when the facilities are large and their future economic impact great, congressional appetites are easily whetted. It is difficult to generalize about how congressional politics affects such decisions because they are made singly, and only one locality can win each contest. Still, there is evidence to support three generalizations. First, Congress unites quickly around the idea that new federal facilities belong anywhere but Washington, D.C. Placing such investments in an area lacking congressional representation is, from the legislators' perspective, a terrible waste. Congress has occasionally enforced this preference with legislation.[10] Second, regional battles sometimes develop where legislators pressure bureaucrats to favor their region, even if they are divided over the optimal location within that region. Mid-

[10] Thomas P. Murphy, *Science, Geopolitics, and Federal Spending* (Lexington, Mass.: Heath Lexington Books, 1971), pp. 265-289.

western congressmen, for example, mounted a (successful) regional campaign for the world's largest proton accelerator, arguing that money for high energy physics was concentrated disproportionately in the Northeast and Far West, to the economic detriment of the Midwest.[11] Third, committee chairmen and other powerful congressional leaders enjoy an advantage when bureaucrats who administer programs under their jurisdiction build new facilities. The NASA facilities built in the 1960s are classic examples—particularly the Manned Spacecraft Center in Houston, home of Albert Thomas, chairman of the subcommittee that appropriates all NASA funds.[12] Although politics clearly affects the allocation of some research funds, the quest for local benefits does not really distort national research priorities. These research programs survive on their general benefits; whatever competition may emerge over local benefits is nothing more than a side game, perhaps with important local economic consequences, but without significant effects on national policy.

Politics leaves an even smaller imprint on research programs that distribute grants and contracts. Here allocational politics is constrained by the existing distribution of suitable research-oriented universities and corporations. It is practically impossible for bureaucrats to spread research funds widely when most of these institutions are clustered. Nevertheless, congressmen are sensitive to inequitable distributions of research funds, whatever the cause, and they have occasionally encouraged bureaucrats to strive for greater equity. One bureaucratic response is to provide technical assistance to help institutions from deprived areas compete more effectively. In any event, these research programs do not appear to have been compromised or distorted by allocational politics. They too survive because of support for their general benefits.

Procurement contracts. The federal government purchases not only ideas but also a tremendous variety of goods, ranging from submarines, missiles, and tanks to desks, hospital equipment, and food. The classic American urban political machine used the strategic purchase of goods and services to maintain its power. Do such purchases play a similar role in American national politics, helping to create and maintain majority coalitions in Congress? In most cases, they do not. The purchases are viewed as the incidental consequences of government programs which themselves serve important ends. Although congressmen enjoy having government purchases made in their

11 Ibid., pp. 291-326; Theodore J. Lowi and Benjamin Ginsberg, *Poliscide* (New York: Macmillan, 1976), pp. 87-107.
12 Murphy, *Science, Geopolitics, and Federal Spending*, pp. 210-218.

districts and are eager to claim credit for whatever procurement contracts come their way, these local benefits seldom create support for a program that otherwise might falter.

Sometimes local benefits do permit programs to survive longer than their general or group benefits would justify. This happens frequently for very large defense contracts that have been the lifeblood of local economies. When termination is proposed, the affected congressmen mobilize to keep the assembly lines open. They usually couch their arguments in terms of general benefits, emphasizing how desperately our arsenal needs additional X-weapons; but the local benefits are their incentive. The Texas congressional delegation, for example, kept the Fort Worth plant of General Dynamics open and producing F-111s for four years after the Defense Department requested termination.[13] Similarly, Senators Jackson and Magnuson (Democrats, Washington) helped sustain for a few years massive federal support for the development of Boeing's supersonic transport, long after its economic and environmental problems had weakened the coalition that had favored it. Such feats are easiest when contractors have had the foresight to spread subcontracts throughout the country, giving many congressmen a vital interest in continuance. The fine art of placing subcontracts for future political use is a skill that few major defense contractors could do without.[14]

Congressmen's efforts to keep local procurement benefits flowing into their districts can severely distort national policy. If successful, they can waste federal money by, for example, compelling the continued production of obsolete or unneeded weapons. This happens infrequently, and principally when large defense contracts with enormous economic consequences are on the line. Yet these are precisely the situations that impose the greatest financial and opportunity costs. Thus, the effects of the quest for local benefits on national policy can be significant when very large procurement contracts are at stake.

Facilities and employment. The federal government directly employs nearly 5 million military and civilian personnel. Where these people work is of considerable interest to congressmen, in part because the government's $80 billion payroll affects some local economies so deeply. Administrative agencies have the right, within limits, to

[13] Peter Ognibene, "Grounding the Texas Air Force," *New York Times* (May 10, 1975), p. 29.

[14] Craig Liske and Barry Rundquist, *The Politics of Weapons Procurement: The Role of Congress*, Monograph Series in World Affairs, vol. 12, no. 1 (Denver: The Social Science Foundation and Graduate School of International Studies, University of Denver, 1974), p. 82.

determine where their employees will work. The principal limitation is the need for adequate facilities—office buildings, military installations, and so on. Agencies help decide where these federal facilities will be constructed, but Congress has retained the right to approve individual project decisions. The seriousness with which Congress accepts this task is illustrated by its decision to have two appropriations subcommittees examine the defense budget. One scrutinizes the $2 billion or so proposed for new military construction, while the other scans the $120 billion destined for all other military purposes.

Congressmen can easily rationalize extensive involvement in decisions about where new facilities will be built, and hence where federal employees will work, because such decisions are easily divorced from the question of what those workers will do. Processing tax returns, writing social security checks, drawing maps, distributing consumer information, drafting environmental regulations, reviewing contract compliance, storing ammunition, issuing licenses, testing automobile emissions, and maintaining historical archives are activities that can be performed almost anywhere. Governmental effectiveness and efficiency are relatively independent of location for a wide range of government activities such as these. Lacking good, program-related reasons for locating federal facilities in any particular place, congressmen are only too happy to volunteer their districts. These facilities are especially desirable because, unlike procurement contracts, they generally represent long-term commitments of federal funds.

Exactly how influential congressmen are in the allocation of new facilities is not the principal question here. Elsewhere I have shown that members of the House Armed Services Committee had a slight edge over others in attracting new military installations to their districts during the 1950s; and members of other committees probably have similar advantages, though there are no empirical studies to confirm the anecdotal evidence.[15] Here the question is whether this form of competition for local benefits affects the shape of national policy significantly. In most cases it does not. The question of where a few thousand office workers will be located is usually secondary to the issue of exactly what they will do; it is difficult to imagine Congress enacting many programs just because a few lucky congressmen could see new administrative headquarters in their districts. Similarly, proposals in the 1950s to expand the air force appear to have been considered on their merits, unencumbered by congressional jockeying for new bases. Although the competition for these local benefits is

[15] R. Douglas Arnold, *Congress and the Bureaucracy: A Theory of Influence* (New Haven: Yale University Press, 1979), pp. 115-119.

frequently intense, it ordinarily comes after basic policy decisions are made.

Two situations arise that can distort national policy choices. First, agencies sometimes build facilities in areas where there is little objective need but great political merit. Shortly after F. Edward Hébert (Democrat, Louisiana) became chairman of the House Armed Services Committee, the navy suddenly decided that his hometown, New Orleans, was a good place to move various naval headquarters and build a new hospital. Although the transfers became unnecessary after Hébert lost his chairmanship a few years later, it was too late to stop the hospital. New Orleans now boasts one of the newest, finest, most underused hospitals in the nation (12 percent occupancy rate).[16] Admittedly these cases occur infrequently. The inefficiencies, however, are unquestioned. Second, after federal facilities are built, both congressmen and their constituents quickly become accustomed to regular flows of funds. They work strenuously to maintain these local benefits whenever they are threatened either by termination or by a relocation of facilities. For two decades, congressmen have resisted the Pentagon's efforts to close military installations in their districts. Although the Pentagon has succeeded in closing hundreds of installations, congressmen on important committees have helped spare their districts this agony.[17] The consequences of such favoritism are minimal (except for the local communities) if the installations spared are at least as good as the condemned ones. When they are inferior, the costs incurred in upgrading them can be substantial.

Intergovernmental Grants

The world of grants to state and local governments is considerably different from that of direct federal spending. If anything, it resembles the politics of water projects more closely than it does the politics of research, procurement, employment, or facilities. Local benefits abound, and they frequently overshadow whatever general benefits there may be.

For most programs of direct federal spending, congressmen can separate questions of purpose from questions of location. They can (and do) debate issues related to national defense, medical research, care of veterans, space exploration, and geological surveys without first knowing where money will be spent. Furthermore, their voting decisions on such matters do not depend on whether (or how much)

[16] *Congressional Quarterly, Weekly Report* (May 6, 1978), p. 1112.
[17] Arnold, *Congress and the Bureaucracy*, pp. 107-115.

money is spent in their own districts.[18] For programs giving assistance to state and local governments, by contrast, congressmen seldom distinguish between location and purpose. The issue of location dominates debate, and it dominates legislators' voting decisions (as I shall demonstrate). Few congressmen see merit in grant programs that do not benefit their districts, and few fail to see a program's virtues when it includes "fair shares" for all.

Programs that call for direct federal spending usually attack the broader problems of society and provide substantial general and group benefits. Local benefits are merely an incidental consequence of the means adopted to achieve these ends. Districts that lack shares of local spending still profit from the collective goods provided. Intergovernmental grant programs, on the other hand, often attack problems of narrower scope. However much we may think of education, housing, highways, and poverty as national problems worthy of national solutions, their primary impact is local and their spillover effects (by comparison) few. Ameliorating educational problems in a single district, for example, provides relatively little of value for the remaining 434.

The abundance of local benefits and the scarcity of general benefits make the politics of grant programs revolve around the local benefits to be allocated. Careful allocation is crucial to congressional support. Congress can choose to allocate benefits itself, or it can delegate the task to agencies, usually with some type of instruction and always with congressional oversight. Congress is ill-equipped to allocate grants individually, project-by-project, as it does for water projects. The volume is simply too great. Instead, it writes formulas, based on objective criteria such as population, income, and unemployment, that determine exactly how much each eligible area will receive. Agencies, with their hierarchical organizations and elaborate divisions of labor, are well suited to making individual project decisions. Most agencies that are given authority to allocate benefits do so with project decisions, though occasionally they devise formulas. Essentially, then, the choice is between allocation by congressional formula and allocation by project with bureaucrats making the selections. Each approach allows for careful, strategic allocations of benefits. The actual patterns of decisions, however, differ fundamentally, and so does the impact of local benefits on the shape of national policy.

Until recently all grants were categorical, providing states and localities with funds for specific, narrowly defined purposes such as

---

[18] Wayne Moyer, "House Voting on Defense: An Ideological Explanation," in Bruce M. Russett and Alfred Stepan, eds., *Military Force and American Society* (New York: Harper and Row, 1973), pp. 106-141.

preventing alcoholism, educating the handicapped, protecting hunters, controlling rats, building highways, or providing breakfasts for school children. In the last decade, a handful of general-purpose and broad-based grants have emerged that distribute funds for broadly defined functions such as employment and training, community development, and local public works. Here recipients are free to determine specific purposes. The distinction between categorical and broad-based grants is crucial, for the former also provide benefits to organized interest groups, along with the obvious local benefits, whereas the latter provide local benefits exclusively. The existence of group benefits has made allocational politics for categorical programs more restrained than it has been for the broad-based programs.

In fiscal year 1980 intergovernmental grant programs distributed $83 billion to state and local governments in approximately 500 separate programs. About one-fifth of the funds were distributed by a half-dozen or so new broad-based (formula) programs. The rest were categorical grants. Among these, project grants outnumbered formula grants (67 percent versus 33 percent), but the formula grants were far larger and distributed more funds (69 percent versus 31 percent).[19]

Twelve grant programs provided benefits directed at individuals, through programs administered by state and local governments. These welfare-type programs included public assistance, Medicaid, and payments for children's nutrition, and accounted for one-third of all expenditures. The political logic of these programs resembles the politics of transfer payments to individuals more closely than it does the politics of intergovernmental grants. Throughout this chapter I treat them as benefits to individuals rather than grants to state and local governments, following their political logic rather than their accounting definitions.[20]

Old Formula Programs. Categorical programs meet specific demands for governmental services. Originally these demands may be articulated by users of services (motorists, say), by service-providers (highway contractors), or by legislators who are sensitive to citizens' latent needs. Whatever their origins, the demands usually center on particular solutions (more money for better roads) rather than open-ended requests for assistance in solving general problems

---

[19] Advisory Commission on Intergovernmental Relations, *Categorical Grants: Their Role and Design* (Washington, D.C.: Government Printing Office, 1978), p. 92.

[20] This is the current practice in the government's own *Special Analyses of the United States Budget, 1980*. These programs are listed at pp. 235-242.

(do something to improve transportation). Once established, few grant programs ever die, for they provide not only local benefits to congressmen, but also valuable group benefits to service-users and service-providers, many of whom organize to protect their interests. Over time, grant programs proliferate, as additional ones are created to fund new solutions to recurrent problems.

Congress decides whether new categorical programs will allocate local benefits by formula or on a project-by-project basis. Generalizing about those choices is not easy, for Congress displays the typical inconsistencies of a large, decentralized body. In the beginning, formula programs were in vogue. The first major assistance program, the Federal Aid Road Act of 1916, employed a formula, as did the Smith-Hughes Act of 1917, which subsidized salaries for teachers of industry, trade, and home economics. In general, formulas were preferred when states were the recipients, when most recipients were already performing the designated functions, and when all eligible areas were to receive shares of benefits. Project grants emerged repeatedly during the depression, when the necessity of concentrating funds in the most desperate areas was apparent. During the 1960s when grant programs multiplied most rapidly, newly established project grants outnumbered new formula programs four to one. Project grants are preferred especially when the recipients are local rather than state governments, when the federal government seeks to stimulate new activities or prompt the development of new solutions to old problems, and when the aim is to distribute funds selectively among eligible areas.

Allocational formulas are inclusive: all eligible areas receive shares of benefits. Exactly how much each receives depends on how it "scores" on the various objective criteria chosen. There are three approaches to the construction of formulas. One, the "merit" approach, uses criteria that represent important differences in recipients' needs, capabilities, fiscal capacities, or accomplishments. Such formulas rest on the notion that the federal government ought to help equalize disparities among recipients, or reward them according to their own efforts to tackle problems, or somehow help compensate for their differing needs and capabilities. The second, the political approach, involves criteria that produce politically pleasing allocations and thus help a program win congressional support. The third, the group approach, makes geographic allocations consistent with the needs of the interest groups that benefit from a program and that provide its core of support. The three approaches build upon the distinctions I have been emphasizing between general, local, and group benefits.

Actual formulas do not always reveal their connections to these three approaches as clearly as one might hope. Nevertheless, one can infer something about the intentions of their designers simply by inspecting the 140 or so formulas now in use.[21] This is what I have done. My most striking discovery is how infrequently formulas are constructed around merit criteria. One justification for federal assistance is to help poorer states provide services that richer states provide without outside assistance, yet only one-seventh of all formulas explicitly include factors that steer funds to less fortunate areas. As recently as 1975, it was the highest-income states that received the most grants per capita (from all sources).[22] Redistribution sometimes occurs, but not always toward the needy.

Similarly, one expects to find formulas which reflect the fact that most programs' potential beneficiaries are not distributed uniformly throughout the population. In actuality, many programs ignore legitimate differences in demand. The program whose purpose is to make railroad crossings safer hands out funds under a formula that counts population, area, and postal-route mileage but not railroad crossings. Law enforcement grants reflect population, not the incidence of crime. Hunter safety grants ignore the concentration of hunters in rural areas. Urban mass transit grants reflect urban population and density, but not how many people actually use mass transit. New York, a city built around mass transit, receives a subsidy of two cents per transit passenger, while Grand Rapids, a product of the automobile, reaps forty-five cents per passenger.[23]

Many programs do include formulas that reflect differences in the demand for services. Grants for various types of special education, for example, take account of the number of children from poor, migratory, or disadvantaged families, or the number of pre-school or college-age youth. Similarly, social welfare programs in-

[21] The programs are those listed in Advisory Commission on Intergovernmental Relations, *Categorical Grants*, pp. 128-137. Formulas are contained in U.S., Congress, House, Committee on Post Office and Civil Service, Subcommittee on Census and Population, *Federal Formula Grant-in-Aid Programs that Use Population as a Factor in Allocating Funds*, Committee Print, 94th Congress, 1st session, October 24, 1975; and Office of Management and Budget, *Catalog of Federal Domestic Assistance* (Washington, D.C.: Government Printing Office, 1979).

[22] Sophie R. Dales, "Federal Grants to State and Local Governments, Fiscal Year 1975: A Quarter-Century Review," *Social Security Bulletin* 39 (September 1976), p. 31, as quoted in Advisory Commission on Intergovernmental Relations, *Categorical Grants*, p. 39.

[23] William C. Freund, "Can Quotas, Tariffs, and Subsidies Save the Northeast?" in George Sternlieb and James W. Hughes, eds., *Revitalizing the Northeast* (New Brunswick: Center for Urban Policy Research, 1978), p. 204.

clude criteria related to poverty, concentration of elderly individuals, and the like. Even so, such criteria frequently play only a small role in actual allocational decisions. Grants for drug abuse treatment, for example, allocate but a third of the available funds according to the incidence of chronic drug abuse, with the rest according to population and other factors.[24]

Why does Congress design only some formula programs to reflect differences in demand? A complete answer awaits more careful research. After spending a few days immersed in some 140 formulas, however, I can offer at least the strong suspicion that programs tend to be closely tailored to demand when either the service-users or the service-providers are well organized. Teachers and social workers, for example, have long been organized and active in policy formulation. They have an obvious interest in the appropriate allocation of group benefits, and they are unwilling to consign allocational decisions completely to congressmen who, left to their own devices, might be blinded by the need to win local benefits. Drug users, mass transit riders, and the victims of either train accidents or crime are unorganized and thus ineffectual in the allocation game. Their interests are easily overlooked by congressmen eager to guarantee their districts generous shares.

Most formula building is not a clash between rival claimants calculating how to capture all of a limited stock of benefits for themselves. Rather it is a politics of accommodation; the central debate is over what constitutes an equitable allocation of benefits. Members of the House see equity in terms of population. What could be more equitable, in their view, than equal shares for districts that are approximately equal in population? Senators prefer thinking about the fundamental equality of states. Those from Alaska, Vermont, and Wyoming are unpersuaded that New York and California deserve fifty or sixty times as much assistance as their great states.

How can these divergent views of equity be reconciled? Conference committees have a favorite solution. They accept the House notion that population should be an important component in any formula. But then they add both a minimum allocation for each state, which gives the least populous states far more than their entitlements, and a maximum allocation, which denies the most populous states their "fair" shares. Population is actually the most common factor in allocational formulas, figuring in about 60 percent of them. Minimums appear in nearly half, and maximums in about one-eighth.

[24] Committee on Post Office and Civil Service, *Federal Formula Grant-in-Aid Programs*, p. 123.

The ceilings usually affect only the largest two or three states and thus do little to diminish House majorities. The floors, which benefit perhaps a dozen small states, contribute generously to Senate majorities. These simple maneuvers, though difficult to defend on policy grounds, consistently yield large, stable congressional majorities.

Allocational formulas, then, combine elements from the merit, group, and political approaches. But how deep an imprint does politics leave on these policies? Its principal effect is to discourage Congress from designing formulas that reflect vast differences either in the demand for services or in the capacity of governments to tackle them alone. Small deviations are possible, but the need for political equity precludes anything major. A secondary effect is that small states benefit disproportionately, a consequence of their equal representation in the Senate.

The politics of formula building for most categorical programs has not (yet) degenerated into the game that has become standard for broad-based grants: congressmen consider an endless series of formulas and each chooses the one that provides a few more pennies for his district. First, the information required for this kind of haggling has not been available (until recently). Evaluating increasingly complex formulas requires computers to calculate exactly how each legislator's district will fare under a given plan. More important, the organized interests that benefit disproportionately from narrow categorical programs tend to seek an equitable distribution among their members and are unlikely to enjoy, as congressmen do, endless jockeying for local advantage.

Project Grants. Formula programs embrace all-inclusive criteria from the start; congressional politics then dictates that liberal doses of "equity" be added. The philosophy behind project grants, by contrast, allows that not all eligible areas need receive shares, and these shares need not be equal. But here, too, congressional politics leaves its imprint, introducing more inclusive criteria and notions of political equity where none were intended.

The point of project grants is that, unlike formula grants, they can be molded to fit the recipients' peculiar problems, they can be used to encourage policy innovation, and they can easily be targeted to the areas of greatest need. They are particularly valuable for research and demonstration programs, for which formula grants are cumbersome. Although project grants have been used for dozens of purposes, their most prominent uses have been in urban and community development, economic and regional development, health, education, and all forms of public works construction. Well-known programs include urban renewal, model cities, Appalachian development, area redevelopment, and water and sewer construction.

In the abstract, the philosophy of project grants may be attractive. Unfortunately, their most distinctive features create instant congressional problems. Targeting benefits implies that not all legislators will receive local benefits. If the criteria for targeting are known, excluded congressmen will quickly discover their fate and, lacking compelling reasons to the contrary, will oppose the whole program. If the criteria are nebulous, the general uncertainty may produce even more opposition, with everyone assuming the worst. The more congressmen expect allocations to diverge from standards of political equity, the more substantial the opposition is likely to be. A related problem is that the allocation of benefits is separated from the enactment of programs in both time and space. Enactment is a congressional function, while allocation takes place months (perhaps years) later in administrative agencies, after state and local governments have submitted detailed proposals. Thus, congressmen can only imagine what a program might some day deliver; they derive no guaranteed local benefits from their support.

These problems can be overcome and coalitions assembled in two fundamentally different ways. First, disparate programs can be gathered together so that congressmen will evaluate and vote on the package as a whole. The objective is for congressmen to see benefits for their districts in at least some programs, and thus decide to support the entire package. Education bills typically include programs benefiting every educational and geographic interest, and they do very well indeed. A variant of this approach is for blocs of congressmen to agree to support each other's favorite programs, even though the various programs are considered in different bills and at different times. The logic is identical, but policing the agreements is more difficult. The Democratic party once provided an umbrella coalition for blocs of urban and rural congressmen who supported programs benefiting each other. This coalition, however, has little force today.

The alternative approach to coalition building is for congressmen to shape the allocational process to their liking. Bureaucrats will still make the final decisions, but Congress can limit their discretion. One tactic is to broaden a program's eligibility criteria so that more localities may apply for grants. Urban programs frequently are redesigned so that even tiny hamlets will be eligible—and congressmen from rural areas will find them attractive. A second tactic is to manipulate the number of grants to be awarded, either by increasing total funding or by limiting the size of individual grants. The idea is that the more grants are available, the greater each congressman's chances of receiving one. A third tactic is to reserve some fraction of all grants for localities with particular characteristics—usually areas the bureaucrats are least likely to favor. Finally, Congress can convey to the implementing agency its sense that targeting benefits should not go too far and that some consideration should be given to broadening the distribution. Bureaucrats are ordinarily quick to pick up such hints, for it serves their interests. In fact, they hardly need congressional directives. Some bureaucrats have developed sophisticated allocational strategies that anticipate congressmen's needs.[25]

These tactics are used frequently to help assemble support for new programs and to shore up shaky coalitions for established programs. The model cities program (1966) illustrates their effects. The idea behind model cities was to create a demonstration program pouring massive federal funds into a handful of troubled cities. Congress transformed it completely by providing for 150 cities, making small cities eligible, and limiting any state's share to 15 percent of the total funds. Bureaucrats then selected the cities strategically, for maximum political effect, spreading the benefits among as many of the program's congressional supporters as possible, even selecting a handful of villages with populations under 5,000. Similarly, a water and sewer program (1965) conceived to help rapidly growing areas was transformed so that all areas were eligible. The Appalachian regional development program (and most other economic development programs) have been broadened to include less distressed areas. The poverty program (1964), conceived as an experiment that would concentrate funds in pockets of poverty, evolved into a program with benefits spread thinly across the country. The list could go on.

The extent to which their preoccupation with local benefits can dominate congressmen's attitudes toward categorical programs is illustrated by the Urban Development Action Grant program (1977), the Carter administration's major urban initiative. Actually, there was little congressional debate on the program's intent, methods, or purpose. Attention focused on how the grants would be parceled out. Although it had already been established that cities of all sizes would be eligible, legislators from rural areas were dubious about their districts' chances in the competition. An amendment to guarantee 25 percent of all funds for cities under 50,000 population strengthened the coalition considerably. As table 8–1 demonstrates, congressmen had little trouble perceiving their districts' interests: those from rural areas were united in support (86 percent) while those from the most

[25] Arnold, *Congress and the Bureaucracy.*

TABLE 8–1

Districts' Interests and Congressmen's Votes on Urban Development Action Grant Amendment Reserving Funds for Smaller Cities

% of District Population in Central Cities	Congressmen's Positions on Amendment		Number of Districts in Category	% Supporting Amendment
	For	Against		
0–19	164	26	190	86
20–39	69	18	87	79
40–59	32	24	56	57
60–79	9	14	23	39
80–100	5	47	52	10
All districts	279	129	408	

NOTE: The amendment required that 25 percent of funds be used for cities under 50,000 population (May 11, 1977).

SOURCES: *Congressional Quarterly, Weekly Report* (May 14, 1977), pp. 940-941; *The Almanac of American Politics* (1978).

urban areas were equally unsupportive (10 percent). The question whether separate benefit pools made good economic policy was never raised, for the political logic was compelling.[26]

Congressional politics can quickly dismantle any scheme for carefully targeting the benefits of grant programs and replace it with one more congenial to legislators' standards of political equity. At the same time, however, Congress tolerates a modest amount of political targeting, with members of important committees, coalition leaders, and crucial supporters profiting from bureaucratic largess.[27]

Does all this transform project grants into nothing better than formula grants, with their similar emphasis on all-inclusiveness and political equity—or perhaps something worse, since project grants permit precise political targeting while formula grants do not? Not necessarily. Even after all these political maneuverings, bureaucrats still have immense freedom to apply merit criteria in selecting projects and allocating benefits. Although political criteria may dictate that all (or most) congressmen ought to receive grants, bureaucrats still determine which applicants within each district most deserve benefits, and they may adjust the amount of each award appropriately. Furthermore,

[26] *Congressional Quarterly, Weekly Report* (May 14, 1977), pp. 891-892.
[27] Arnold, *Congress and the Bureaucracy*, pp. 95-206.

273

they can deny benefits to the most unworthy areas without running any great risk. Bureaucratic decision making, one step removed from coalition building in Congress, allows such choices, whereas formula drafting, centered in Congress, does not.

All this follows when a coalition is assembled to back a single categorical program. But what happens when an umbrella coalition is put together, embracing disparate programs? The consequences are necessarily less severe. Inclusiveness and political equity must still prevail, but over a whole package of programs; they need not be imposed on each. Individual programs can target benefits according to merit criteria. Unfortunately, this strategy is used infrequently today. It is still chosen when separate programs logically belong in the same bill, but seldom for programs included in different bills. One obvious reason is the diminished role of party leaders in Congress. Democratic leaders once helped manage umbrella coalitions, arranging the complex trades necessary to keep farm, city, labor, and western congressmen together in support of various targeted benefits, but they no longer do.[28] A second reason is that today more congressional votes are recorded and potentially visible to constituents. Rural congressmen, for example, might find it difficult to explain to their constituents how all the urban-oriented votes they have cast really benefit rural areas.

New Formula Programs. Categorical programs mushroomed during the 1960s, with a record of 109 new programs in 1965, the most frantic year of the Great Society, and with over 400 programs in operation at the end of the decade. Each program sustained the interests of some narrow group. Not everyone was pleased by the system, however. Though they enjoyed the flow of federal money, governors, mayors, and county executives resented the extent to which their own spending priorities were dictated by the availability of federal grants. More money with fewer strings became their rallying cry.

The idea was advanced by their own "public interest" groups, the National Governors' Conference, the National League of Cities, the United States Conference of Mayors, and others, and quickly picked up by the Nixon administration and various Republicans who found congenial (and politically opportune) the notion of less federal control.[29] Eventually, it evolved into proposals for two types of

---

[28] David R. Mayhew, *Party Loyalty Among Congressmen: The Difference Between Democrats and Republicans, 1947-1962* (Cambridge: Harvard University Press, 1966).

[29] Donald H. Haider, *When Governments Come to Washington* (New York: The Free Press, 1974).

programs. General revenue sharing, a proposal with a bipartisan history, would distribute funds by formula to state and local governments, with few, if any, restrictions on the purposes for which they could be spent. Block grants would also distribute funds by formula for recipient-determined purposes, but there would be separate programs for broad areas such as employment and training, community development, and law enforcement assistance. Each program would replace a raft of narrow categorical programs in the same functional area.

The question of how local benefits would be allocated under revenue sharing or the various block grant programs was central. Clearly, these programs promised few general benefits. They could no more survive in Congress on their general benefits than could categorical programs. Neither did they promise any new benefits for groups of service-providers or service-demanders, unlike the categorical programs, which thrived on group support. Aside from the associations of government executives, few groups saw advantages in a system that guaranteed them nothing but the right to compete with others at the local level. In the absence of significant general or group benefits, Congress naturally concentrated on the allocation of local benefits.

On this matter the associations of government executives were divided. Governors thought the states should be the principal recipients, mayors sought guaranteed shares for cities, and county executives defended their turf. More difficult was the question of how funds would be allocated among the various cities or states or counties. Mayors might agree that cities deserved larger shares, but they quickly parted over how to distribute those shares among them. New York and Houston inevitably diverge on what constitutes fair division. Public interest groups fought for what united them (more money for their members collectively), while their individual members lobbied their congressmen to manipulate the formulas until they produced more pleasing decisions for their localities.

In general, conflict over formulas is more intense for broad-based programs than it is for categorical programs. First, the stakes are larger. Individual broad-based programs can dispense billions. Second, everyone knows the stakes, because computers can calculate quickly the local implications of every imaginable formula.[30] Congressmen can only guess how much their districts will receive from project grants, since actual allocations depend on both local initiative and

30 Stephen E. Frantzich, "Computerized Information Technology in the U.S. House of Representatives," *Legislative Studies Quarterly*, vol. 4 (May 1979), p. 266.

bureaucratic choice. They could forecast their shares of early formula grants, but not with speed or precision; they could not tinker endlessly with the formulas, searching for optimal political allocations, because there was no way to calculate quickly the local consequences. (They were also dissuaded from playing this game by the existence of substantial group benefits, which threw them into alliance with organized interest groups whose notions about allocation diverged from their own.) For the new broad-based grants, however, there are no such constraints.

Not only do congressmen know the incidence of local benefits under alternative formulas, but so do local officials, interested constituents, and potential opponents. The extent of information about local benefits, coupled with the absence of significant general or group benefits, impels congressmen to protect their districts' immediate interests to a degree unusual in congressional politics. They operate under the watchful eyes of covetous local officials, and in dread of future opponents' unearthing votes they cast for formulas that denied their districts maximum shares. What legislator wants to hand an opponent an issue so simple that no voter could fail to comprehend it? Given this, a congressman is practically forced to support the formula that maximizes his district's share of benefits, at least when the votes are public and recorded. There is little room for logrolling or for voting one's conscience when the stakes are so clear and so great.

Some might deny that congressmen are actually this calculating of local advantage when they design allocational formulas. Part of the reason is that congressional debate is seldom so crude. Congressmen debate behind a smokescreen; abstract concepts of fairness, need, justice, and hardship obscure the real issues of local advantage. Few misunderstand the code. When Senator Bentsen (Democrat, Texas) proposed in 1978 that even booming cities with low unemployment deserved countercyclical aid because they had "pockets" of poverty, all were aware that the real issue was not poverty but benefits for Houston and other economically healthy cities in the South. One clue is that the support Bentsen garnered came from those representing these prosperous areas, not from traditional champions of the poor.[31]

The best evidence of congressmen's preoccupation with local effects comes from recent roll call votes in which districts' interests were unambiguous. Most compelling was the formula fight in 1979 for a new $1.35 billion block grant program for states designed to

[31] *Congressional Quarterly, Weekly Report* (August 19, 1978), p. 2220.

TABLE 8–2

DISTRICTS' INTERESTS AND CONGRESSMEN'S VOTES ON AMENDMENT TO
FUEL ASSISTANCE FORMULA THAT FAVORED COLDER STATES

Location of District	Congressmen's Positions on Amendment		Number of Districts in Category	% Supporting Amendment
	For	Against		
Sunbelt[a]	4	90	94	4
Frostbelt[b]	178	13	191	93
Total	182	103	285	

NOTE: The amendment specified a formula weighted toward states with colder weather to be used to distribute $1.35 billion in fuel assistance funds for the poor (November 9, 1979).

[a] Sunbelt: California plus the fourteen states below 37° latitude (Alabama, Arkansas, Arizona, Florida, Georgia, Hawaii, Louisiana, Mississippi, New Mexico, North Carolina, Oklahoma, South Carolina, Tennessee, Texas).

[b] Frostbelt: The remaining thirty-five states.

SOURCE: *Congressional Quarterly, Weekly Report* (November 17, 1979), p. 2614.

help the poor pay their heating bills. Although few disputed that colder areas "deserved" more assistance per capita than warmer areas, legislators divided over how much more. As table 8–2 demonstrates, frostbelt congressmen were practically unanimous (93 percent) in their support of a formula weighted toward colder states, while sunbelt congressmen were equally united (96 percent) in opposition.[32] All this when there were excellent objective data on just how much residents of various states actually spent on heat. The point is that in formula fights, especially when information on local impact is clear, congressmen vote their districts' interests, with less than usual attention to questions of merit.

With congressmen all looking out for their districts' interests, what kinds of policies are produced? Typically there is little consensus on their fundamental purposes or long-term goals, but only short-term agreement on how benefits are to be allocated. In the absence of any unity of purpose, it becomes legitimate to break open the allocational formulas now and then and relaunch the fight for local advantage. The recurrent controversy over Community Development Block Grants illustrates well the dominance of allocational politics over common purpose.

[32] Ibid. (November 17, 1979), pp. 2593-2595.

277

Community Development Block Grants were proposed by the Nixon administration to consolidate ten existing categorical programs, including urban renewal and model cities. The formula itself, which allocated funds according to population, the overcrowding of housing, and poverty, drew relatively little fire in 1974 when Congress enacted the program. Congressmen were far too busy arranging for a "hold harmless" clause guaranteeing for three to six years that no community would receive less under the new program than it had under the ten categorical programs. This issue was pressing because many communities, especially the 150 model cities and those with large urban renewal projects, would face large cuts under any formula since formulas inevitably spread benefits widely. At this stage, protecting cities from immediate reductions was more important to many congressmen than carefully shaping a formula that would not take full effect for at least three years. In 1977, as the hold harmless clause was being phased out, congressmen from the Northeast and Midwest realized that the formula, with its emphasis on population, poverty, and overcrowding, actually benefited the sunbelt and that this advantage would increase with time as the frostbelt continued to lose population. With the support of the Carter administration, they moved to alter the formula. The new formula included two additional factors, age of housing and growth lag, which redirected benefits to the frostbelt. In order to soften the impact on the sunbelt, both formulas were adopted, the existing one and the new one, with each community using whichever was more advantageous. Even so, sunbelt congressmen worked to overturn the new formula on the House floor, while congressmen from the Northeast and Midwest united to protect it (see table 8–3).[33]

Decisions for other formula programs have followed the same patterns. A hold harmless provision is usually adopted when changes are made in an allocational formula, as the soon-to-be-deprived congressmen stand together to protect their districts from the unspeakable crime of reduced federal spending. It is often necessary to increase total funding for a program when a formula is changed, to allow both for the new beneficiaries and for those protected by grandfather clauses. Dual formulas are also common. General revenue-sharing funds, for example, are distributed among states according to two formulas: a five-factor formula, designed in the House, that favors the more populous, urban states, and a three-factor formula, product of the Senate, that favors more rural areas, especially in the South. The House-Senate compromise bestows upon each state an

[33] *Congressional Quarterly Almanac* (1974), pp. 345-363; (1977), pp. 126-137.

TABLE 8–3

DISTRICTS' INTERESTS AND CONGRESSMEN'S VOTES ON AMENDMENT TO
DELETE FORMULA FOR COMMUNITY DEVELOPMENT BLOCK GRANTS

Location of District	Congressmen's Positions on Amendment		Number of Districts in Category	% Opposing Amendment
	For	Against		
Northeast	1	110	111	99
Midwest	7	108	115	94
West	45	23	68	34
South	96	20	116	17
Total	149	261	410	

NOTE: This amendment was designed to delete a new alternative formula for allocation of community development block grant funds that was advantageous to communities with older housing stock or a lag in population growth (May 10, 1977).

SOURCE: *Congressional Quarterly, Weekly Report* (May 14, 1977), pp. 940-941.

allocation from the more advantageous formula.[34]

Broad-based programs do sometimes reflect more general concerns, providing extra benefits for poorer areas, or rewarding localities according to their own tax effort. But these differential effects are rarely very pronounced. The politics of formula design practically guarantees that any redistribution will be mild. Those who propose programs to target funds to distressed areas usually find their good intentions thwarted by political realities that dictate a wide distribution of benefits.

The Imprint of Local Politics

The congressional quest for local benefits leaves an uneven imprint on public policy. Where the impressions are deep and durable, understanding how congressmen compete for local benefits and how their conflicts are resolved is the key to understanding policy making. Where the impressions are faint, policy making and competition for local benefits can be analyzed as separate processes, with little mutual impact.

The effects of the quest for local benefits on public policy vary according to differences in the composition of programs' benefits and

[34] Paul R. Dommel, *The Politics of Revenue Sharing* (Bloomington: Indiana University Press, 1974), pp. 156-164.

279

costs, differences in the process by which local benefits are allocated, and differences in interest group forces. Most important is whether a program provides substantial general benefits. Programs that are valued by the public regardless of where funds flow generate congressional support quite easily; general benefits distract legislators from their concern for local benefits. National defense, medical research, and national parks are good examples. Programs that concentrate most of their benefits in the areas where the funds are actually spent have no such natural supporting coalition. They tend to survive and prosper only when congressmen are satisfied with the distribution of local benefits. Public works and most intergovernmental grant programs belong in this class. Substantial group benefits can also help restrain congressmen from full-scale battles for local benefits. Interest groups usually have their own ideas about proper allocation, and they seldom coincide with congressmen's predilections.

The impact of the quest for local benefits also depends on where and how allocational decisions are made. When they are made in Congress concurrently with other decisions on programs the imprint tends to be greatest. It tends to be least when they are made later, in administrative agencies. Part of the reason is circular: Congress chooses to retain full allocational control when it cares most about allocation. But proximity in time and space also plays a part. The pressures on a congressman to protect his district's interests are greatest when he participates in decision making, and particularly when he must vote publicly on alternative formulas with precisely identifiable local consequences. Local pressures are less when bureaucrats allocate benefits. Congressmen profit either way. They claim credit when the bureaucrats' choices please them, and rail against them when they do not. There are no losing outcomes comparable to a wrong vote on a formula or repeated failure to obtain congressional authorization for a particular project.

Together these factors determine how much local benefits affect the shape of public policy. It may help to imagine a continuum of spending programs ranging from those scarred most deeply by the scramble for local benefits to those unaffected by it. Water projects lie at one end of the continuum, for they provide few general benefits and immense local benefits. They are everyone's favorite example of the congressional pork barrel. After water projects come intergovernmental grants, ranging from broad-based formula programs, where competition for local benefits leaves deep impressions, to categorical formula grants, where the impressions are somewhat less pronounced, and finally to project grants, where they are even less noticeable. Next along the continuum are the construction and staffing of federal facilities, where substantial agreement on general benefits reduces some of the perverse effects of the quest for local benefits. These perverse effects are even further reduced for most procurement contracts. Anchoring this end of the continuum are defense, medical, and scientific research, where the impressions are practically imperceptible.[35] Completely off the continuum are the vast programs of transfer payments made directly to individuals. Here there are no geographically specific local benefits and thus no corresponding blemishes on public policy.

Changing Patterns of Federal Expenditures. A popular misconception about Congress is that it has turned increasingly to particularistic programs, so that each congressman can bring home ever more attractive packages of local benefits. Those who believe this to be true see innumerable perverse consequences. Fiorina argues that the greatly expanded pork barrel of recent years ("full to overflowing") has been transformed by clever congressmen into electoral dividends and that this expansion explains (in part) the increased safety of incumbents.[36] Elsewhere he argues that governmental growth can be traced back (in part) to the fundamental conflict between legislators over local benefits, a conflict resolved by overspending in each member's district in accordance with norms of reciprocity and universalism.[37]

Unfortunately, the notion that federal expenditures are increasingly shaped by congressional competition over local benefits is inaccurate. Figure 8–1 shows how the composition of the federal budget has changed during the past thirty years.[38] The eight analytic cate-

[35] It is worth reemphasizing that this essay is about how congressmen's quests for local benefits affect fundamental policy choices, not simply how congressional politics affects the allocation of local benefits (the subject of my previous work). The distinction is important. There may still be intense political competition over the location of a research or defense installation. But as long as this competition does not distort research priorities or decrease efficiency in achieving defense goals, we ought not be too concerned; it is a harmless political game, with no more than local consequences. My indignation is reserved for instances where competition for local benefits disfigures public policy, as when federal money is distributed according to political criteria, with scant attention to where the most pressing problems are located.

[36] Morris P. Fiorina, *Congress: Keystone of the Washington Establishment* (New Haven: Yale University Press, 1977), p. 48.

[37] Fiorina, "Legislative Facilitation of Government Growth."

[38] One could create a very different impression if one looked at gross, unadjusted expenditures. Naturally, practically all governmental expenditures increase over time, as do most nongovernmental expenditures. Examining the composition of federal expenditures is less misleading because the effects of population growth, economic growth, and inflation are removed. Federal expenditures as a proportion of the gross national product have increased very gradually from 18 percent in the early 1950s to about 22 percent today.

FIGURE 8–1

Composition of Federal Expenditures, 1950–1980

Federal Expenditures (%)

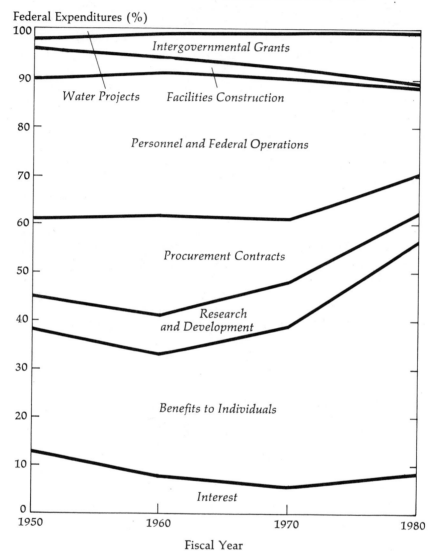

Fiscal Year

NOTE: The eight categories of expenditure are listed in order of the degree to which the quest for local benefits leaves its mark on public policy. Water projects are the most sharply affected, research and development least so; interest and benefits to individuals are unaffected. See also footnote 39 in the text.

SOURCE: U.S. Office of Management and Budget, *The Budget of the United States,* Special Analyses and Appendix, fiscal years 1950, 1960, 1970, and 1980.

282

gories are ordered according to the degree to which the quest for local benefits leaves its mark on public policy (using the continuum developed in the previous section). Note that the principal source of change has been the growth in direct benefits to individuals.[39] These programs, including social security, public assistance, Medicare, and Medicaid, now account for nearly half of all federal expenditures. Allocating benefits directly to individuals dampens any congressional competition over shares of local benefits. From this perspective, the impact of the congressional quest for local benefits on federal expenditures seems to be diminishing.

The shifts among the remaining types of expenditures are mixed, and some of their effects cancel out. Within the category of intergovernmental grants, the scramble for local benefits seems to be making even deeper impressions on public policy, as broad-based formula grants, with their all-inclusive allocational criteria and standards of political equity, displace project grants (see figure 8–2). Conversely, the sharp decline in water projects (from 2 percent of total expenditures to 0.5 percent) suggests a major reduction in that classic American pork barrel where the quest for local benefits has always been so overpowering. On the whole, the shift away from the construction of water projects and other federal facilities toward intergovernmental grants has probably deepened only slightly the impressions that the congressional quest leaves on domestic policy.

The argument that these shifts have somehow allowed congressmen greater opportunities for credit claiming and, therefore, that they have contributed to the remarkable electoral security of congressmen in recent years does not rest on firm evidence. In fact, these shifts have produced a relative decline in the volume of particularized benefits: water projects, project grants, construction and staffing of federal facilities, and procurement contracts all have been declining in relative magnitude, and these are the outlays where a legislator "can believably generate a sense of responsibility" for a particular decision.[40] They have been displaced by the growth in formula programs (such as revenue sharing) and entitlement benefits for

---

[39] For all years, I have counted as "benefits to individuals" those intergovernmental grant programs that provide payments to individuals, such as Medicaid and public assistance. This is consistent with current accounting practice in *Special Analyses*. I have reclassified such programs in earlier years so that only substantive changes in expenditures are reflected, not changes in methods of accounting. The distinction between procurement contracts and expenditures for personnel and operations is not well maintained in earlier years. Fortunately, it is not important to my basic argument.

[40] Mayhew, *Congress: The Electoral Connection*, p. 53.

FIGURE 8–2

FEDERAL EXPENDITURES FOR INTERGOVERNMENTAL GRANTS, BY
ALLOCATIONAL METHOD, 1964–1980

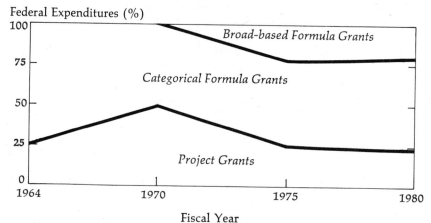

SOURCE: U.S. Office of Management and Budget, *The Budget of the United States,*
Special Analyses, fiscal years 1973, 1970; Donald H. Haider, *When Governments
Come to Washington* (New York: The Free Press, 1974), p. 55; Advisory Com-
mission on Intergovernmental Relations, *Categorical Grants: Their Role and
Design,* pp. 32, 92.

individuals (such as Medicare). These newer programs deliver benefits as a matter of right, not privilege, and congressmen have fewer
opportunities to claim responsibility for them.

There is even less support for the argument that congressmen's
incessant quests for local benefits has somehow contributed to growth
in government spending. Actually, the magnitude of growth is relatively small. Federal outlays as a percentage of the gross national
product since 1955 have amounted to: 18.1 percent in 1955, 18.5 percent in 1960, 18.0 percent in 1965, 20.5 percent in 1970, 22.9 percent
in 1975, and 21.7 percent in 1980.[41] The great engine of change,
however, has been the growth of transfer payments to individuals.
These payments have increased from 25 percent of federal spending
in 1950 to 48 percent today (see figure 8–1). The pork barrel simply
has not been expanding.[42]

[41] *Budget of the United States* (1973), p. 552, (1980), p. 577.

[42] For a more rigorous analysis of the argument, see R. Douglas Arnold, "Legislatures, Overspending, and Government Growth" (Paper presented at the conference on the causes and consequences of public sector growth, Dorado Beach,
Puerto Rico, November 1978).

The Politics of Inclusion. Congress has always had trouble targeting benefits to areas where they are most needed. The whole notion goes against the congressional grain. Unfortunately, recent changes in Congress have made such targeting less likely than ever, especially for intergovernmental grants. More and more, Congress produces homogenized grant programs that distribute small packages of benefits (relatively) uniformly across the country, where once it made greater efforts to concentrate benefits. The sources of change are many, though interrelated.

One source is the shift from the project grants of the 1960s to the broad-based formula grants of the 1970s. Of course, it is fashionable today to deride project grants, by creating images of pointy-headed bureaucrats dictating how communities can spend their own federal tax dollars. What is often overlooked, however, is that bureaucrats are much more likely than congressmen to target funds according to need. Bureaucrats are not unconcerned with political realities; in fact, most are quite talented at melding political and merit criteria. But they are free to make individual project decisions. They are not faced with the task of writing blanket formulas suitable for every case. To illustrate: congressmen may write a formula that spreads funds fairly evenly among 3,000 counties; bureaucrats, on the other hand, may allocate funds according to whatever merit criteria they choose, subject to the constraint that most congressional districts contain at least one "needy" county. Politics is only one of many considerations entering into the allocation of projects, whereas it can become the principal determinant of a formula designed by Congress.[43]

Although it is easier to tailor allocations to the differing needs of beneficiaries through individual project decisions than through formula grants, Congress could still design more effective formulas than it does. Unfortunately, still other changes in Congress preclude this. Ordinarily, better information makes for better decisions. Here, vast improvements in the information available to congressmen have had the opposite effect. When computers inform everyone (congressmen, constituents, and future opponents) of the incidence of local benefits under every imaginable formula, the stage is set for the complete dominance of local politics. When congressmen are forced to vote publicly on alternative formulas under the watchful eye of

[43] There are, of course, countervailing arguments in favor of broad-based formulas. Their advocates usually emphasize the virtues of decentralization and the value of local control over how federal money is eventually spent. My point here is that this decentralization in spending authority has come at the price of greater politicization in the allocation of funds among recipients.

285

voracious local officials, that dominance is all but assured. All these changes have occurred. Computers are now well entrenched on Capitol Hill. Formula fights have moved from the committee rooms to the floor. Recorded votes are demanded increasingly. Cities, states, and counties have established their own Washington offices, and they keep careful track of their congressmen's actions. Ignorance is not bliss, but neither does perfect and complete information necessarily produce more enlightened public policy.

The decline of political parties in American society has been well chronicled, as has their diminishing role in Congress. This decline removes one of the few forces working to impede the politics of inclusion that now transforms every narrow program into one dispensing benefits universally and uniformly. Parties restrained such actions, not because they substituted noble objectives for local self-interest, but rather because they allowed congressmen to pursue policies offering greater local advantages than the politics of inclusion. Today most coalitions are assembled ad hoc, one program at a time; congressmen's support is contingent upon their receiving satisfactory shares of benefits for their districts. The result is hundreds of programs dispensing tiny shares to everyone: urban programs that encompass rural hamlets, law enforcement programs that benefit localities where crime is a minor issue, economic development programs that embrace economically healthy areas, and fuel assistance programs for regions where heating costs are not onerous. The present arrangements should not imply that citizens actually prefer small portions of every item on the menu or that this constitutes a healthy diet. It is simply the inevitable consequence of a system where congressmen have to look out for their district's interests program by program.

Concentrating each program's benefits where they are most needed requires controlled logrolling, and that functions best when party leaders are strong enough to arrange and enforce agreements among legislators. Logrolling has a poor reputation, no doubt because it is associated with rivers and harbors bills funding scores of unjustifiable projects. But logrolling has its virtues. It can draw under a single umbrella coalition a whole series of programs, each of which targets funds according to need. Districts then receive substantial benefits where their needs are greatest and nothing where they are marginal.

The rise of broad-based formula grants and the decline of project grants in the last decade may not serve the public interest well. It is now extremely expensive to deliver funds to the most desperate areas because funds must be included for all the less needy areas. Under categorical grants, a small portion of funds had to be allocated for political reasons—to grease the congressional wheels. Under the new formula programs, however, that political portion has multiplied many times. Universalism and uniformity threaten to displace need as allocational criteria.

Neither does the rise of these formula grants necessarily serve congressmen's individual political ends. The conventional wisdom is that congressmen prefer categorical project grants. They enjoy creating them because important interest groups are watching, and they enjoy obtaining projects for their districts because they can claim credit for bringing home the bacon. They can earn credit year after year because localities must continually reapply for these project grants. Under formula grants, once programs are enacted the benefits flow automatically. Congressmen can no more claim credit for the repeated delivery of revenue-sharing checks than they can for social security.

But then why has Congress been approving broad-based formula grants? The best explanation is that outside pressures have counted for more than calculations of political advantage. Outside groups struggled to place these proposals on the agenda; once they were there, congressmen had little choice but to approve them, for no one wanted to vote publicly to deny his district money. The outside groups were the new public interest groups, representing state and local officials, who saw more money with fewer strings attached for their members, and Republican politicians, who saw political advantage in proposing alternatives to the Democrats' centralized programs.

9

The Three-Ring Budget Process:
The Appropriations, Tax,
and Budget Committees
in Congress

Allen Schick

For more than a century—from the Civil War until the Congressional Budget Act of 1974—Congress had a relatively stable committee structure for making spending and revenue decisions. Most expenditures were within the province of the appropriations committees, while revenue measures were handled by the House Ways and Means and Senate Finance committees. The Budget Act disrupted this symmetrical division of labor by vesting a third set of committees with a role in financial policy.

The House and Senate budget committees established by the 1974 act operate in addition to the older tax and appropriations committees. The budget committees lack legislative jurisdiction. Their principal job is to prepare two (or more) budget resolutions each year. These resolutions (which do not have the force of law) set forth total revenues, total outlays and budget authority, the budget's surplus or deficit, and the public debt of the United States. Each resolution also divides total spending (budget authority and outlays) among almost twenty functions—defense, health, agriculture, and so on. But despite their limited jurisdiction, the budget committees are actively involved in matters handled by the tax and appropriations committees because the content of a budget resolution intrudes on the central business of these older committees.

This chapter is concerned with why Congress found it suitable to complicate legislative operations by creating a budget process and with the implications of that process for the appropriations and tax committees. The usual explanation for the establishment of the congressional budget process focuses on the impoundment battles between President Nixon and the Democratic Congress in the early 1970s. This is a patently incomplete explanation, for while it accounts for the impoundment control segment of the Budget Act, it does not explain why Congress went through the distasteful task of imposing controls on its own budget powers.[1] Of course, impoundment was a powerful spur to congressional action; arguably, Congress might not have acted had it not been for this issue. Nevertheless, when it wrote the Budget Act, Congress was much more concerned about the distribution of power within its own ranks than between it and the executive branch.

The Congressional Budget Act of 1973 was born during a period of budgetary conflict in Congress. The confrontation most relevant to this study was between the appropriations and the tax committees over efforts to limit federal spending. Although they clashed over budget policies, these powerful committees were principally concerned about their jurisdiction and responsibilities. When they could not compose their difference, Congress intervened by devising a budget process which coordinated the committees' legislative activities without impairing their basic jurisdiction.

Conflict in Congress during the years before the Budget Act was a byproduct of legislative change and impotence. The power and status of the appropriations committees were impaired by spending pressures which buffeted Congress, while the operations of the House Ways and Means Committee were altered by legislative reform. When the Budget Act was passed, these bulwarks of legislative power were less cohesive and less dominant in their spheres of operation than they long had been been reputed to be. The Budget Act was an attempt to reestablish legislative power of the purse by chartering new committees to exercise it in behalf of Congress. But as we shall see, the coexistence of the old and new centers of power has generated fresh opportunities for strife.

The Appropriations versus the Tax Committees

Until the Civil War, the House Ways and Means and the Senate Finance committees handled both the revenue and the spending sides of the budget. This convenient arrangement was ended by wartime growth in the federal budget and, hence, in the workloads of these committees. But when Congress created separate committees to handle appropriations, it did more than divide its burgeoning workload. It also dispersed budgetary power among a broader circle of committees and members than before.

For many years, the division between the tax and appropriations

---

[1] The Congressional Budget and Impoundment Control Act of 1974 has ten titles. The first nine deal with the congressional budget process and related matters; Title 10 is a separate law, the Impoundment Control Act.

committees helped to mitigate budgetary conflict within Congress. By separating revenue and spending decisions, Congress could avoid explicit responsibility for the deficits which often ensued. Taxes could be raised and spending cut, with each side ritualistically complaining about the red ink.

In the years immediately preceding the Budget Act, however, massive increases in the size of federal deficits disturbed this "no fault" arrangement. During the seven years from 1960 through 1966, the deficit averaged about $3.5 billion a year. Then came escalating American involvement in Vietnam, pressure to spend on "guns and butter," and a slowdown of economic growth combined with an increase in inflation, and the deficit soared to a $13.5 billion average over the next seven years. To make matters worse, during the early 1960s, the president requested and Congress enacted a substantial tax cut; during the last years of the decade, the president called upon Congress to impose a surtax.

With the shift in fiscal fortunes, responsibility for the budget totals could no longer be avoided. As Congress became more sensitive to the deficit, the appropriations committees found themselves increasingly blamed for the unsatisfactory condition of the budget. But the tax committees were implicated too because they had jurisdiction over debt legislation. Periodically Ways and Means and Finance had no choice but to report unpopular legislation raising the statutory limit on the public debt.[2] In an era of deficit spending, the tax committees became convinced that since the federal government would spend all that it took in or more, the best way to hold down expenditures was to keep a lid on revenues. Even if this meant chronic deficits, at least spending would be lower than would be likely with higher revenues.

Concern over the budget deficit posed special problems for the appropriations committees. They have long operated as clusters of semiautonomous subcommittees, each preparing its own appropriations bill. The full committees consider individual appropriations bills, not spending as a whole. Another problem was that although budget watchers are primarily interested in federal outlays, sums actually spent, the appropriations committees deal almost exclusively with budget authority, the sums "provided for obligation."[3] As a

[2] The permanent statutory limit on the public debt is hundreds of billions of dollars below the temporary limit. Consequently, when the temporary limit expires, or has to be raised in order to finance the deficit, Congress must pass a new debt limit bill.

[3] Appropriations are the principal form of budget authority, which is defined in the Congressional Budget Act as "authority provided by law to enter into obligations which will result in immediate or future outlays involving government funds."

result, a cut in appropriations is rarely matched dollar for dollar by a reduction in outlays.

Yet Congress is mostly interested in outlays. On five occasions between 1967 and 1973, it acted on proposals to limit total federal spending. The first of these, in 1967, occurred shortly after President Johnson asked for a 10 percent tax increase and warned that the deficit might reach $29 billion if Congress failed to act.[4] This proposal triggered a Republican attempt to attach a spending limitation to a continuing resolution providing interim funding for federal agencies which had not yet received their regular appropriations for the fiscal year. During floor debate, Chairman George Mahon defended the performance of the House Appropriations Committee and claimed that it had already cut $4 billion from agency budget requests. However, in a vote that split the normally nonpartisan House Appropriations Committee along party lines, the House voted 202–182 to recommit the continuing resolution.

The issue was renewed one week later (October 3, 1967) when the House reversed itself and passed a resolution continuing the funding of federal agencies through October 10.[5] Immediately after this, Congressman John Byrnes, ranking Republican on the Ways and Means Committee, announced that the committee

> has just met in executive session and has adopted a motion that the committee temporarily lay the tax matter on the table, and that further consideration of the tax increase be deferred until such time as the President and the Congress reach an understanding on the means of implementing more effective expenditure reduction and control as an essential corollary to further consideration of a tax increase. . . .[6]

Here was direct confrontation between two House committees. Ways and Means was putting Appropriations on notice that its quid pro quo for a surtax was a ceiling on expenditures. The conflict cooled for a brief period when the Senate adopted a continuing resolution with interim funding, a device which was twice extended.[7] The Senate, however, was reluctant to approve any spending limitation. Its Appropriations Committee insisted that spending cuts "should be made

---

[4] For an informative and detailed account of tax and spending conflicts in 1967 and 1968, see Lawrence C. Pierce, *The Politics of Fiscal Policy Formation* (Pacific Palisades, Calif.: Goodyear Publishing Company, 1971) pp. 148-72.

[5] In order to enable members to vote for the continuing resolution without opposing the spending limitation, the measure was considered under a rule which precluded the spending limit amendment.

[6] *Congressional Record*, vol. 113 (October 3, 1967), p. 27659.

[7] P.L. 90-102.

in the appropriation bills and not by across-the-board reductions in a continuing resolution."[8] The stalemate was finally broken by an administration proposal to reduce personnel costs by 2 percent and other obligational authority (the term then used for budget authority) by 10 percent. Significantly, Congress could not end its internal conflict without White House intervention. Significantly, also, the administration's proposal to cut spending was made at a hearing before the Ways and Means Committee, not to either of the appropriations committees.

Enactment of the continuing resolution provided only a brief respite in the battle over budget cuts. Ways and Means still insisted that the president come up with a spending control proposal before it would consider his surtax legislation. Chairman Wilbur Mills took the floor in February 1978 to restate his position "that any income tax increase should be coupled with actions evidencing firm control over the expenditure side of the budget both in spirit and deed."[9]

There was, however, a formidable obstacle to a surtax-spending ceiling package: the surtax was under one committee's jurisdiction, the ceiling another's. After months of fruitless bickering in the House, this difficulty was finally surmounted in the Senate by the adoption of a floor amendment attaching a combined surtax and spending limit to an extraneous bill. Senator Warren Magnuson of the Appropriations Committee objected to this unusual maneuver and warned that its effect "would be to say to the Appropriations Committee, 'Let's forget about you people meeting and going over these items one by one and looking at them and shaping them at least within the framework of the fiscal condition of the Nation.' "[10]

The Senate rejected this plea and went on to adopt the floor amendment. In conference, extensive negotiations among administration and congressional leaders produced a package satisfactory to both the House Ways and Means and the appropriations committees. House Appropriations adopted a "sense of the Committee" resolution committing itself to substantial budget reductions.[11] This helped pave the way for resolution of the protracted conflict in June 1968, but it could not detract from the fact that enactment of a spending reduction had effectively bypassed the appropriations process.

In 1969 and 1970, the appropriations committees supported spending limitations without a fight. Chairman Mahon announced that he had come to:

[8] *Congressional Record*, vol. 113 (October 25, 1967), p. 30109.
[9] *Congressional Record*, vol. 114 (February 29, 1968), p. 4704.
[10] *Congressional Record*, vol. 114 (March 26, 1968), p. 7719.
[11] See *Congressional Record*, vol. 114 (June 20, 1968), p. 18059.

292

the conclusion that an expenditure ceiling can be meaningful, and that it will encourage greater focus of attention by
Congress and the country and the press upon spending.
But . . . the best means and most appropriate and effective
way to reduce Government spending is to hold the line on
authorizations and appropriations. [12]

Despite Mahon's conversion to expenditure controls, a new battle
erupted in September 1972, complicated this time by President Nixon's
demand for unrestrained discretion to enforce a $250 billion limit on
total spending. Once again, the appropriations committees were bypassed; once again there was bitter controversy between the revenue
and spending committees. The battle lines were drawn when Ways
and Means attached a spending limit to legislation dealing with the
public debt. The bill would have authorized the president "notwith-
standing the provisions of any other law" to withhold such amounts
as may be necessary to maintain the $250 billion ceiling. During
floor debate, Appropriations Committee Chairman Mahon, a courtly
member known for his dislike of personal or institutional combat,
openly attacked the Ways and Means Committee. His accumulated
grievances could not be held back any longer:

It surprises me a bit that my good friend from Arkansas
[Wilbur Mills, Chairman of Ways and Means] would speak
so fervently about economy and a balanced budget when he
has led the fight to bring about the condition with which we
are confronted today. Yet he talks about economy and points
the finger at the Appropriations Committee, and yet the
gentleman from Arkansas has led the fight over the last 10
years that has reduced the revenues of this Government by
the equivalent of $50 billion for the forthcoming fiscal year.
Except for those reductions, we would be in the black, provided the economy would have behaved as it has.

Yet the gentleman points his finger at the Appropriations
Committee. This is not where the problem is. The cutting
of revenues and the increasing of spending through the
Committee on Ways and Means, through the leadership
of the gentleman from Arkansas, have helped bring us to
this day of crisis.[13]

Despite Mahon's impassioned plea, the spending limit was passed by
the House. However, the Senate added an amendment requiring
the president to make proportional cuts in programs and barring re-

---

[12] *Congressional Record*, vol. 115 (May 20, 1969), p. 13125.
[13] *Congressional Record*, vol. 118 (October 10, 1972), p. 34599.

ductions of more than 10 percent in any activity or item. Faced with pressure to adjourn, Congress, on the last day of the session, passed a bill with contradictory provisions estabishing and voiding a ceiling on expenditures.[14]

Five attempts were made to impose ceilings on expenditures during the 1967–1972 period:

- In 1967, the spending reduction was attached to a continuing resolution.
- In 1968, spending limits were combined with tax legislation.
- In 1969 and 1970, limitations were written into supplemental appropriations.
- In 1972, outlay limits were added to a debt ceiling bill.

All this not only generated intense conflict; it also demonstrated Congress's lack of procedures for considering spending limitations.

The Loss of Control over the Budget. Why did the appropriations and tax committees fight so often and so bitterly over spending limitations? An easy answer is that each set of committees wanted to expand (or protect) its jurisdiction vis-à-vis the other. Jurisdictional squabbbles are common on Capitol Hill, especially when (as in the case of spending limits) no committee had a clearly-established claim to the legislation. But this answer invites another question. Why were the tax and appropriations committees so concerned about spending limits? They had avoided this troubling issue for a full century, and there appeared to be little outside pressure on them to take up the cause.

The condition of the federal budget during the tumultuous years from Vietnam to Watergate was one source of Congress's concern. As we have noted, federal deficits grew during the years under review here. The "guns versus butter" debate at the close of the Johnson era was an indication of the financial strain facing the nation. Incremental resources—traditionally the chief means of dampening budgetary tensions—were no longer abundantly available for satisfying new claims without depriving old ones. An increasing portion of the budget became uncontrollable, because of past commitments or legislation mandating expenditures. In fiscal 1967, the first year for which annual statistics were regularly published, almost 60 percent of federal outlays were listed as uncontrollable under existing law. Uncontrollability made it harder for liberals to channel funds to

---

[14] P.L. 92-599. Section 201(a) established a $250 billion spending limitation for fiscal 1973; section 201(b) terminated the limitation "one day after the date of enactment."

their favored programs and for conservatives to limit total spending. None of the spending limitations enacted between 1967 and 1972 achieved its intended effects. Uncontrollable spending continued to soar and usually was exempted from the limitations. Many committees and members adapted to tight budgets by promoting backdoor legislation which escaped review by an appropriations committee. According to one estimate, the appropriations committees cut $30 billion from the budget between 1967 and 1973—about the amount Congress added through backdoor devices such as contract authority, borrowing authority, and entitlements.[15]

At the same time that fewer resources were available for responding to claims on the budget, Congress was becoming more open to demands. Historically, the budget was shielded from outside scrutiny by its inherent complexity, the obscurity of budget documents, the impenetrability of the tax laws, and the failure of most affected interests to invest in budget research and data. The House appropriations subcommittees amassed budgetary power through their mastery of the details of expenditures. On the tax side, the Ways and Means Committee's status was protected for many years by a monolithic committee structure (no subcommittees), closed rules (no floor amendments), and privileged access to expert staff. For most outsiders, the budget was an intimidating document, a curtain of numbers that was difficult to penetrate. As we shall see, however, this situation was eroded in the years preceding the passage of the Budget Act by changes in the structure and behavior of key congressional committees. The next section deals with changes in the appropriations process during the years before the Budget Act; the following section looks at the tax-writing process in the same period. Both sections focus on the relevant House committees because these were the main points of budget control in Congress.

The House Appropriations Committee

Richard Fenno's magisterial study of the appropriations process identified budget cutting as the foremost operational goal of the House Appropriations Committee. For generations, a commitment to budget cutting was the yardstick by which the committee's effectiveness was measured. Year after year, House Appropriations produced figures showing how much it had cut from the president's budget—proof that the committee had stood its ground in the face of spending demands.

[15] See Joint Study Committee on Budget Control, *Interim Report*, February 7, 1973, p. 21.

Budget cutting via the appropriations process served two basic legislative expectations: to guard against waste and extravagance and to check the executive. But the appropriations process had another legislative purpose, directed at Congress itself rather than at the executive branch. House Appropriations also functioned as a guardian against the spending interests of Congress itself. Over the past century, Congress has bolstered the Appropriations Committee when it has wanted budgetary discipline; it has weakened the committee when it has preferred a freer rein to spend. The vacillating fortunes of this committee depend on the market in Congress for spending control. But even when it has wanted effective guardians, Congress has been reluctant to unleash Appropriations to work its will on the federal budget. Guarding the Treasury is but one of the goals pursued by Congress; spending on favored programs is another. As Fenno pointed out, House Appropriations has been buffeted by the same tensions which have beset Congress: "the Committee is subject to two sets of expectations—one holding that the Committee should supply money for programs authorized by Congress and one holding that the Committee should fund these programs in as economical a manner as possible."[16]

Fenno's study was published in 1966 (though most of the research was completed several years earlier) shortly after the chairmanship of the House Appropriations Committee passed from Clarence Cannon to George Mahon. When Mahon became chairman during fiscal 1965, federal outlays were $118 billion; when he retired in fiscal 1979, expenditures were nearing the $500 billion mark. For a committee which defined its purpose as "guarding the purse," this spending rise was a difficult experience. It meant not only that the committee had lost some of its effectiveness as guardian, but that the role of House Appropriations had changed in response to pressures from the parent chamber.

On the surface the appropriations process has not changed much over the years. Each agency still appears before its appropriations subcommittee with voluminous justification books detailing what it spends and explaining the changes requested in its items of expenditure. Each subcommittee marks up its bill and sends it to the full committee, which makes few or no changes. Behind the façade, however, changes in its role, operations, and composition have weakened House Appropriations as guardian of the purse. Let us look now at some of those changes.

[16] Richard F. Fenno, *The Power of the Purse: Appropriations Politics in Congress* (Boston: Little, Brown, 1966), p. 355.

1. Authorizations are powerful claims for federal dollars and, as Fenno noted, convey "the expectation . . . that the Appropriations Committee should provide support for the activity specified therein."[17] Until the 1950s, most authorizations were permanent and for indefinite amounts—"such sums as may be necessary." Over the past three decades, Congress has moved toward temporary (annual and multiyear) authorizations, usually for specific amounts. This shift has increased the pressure on Appropriations to fund the programs established by Congress.

2. Congress sometimes does more than merely signal its expectations to the appropriations committees; it bypasses them altogether through backdoor legislation. Backdoors represent a congressional determination to shelter certain programs from Appropriations's review and control. Moreover, many backdoors are permanent appropriations which automatically become available each year without action by Congress. The combined effect of backdoors and permanent appropriations has been the removal of more than half of the budget from Appropriations's control. The unmistakable message to House Appropriations has been that if it tried to be a stern guardian, Congress would respond by removing coveted programs from its effective jurisdiction.

3. In order to guard against Congress's inclination to spend, the appropriations committees have to be sheltered from some of the pressures which buffet Congress. Otherwise, their budgetary preferences probably would not differ much from those of Congress itself. Over the years, the House Appropriations Committee was protected by various arrangements which enabled it to rebuff spending pressures. These protective features can be summarized as follows:

The House Appropriations Committee carefully selected its members from relatively "safe" districts. Because their reelection prospects were good, these members could afford to resist pressure from interest groups. Turnover on the committee was low, and new members went through a prolonged apprenticeship before they gained positions of authority. By the time they became subcommittee chairmen or ranking minority members, most Appropriations committeemen had been socialized to conform to the group's norms, including the imperative of sticking together in order to beat back the pressures from outside. On occasion, the committee applied sanctions against members considered to be unduly supportive of programs within their subcommittee's jurisdiction. These included abolishing subcommittees, changing their jurisdiction, or altering their membership. Committee and subcommittee meetings were almost always held behind closed doors,

[17] Ibid., pp. 7-8.

beyond the easy reach of interest groups. Committee members rarely filed dissenting opinions, though they sometimes "reserved" the option of reopening an issue on the floor. Floor consideration in the House was in the Committee of the Whole where the individual votes of members were not recorded. As a consequence, congressmen were able to hide their opposition to spending proposals in the anonymity of voice or other unrecorded votes. Comparatively few recommendations of the House Appropriations Committee were overturned on the floor.

Many of these protections were eroded by the reform movement that swept through the House of Representatives in the early 1970s, leaving the Appropriations Committee less able than before to withstand congressional spending demands.

4. Every one of the more than 700 meetings of the House Appropriations Committee in the 91st Congress (1969 and 1970) was closed; Senate Appropriations closed about three-quarters of its meetings.[18] However, in a series of moves, the House and Senate chipped away at rules permitting or mandating closed sessions. By the mid-1970s, the rule was firmly established in both chambers that committee meetings must be open except in special cases where the committee formally votes to meet in executive session. Within the space of a few years, House Appropriations was transformed from a sheltered to a public group. The audience at appropriations hearings is informed, attentive, and prepared to advance its causes. The chilling effect on opposition to spending proposals was described by a subcommittee clerk who clearly was unhappy about the change:

> The House Appropriations Committee is weaker now. The members seem to be playing to the audience. They are not prone in an open markup or conference to say what they want to say. This year we had five or six members who showed up at our conference and some of the projects they wanted were dogs. But our members are not likely to criticize another member's feelings, so you don't have the kind of exchange we used to have when markups and conferences were closed.[19]

5. For many years, House Appropriations had strong chairmen who had been schooled in the budget-cutting norms of the group and

---

[18] According to Fenno (ibid., p. 113), House Appropriations "members believe . . . that closed, executive sessions are necessary to protect Committee deliberations from pressure generated through publicity which would, in their view, increase appropriations and prevent them from protecting the Treasury."

[19] Throughout this chapter, unless otherwise noted, quotations are from author's interviews with members and staff in 1977 and 1978.

thrust their views on their colleagues. Along with the chairmanship of other House committees, that of Appropriations was invariably determined by seniority. With few exceptions, much the same applied to the selection of subcommittee chairmen. In 1971, however, the Democratic Caucus breached the seniority rule by establishing a procedure whereby it could select chairmen on grounds other than seniority. The seniority rule was further eroded at the start of the 94th Congress when the Democratic Steering and Policy Committee was given a role in recommending committee chairmen and assigning members to committees. Three longtime Democratic chairmen were deposed in 1975, signaling that the Caucus was willing to use its new muscle against senior members who were out of touch with rank and file congressmen or party policy. Chairman Mahon was reelected by the Caucus, his survival probably due to his permissive leadership of Appropriations as well as to his polite manner. As chairman, Mahon rarely tried to force his views on other committee members and, like a good team player, he usually went along with the majority when he was outvoted. Mahon survived, in other words, because he posed no obstacle to the spread of liberal budget views on appropriations.

The Caucus broke new ground in 1975 by extending its election process to the chairmen of House Appropriations subcommittees. Appropriations was the only committee for which the Caucus seized this role. It justified this extraordinary intrusion into the internal affairs of a committee on the ground that Appropriations subcommittees are virtually autonomous and function almost as if they were full committees. But there was another unstated motive behind this move. The subcommittee chairmen were among the most conservative members of the House Appropriations Committee. In the 93rd Congress, only one of the thirteen subcommittee chairmen had an ADA score—Americans for Democratic Action—above the average for all Democrats on the committee. By reserving to itself the power to dismiss chairmen, the Caucus was putting the conservatives on notice that they would risk losing their posts if their subcommittees blocked liberal spending proposals. Here, too, the result was a weakening of the committee as guardian. As a veteran staffer explained:

> All of a sudden, the subcommittee chairman is playing to an audience and that audience has to vote on him every two years to put him back in his chair. That has a great deal to do with how the committee is reacting to the fiscal situation. There doesn't seem to be a tendency in the committee to cut so much anymore because they are doing what the Democratic Caucus wants them to do.

6. Although election by the Caucus was undoubtedly a constraining influence, the decline in the role of the chairman was due more to changes within the committee than to pressures from without. During the Mahon era, the full committee chairman became little more than one among equals, certainly less influential in particular spending areas than the relevant subcommittee chairmen. Mahon probably had a greater say in appropriations decisions by virtue of his chairmanship of the defense subcommittee than because of his leadership of the full committee. Before Mahon, one of the levers held by the chairman was the periodic restructuring of subcommittees, enabling him to reward cooperative colleagues (those who cut the budget) and penalize recalcitrant ones. However, during the Mahon years, the number of subcommittees stabilized and jurisdictional shifts were increasingly rare. One of the few changes was the transfer of environmental programs from conservative Jamie Whitten's agriculture subcommittee to the Housing and Urban Development subcommittee headed by Edward Boland, the subcommittee chairman with the most liberal voting record. Thus, rather than using internal sanctions to dampen spending pressures, Appropriations used them to ensure that liberal programs were not blocked by fiscal guardians.

A further weakening of committee leadership resulted from a change in the procedure for allocating subcommittee seats among Appropriations members. Under Mahon's predecessor, the chairman and ranking minority member had a major role in deciding who sat on which subcommittee. On occasion, members were deliberately placed on subcommittees in which they had little initial interest. During Mahon's tenure, however, members were allowed to pick their subcommittees in accord with a seniority-based procedure. Inevitably, this self-selection process led to the placement of program advocates on subcommittees. A staff assistant to Chairman Mahon explained the result:

> What we find is that city and inner-city guys are all on Labor-HEW, all of the hawkish guys go to Defense, and the big [full] committee chairman no longer has the power to take the guy who has a defense interest and say, "you serve on the Agriculture subcommittee and do the public some good."

7. The triumph of individualism is reflected in the new acceptance of public dissent in committee reports. During the sixteen years from 1947 through 1962, only twelve minority reports were issued by members of the House Appropriations Committee. According to Fenno's computations, 94 percent of the appropriation bills reported

by the committee received unanimous endorsement. However, three-quarters of the appropriation bills reported by House Appropriations for fiscal 1975 and 1976 carried a separate expression of opinion by one or more committeemen. More additional and dissenting views were filed during these two years than in all the years covered by Fenno's study.

The decline of the chairmanship went hand in hand with the rising independence of members, eroding Appropriations's control of the purse. Mahon, along with other fiscal conservatives, was frequently outvoted in committee but went along with the majority when the appropriations reached the floor. One such instance provoked a revealing exchange between Mahon and conservative Republican Bob Michel, the ranking minority member on the Labor–Health, Education, and Welfare subcommittee. Mahon endorsed a conference report on a Labor-HEW bill even though he was unhappy with the high spending level. It "troubles me a great deal," he told the House, "because it is far above the President's budget and in my judgment too high."[20] Despite his misgiving, Mahon signed the conference report, provoking Michel to speculate on why spending control had diminished on Appropriations:

> Under the old rules under which we were operating I felt much more confident that when we really got to the nitty-gritty, the committee chairman would stand up with some of us and really keep these figures limited to what he and I both would, as a matter of personal philosophy, prefer. The fact is though, that there is a process on that side of the aisle of electing chairmen and subcommitee chairmen from among the whole membership, and that has had the very kind of effect that I am talking about here.
>
> That effect is that we do not have any more of that "College of Cardinals" that was in a position where chairmen could take a traditional hard stand on spending by the Federal Government.

With characteristic modesty, Mahon offered his own explanation for the loss of control:

> Mr. Speaker, the committee chairman has never had the ability to dictate the policy of the committee. . . . Certainly the chairman of a committee has more clout than a non-chairman, but all one can do is his best under the circumstances. I have wrestled with these problems through the years, just as the gentleman from Illinois has. The gentle-

[20] *Congressional Record*, daily edition, vol. 122 (August 10, 1967), p. H 8624.

man from Illinois has seen new Members come, and, generally speaking the new Members are more liberal than the
ones they replaced.[21]

8. As Mahon noted, the reorientation of the committee was
facilitated by changes in its membership. The critical changes came
about through the addition of liberal congressmen, not by the dis-
placement of old members. Senior Democrats on the Appropriations
Committee were clustered near the top of the longevity list in the
House of Representatives. Eight of the twenty-three longest-serving
Democrats in the House in 1977 sat on Appropriations. More than
half of the subcommittee chairmen in 1967 were still holding on to
their posts a decade later. The senior Democrats also happened to
be among the most conservative members of the Appropriations Committee. The ADA average for the ten "oldest" Democrats in 1977
was below the average for all of the Republicans on the committee
in the same year.

Nevertheless, a change in the party ratio weakened the influence
of conservative Democrats on Appropriations. In 1967, the ratio was
thirty to twenty-one, a Democratic margin of only nine which enabled
conservative Democrats to link up with Republicans and dominate the
committee. By 1977, the majority's advantage had been stretched to
thirty-seven to eighteen, a spread of nineteen seats, more than double
the earlier margin. This shift was due primarily to a Democratic
Caucus decision that Appropriations along with other key House
committees should have at least a two-to-one party ratio. This change
in the composition of Appropriations vitiated the conservative Demo-
crat-Republican coalition. Even when conservative Democrats sided
with committee Republicans, they were outvoted by the liberals.
Equally important, the Democrats extended their better than two-to-
one edge to the subcommittees where the bulk of appropriation decisions are made. In 1967, for example, the Democrats had a bare
five-to-three edge on Labor-HEW; in 1977, they enjoyed an eight-to-
three advantage.

The addition of liberal Democrats did more than change the
political complexion of the committee. It also obstructed the socializa-
tion and cooptation of new members. With so many newcomers joining the committee in each Congress, it was not possible for the slow
"learning" process successfully to educate the recruits to committee
norms. Moreover, a good number of the new Democrats joined the
committee in order to subvert its traditional posture. They knew that
Appropriations was oriented to conservative values and they wanted
to change its posture on spending issues.

[21] Ibid.

Although the Senate Appropriations Committee did not have the budget-cutting role associated with the House committee, it too underwent a shift in membership between 1967 and 1977 which had the effect of liberalizing its attitudes toward the budget. The composition of the Republican group changed dramatically over the decade. In 1967, only two of the committee's nine Republicans had liberal voting records; in 1977, more than half of the Republicans could be classified as liberals. As a group, the Republicans on Senate Appropriations were unrepresentative of their party in the Senate. As measured by ADA ratings, five of the seven most liberal Republican senators were on the Appropriations Committee.

9. Longtime participants in the appropriations process invariably express the view that there was a sharp upsurge in the number of floor amendments in the 1970s. The floor record of appropriation bills (and other legislation) was affected by the Legislative Reorganization Act of 1970 which provided for recorded votes in the Committee of the Whole. The procedural change was accompanied by the relaxation of informal inhibitions against floor challenges to committees. The steep spiral of roll calls in both the House and Senate suggests that the customary deference accorded committees no longer restrains congressmen from trying to get their own way on the floor. The legislative norms (apprenticeship, reciprocity, and specialization) which held members' independence in check and enabled committees to steer their work through Congress without much floor opposition have been eroded by the "democratization" of the House and Senate and the yearning of junior congressmen for a greater share of legislative power.

Short of restrictive rules which limit floor action, the best protection for a committee determined to avoid serious floor challenge is to produce a bill that satisfies the expectations of its chamber. In the floor exchange quoted earlier between Mahon and Michel over the Labor-HEW appropriation, the chairman alluded to his committee's subservience to congressional interests:

> We do need to impose greater discipline on ourselves. . . .
> But when we deal with all of the 435 Members of this body
> and the Members of the other body, then we have to do the
> best we can under the circumstances. The Congress and the
> country must come to the position of supporting a greater
> degree of restraint than we have now.[22]

The plain implication of this statement is that despite its reputation for power, the Appropriations Committee is beholden to Congress.

[22] Ibid., p. H 8625.

The committee cannot be a more restrictive guardian than Congress wants it to be. As Congress became more favorably inclined toward spending, so too did its appropriations committees. Even as they defended the appropriations process with statistics showing how much had been cut from the budget, conservatives on Appropriations knew that it had lost effective control. In the aftermath of the 1972 battle over the $250 billion spending limit, Congress established a Joint Study Committee on Budget Control to devise new means of controlling federal expenditures and deficits. Fourteen of the most senior and most conservative members of the House and Senate Appropriations committees (almost half of the members of the Joint Study Committee) signed a unanimous report which opened with a recitation of chronic budget deficits and an attack on their causes:

> The constant continuation of deficits plus their increasing size illustrates the need for Congress to obtain better control over the budget. . . . The present institutional arrangements in many cases appear to make it impossible to decide between competing priorities with the result that spending is made available for many programs where the preference might have been to make choices among the programs rather than providing for spending in all cases.[23]

The appropriations process is not mentioned in this statement (though it figures prominently in other sections of the report), but there can be no doubting the Joint Study Committee's conviction that the appropriations committees were no longer able to withstand spending pressures within Congress. This perception of the appropriations process also was held by conservative interests disturbed over persistent budget deficits. One of the reasons "the financial circles in this country wanted the Budget Act," a Senate Appropriations aide argued, was that "the appropriations process had been penetrated by liberals to a point where they were able to get funding for a lot of their programs." This interpretation overstates the extent to which outside interests were active in the development of the Budget Act, but it accurately captures the prevailing view that Congress's ability to keep a lid on appropriations had diminished.

The Ways and Means Committee

Changes comparable to those on the spending side of the budget also affected tax legislation during the tumultuous years before the Budget Act. Just as Congress lost some of its control on spending, it also

[23] Joint Study Committee on Budget Control, *Interim Report*, p. 1.

lost some of its ability to withstand pressure for reduced taxes. There was a major difference, however, between spending and tax controls: whereas Congress had no choice but to make annual appropriations, it had the option of leaving the tax code unchanged. Thus the main way of resisting pressure for lower taxes was to do nothing; this "nondecisional" approach was associated with the House Ways and Means Committee. In the congressional division of labor, the Senate Finance Committee had the task of accommodating the pressures for lower taxes. Thus Congress could strike a balance in conference.

Until the 1970s, Congress did not make major changes in tax policy every year. In most years, revenues were the "givens" of federal budgeting, and budget activity was concentrated on the spending side of the ledger. The president's budget estimated the expected revenues, and Congress did not have to produce estimates of its own, though it normally did so as part of its ritual adjustment of the public debt limit.[24] In nondecisional years, Congress often made minor changes in the tax code, but these affected only a small number of taxpayers and small amounts of money.

Non–decision making assured a relatively stable tax structure, a condition widely regarded as desirable for business investment and capital formation. By accepting the tax structure unchanged, Congress spared itself an arduous and potentially divisive reconsideration of the internal revenue code every year or two. It could afford to simplify its workload in this manner because of the elasticity of federal revenues. Receipts grow faster than gross national product, thereby enabling Congress to finance budgetary expansion with incremental revenues from existing sources. Congress could satisfy its program interests without having to charge the taxpayers explicitly for the added costs.

Non–decision making was a welcome strategy because it avoided the political and economic liabilities associated with active tax policy. When it takes up broad tax issues, Congress has three options: it can raise taxes, it can lower them, or it can redistribute the tax burden. The understandable political distaste for higher taxes rules out the first course of action except under special circumstances. Since World War II, Congress has raised broad-based taxes only in time of war or to finance social security expansion. The second option—to lower taxes—is almost always politically attractive, but it opens up the possibility of a "raid" on the Treasury by con-

[24] For a perceptive analysis of non–decision making, see Matthew A. Crenson, *The Unpolitics of Air Pollution* (Baltimore: Johns Hopkins University Press, 1971), pp. 1-24.

gressmen responding to pressure from taxpayers. The federal government simply cannot afford a free fight every year over the size of the tax burden; the outcome would usually be a loss in federal revenues. The government's ability to tolerate a deficit actually whets the legislative inclination for tax reduction. By foreclosing large-scale action on taxes in most years, the president and Congress protect the Treasury against a potential loss in revenues. When policy is made by nondecision, Congress can sidestep the persistent pressure for tax cuts.

The third form of tax action is redistribution—shifting the burden of taxation from one group to another without significantly altering the overall yield to the Treasury. But redistributive issues are among the most contentious faced by Congress, which excels as a distributor of public benefits. As things have turned out, Congress has redistributed the tax burden from time to time but usually as part of an overall reduction in tax liabilities. Everybody gains, but not equally. Potential conflict is defused, though some taxpayers may be relatively worse off.

Congress was able to respond selectively to pressures on the tax structure by approving various "members" bills, items of interest to no more than a few congressmen. These measures did not threaten the Treasury with significant revenue losses, and they usually were rushed through Congress without any hearings in committee or much debate on the floor. They did not breach the pattern of non–decision making in Congress.

Within Congress, the tax-writing process was fitted with various dampers which limited the opportunity for action. Although the constitutional requirement that revenue measures originate in the House (Article I, Section 7) did not shut off Senate initiative, it definitely restricted the flow of tax legislation through Congress. The Senate was adept at attaching nongermane tax amendments to minor bills, but without the constitutional inhibition, there probably would have been more tax activity in both the Senate and the House.

As the congressional point of origin for major tax legislation, the House Ways and Means Committee was in a position to determine whether or not tax policy would be actionable in a particular year. During the long tenure of Wilbur Mills as its chairman (1958–1974), Ways and Means functioned without subcommittees; tax matters along with its other legislative business were handled by the full committee. The jurisdiction of Ways and Means during those years was extraordinarily broad. In addition to revenue measures, it covered all of social security (including public assistance, Medicare, Medicaid, and work incentive programs), unemployment compensation, the public debt, international trade, and revenue sharing. Ways and Means was responsible for more than one-third of the direct expenditures of the federal government and all of its revenues, a massive concentration of power for a legislative body in which power is supposed to be widely shared.

Its lack of subcommittees compelled Ways and Means to process major legislation on a "one at a time" basis. By forgoing the conventional division of labor among subcommittees, Ways and Means was able to restrict its output. If Chairman Mills decided that the main item of business during the next year would be social security, he thereby foreclosed consideration of major tax legislation. There was no subcommittee to challenge his agenda or to take the initiative. Of course, Mills was not impervious to pressures from other committee members or from the House, and he sometimes adjusted the agenda to accommodate fellow congressmen or the president. Nevertheless, the overall effect was to close off major tax action in most years.

When Ways and Means chose to act, it maintained effective control over floor action by insisting that its tax bills be considered under a "closed rule." The rules of the House accord privileged status to revenue measures; they can be called up for floor action without first being cleared by the Rules Committee. But this procedure would open up tax bills to an unlimited number of floor amendments and would threaten the ability of Ways and Means to control the final product. By obtaining a closed rule, Ways and Means limited the House to two options: to approve the bill as reported by committee or to reject it. With rare exceptions, the House approved tax legislation exactly as recommended by Ways and Means. (Minor tariff and tax bills generally are considered under suspension of the rules, another procedure which bars floor amendments.) One cannot avoid the conclusion that the terms of accommodation between Ways and Means and the House were markedly different under the closed rule than they might have been if the full chamber had had an unrestricted choice. To assess the restrictive impact of the closed rule, one need only compare the controlled action on tax bills in the House with the free-for-all in the Senate; major tax bills sometimes provoke dozens, and even hundreds, of floor amendments in the Senate.[25]

[25] Fenno and Manley have contended that Ways and Means's success with the closed rule manifested the confidence of the House in the committee and its chairman. See Richard F. Fenno, *Congressmen in Committees* (Boston: Little, Brown, 1973), and John F. Manley, *The Politics of Finance* (Boston: Little, Brown, 1970).

Non–decision making was fostered by the centralization of tax information and expertise within Congress. Neither Ways and Means nor Finance had its own tax staff; lacking subcommittees, they also lacked the specialized staffs often associated with these units. Since 1926, the two committees have shared a single tax staff—the Joint Committee on Taxation,[26] a group renowned for its nonpartisanship and professional competence. In 1973, half of the House committees had larger staffs than Ways and Means, and thirteen of the seventeen standing committees in the Senate had larger staffs than Finance. Although these statistics do not take into account the Joint Tax Committee, they indicate that both Ways and Means and Finance were modestly staffed compared with congressional committees with much narrower jurisdictions. Although it serves all the members of Ways and Means and Finance, the joint committee is most responsive to the chairmen of its parent committees. Wilbur Mills's and Russell Long's reputed mastery of tax law owed a great deal to their preferential access to the joint committee's tax experts.

If tax information was controlled within Congress, it was substantially lacking outside. Because Ways and Means and Finance marked up tax legislation in executive session, only interests with access to the right congressmen were in a position to influence the process. Often, the legislative aides of committee members were not permitted in the meeting room, though Treasury officials sat at the staff table alongside the specialists from the joint committee and participated in the markup. Outsiders did not have timely reports of committee deliberations, nor could they rely on tax groups (comparable to the numerous associations active on the state and local levels) to represent their interests. Of course, many interest groups monitored congressional tax activity and lobbied in behalf of legislation favorable to their constituents, but virtually all confined their interests to the particular matters in which they specialized—agriculture, business, labor, and so on, across the whole spectrum of American politics. By selectively responding to these special interests, Congress could deflate pressure for a comprehensive review of the tax laws.

Non–decision making no longer dominates tax policy in Congress. The federal government's role in managing the economy and redistributing income has compelled it to make frequent adjustments in the tax laws. During the 1970s, the ability of Ways and Means to control tax legislation in the House of Representatives was sub-

[26] Until 1977, this committee was known as the Joint Committee on Internal Revenue Taxation. The committee has no legislative jurisdiction and merely functions as the tax staff for Ways and Means and Finance.

stantially weakened. Some of the changes affecting Ways and Means were specifically directed at this powerful committee, but others emanated from a broader reform movement in the House.[27]

1. In December 1974, the Democratic Caucus expanded Ways and Means from twenty-five to thirty-seven members and changed the party ratio on the committee from fifteen Democrats and ten Republicans to twenty-five Democrats and twelve Republicans. All but two of the dozen new seats on the committee were awarded to Democrats. When Ways and Means was organized at the start of the 94th Congress (in January 1975) more than half of its members were newly appointed. This infusion of new members was remarkable: during the preceding dozen years, turnover on Ways and Means had averaged 20 percent per Congress; now in a single upheaval, almost 60 percent of its members were new appointees. The enlargement of the committee compelled Ways and Means to relax its preference for members with substantial congressional service. In the preceding three decades, members had averaged more than three terms in the House before appointment to Ways and Means; those appointed to the committee in 1975 had served less than two terms in the House. The new members included several freshmen (virtually unprecedented on Ways and Means), a black, and a woman. In the past, Ways and Means had recruited members from "safe" districts, but half of the 1975 appointees had a winning margin of 55 percent or less in their most recent election. The new Democrats on Ways and Means were slightly more liberal and voted more consistently with their party's majority than their counterparts on the committee had in the past.

The expansion of Ways and Means broke the pattern of consensual decision making practiced by the committee during the long chairmanship of Wilbur Mills.[28] When the committee was divided on an important issue, Mills generally tried to develop a middle ground that could accommodate both Democrats and Republicans and attract overwhelming support. He preferred to avoid close votes in committee, fearing that they would spell trouble for Ways and Means

[27] Informed and perceptive analyses of these developments are provided in Catherine E. Rudder, "The Reform of the Committee on Ways and Means: Procedural and Substantive Impact, 1975" (Paper presented at the Southwestern Political Science Association, April 1976); and M. Kenneth Bowler, "The New Committee on Ways and Means: Policy Implications of Recent Changes in the House Committee" (Paper presented at the 1976 annual meeting of the American Political Science Association).

[28] Manley, *Politics of Finance*, characterized the work of Ways and Means as restrained partisanship; Democrats and Republicans would differ but still unite to obtain a committee majority in support of a consensus bill.

309

legislation on the floor. But consensus has been much more difficult to secure in the thirty-seven-member committee, not only because of its larger size but because many of the newcomers have been unwilling to accept "followership" roles. Some of the new recruits have been among the most active committee members, particularly with regard to tax reform issues. In 1975, the roll call replaced consensus as the predominant decision-making mode of the committee.

2. In a move clearly aimed at Ways and Means, the Democratic Caucus in 1974 ordered all House committees to establish at least four legislative subcommittees. Ways and Means responded by establishing six subcommittees, but it continued to handle tax legislation in the full committee. With its subcommittees, Ways and Means more than doubled its staff size. No longer forced to consider one big bill at a time, the full committee now can deal with tax legislation while its subcommittees are working on other measures. Because of subcommittees (and other changes), Ways and Means now holds many more meetings than in the past.

3. In 1973, the Democratic Caucus established a procedure to break the closed rule. Upon petition of fifty or more Democratic congressmen, a Caucus majority can instruct the Rules Committee to write a rule allowing a floor vote on a particular amendment. This "appeals" procedure has enabled Ways and Means Democrats to get floor votes or amendments rejected in committee. Rather than face defeat in Caucus, Ways and Means has adopted the practice of seeking "modified" rules allowing floor consideration of a limited number of hotly contested amendments. This procedure preserves a modicum of control for Ways and Means over tax legislation and averts direct challenges to its judgment.

4. The opening of committee meetings to the public has affected both Ways and Means and Finance. In 1972, two-thirds of the sessions held by Ways and Means were closed; in 1975, all but 2 percent were open. Finance changed from a 77 percent closed rate in 1972 to only 4 percent three years later. The open meetings have enabled staff aides to attend committee markups, and this has encouraged members to participate more actively and independently.

5. In the wake of personal tragedy, Wilbur Mills resigned as chairman in 1974, thus ending his legendary domination of the committee and of tax policy in the House. Al Ullman (who had served briefly as the first chairman of the House Budget Committee) has not exercised a commanding role in committee deliberations, and it is not likely that any chairman will again rule Ways and Means with the authority Mills had. There has been too much diffusion of

power for a single legislator to control committee members and their output.

The various developments recounted in this section diminished the ability of Ways and Means to maintain tax policy as a nondecision. In the words of Catherine Rudder, "There are more opportunities for more people and groups to register their positions on issues considered by the Ways and Means Committee. . . . The committee is more porous, more open to diverse influences,"[29] and not as beholden, therefore, to nondecisional routines. The new members of Ways and Means were significantly more reform-minded than oldtimers on the committee were. Ways and Means could no longer shut off tax reform issues with a bipartisan coalition of conservative Democrats and Republicans, but liberals in favor of tax reform could not consistently marshal a committee majority behind their position.

Despite its traumas, Ways and Means has remained one of the most powerful congressional committees, if only for its still enormous jurisdiction: virtually all federal revenues, most of the social security system, and much foreign economic policy. One should not leap to the conclusion, expressed in the *National Journal* after the 1974 Caucus actions, that this committee "now is no more than one among equals."[30]

The New Guardians

The Congressional Budget Act of 1974 was developed during a period of change in the handling of tax and spending legislation. Controls built into the appropriations and tax-writing processes had been weakened and, as a consequence, Congress was exposed to pressure for higher spending and more tax benefits. The Budget Act can be regarded as an attempt to establish new controls in place of the older ones. The new controls are part of a budget process which relates spending and revenues to one another and to the total financial condition of the federal government. The budget process has the following salient features.

New budget committees were established in the House and Senate, in addition to the older tax and appropriations committees. The main job of the budget committees is to produce at least two budget resolutions each year, one scheduled for adoption before the

[29] Rudder, "Reform of the Committee," pp. 30-31.
[30] Michael J. Malbin, "New Democratic Procedures Affect Distribution of Power," *National Journal*, vol. 6 (December 14, 1974), p. 1881.

House and Senate consider spending or revenue legislation for the next fiscal year, the other shortly before the start of the fiscal year. The first resolution provides targets for subsequent budget-related legislation but does not bar Congress from taking any revenue or expenditure action it deems appropriate. The second resolution sets a ceiling on total outlays and a floor on total revenues. After this resolution is approved, Congress cannot violate its self-imposed budget constraints. However, Congress can revise its budget decisions by adopting a new resolution any time during the fiscal year.

Revenues and expenditures are treated differently in the budget resolutions. Total spending (budget authority and outlays) is divided into nineteen functional categories—defense, agriculture, health, and so on. Care was taken in the Budget Act to structure these budget decisions independently of the categories used for appropriations decisions, though some areas (such as defense) overlap considerably. The budget and appropriations structures are linked by "crosswalk" procedures which divide the budget allocations among the various appropriations subcommittees. However, only total revenues and the amount by which the total would be increased or decreased by changes in the tax laws are shown in the budget resolutions. The purpose of this arrangement is to deprive the budget committees of any direct say with respect to the particulars of tax legislation. For the same reason, data on tax expenditures (preferential provisions of the tax code) are relegated to committee reports but are not presented in the budget resolutions.

The budget committees are the guardians of the purse in the congressional budget process. Their large staffs closely monitor revenue and spending legislation being developed by House and Senate committees and (with the assistance of the Congressional Budget Office) they "keep score" on the status of the budget and on the budgetary impact of legislation. The House Budget Committee conducts "early warning" sessions during which it reviews revenues and appropriation bills and other legislation scheduled for floor action. The Senate Budget Committee issues scorekeeping reports which compute the budgetary impact of enacted and pending legislation. And both committees frequently inform their respective chambers as to whether particular measures are in accord with the latest budget resolution. Although the Senate Budget Committee has taken a more public enforcement posture than the House Committee, both issue floor comments when appropriation and revenue measures are under consideration.

The new budget committees did not enter a legislative vacuum when they started to function in 1974. The appropriations and tax committees were well established and protective of their turf. Nothing in the Budget Act ordained specific changes in the behavior of the older committees; the act itself could not ensure that appropriations or tax decisions would be made differently from the way they were made before Congress had its own budget process. What the Budget Act created was an opportunity for change. The next sections examine the way the appropriations and tax committees have adapted.

The Appropriations Committees in the Budget Process. The Budget Act implicitly redefined the role of the appropriations committees. They are no longer regarded as protectors of the purse; rather they are cast as claimants whose striving for higher spending is to be policed by budget controls. Like other legislative claimants (such as authorizing committees), the appropriations committees must file reports by March 15 indicating the amounts they want to spend on their programs. They dare not claim too little, lest some of their spending proposals be crowded out later in the year by low budget allocations. Like other claimants, they hedge by asking for amounts sufficient to cover possible initiatives. Before they can report any of their regular bills, the appropriations committees must notify Congress of how they expect to allocate their share of the budget among their subcommittees. Before it brings a single bill to the floor, House Appropriations is supposed to mark up all its regular bills and report to Congress on how the total compares with the allocations in the congressional budget. Every appropriation measure comes to the floor with a scorecard showing its relation to the numbers in the congressional budget. Actions of the appropriations committees are monitored by controllers from the budget committees to ensure that the budget targets and ceilings are protected. When an appropriation bill is debated in the House or Senate, the chairman of the appropriate budget committee usually takes the floor to announce whether the appropriations committee has complied with or violated the budget controls.

These procedures are built on an expectation that the appropriations committees cannot be trusted to abide by the congressional budget unless their actions are watched and controlled. To put the matter bluntly, the budget process exists to prevent budget busting by the appropriations committees (or by other congressional spenders). The transformation of the former guardians into claimants is the logical culmination of the changes in the appropriations process during the pre–Budget Act years.

As part of their claimant role, the appropriations committees monitor the formulation of budget resolutions to ensure that there

313

is enough room for their bills. In April 1979, for example, when the House Budget Committee was developing a revised resolution for the fiscal year then in progress, Chairman Jamie Whitten of House Appropriations was alarmed that the new resolution might not be sufficiently generous to accommodate many of the supplemental requests his committee was considering. Whitten thereupon wrote a letter to Speaker Thomas P. O'Neill protesting that the Budget Committee's proposal

> would require budget cuts in the pending discretionary sup-
> plementals of some 61 percent in budget authority and 58
> percent in outlays. While I have little doubt that some reduc-
> tions can and should be made, cuts of such magnitude as are
> being considered by the Budget Commttee will be difficult to
> achieve.[31]

When they behave as claimants, the appropriations committees ordinarily do so by choice, without overt pressure being applied by other legislative participants. But because it is still ambivalent about spending, House Appropriations sometimes returns to its old guardian ethic. Thus, early in 1977, shortly after Congress had adopted a "third" resolution making room for additional spending which had been agreed upon in negotiations between President Carter and Democratic leaders, House Appropriations reported a supplemental bill which was hundreds of millions of dollars below the amount allowed by the resolution. In the committee's view, it was merely fulfilling its traditional budget-cutting role by appropriating less than the president had requested. But Appropriations was forced to back down. When Chairman Robert Giaimo of the House Budget Committee was apprised of this move, he strongly protested to Speaker O'Neill that the economic stimulus program was being vitiated by the Appropriations Committee. Congressman Mahon and others from House Appropriations were then summoned to the Speaker's Office where they were told to put back the funds cut from the stimulus package. Appropriations was given two options: to propose restoration of the funds on the floor (it was too late to do it in committee) or to have an amendment to this effect offered on behalf of the Democratic leadership and the Budget Committee. Appropriations took the first course of action when the bill reached the floor on March 15, 1977. Chairman Mahon only obliquely referred to the heated confrontation: "Now, we are going to have a rather awkward

---

[31] Letter from Congressman Jamie Whitten to Speaker Thomas P. O'Neill, April 4, 1979.

operation this afternoon."[32] One by one, the chairmen of the relevant appropriations subcommittees dutifully sponsored amendments adding about $700 million to the supplemental bill. Everything went according to script and not a public word was uttered about the showdown in the Speaker's Office. Congressman Giaimo complimented

> the various subcommittee chairmen for their willingness to offer these amendments in order that the economic stimulus package we have agreed upon can be promptly implemented. . . . I urge their adoption, and once again commend the Appropriations Committee for its responsiveness to the needs of the economy as expressed through our budget process.[33]

After it was over, participants from the House Budget and Appropriations committees insisted in interviews that economic stimulus was a special case because that appropriation bill was a response to a just-adopted "third" resolution in which Congress had made an explicit decision as to the amount of stimulus that should be pumped into the economy. They suggested that the Appropriations Committee would have more leeway in making "micro" decisions than in setting spending levels. But even as a special case, the incident showed how expectations about the appropriations process had been changed by the new budget rules.

Despite the budget process, the appropriations committees have persisted in orienting their decisions to the president's budget estimates rather than to congressional budget allocations. From the moment the executive budget is released through the end of the appropriations process, these committees direct their attention to the president's numbers. The first thing Appropriations members and staff do when they get the executive budget is to comb through the documents to find out what the president has cut or added. This orientation continues during the hearings. "We are still dealing with the President's budget," an Appropriations committeeman admitted. "We are hearing the President's budget and that is what we are scoring against." At every turn, the questioning relates to what the budget includes or fails to include. One can read thousands of pages of appropriations hearings without encountering a single mention of the congressional budget process or of the amounts allocated in budget resolutions.

The primacy of the president's numbers persists during the markup of appropriation bills. "I attend a lot of markups of the various subcommittees," a senior member boasted, "and we rarely

---

[32] *Congressional Record*, daily edition, vol. 123 (March 15, 1977), p. H 2079.
[33] Ibid., p. H 2085.

even refer to the fact that the budget committees exist." This "benign neglect" was confirmed by a fellow committeeman who also had a leading role in the budget process. "They [Appropriations] are always talking about the President's budget. They hate to acknowledge the existence of the Congressional budget." An important staff aide who has participated in hundreds of markups recalled that "the budget resolution numbers were mentioned at most once or twice during markup and that was by staff dragging it up. Afterwards, there was stony silence and they went on to other stuff."

As appropriation levels approach congressional budget targets, attentiveness to the congressional numbers increases. But these numbers are used selectively, not as an absolute veto against proposals that might bust the target. A staff assistant explained that "subcommittee clerks and members added the Budget Act to the armament of reasons for stiffing a request that they don't want to fund." One of the clerks explained how this works:

> The budget resolution has given the subcommittee and the full committee a tool to resist increases over and above what the committee would otherwise recommend. We've used it this year saying, "Gee whiz, we'd like to put that in but we've got the budget ceiling and it would take us over." It has given the committee a crutch to resist what they might want to resist anyway.

Even if they consider the congressional numbers during markup, the appropriations committees return to an executive focus in their reports. For each appropriations account, the report compares the committee's recommendation with the amount requested by the president (as well as with the amount appropriated for the prior year). The committee then discusses the major differences between the budget estimate and its recommendation, usually concentrating on proposed increases that have been disallowed, the items it has added, and restrictions on use of the funds. Each report also contains a "comparative statement of budget authority," a tabular comparison of the budget estimates, and the committee's recommendations. The only concession to the Budget Act is a short table comparing the total in the bill with the funds allocated pursuant to the most recent budget resolution.

The continuing dominance of presidential numbers is as much a matter of habit as anything else. The appropriations committees simply would not know how to tackle the mammoth federal budget if they were bereft of the decisional methods that served them so well in the past. They could, of course, devise new methods, but the budget process offers them meager incentives to do so. They can comply with the requirements of congressional budgeting while holding on to their traditions. Moreover, the new budget process encourages the appropriations committees to continue using the president's budget as their guide. The main reason is that the highly aggregated budget resolutions are not directly relevant to the discrete choices facing the appropriations committees. These committees mark up their bills item by item, delving into the lines that constitute the various appropriations accounts. The budget committees, an appropriations staffer explains, "are dealing in macroeconomic policy, in billions of dollars; we are usually dealing in 5 or 50 million dollar issues." Another staffer put the matter quite succinctly: "The budget numbers are just a bunch of big numbers." For committees that have to make thousands of little decisions each year, the functional allocations in the budget resolutions are not useful guidelines.

The fact that the congressional budget is rarely mentioned during their hearings and markups or in their reports does not mean that the appropriations committees are unaware of or do not care about the spending decisions made in the budget process. They care very much and work behind the scenes to get budget numbers compatible with their preferences and with the appropriation bills they expect to report in the months ahead. The congressional budget is now an unarticulated fact of the appropriations process. It is there and everybody knows it. Silence is Appropriations's way of coping with the traumas of this new process, an effort to preserve a maximum of autonomy for the appropriations committees.

Silent accommodation is viable because for the most part the appropriations committees have lived within their budget allocations, not only with regard to spending totals but for individual bills as well. Although they rarely cite the budget numbers as justification for what they do, the appropriations committees generally make an effort to comply with the congressional budget. Even though the appropriations subcommittees are well advanced in their work by the time the first budget resolution clears Congress, the resolution's basic shape is known long before Congress takes final action. Appropriations members know (or can figure out without much difficulty) what is assumed to be in or excluded by the budget resolution. They know when appropriation bills are approaching the budget targets and they know whether programs that are being talked about can be fitted into the budget.

Silent accommodation is facilitated by the stability and predictability of the appropriations sector of the federal budget. Experienced participants can usually project total regular appropriations for the next fiscal year with a margin of error of not more than a few billion dollars. After a quick examination of the president's requests, appropriations veterans can predict which cuts are likely to be restored and the increases likely to be disallowed or scaled down. These expectations are transmitted to the budget committees (which do their own anticipating), and the staffs of the two committees cooperate to develop a budget resolution which holds few surprises for the appropriations committees. Because they know what the budget resolutions portend, the appropriations committees do not have to talk much about them.

If budget levels were to become a big issue during appropriation markups, it would spell a breakdown in the cooperative relationships between the appropriations and budget committees. As long as the two processes successfully anticipate and accommodate each other, silence will represent grudging acceptance of the new realities by the appropriations committees.

The appropriations committees give selective attention to the budget process, and the budget committees respond selectively to appropriations actions. Both parties try to accommodate each other's interests and usually find themselves on the same side of the issue. They can operate in this manner because their substantive interests (as opposed to jurisdictional ones) do not diverge very much. The budget committees could not be conciliatory on the floor if their resolutions were ravaged by the appropriations committees; the appropriations committees could not silently conform to the budget process if their preferences were foreclosed by draconian budget targets. Thus far, the politics of accommodation has not required either side to bend very much.

The Tax Committees in the Budget Process. The Budget Act subjects revenue and spending legislation to similar procedural and substantive constraints. Except for the fact that the budget resolutions deal only with total revenues, the rules are pretty much the same for both sides of the budget. This symmetry arose out of the conviction that revenues were also in need of budgetary discipline.[34] By setting a floor on revenues, the budget resolutions would limit the amount of benefits that Congress could provide through tax reductions or through the enactment of tax expenditures.

During the years 1974–1978, Congress approved seven major tax bills; an eighth was passed by the House but died in the

[34] See the report of the Senate Committee on Rules and Administration on S. 1541, S. Rept. No. 93-688, 1974, pp. 18-19.

Senate. This spurt of legislative activity significantly affected the tax burdens of most Americans, redistributed tens of billions of dollars, and curtailed some tax expenditures and started others. If ever there was an opportunity for the congressional budget process to influence tax policy, it came right at the start.

The effect of budget decisions on tax legislation depends on the type of revenue action taken by Congress. When Congress considers special tax legislation which uses the tax laws to achieve substantive policy objectives, the budget process has relatively little influence. When substantive concerns are dominant, the budget process has no special claim on Congress; rather, the particular interests relevant to each issue determine the outcome. Thus, when Congress considers energy tax legislation, the ostensible purpose is not to raise or lower federal revenues (although this might be one of the significant results) but to influence the use and development of energy resources.

However, the relevance of the budget process to tax legislation increases when the measure raises fiscal rather than substantive issues and when the revenue impact is substantial. Both of these conditions were present in the four tax reductions enacted between 1975 and 1979. Tax cuts are clearly within the province of the budget committees, which can specify the amount of reductions in their resolutions. The Budget Act—through its prohibition of tax cuts below the amount set in the second resolution—has cast the budget committees as guardians against unbudgeted tax reductions. Forcing Congress to resist the temptation to treat revenue legislation as an opportunity to benefit the taxpayers has not been an easy or popular role, but the budget committees have stuck to it.

A third type of tax action in Congress deals with the distribution of the tax burden. This issue arises from time to time through efforts to reform the tax code by curbing tax expenditures. However, since they are confined to setting revenue totals, the budget committees have less say in these distributive matters than they do with respect to the distribution of direct expenditures. When they have tried to expand their role, the committees have met strong resistance from Ways and Means and Finance.

Taxation versus budgeting: a case study in legislative conflict. Conflict in the Senate over 1976 tax legislation demonstrated the limited role of the budget committees in distributing tax burdens and benefits. The Senate Budget Committee, in that year, found itself under heavy pressure from reformers to include a limitation on tax expenditures in its budget resolution. In an effort to avoid a confrontation on this difficult issue, Senator Long, chairman of the Finance Committee, appeared at the Budget Committee's markup session. He began his statement by defining the relationship between the two committees: "I am simply here to urge that the budget committee stay within its jurisdiction . . . and that we stay within our jurisdiction."[35] Long was prepared to do battle over the thing that mattered most to him: not a provision of the tax code—there are many ways to resolve that kind of dispute—but his committee's position and what he saw as an effort to chip away at its power. By defining the issue as a jurisdictional squabble, Long shifted the argument from fidelity to the new budget process to an invasion of his committee's role in the Senate. Long did more than hoist a warning flag. He specified how the lines between budget and finance must be drawn in order to avoid a conflict:

> Now, what we fully expect to do is to tailor the tax bill that will be reported to whatever figure this budget committee arrives at. You tell us how much revenue you expect and how much spending you expect, and we will undertake to tailor our activities to meet that. . . . We on the tax committee can live with whatever figure you recommend here, as long as you put a figure on it.[36]

Senator Edmund Muskie sought to ease the tension by claiming that the Senate Budget Committee was doing nothing more with regard to taxes than Congress had already accepted as its proper role on the expenditure side of the budget:

> I agree that we are not a tax-writing committee. Neither are we an appropriations committee. Neither are we an authorizing committee. Our jurisdiction is an overall one . . . [but] we have responsibilities beyond simply adding up the numbers dictated by current law.[37]

The Budget Committee's "responsibilities beyond simply adding up the numbers," in Muskie's judgment, meant indicating how it had derived the revenue total and the reductions in tax expenditures that should be achieved:

> If you really want to influence the finance committee and the Congress on the question of tax expenditures . . . we have some obligation . . . to indicate what proportion of that revenue number is expected to be achieved by reform in the

[35] U.S. Senate Budget Committee, "Markup of the First Concurrent Resolution for Fiscal 1977," transcript, pp. 551-52.
[36] Ibid., pp. 553-54.
[37] Ibid., p. 555.

tax law, with whatever detail it pleases the [budget] committee to include.[38]

Battlelines, thus, were drawn between Long, who would have restricted the budget resolution to a single revenue number, and Muskie, who wanted the Senate Budget Committee to specify some of the details of tax policy as well. Long realized that the higher the revenue gain projected in the budget resolution, the more difficult would be his committee's task in meeting it. Revenue increases, he argued, generally are made effective at the start of the next calendar year while losses are often given retroactive effect. He warned, therefore, that even if changes in tax expenditures would produce long-term revenue increases, they might show a first-year loss. The committee disregarded Long's argument and voted for a $2 billion reduction in tax expenditures, the amount fixed by the House committee in its resolution.[39]

Perhaps without realizing it, the Senate Budget Committee was seeking to force an abrupt change in the role of the Finance Committee and in the relationship between the House and Senate Tax committees. On every major tax bill over the previous twenty years, the legislation reported by Finance would have produced less first-year revenue from reform (or lost more revenue because of new tax subsidies) than the bill passed by the House. Senate Finance (like Senate Appropriations) functions as a sort of "court of appeals," trimming back some of the reform-induced tax gains voted by the House. But the 1976 tax reform bill, approved by the House, was itself at least $400 million below the $2 billion reform target set in the first budget resolution. For Finance to straightforwardly conform to the budget target would have meant a radical disruption of roles and expectations. Finance would have had to take a harder line on tax subsidies than the House had, something it had not done in many years.

During the Finance Committee's markup of the tax bill, Long tried to hold down the deviation from the budget target. Long, however, was wedged between his commitment to conform to the "bottom line" in the budget resolution and the prospect that Finance's bill would be substantially below target. He realized that outright disregard of the budget resolution would pose a dangerous threat to the jurisdiction of his committee. With Congress still enamored of its new budget process, Long sensed that the best way to protect Finance's interests would be through at least nominal adherence to the requirements of the budget resolution.

[38] Ibid., p. 901.
[39] Ibid., p. 903.

Finance, therefore, contrived to arithmetically meet the revenue target by (1) extending the temporary tax cuts then in effect through only nine months of the fiscal year, and (2) making revenue gains effective at once while deferring the effective dates for revenue losses. As a consequence of this tampering with effective dates, the bill Finance reported conformed to the overall revenue level of the budget resolution, even though the first-year revenue gain from tax reform was less than half the $2 billion target.

Shortly before the tax bill was scheduled for floor debate, Muskie convened a meeting of the Senate Budget Committee at which he strenuously objected to Finance's legerdemain and argued that it violated the spirit of the budget process. "We have an obligation as a committee to make clear . . . that the finance committee bill does not meet the requirements, at least the clearly stated policy direction, of the first concurrent resolution."[40] The Senate Budget Committee knew that Finance had produced a revenue loss, not the revenue gain it purported to have devised. By back-dating the reductions in tax expenditures but leap-frogging the next fiscal year for some of the new credits, Finance conveyed an erroneous impression of its action. The bill actually would have lost revenue in the years beyond the reach of the budget resolution. If Finance could satisfy the dictates of a budget resolution merely by manipulating the effective dates, it could nullify the budget process.

Excited by this apprehension Senators Muskie and Bellmon circulated a "dear colleague" letter to all senators, announcing that they would challenge the tax bill when it reached the floor. "This is not a contest between the budget and finance committees," they wrote. "The question before the Senate is whether to sustain the congressional budget."[41] But once the Senate Budget Committee had attacked Finance's handiwork, a contest between the two committees was unavoidable. Long—in his own "dear colleague" response—exploited this conflict by broadening the jurisdictional issue to cover all congressional committees.

> The Senate will have to decide whether the function of the budget committee is to recommend target figures within which each committee will live, or whether the budget committee, in addition, is to write the specifications for the bills of other committees within the area of their jurisdiction. This is not an issue involving the integrity of the congressional budget process. That process is secure and we firmly

[40] U.S. Senate Budget Committee, transcript of meeting on June 15, 1976, p. 11.
[41] See *Congressional Record*, daily edition, vol. 122 (June 16, 1976), p. S 9569.

support it. Instead, this is an issue involving the proper jurisdictional functions of the Senate's committee. . . .

Is the Senate to respect the right of each committee to make its recommendations? Or is the Senate to expect a single committee to tell all other committees in advance what they would do, in detail, and police them to see that they do precisely that?[42]

When the fight reached the floor, it turned into a contest between two willful chairmen. Muskie tried to force an early vote on a full-year extension of the tax cuts in order to show the likely effect of Finance's bill on federal revenues; Long riposted by accusing Muskie of being a "budget buster." Through four days of sharp exchanges punctuated by procedural maneuvers, Long insisted that the budget process had been complied with and Muskie argued that it had been breached. After votes in favor of Long's position, Muskie withdrew his amendment.

Just before final passage of the tax bill, Long offered an amendment expressing the "sense of the Senate" that its conferees produce legislation holding the fiscal 1977 revenue loss to $15.3 billion, the exact amount specified in the first resolution. This was another way of reminding the Senate that Finance would live up to the revenue level in the congressional budget provided that Senate Budget not try to dictate the details. The revenue number binding on the Senate, he once again admonished his colleagues, is "what the budget resolution said, not what the fine print inside the budget committee report said." Long might have had another purpose in his "sense of the Senate" amendment, to signal the Senate that the real tax bill would be the one worked out in conference, not the one marked up by Finance and dotted with floor amendments. As he would do one year later on an energy tax bill, Long was willing to load the tax reform legislation with costly provisions that would have to be abandoned in conference. These "bargaining chips" would help produce an outcome more in conformance with his own preference than might be achieved if the Senate strictly conformed to the budget levels.

As Long had promised, the bill produced in conference was substantially in compliance with the requirements of the budget resolution.[43] This strategy put the Senate Budget Committee in an uncomfortable quandary: if it chose to disregard noncompliance in the expectation that the problem would be remedied in conference, it would have tolerated violations of the budget process; if it were to

---

[42] Ibid., p. S 9570.

[43] Several of the tax reforms were repealed or scaled down in subsequent years, however.

challenge such violations, it would probably be rebuffed by the "wait for the conference" argument which Finance adroitly used a year later in an energy bill. But after the conference is over, it may be too late to do much about tax measures still at variance with the budget resolution.

Taxation with budgeting: an unbalanced relationship. After it was all over, a Senate Budget Committee staff leader said, "We lost every battle and won the war." But it was a limited, costly victory at best, perhaps even a pyrrhic one. Nothing really was changed by the outcome, certainly not the relationship between the budget and tax committees. The budget committees barely established a jurisdictional foothold in the tax field; they were still outsiders pressing for recognition against the superior positions of Ways and Means and Finance.

Because congressional committees protect their legislative territory, it is understandable that Ways and Means and Finance have not welcomed the new budget entities with open arms. But one might have expected the kind of peaceful coexistence that has developed between the budget and appropriations committees to have emerged in the tax field as well. This has not happened. Even in the House where the budget committee has maintained a cautious and deferential posture, it has had, in the opinion of one of its top staffers, "more fights with Ways and Means than we will ever have with Appropriations. Every time we turn around, we have an issue with the Ways and Means Committee."

On every tax issue in Congress, the budget and tax committees can veer toward confrontation or accommodation. If the budget committees had a voice in the 1976 outcome, it was by dint of confrontation. They had to fight for what they got, with the House Budget Committee applying quiet pressure and Senate Budget sounding the battle cry. But no successful legislative committee could function on these terms for long. In the pluralist environment of Capitol Hill, success is not bought in the currency of war but in the deference accorded to committees (and members) by virtue of their expertise in particular areas of legislation. A committee that has to keep score in order to know whether it is making a difference is a committee uncertain of its position in Congress. At least in the tax field, the budget committees cannot live by peace alone, merely going along with what others would do without a budget process. But they cannot be at war all the time either. A committee which repeatedly has to battle its peers is a committee with no sure jurisdictional claim of its own, no uncontested piece of the legislative process.

Victories won by such committees have no halo effect. The budget committees were not enriched in will or resources by their 1976 accomplishment. The Senate Budget Committee put up a dispirited fight when energy and social security tax bills were rushed through the Senate in the final days of the 1977 session. When Senator Long engineered an egregious evasion of the budget process in the 1977 energy tax legislation, many senators just were not interested in hearing any more about the problems and prerequisites of the budget process. Senate Budget had paid a price for its 1976 triumph; it was now seen by many as an overreaching, combative committee, not merely as the guardian of the congressional budget.

The tax committees do not generally need budgetary allies. They rank among the truly powerful congressional committees, in terms of both scope of jurisdiction and ability to move their bills on the floor. There is very little that the budget committees could do for Ways and Means and Finance to foster a sense of interdependence.

Budget Control and the Diffusion of Legislative Power

In establishing a process that would coordinate the budget policies and priorities of the national government, Congress sought to preserve its essential character as a legislative body. It sought to balance budget control with other legislative values. This has not been easy. Power is widely dispersed in Congress, there are multiple opportunities for access and influence, and important decisions are often made piecemeal, in an inconsistent manner. These characteristics are political imperatives for a legislature whose distinctive role is the representation of diverse interests. Before the Budget Act was passed, Congress diffused its budgetary power by separating tax from spending decisions, setting up parallel authorizing and appropriating processes, and splitting its spending business among more than a dozen appropriation bills (and subcommittees) and "backdoor" legislation outside the appropriation process. Power over the finances of the federal government was broadly, though not evenly, distributed on Capitol Hill. Just about every committee and member had some piece of the action.

But while legislative norms have propelled Congress toward the fragmentation of power, budgeting calls for the concentration of power. Budgeting's essential purpose is the coordination of many decisions and many decision makers to achieve a reasonably comprehensive and consistent outcome. Budgeting requires attention to how the parts relate to the whole and to the relationship between tax and spending policies. Because it is integrative, budgeting was long regarded as an executive rather than a legislative function.

The Congressional Budget Act sought to reconcile the legislative imperative for fragmentation with the budget's tendency toward integration. Congress recognized in 1974 that the new process could not succeed if it tried to concentrate legislative power over money in a few hands. Accordingly, even as it chartered new budget committees, the act continued separate authorizations, appropriations, and tax committees, along with their specialized processes. By simply adding a layer to the preexisting processes, the 1974 legislation sought to accommodate both the budget's need for fiscal cohesion and Congress's need for legislative collegiality.

The Budget Act was purposely cast in distributive terms. It defined the mission and scope of the budget committees and generally avoided explicit redistributive decisions about the powers to be surrendered by the older committees. In fact, the Congressional Budget Act expanded the budgetary roles of the tax and appropriations committees by recognizing them as claimants in the process.

However, this blueprint for budgetary reform invites a clash of interests within Congress between those who are posted to guard the Treasury and those who would open the coffers to favored interests. The budget committees are positioned (to borrow Mayhew's term) as "control committees" striving to deter Congress from doing what it might in the absence of budgetary discipline.[44] The job of the budget committees is to guard Congress against itself. They could succeed only by waging endless conflict on Capitol Hill. Lacking any matter (other than budget procedure) exclusively their own, the budget committees have to trespass on the interests of other committees in order to have an impact on legislative outcomes. The Budget Act thus does more than merely recognize the inevitability of conflict; it seeds new opportunities for confrontation into the legislative process. Yet budgets have to get settled and legislators need means for resolving their differences. In order for the new process to survive, Congress will have to establish budgetary control over revenue and spending decisions, while allowing jurisdictional independence to the appropriations and tax committees. It will have to balance these competing drives without opening itself to internecine warfare. The first years of congressional budgeting show that Congress is at least willing to try.

If it succeeds, Congress will end up with less control over the budget than some reformers and critics would like it to have. The budget committees will not prevail in every confrontation, nor will Congress always abide by the dictates of its budget decisions. In

[44] See David R. Mayhew, *Congress: The Electoral Connection* (New Haven: Yale University Press, 1974).

some instances, Congress will uphold its new budget guardians and insist that other committees rein in their spending ambitions or desires for tax cuts in order to live within the budget's constraints. On other occasions, Congress will brush aside objections from its budget enforcers in order to legislate tax reductions or higher spending. It would be folly to regard every outcome as a test of the strength or staying power of the budget process. Like other congressional committees, the budget committees can survive and succeed without winning every battle.

Most budget outcomes are likely to turn more on external events than on operations within Congress. As political and economic conditions change, so too will the effectiveness of the budget process. In some years, the political "market" will favor tighter budgets and lower (or no) deficits. Under such circumstances, the budget committees might be able to exert more effective control over peer committees than when pressures for spending increases or tax cuts are dominant. It would be a mistake to credit or blame the budget committees for every result without taking account of the larger environment within which congressional budgeting is practiced.

A Republican Budget Process?

The budget process was inaugurated during a period of Democratic hegemony in Congress. The 1980 elections, however, gave Republicans control of the White House and the Senate and sufficient strength to resurrect the conservative coalition in the House. It is not likely that congressional budgeting will take the same path in the early 1980s that it carved out in the late 1970s. Much more is involved in the passage from Democratic to Republican hands than a change in political leadership. Many Republicans, especially the more conservative ones, want budget limitations, not a budget process. They see the Budget Act with its empowerment of the majority to make any financial decision it wants as an invitation to fiscal irresponsibility. They do not want to vest Congress with the power to make any budget that it wills; rather, they want to restrict the legislative power of the purse through constitutional or statutory fetters that would ordain balanced or smaller budgets.

If House Republicans persist in virtual *en bloc* opposition to budget resolutions, the chamber might not be able to muster a majority in support on any set of revenue and spending plans. The process faces less risk in the Senate, where bipartisan majorities endorsed budget resolutions in the past.

Yet the congressional budget offers newly risen Republicans an opportunity to write their fiscal and program preferences into law. In accord with their professed political aims, House and Senate Republicans can tilt budget resolutions in favor of defense spending. If they have the votes, they can pass balanced budgets, but without a budget process, they would lack the means of enforcing that balance. They would face the prospect of authorizing and appropriating committees, even under Republican domination, pressing ahead with their spending ambitions and making a nullity of the coveted budget balance. In sum, Republicans might want budget limitations rather than budget resolutions, but without the latter, they might not be able to enforce the former.

10

Trade Consensus, SALT Stalemate: Congress and Foreign Policy in the 1970s

I. M. Destler

On Thursday, January 3, 1980, President Carter asked the United States Senate to defer consideration of the SALT II treaty until the international situation had clarified itself. The immediate cause was the Soviet invasion of Afghanistan, which followed upon the continuing crises of the hostages held at the U.S. Embassy in Iran. But Carter's temporary abandonment of the centerpiece of his foreign policy reflected a broader domestic deadlock as well. For despite two-and-one-half years of negotiating, followed by six months of congressional explanation and exhortation, the administration had not come close to building a solid, two-thirds majority in support of SALT II ratification.

Two days before, on the first of the year, there entered into effect the major results of the comprehensive multilateral trade negotiations (MTN) completed nine months earlier at Geneva. Here, unlike on SALT, the executive and legislative branches were able to arrive at a common outcome, a consistent U.S. foreign policy stance. Here the outcome was not stalemate but productive compromise, on the handling of economic relations overseas and on the resolution of related issues at home.

How does one explain these divergent experiences? And what, more generally, was the impact of the "new Congress" on American foreign policy making in the 1970s?

The Democratic Dilemma

"It is most especially in the conduct of their foreign relations that democracies appear . . . to be decidedly inferior to governments car-

This chapter draws substantially on interviews and informal conversations with legislative and executive branch officials involved in the issues treated. I am grateful also to John Ikenberry, my former Carnegie intern, for his research support and cogent criticisms of an earlier draft.

ried on upon different principles."[1] Foreign policy brings a need for "energy in the executive," for "decision, activity, secrecy, and dispatch."[2] Yet the United States Constitution is "an invitation to struggle for the privilege of directing American foreign policy."[3] Can we "leave vast and vital decision-making powers in the hands of a decentralized, independent-minded, and largely parochial-minded body of legislators"? Can we conduct "American foreign policy in the twentieth century under an eighteenth century constitution"?[4]

The questions are hardly new. Connoisseurs of quotations will recognize that the last (and most recent) was uttered by Senator J. William Fulbright eighteen years ago; the others come from de Tocqueville's *Democracy in America*, Alexander Hamilton's *Federalist* No. 70, and Edwin S. Corwin's classic study of the presidency. But the 1970s brought new relevance to this old issue. After two decades of substantial deference to presidential leadership, a "new Congress" moved to reassert its foreign policy powers. This reassertion had two basic sources. One was disillusionment with the content of U.S. foreign policy, with what presidential dominance had wrought. The other was the broader revolt among junior members against the congressional power structure, leading to a dispersion of influence on Capitol Hill.

The Resurgence of the 1970s. What spurred the *foreign policy* reaction was, of course, Vietnam. The movement to limit, then terminate, American involvement in the war gained force, culminating in the Indochina bombing prohibition of 1973. Defense budgets and specific weapons systems came under unprecedented challenge. Foreign assistance acts became even harder to pass, and encumbered with restrictions. And congressional activism spread from specific policies to the instruments of executive flexibility which had helped make Vietnam possible. Through the War Powers Resolution of 1973, Congress sought to constrain presidential capacity to send troops into combat. The Foreign Relations Committee challenged the widespread use of executive agreements instead of treaties. Special Senate and House committees investigated the intelligence community, and perma-

[1] Alexis de Tocqueville, *Democracy in America*, trans. Henry Reeve (New York: The Colonial Press, 1900), vol. 1, p. 237.

[2] Alexander Hamilton, John Jay, and James Madison, *Federalist* No. 70 (New York: Modern Library, 1964), pp. 454-455.

[3] Edwin S. Corwin, *The President: Office and Powers* (New York: New York University Press, 1940), p. 200.

[4] J. William Fulbright, "American Foreign Policy in the Twentieth Century Under an Eighteenth Century Constitution," *Cornell Law Quarterly*, vol. 47 (Fall 1961), p. 7.

nent committees were created to constrain it. Military assistance and arms sales were more closely regulated.

In several important cases Congress acted by imposing new procedures, which did not dictate policy in advance but gave legislators a handle on executive decisions as they were made. The War Powers Resolution requires the president to report to Congress whenever American troops are deployed in combat and requires Congress to approve such engagement if it continues more than sixty days. The Nelson-Bingham amendment to the Arms Export Control Act requires that the administration report all offers of large arms sales (except certain sales to NATO and other allies), with Congress empowered to veto them by concurrent resolution within thirty days. The Hughes-Ryan amendment required that CIA covert operations not be conducted "unless and until" they are reported "to the appropriate committees of Congress."

In the beginning, this congressional reassertion was centered in the responsible committees, Senate Foreign Relations and House Foreign Affairs, and encouraged by Majority Leader Mike Mansfield. But as democratization spread on Capitol Hill, initiatives came importantly from members outside these committees. Senator Henry Jackson, a member of neither Foreign Relations nor Finance, won adoption of his amendment to the Trade Act of 1974 linking U.S. trade concessions to Soviet emigration policy; the immediate result was Soviet renunciation of the previously negotiated bilateral trade agreement, a major setback to the Nixon-Ford-Kissinger détente policy. Senator Nelson, who served on neither Foreign Relations nor Armed Services, got his arms sales amendment adopted on the floor after Foreign Relations proved uninterested. An ad hoc group of outraged, rebellious House members was the driving force behind the congressionally imposed embargo on arms sales to Turkey in 1974, after that country's occupation of a large part of Cyprus. Senator Tunney of California, whose major committees were Commerce and Judiciary, initiated the amendment which terminated covert U.S. involvement in the Angolan civil war. Congressional pressure for greater concern with human rights came originally from members like Don Fraser of House Foreign Affairs; later the initiative was seized by outsider Tom Harkin, who used open floor procedures to win enactment of more constricting statutory requirements.[5]

More and more, the floor became where the action was. When in 1978 Foreign Relations voted fifteen to one for ratification of the

[5] For good accounts of many of these episodes, see Thomas M. Franck and Edward Weisband, *Foreign Policy by Congress* (New York: Oxford University Press, 1979).

Panama Canal treaties, no one was impressed; it was clear that the real arena would be the Senate as a whole. In fact, Majority Leader Robert Byrd and Minority Leader Howard Baker asked that Foreign Relations *not* formally adopt their "leadership amendments" crucial to building the needed two-thirds majority, so that senators could participate in this action through their floor votes. Foreign Relations regained some dynamism when Frank Church replaced John Sparkman as chairman in 1979. But partisan division increased with the addition of three conservative Republicans and the creation, for the first time, of a minority staff. The impact of the foreign policy committees in both houses was limited not just by decentralization of power and changes in leadership but by the enduring structural problem of jurisdiction. Inevitably, committees like Armed Services, Appropriations, Finance, Ways and Means, Energy, and Banking possessed important powers relevant to foreign policy.

A final institutional development was the growth of congressional foreign policy staffing. The number of committee aides multiplied. It also became the norm for each senator to have a foreign policy specialist on his personal staff, something highly unusual in 1965, and a growing number had more than one. This also helped to disperse power, by giving junior and noncommittee members the resources to compete with their seniors, and by making a number of the more successful aides important foreign policy actors in their own right.

Thus the foreign policy Congress of the 1970s was active, skeptical, decentralized, unpredictable, and amply staffed. It was also increasingly conservative. The favored causes in the early 1970s had been those of the left, in reaction to Vietnam, Watergate, Kissinger's expansion of arms sales and neglect of human rights, and so on. But the Carter administration generally found the winds blowing from a different direction, as it faced a strong right-wing campaign to keep the "American Canal in Panama," a House contesting withdrawal of U.S. troops from Korea, and a Senate calling for removal of sanctions against Zimbabwe-Rhodesia.

Into this foreign policy arena in 1979 came two major executive foreign policy achievements, the multilateral trade agreements and the SALT II treaty. Both were careful, conservative products, very much in the mainstream of postwar American foreign policy. Each had been under negotiation for most of the decade, initially in the Nixon administration, and neither would have been fundamentally different had Gerald Ford mustered twenty-nine more electoral votes in 1976. But with the importance of the issues involved and the nature of the "new Congress," each posed a serious challenge to both branches. Would the executive be able to manage its politics effectively, in relation to both the legislature and the broader national political arena? Would the Congress prove institutionally capable of addressing the issue coherently and effectively? Would the two branches be able to reach a common policy outcome? Could the United States, on either issue or both, achieve a constructive resolution of the democratic dilemma, combining active congressional engagement with pursuit of coherent, sustainable lines of foreign policy action?

Consensus on the Multilateral Trade Negotiations

Background. The multilateral trade negotiations were formally inaugurated at a conference in Japan in September 1973—hence the name Tokyo Round, though Geneva was the actual locus of the talks. The goal was the reduction of barriers to international trade; thus the MTN was successor to the Kennedy Round of 1963–1967, which had produced an average cut of 36 to 39 percent in tariffs imposed by major industrial countries.[6]

But there was a major difference. The Kennedy Round, like major trade negotiations before it, had dealt predominantly with tariffs and (together with its predecessors) had reduced tariffs so much that they were no longer viewed as the primary barrier to international trade. The emphasis had shifted to a range of nontariff barriers (NTBs) and other trade-distorting devices, the products of extensive government interventions in national economies. As Senator Russell Long stated the problem from the U.S. vantage point, "We can no longer expose our markets, while the rest of the world hides behind variable levies, export subsidies, import equalization fees, border taxes, cartels, government procurement practices, dumping, import quotas, and a host of other practices which effectively bar our products."[7]

Thus the MTN's goal was not only further reductions in tariffs, but agreement on a series of arrangements to codify and constrain trade-distorting government interventions. This lent particular technical complexity to the talks. Moreover, dealing with nontariff distortions meant reaching into conflicting rationales and philosophies for national economic policies, and into the delicate political balances supporting such policies. For example, in agricultural trade the United States confronted the European Community's common agricultural

[6] Ernest H. Preeg, *Traders and Diplomats: An Analysis of the Kennedy Round of Negotiations Under the General Agreement on Tariffs and Trade* (Washington, D.C.: Brookings Institution, 1970), p. 257.

[7] U.S. Senate, Committee on Finance, *Hearings on the Trade Reform Act of 1973*, 93rd Congress, 2nd session, 1974, p. 2.

policy, an elaborate trade-distorting system which maintained high and rather stable grain prices within the Community by encouraging production inside and limiting imports to what the domestic producers could not supply. By liberal trade criteria it was an abomination, but it was important as political glue holding the Community together.

Statutory Mandate. Under the Constitution, Congress has original jurisdiction over the regulation of foreign commerce. But beginning in the 1930s, it recurrently delegated to the president the authority to negotiate reductions in U.S. tariffs in exchange for reductions in the tariffs other countries applied to U.S. products. Furthermore, Congress gave the president advance authority to implement, within certain limits, the tariff reductions he negotiated, thus strengthening U.S. negotiating credibility and avoiding the need for Congress to pass on specific tariff reductions which affected interests would oppose.

For the Tokyo Round, the administration also required comparable advance authority, but the question of its form was more complicated. Tariffs were governed by specific trade statutes, and the range of authorized reductions could be set by Congress in advance. Agreements on nontariff distortions, however, would affect a wide variety of U.S. laws, extending well beyond the trade field. The Congress could hardly grant the president a blank check, authorizing him to make any changes in domestic law necessary to implement nontariff barrier agreements. But if Congress took the opposite line, insisting that all specific changes be dealt with by normal legislative action after the negotiation, this would undercut the U.S. negotiators' credibility. Their foreign counterparts remembered how, in the Kennedy Round, U.S. negotiators had agreed to eliminate the controversial "American selling price" system of customs valuation for certain chemicals and other products, only to have Congress fail to pass the implementing legislation.

In April 1973, when it formally sought authorization to enter the Tokyo Round, the Nixon administration proposed what it represented as a middle course. The Congress would authorize negotiated reductions in tariffs, as before, and it would also authorize the president "to negotiate trade agreements with other countries and instrumentalities providing on a basis of mutuality for the reduction, elimination, or harmonization of [nontariff] barriers and other distortions of international trade." The president would notify the Congress upon reaching such agreements, specifying their effects on existing law, and unless either the Senate or the House disapproved a specific agreement within ninety days, it and the specified changes in law would go automatically into effect.

This "one-house veto" formula passed the House in December 1973, but members of the Senate Finance Committee considered it unconstitutional. After rejecting it, they worked with administration officials to devise an alternative, a unique set of procedures for expeditious consideration of nontariff barrier agreements. Essentially, these provided that (as the Finance Committee insisted) Congress would have to approve all NTB agreements and enact the laws necessary to implement them. But it would bind itself (as the administration needed) to act expeditiously, and without amendment, on whatever implementing legislation the administration submitted. Thus, U.S. negotiators could assure their foreign counterparts that any agreements would get a definitive up-or-down vote from Congress within a finite period of time—sixty or ninety legislative days—after the implementing legislation was presented. This approach passed the Senate, was accepted by the House, and was signed into law by President Gerald Ford on January 3, 1975.

Thus, in the Trade Act of 1974, the Congress provided not only substantive guidelines and constraints for the MTN negotiations, but procedures for reviewing their results. It provided also for an elaborate structure of advisory committees representing the private sector, and for official advisory status at the negotiations for members and staff of the Senate Committee on Finance and the House Committee on Ways and Means. Title I of the Trade Act, which dealt primarily with the negotiations, covered thirty-one pages of small print.

Congressional Engagement: 1975–1978. After this substantial trade labor, the Congress rested. Members and their staffs filled their formal roles as advisers to the negotiations. But members of Congress gave little concrete indication, beyond what the Trade Act already signaled, as to what they wanted the specific content of agreements to be. Asked in early 1978 about the nature of key senators' advice to Special Trade Representative Robert Strauss, a well-placed staff aide replied, "It is something like this: They say, Bob, you go out there and do what you think is best, and we will support you unless you make a bad mistake!"

The primary reason for congressional inactivity was the obvious one. Trade was not current legislative business, nor was it, for most, current political business. Thus it got crowded out by all the things that were. In addition, those members of Congress with little interest in trade issues (the vast majority) had several time-tested means of deflecting trade pressures from themselves. Certain complaints could be referred to the International Trade Commission, which passed on claims of injury from foreign competition. Others could be referred to the industry advisory committees set up for the Tokyo Round. Most fundamentally, members of Congress liked to rely on the executive branch to work with and placate particular industry interests, to take the direct trade policy heat. If the major industry groups were then satisfied with the results, legislators were likely to be satisfied also.

To promote this very objective, Congress had insisted in the Trade Expansion Act of 1962 that the president establish a "special representative for trade negotiations" (STR) in his Executive Office who would take overall charge of the Kennedy Round talks. The STR was intended to be responsive (though not necessarily submissive) to domestic economic interests; the State Department was judged too ready to sacrifice these interests for foreign policy goals. The mandate of the special trade representative's office (also known as STR) was protected, and strengthened, in the Trade Act of 1974. Responding to these congressional interests and to the pressure from certain trade-affected domestic industries, STR had moved increasingly into the role of overall U.S. trade policy broker.[8] And STR embarked on the multilateral trade negotiations having been, in fact as well as in form, the executive branch leader in working with Congress to get the Trade Act passed.

In the 1975–1978 period, STR continued to be sensitive above all to the domestic politics of trade policy, chastened by the recognition that whatever the current inattention on the Hill, Congress would ultimately have to approve the MTN results. This meant balancing the claims of particular industries for import relief against the economic and foreign policy interest in trade liberalization, so as to keep the president and his special trade representative solidly in the political center. It meant ensuring that major industries like steel, shoes, textiles, and consumer electronics did not find the administration totally unresponsive to their import problems.

Congressional Engagement: 1978-1979. The multilateral trade negotiations were largely dormant until the spring of 1977, when Robert Strauss became the STR and the Carter administration reinforced the American commitment to success. Thereafter the international bargaining became serious, confronting Congress with the prospect of a completed agreement package sometime in 1978. The question of

---

[8] For more on STR and its evolving role, see I. M. Destler, *Making Foreign Economic Policy* (Washington, D.C.: Brookings Institution, 1980), especially pp. 202-205. For more on the overall MTN process, see I. M. Destler and Thomas R. Graham, "United States Congress and the Tokyo Round," *The World Economy*, vol. 3 (June 1980), pp. 53, 70.

how Congress would respond suddenly took on immediate, practical importance. Substantive guidance from the Hill continued to be general, though it was clear that there was strong concern about combating foreign subsidies of goods imported into the United States. But on process, an important initiative did come from the congressional side, and this initiative was to drive the politics of the MTN thereafter.

In the spring of 1978, the staff of the Senate Finance Committee began to address the question of how the Trade Act procedures for expeditious consideration of nontariff barrier agreements would actually be carried out.[9] The law provided clear guidance on what would happen after the administration completed negotiations and submitted a bill, and it also required that the administration consult with the Congress for at least ninety days prior to these events. But the bill was necessarily vague on the nature of that consultation. Finance aides, led by trade specialist Robert Cassidy, felt that the implementing bill should in fact be drafted on Capitol Hill. Congress had the technical staff capacity; more important, Congress would be less likely to approve the implementing legislation if it were not, in some important sense, its own creation. And these aides knew that the administration recognized its political risks and was determined to limit them. Specifically, they knew that the administration needed the overwhelming endorsement of the responsible committees, Finance and Ways and Means, for the implementing legislation it submitted. Otherwise the requirement for an up-or-down vote could prove a political disaster, with affected industries joining in a coalition to overturn the MTN.

So the committee staff proposed that Finance and its House counterpart plan formal meetings with STR in which they, in essence, would "mark up" the bill before the administration formally submitted it. Insofar as was possible, they would duplicate the normal legislative process. The two committees would make determinations on the substance of the implementing legislation, in the form of advice which the administration would take into account in the implementing bill finally submitted. And after each committee completed these "non-markup" sessions (as they came to be called) there would be a "non-conference" at which they sought to resolve their differences.

After accepting this proposal, the Finance Committee confronted Strauss with it at an executive session late in July. Despite misgivings on *his* staff, Strauss agreed. This agreement was confirmed in

---

[9] For an insider's description, see Robert C. Cassidy, Jr., "Negotiating About Negotiations: The Geneva Multilateral Trade Talks," unpublished paper, 1979. Cassidy was the chief staff aide to the Senate Finance Committee during the multilateral trade negotiations.

an exchange of letters between Strauss and Senator Abraham Ribicoff, chairman of Finance's Trade Subcommittee, in August, which incorporated a timetable worked out by legislative and STR staffs. There was no parallel formal understanding with Ways and Means, but the Finance initiative set the pattern which both committees were to follow.

They did not do so immediately, however, for despite optimistic expectations, the MTN negotiations were not completed in 1978. And as they bogged down over some difficult final issues, two legislative events intervened, neither of which was handled well by either branch. The first was enactment, by both the Senate and the House, of the Hollings-Holland amendment prohibiting any reduction of U.S. textile tariffs in the MTN—despite other countries' insistence on such reductions, and despite the fact that U.S. negotiators had already offered them. The second was congressional failure, in the October adjournment rush, to pass a bill the Europeans deemed essential to completion of the negotiations—one which extended the authority of the administration to waive countervailing duties on imports found to have been subsidized by foreign governments. Such subsidies were a major issue in the negotiations, perhaps the most contentious issue. The Europeans insisted they would not complete the talks if the United States suddenly imposed duties under the old law even as it was negotiating for a new arrangement. But under the Trade Act of 1974, the secretary of the Treasury's authority to waive imposition of such duties expired on January 3, 1979; the 96th Congress was not to convene until January 15.

President Carter vetoed the textile amendment after the 95th Congress adjourned, but the two issues became politically linked. The ranking members of the House trade subcommittee warned that the textile industry could block waiver legislation in the 96th Congress or attach its proposal as an amendment to such legislation. And in fact, Chairman Charles Vanik delayed action on the waiver extension until the textile issue could be resolved.

Strauss promised the Europeans that the administration would press for the waiver when the 96th Congress convened, and the negotiators in Geneva continued to work out the final issues, deferring any formal endorsement of the results. Simultaneously, Strauss negotiated with the textile industry, acceding to its major demands. By February it had gotten most of what it wanted—mainly the extension and strengthening of quota arrangements on textile imports. Thereafter Congress moved expeditiously to extend the countervailing waiver authority, and the two key committees began to address the entire MTN package.

The "Non-Markups." Prior to the "sunshine" reforms of the early 1970s, Congress typically developed legislation in closed committee sessions with attendance confined to members, their staffs, and invited executive branch officials. The Trade Act procedures made it possible to turn back the clock, to return to this earlier, easier way of doing things. Meetings on trade implementing legislation were, in form, advisory—it was the administration, under the Trade Act of 1974, that controlled the language of the implementing bill on which Congress would act. So they were not directly governed by the procedural reforms which applied to regular legislative business. And both congressional and executive branch participants preferred closed sessions, for they rendered the issues politically more manageable for the committees, and for STR as well. There was also, initially, the further rationale that the non-markups concerned confidential matters still under international negotiation, since they began before the formal conclusion of the MTN on April 12.

The Finance Committee held nine days of non-markup sessions, beginning March 6 and ending May 3. Ways and Means held fifteen, between March 13 and May 16. Representatives of the two then held a "non-conference" May 21–23. They did not actually draft the statute in these meetings; rather, they made specific policy recommendations by reviewing options offered up by committee and executive branch aids. Then, as the substantive issues were being resolved, task forces including legislative and executive branch officials worked to put the agreed recommendations into specific statutory language, meeting in the offices of the Senate and House legislative counsels. This latter task proved more complicated than anyone had anticipated; the final bill totaled 173 pages of dense legal prose.

The length reflected, most importantly, the comprehensiveness of the agreements themselves. A title totaling twenty-two pages, for example, dealt with changing the tax and tariff treatment of distilled spirits in the United States to conform to one specialized MTN agreement. The bill's length also reflected Congress's use of its leeway, within the express terms of the agreements, to pursue particular trade policy objectives. For example, Senators John Heinz and John Danforth made a determined effort to tighten antidumping and countervailing duty legislation, reflecting their own policy goals in this area and the interests of the U.S. steel industry in combating what it argued were unfair, subsidized imports. The result was language which, though consistent with the codes, is likely to make relief under these statutes easier for specific industries to achieve. In no case, however, did the committees recommend amendment of agreements reached,[10] nor did the non-conference propose language that was judged by our negotiating partners to be in violation of these agreements. Moreover, the two committees clearly liked the Trade Act procedures, for included in the bill they drafted was a provision extending them for eight more years.

The problem of overlapping jurisdictions was handled differently in the two committees. Senate Finance farmed out certain subjects to other committees—implementation of the code on product standards was handled by the Committee on Commerce, for example. The Ways and Means Trade subcommittee followed the opposite procedure—by inviting members of such committees to join in its non-markup sessions when subjects under their jurisdiction arose.

Finally, the non-markups were essentially a technocratic, staff-managed enterprise, particularly on the Senate side. Few members of the Finance Committee showed detailed understanding of particular issues, let alone of the statutory language they endorsed. Rather, issues were thrashed out by staff specialists on the Hill and those in the executive, working with private trade specialists and lobbyists. And the committee staff members played a key connecting role—in linking the committees to each other, to the executive branch, and to the private trade policy community.

Once the committees had arrived at their recommendations and the drafting process was complete, the administration released a public draft of the implementing bill at the beginning of June. After making modest changes, it submitted the bill formally on June 19 as provided by the Trade Act. Floor debate proved basically laudatory, inconsequential, and anticlimactic. The Trade Act procedures meant that no amendments could be offered, and most important industries had been satisfied—either by language in the bill or by other administration accommodations of their interests. The House passed the bill on July 11 by a vote of 395 to 7; the Senate followed suit by 90 to 4 twelve days later. Five of the eleven negative votes came from members residing in Wisconsin, reflecting the dairy industry's unhappiness with some modest U.S. concessions on cheese imports.

[10] The House Small Business Committee did protest that under the new government procurement code, the United States would expose to competitive bidding contracts previously reserved for minority-owned business. This resulted in an adjustment of the U.S. offer under this code. And the Finance Committee initially recommended a more softly worded U.S. injury requirement than that in the countervailing duty code; the non-conference, however, agreed to employ the wording of the code, "material injury"! For the text of the codes, see "Agreement Reached in the Tokyo Round of the Multilateral Trade Negotiations," Message from the President of the United States, June 19, 1979 (House Document 9G-153, part I).

Deadlock on SALT II

Background. As the Tokyo Round followed, after a few years' lull, the Kennedy Round, so SALT II was the immediate successor to SALT I. In its negotiations with the Soviet Union in 1969–1972, the Nixon administration had achieved a permanent treaty limiting anti-ballistic missiles, but only an interim five-year accord on offensive nuclear weapons. The main agenda for SALT II was to arrive at a permanent, or at least long-term treaty on offensive weapons—missiles and intercontinental-range bombers—capable of delivering nuclear warheads.

Both the ABM treaty and the interim agreement on offensive weapons won overwhelming congressional endorsement—the Senate vote was, in each case, 88 to 2. This exaggerated their popularity, since it reflected the advantages of a president with strong conservative credentials in selling such measures. But it reflected also a broad bipartisan endorsement of arms control, facilitated by a relatively benign climate of overall U.S.-Soviet relations.

Statutory Mandate. If trade is an area where Congress has constitutional primacy, strategic arms limitation is one where the executive branch has greater relative advantages. This is high foreign policy; it engages the treaty-negotiating power of the president, in a policy area where he has traditionally been accorded deference. When asked by a new congressman which committee he should join, President Eisenhower recommended Ways and Means; he said that "on taxes Ways and Means was king, whereas on foreign relations, he was."[11] And on arms control during 1969–1977, the most careful and comprehensive published study concludes that "the executive branch by and large shaped U.S. policy while the Congress consistently acquiesced in executive dominance."[12]

Formal congressional policy guidance for the conduct of SALT was as meager as that for the MTN was ample. The Senate Foreign Relations Committee had unanimously recommended both the SALT I treaty and the interim agreement "without encumbering reservations or understandings of any kind."[13] But Senator Henry Jackson, fastening on the fact that the interim agreement allowed the Soviet Union significantly more missile launchers than it allowed the United States, secured Senate adoption of an amendment to the resolution of ratifica-

[11] Richard Fenno, *Congressmen in Committees* (Boston: Little Brown, 1973), p. 30.
[12] Alan Platt, *The U.S. Senate and Strategic Arms Policy, 1969-1977* (Boulder, Colo.: Westview Press, 1978), p. 5.
[13] Senator J. William Fulbright, on the Senate floor, quoted ibid., p. 27.

tion declaring that the Congress "urges and requests the president to seek a future treaty that, inter alia, would not limit the United States to levels of intercontinental strategic forces inferior to the limits provided for the Soviet Union." Jackson was concerned, moreover, not just with numbers of missiles but with their size—the "throw-weight" they could deliver. His amendment, the language of which was negotiated with and then endorsed by the Nixon administration, was the most important specific policy guidance in the resolution of ratification, which totaled approximately three pages. (Other guidance included a provision urging the president to "seek at the earliest practical moment strategic arms reduction talks (SART) . . . and simultaneously to work toward reductions in conventional armaments.")

Nor were any specific procedures provided for consideration of future arms control agreements. The Arms Control and Disarmament Act of 1961 provided "that no action shall be taken under this or any other law that will obligate the United States to disarm or to reduce or to limit the armed forces or armaments of the United States, except pursuant to the treaty-making power of the president under the Constitution or unless authorized by further affirmative legislation by the Congress of the United States."[14] The 1972 ABM accord had been a treaty requiring ratification by two-thirds of the Senate—the limited-duration offensive arms accord had been an agreement endorsed by a majority of both House and Senate. It was widely assumed that SALT II (on offensive arms) would be a treaty, because a permanent or long-duration pact was the goal. But this was not a clear legal requirement. Nor was there any particular procedural arrangement on how, or how fast, Congress would act on a SALT II pact once submitted.

Congressional Engagement: 1972–1979. In the first four years of the SALT II negotiations, under the Nixon and Ford administrations, congressional involvement was relatively limited. Very few senators kept themselves continuously informed, and the negotiations were conducted in secrecy by the executive branch. Secretary of State Henry Kissinger took personal charge, consulting with members of Congress at times and places of his choosing. The major achievement was the interim Ford-Brezhnev accord reached in November 1974 at Vladivostok. This called for a treaty, lasting through 1985, which would limit each country to 2,400 strategic delivery vehicles, only 1,320 of which could have multiple independently-targeted reentry vehicles

[14] Public Law 87-297, 75 Stat. 631, Sec. 33.

(MIRVs). The equal aggregate levels responded to the Senate guidance provided in the Jackson amendment.

But Jackson, by far the most assertive senator on SALT during this period, was not appeased; for one thing, the accord did not cut into the Russians' throw-weight advantage.[15] He and his staff aide for SALT, Richard Perle, worked with a growing outside community of conservative critics to influence the outcome of the conflict within the executive branch over the content of SALT II, buttressing those (particularly in the Pentagon) who opposed U.S. concessions on the weapons systems not addressed at Vladivostok—the Soviet backfire bomber and the American cruise missile. And Ford, facing Ronald Reagan's strong challenge from the right, decided not to accept the political risks involved in following Kissinger's recommendations for completing a SALT II accord.

Jimmy Carter thus inherited from his predecessor a nearly completed SALT II treaty and a national security community deeply divided about its contents, in both the executive and legislative branches. This division surfaced dramatically in the battle over the nomination of Paul Warnke—a committed, formidable advocate of arms restraint—as strategic arms negotiator in February 1977. Jackson led the campaign against Warnke's nomination, and forty votes were cast in opposition—enough to block ratification of a treaty.

The president was sensitive to this division. He elicited Jackson's views and received a twenty-three-page memo, drafted by Perle, calling for major additional constraints on Soviet forces. Moreover, Carter and a number of the members of his new foreign policy team were themselves not all that happy with the Vladivostok terms. They were dissatisfied with the large number of strategic delivery vehicles allowed each side and concerned about the future threat of MIRVed Soviet land-based missiles to the U.S. land-based missile force. Thus, in March 1977, Carter sent Secretary of State Cyrus Vance to Moscow with a comprehensive new arms reduction proposal which Jackson called "eminently reasonable and sensible." Unfortunately, the very things that made the proposal attractive to both hawks and doves in Washington made it unacceptable in Moscow, since it would, in practice, have cut far more into Russian than into U.S. nuclear forces. The Soviet government denounced it as a "cheap and shady maneuver," rejecting also a U.S. fallback proposal presented as an alterna-

15 The United States opted for light, solid-fuel missiles in the 1960s, while the Russians—partly because of a technological lag—built more cumbersome "heavy missiles." With the development of MIRVs, however, heavy missiles had the capacity to carry more warheads. U.S. analysts differed on the strategic importance of this advantage, but just about no one was urging that the United States build new "heavy missiles" itself.

tive; when serious arms talks resumed later in the year, it was on the basis of an approach far closer to Vladivostok. This rekindled the strategic debate in the United States, with a new element added: hawks now charged the administration with retreating from a solid proposal in order to accommodate the Russians.

Substantive division was both reflected in, and exacerbated by, jurisdictional conflict on Capitol Hill. Formal Senate responsibility for reviewing and reporting on all treaties rested with the Committee on Foreign Relations, but the most active and critical congressional SALT engagement was coming from Jackson's arms control subcommittee of the Committee on Armed Services, which held separate hearings on the Warnke nomination and sought to become the focal point for administration consultation on SALT II. Lending substance and prestige to the critics' case was former Deputy Secretary of Defense Paul Nitze, now a voice for the Committee on the Present Danger, who issued bleak periodic reports on the strategic balance and the state of the SALT II negotiations.

Pro-SALT senators and aides mobilized to combat the critics. Their prime vehicle was not the Foreign Relations Committee but the informal "Cranston group," nurtured by Majority Whip Alan Cranston. Through regular meetings of about eighteen senators and their staff aides (including some who were undecided about ratification), the group sought to strengthen senators' understanding of the issues and their self-confidence in tackling them. Key senators in this group included Armed Services Committee members John Culver and Gary Hart. A major behind-the-scenes role in this and more general pro-SALT activity was played by Larry K. Smith, first an Armed Services Committee aide and later Hart's administrative assistant, who emerged as the staff leader of the pro-SALT forces.

The administration gave considerable energy to its congressional problem. At Warnke's invitation, twenty-five senators were designated as advisers to the SALT II delegation, and a number traveled to Geneva to sit in on formal negotiating sessions. By mid-1978, the administration had put together, through the combined effort of State and Arms Control and Disarmament Agency (ACDA) staffs in cooperation with Defense and the White House, a coherent, persuasive case for the emerging SALT II treaty. But the administration had no senior official to play the role on SALT that Strauss had played on trade—that of policy leader in the executive branch and negotiator both in Geneva and on Capitol Hill. Negotiator Warnke was too closely identified with one side, as was his Arms Control and Disarmament Agency. Senate SALT supporters urged repeatedly that the president designate a "SALT czar" and give him clear authority over both the substance of the negotiations and their congressional politics. But no such action was taken until the negotiations were completed.

Instead, the administration was divided—and came across publicly as divided—on the two larger issues affecting SALT, U.S.-Soviet relations and U.S. defense policy. There was an evident tension in perspectives on the Soviet Union between Secretary of State Vance and National Security Assistant Zbigniew Brzezinski, and the president did not embrace, in a clear and consistent fashion, either of these approaches or either of these men. This tension reached a peak in the late spring of 1978, when Brzezinski sought to link SALT progress to Soviet geopolitical behavior, and key State and ACDA officials believed that he might even be attempting to prevent a successful conclusion of the negotiations. On defense, a series of discrete decisions and actions—cancellation of the B-1 bomber, deferral of the development of the neutron bomb—strengthened the conservatives' argument that the Carter administration was soft on defense. Increasingly, Republicans saw defense as a promising partisan issue. In May 1978 Senate Republicans unanimously denounced what they called the administration's "frightening pattern of giving up key U.S. weapons systems for nothing in return."[16] The following January, Minority Leader Howard Baker declared that the era of bipartisanship in foreign policy was over: "Vandenberg was right in his time, and I think I am right in my time."[17]

The administration was thus on the defensive on two key fronts—defense policy and U.S.-Soviet relations. It also sustained some unnecessary collateral damage when the president insisted on retaining, at least formally, the option of submitting SALT II as an agreement rather than a treaty, signalling lack of confidence in its ability to win two-thirds support. And finally, the administration's position was weakened because the conclusion of the SALT treaty dragged on—and on. As early as the fall of 1977, the president was declaring that a final accord was "in sight"; by December 1978, it truly looked imminent, and might in fact have been completed had not Carter announced the agreement to normalize relations with China just days before Vance left for crucial SALT negotiations in Moscow. Without an actual treaty to defend, senior administration officials and White House aides were reluctant to inaugurate an all-out campaign for ratification, and because the treaty seemed within reach, it made sense to wait until it was actually in hand. But as the wait stretched

[16] U.S. Senate Republican Policy Committee, "U.S. Senate Republican Declaration on National Security and Foreign Policy," May 1978, p. 27.
[17] Comments on "Meet the Press," January 14, 1979.

over months and over years, critics were able to raise question after question, without the president and his top aides' being fully mobilized to provide answers or rebut unfounded attacks.

One reason for the protracted negotiations, ironically, was that the administration was taking a tough negotiating stance on a number of issues, partly to respond to congressional concerns. On matters like Soviet agreement to facilitate verification of the treaty (through noninterference with various sophisticated U.S. monitoring practices) or flexibility to deploy the cruise missile and a new land-based missile system, U.S. negotiators pressed hard—and achieved good compromises. Yet the effect was not to build a broader base in congressional support. Consultation and limited accommodation did not lead to consensus; instead, critics simply moved on to new points of attack. Thus in the months before the SALT II treaty was finally signed at Vienna in June 1979, the two sides used the time to hone their arguments and mobilize their supporters. And the thirty to forty genuinely undecided senators, who held the balance in everybody's vote counts on ratification, remained undecided and, for the most part, unengaged.

Congressional Engagement: Reviewing the Treaty. On June 18, 1979, Jimmy Carter and Leonid Brezhnev signed the SALT II treaty in Vienna; that same day, Carter returned to the United States to report to a joint session of Congress on the treaty's terms. It was an unusually complicated document.[18] Attached to the nineteen-article treaty were ninety-eight "agreed statements and common understandings" which spelled out how particular weapons, testing practices, and so on would be defined. The major restrictions were to last until December 31, 1985. Attached to the treaty was a brief, four-article protocol prohibiting deployment until 1982 of certain weapons for which longer-term agreement was not possible: mainly mobile ICBM launchers and ground- or sea-launched cruise missiles with ranges greater than 600 kilometers. There was also a "joint statement of principles and basic guidelines for subsequent negotiations on the limitations of strategic arms." This set forth, among other things, the goal of "significant and substantial reductions in the numbers of strategic offensive arms."

The main treaty was an elaboration on, and strengthening of, the Vladivostok terms. By 1981, each side would be limited to a

[18] For the text of the treaty and companion documents, together with interpretive comments by the executive branch and the Foreign Relations staff, see U.S. Senate Foreign Relations Committee, *The SALT II Treaty* (Exec. Report 96-14), November 19, 1979, pp. 319-453.

total of 2,250 strategic nuclear delivery vehicles (heavy bombers, launchers of intercontinental ballistic missiles [ICBMs], and submarine-launched ballistic missiles [SLBMs]). Within this there were various sublimits—1,320 launchers equipped for multiple warheads (MIRVs) plus bombers with cruise missiles; 1,200 MIRVed missiles; 820 MIRVed ICBMs; 308 "heavy" ICBMs (which only the Soviet Union possessed). MIRVing was also regulated through "fractionation limits": No ICBM or SLBM could have a larger number of independent reentry vehicles than the number for which it had been flight-tested as of May 1, 1979. Thus, for example, the Soviet heavy missile, the SS-18, could only carry 10 reentry vehicles, even though its huge throw-weight made it practical to deploy 20 to 40 warheads on it. There were many other specific provisions: counting rules to facilitate monitoring, for example, as well as a general prohibition on interference with one another's technical means of verifying treaty compliance.

The treaty addressed only those systems it classified as "strategic offensive arms"; it excluded, therefore, most U.S. nuclear weapons based in Europe, and Soviet theater nuclear weapons as well. This generated considerable controversy in the case of the Russian backfire bomber, which had been developed and deployed essentially for theater operations but had the capability of reaching the United States under certain flight patterns. The Russians were adamant about not including the backfire under the SALT II limits, but Brezhnev did issue a unilateral statement at the Vienna summit promising not to increase its production rate (thirty per year), and stating that the Soviet Union "does not intend to give this airplane the capability of operating at intercontinental distances." And Carter stated that the United States considered "the carrying out of these commitments to be essential to the obligations assumed under the Treaty."[19]

The Senate Foreign Relations Committee began hearings promptly, on July 9. They consumed fourteen days in July and August, and thirteen more in September and October. The Armed Services Committee inaugurated parallel hearings two weeks later on the "military implications" of the SALT II treaty, which totaled sixteen days through October.

To coordinate its advocacy of the treaty, the Carter administration enlisted, as special White House counsel, a highly respected Washington lawyer, Lloyd Cutler. Declaring that "there's nothing like starting in your own end zone," Cutler moved quickly to bring order and force to the protreaty cause. The major burden in testimony

---

[19] Both statements are reprinted in ibid., p. 452.

was carried, and very effectively, by Secretary of Defense Harold Brown and by the Joint Chiefs of Staff headed by General David C. Jones. The argument they presented was strong and coherent, if somewhat marginalist: The treaty provided useful restraints on weapons deployment, improving our capacity to manage the arms competition and to monitor what the Russians were doing. It did not keep the United States from pursuing any weapons program it was seriously considering; it limited the Russians to deployment levels well below what they could achieve by 1985 in the treaty's absence, while only slightly constraining U.S. levels; it helped the United States monitor Soviet deployments; it was a necessary step toward discussion of further limits and perhaps reductions in SALT III.

Critics were able to highlight things that this treaty could not accomplish: it did not eliminate the Soviet heavy missiles; it did not include the backfire bomber under the treaty ceilings; it did not lead to a reduction in the number of nuclear warheads each side could point at the other but only slowed the increase, since both sides were moving ahead with MIRVing; it did not guarantee good Soviet behavior on other issues; and the United States could not be certain of detecting all Soviet treaty violations. But the administration and its Senate allies did establish a strong case that, strategically, the United States was better off with the SALT II limits than without. Prominent in establishing this case in the Senate were Foreign Relations Chairman Frank Church and ranking minority member Jacob Javits, with Senator Joseph Biden particularly active in debate. Senator Howard Baker, Republican minority leader, who had announced opposition to SALT II and linked it to his presidential aspirations, did not participate effectively in the hearings. On the Armed Services Committee, while a majority was clearly skeptical, some of the most persuasive individual questioning was conducted by pro-SALT Senators Hart and Culver.

But if the administration was essentially united and effective in presenting its case for SALT II, it was less persuasive on the issues that became linked to ratification—the level of defense spending, the directives to be supplied for future arms negotiations, and the proper extent of "linkage" between SALT II and Soviet world behavior.

Defense spending was the most prominent of these issues. Secretary Brown, bending over backward to appear balanced (and to prevent any large gap between his position and that of the Chiefs), presented a cautious picture of the strategic balance, though he denied there was any serious threat to U.S. deterrent forces taken as a whole. He saw moderate defense budget increases (around 3 percent annually) as adequate to address any future imbalances, if pursued consistently over the long term. The Joint Chiefs did not conceal their view that more was required, and SALT II presented a golden opportunity to get it. On July 25, Senator Sam Nunn, a moderate conservative from Georgia who was one of the Senate's most respected defense experts, explicitly linked his vote on SALT II to the administration's overall defense budget plans—not just on strategic weapons, but on all forces. He called for a 5 percent real annual increase in defense spending and pressed the administration to present its FY 1981 military budget before the Senate acted on SALT II. Former Secretary of State Henry Kissinger, now taking a much more conservative position than in 1976, lent his considerable prestige to this form of linkage; he endorsed SALT II only "if it is coupled with a defense program representing an obligatory understanding between the Congress and the President which overcomes on an urgent basis the grave peril posed by the current military balance."[20] As noted earlier, the administration was poorly positioned to counter such pressure, and as the debate continued, the momentum grew—in September the Senate voted 55 to 42 to support a 5 percent defense spending increase. But this momentum also became, ironically, somewhat decoupled from the treaty, with hard-line SALT opponents like Hollings, Tower, and Jackson joining Nunn in leading the charge.

The other key Senate concern that summer was that SALT II did not restrain arms enough, a criticism endorsed (at least rhetorically) by the right as well as the left. Senators McGovern, Hatfield, and (with typical flamboyance) Moynihan criticized the Vienna pact on this issue, with Moynihan proposing the Senate adopt a reservation requiring agreement on significant arms reductions by 1981; otherwise SALT II would be abrogated. When President Carter, to appease defense hawks, wrote Majority Leader Robert Byrd expressing his determination to go ahead with developing and deploying a powerful new mobile missile, the MX, Moynihan even cited this to argue that SALT would simply perpetuate the arms race unless the process was given the shock treatment that he proposed.

The final matter looming in the background was the relationship of SALT to U.S.-Soviet relations. Kissinger had proposed that SALT ratification be "accompanied by a vigorous expression of the Senate's view of the linkage between SALT and Soviet geopolitical conduct."[21] But this issue—prominent in 1978—received surprisingly little em-

[20] Senate Foreign Relations Committee, *The SALT Treaty*, Hearings, part 3, p. 158.
[21] Ibid.

phasis in the summer 1979 SALT hearings. Indeed, there was a feeling, as the Senate broke for its August recess, that the treaty had considerable momentum on its side. The administration was showing readiness to bargain on the defense budget and future arms control guidelines. Majority Leader Byrd and his deputy, Cranston, had established working groups to explore possible compromises. Cutler was sounding an upbeat note; Cranston was even declaring that his vote counts now showed SALT with about enough support for passage.

In fact, prospects were never this rosy—very few senators not already reckoned as SALT advocates had in fact come forward to endorse the treaty. But the administration did have momentum. Then came the September controversy over a Soviet "combat brigade" in Cuba.

If the administration and its Foreign Relations Committee allies made a good case for SALT II, their handling of the Cuba episode can only be described as a fiasco. This was the latest in a series of reports of Soviet deployments on that sensitive island. In late 1978, for example, the question had been raised whether Soviet MIG-23 fighter planes based there might be nuclear-capable. Then in July 1979, Senator Richard Stone, speaking at least partly to his Florida constituents, expressed alarm about signs that the Russians might be moving to establish a permanent military base in Cuba. In response to new intelligence indications that there might be some sort of Soviet combat presence on the island—in addition to the training forces that the Russians were known to have maintained there since the early 1960s —the administration increased surveillance of Cuba. Before the results were in, Secretary of State Vance unwisely responded to an inquiry from Stone with a letter dated July 27 declaring that U.S. intelligence "does not warrant the conclusion that there are any other significant Soviet forces in Cuba (that is, besides training forces)." Thus, when the intensified surveillance indicated the presence of a combat "brigade," this inevitably generated concern—even though its size (about 2,600) was insignificant, it violated no U.S.-Soviet agreement, and further analysis indicated that it had probably been in Cuba for many years.

When this new intelligence information appeared likely to leak, Under Secretary of State David Newsom telephoned key members of Congress, among them Frank Church, who was in Idaho campaigning against a strong right-wing challenge to his 1980 reelection. Church, who had carefully stressed the need to consider SALT II in its own terms in July and August, now leaped to a self-protective position, breaking the news himself (after alerting Secretary Vance) and declaring that the Senate would certainly not approve SALT II unless the "brigade" were withdrawn.[22]

The administration was immediately thrown onto the defensive, as senator after senator jumped on the issue. Carter himself shortly declared the presence of the brigade "unacceptable" even though the Russians were refusing to admit that there was any brigade in Cuba at all. Through the month of September SALT was stalled while the administration sought ways to climb off the limb it had gotten onto, and ways to help Church climb off. Majority Leader Byrd emerged as the voice of sanity, declaring repeatedly on the Senate floor that this was a "pseudo-crisis," that we did not even know how long these troops had been there or exactly what they were, that we had no specific information that they had violated any agreement between the United States and the Soviet Union, that they were far less of a threat to the United States than any of the missiles SALT would regulate. Finally, on October 1, the president made a carefully balanced speech denouncing the Soviet troop presence, saying that it posed no direct threat to the United States, indicating that the Russians had made some useful—if insufficient—statements "about the future non-combat status of the unit," that the United States was undertaking a set of offsetting military measures in the Caribbean region, and that ratification of the SALT treaty remained vital.

Now the Foreign Relations Committee moved to begin actual consideration of SALT II, beginning its markup sessions on Monday, October 15. It held sixteen open markup sessions and six closed sessions before voting a resolution of ratification on November 9. The treaty received exceptionally thorough treatment. Committee members returned day after day to hear it read article by article. Reservations, understandings, and declarations were proposed in reference to specific articles, and senators and administration advocates, led by Cutler, debated these proposals. When minority senators complained that the administration presence made things one-sided, the committee appointed as a consultant General Edward Rowny, former Joint Chiefs of Staff representative to the strategic arms limitations talks, who had become an outspoken SALT II opponent. The senators developed a considerable grasp of the technical issues involved—much more, for example, than did Senate Finance members working on trade. Certain proposals by verification-buff John Glenn were technical indeed, such as one defining how the United States

---

[22] Neither Newsom nor Vance seems to have asked Church the crucial question—what he would say if he released the information—let alone suggesting ways he might press the issue without painting himself, and the administration, into a corner.

would interpret "maneuvers of a missile associated with targeting and releasing or dispensing" warheads.[23]

The committee adopted twenty specific provisions in its proposed resolution of ratification. Thirteen of these were "Category I" understandings stating unilateral U.S. interpretations and declaratory policy. These included an insistence that nothing in the treaty would impede "existing patterns of collaboration and cooperation" with U.S. allies on nuclear weapons; that the protocol to the treaty could only be extended beyond 1981 with the consent of two-thirds of the Senate; that future negotiations should "pursue continuous year-by-year reductions in the ceilings and subceilings under the Treaty"; and that it was the sense of the Senate that it would, with House concurrence, "authorize and appropriate funds for such nuclear arms and programs as may be necessary to insure essential equivalence," including "the MX ICBM, deployed in a survivable basing mode."[24] There were five "Category II" understandings which the president would be required to communicate to the Soviet Union (but which would not require Soviet assent), including an interpretation of certain provisions of the treaty regarding missile range and testing and a declaration of the intention of the United States to deploy a mobile ICBM system with specified characteristics. And there were two "Category III" reservations requiring explicit Soviet assent, both of them clarifying the legal status of language previously agreed to, most importantly Brezhnev's statement on the backfire bomber. The committee rejected a number of more consequential amendments, including a proposal to count the backfire bomber under the strategic ceiling and a reservation giving the United States a right to deploy heavy ICBMs (whose proponent, Senator Baker, admitted that the United States was unlikely ever to exercise this option).

If one looked at the committee's work alone, one could not help but be impressed. It had responded to a range of legitimate concerns about the treaty, strengthening it in ways that would probably have proved acceptable in Moscow. It had rejected proposals that seemed impossible to negotiate, that would have forced the United States to give up something more important in return or that would claim rights that the United States did not wish to exercise. Finally, the committee supported its actions with a detailed, carefully worded 550-page report that went out of its way to present both sides of all contested issues and the rationale for specific committee decisions.

[23] Senate Foreign Relations Committee, *Salt II Treaty*, p. 39.
[24] The proposed resolution of ratification approval by the committee is in ibid., pp. 72-78.

Yet this careful effort did not significantly broaden the consensus favoring the treaty. The understandings and reservations adopted did not prove to be vehicles by which undecided senators could justify their support; more often they ended up as vehicles for pro-SALT senators to show that they were not simply rubberstamping the administration's work. Thus the vote in favor was only nine to six, in a committee slightly more liberal in its membership than the Senate as a whole. And the only one of the nine not counted as a supporter from the start, Edward Zorinsky, explicitly stated that he might oppose the treaty on the floor unless further conditions were adopted. (On the other side, Senator Glenn, who voted "no" because he felt that all the capabilities that the United States needed to verify the treaty were not yet in place, suggested that he might vote "yes" on the floor if this criterion were met.) After the Foreign Relations report was issued, SALT critics on Armed Services rallied behind a counter-report drafted by Jackson aide Richard Perle, which called the SALT treaty totally unacceptable without "major changes." Despite Chairman John Stennis's resistance to this proposal on both procedural and substantive grounds, the committee voted in favor of it by ten to seven.

Thus as 1979 drew to a close, the treaty seemed likely to be brought to the floor with far fewer than sixty-seven votes lined up for ratification. The strategy of Majority Leader Byrd, who strongly endorsed the treaty in late October, seemed to be to force senators to confront both the terms of SALT II and the consequences of its rejection. Then the necessary compromises would have to be hammered out on the floor, with the administration (and the leadership) working with ad hoc groups of senators to develop vehicles to justify or rationalize their support, with the disadvantage that the Foreign Relations Committee had grabbed up all the easy ones itself. The most promising focal point was a group organized by Senator Nunn. Somewhat appeased by the administration's new defense budget (submitted in advance at his urging), Nunn sent a letter to President Carter, dated December 17, and signed by eighteen colleagues, in which they expressed a range of SALT concerns and a desire to discuss them.

Carter indicated receptiveness to this initiative. But then came Afghanistan. The Iran hostage crisis had already caused problems for the SALT II treaty by underscoring American weakness and vulnerability. The movement of Russian tanks into Kabul transformed SALT politics in a much more fundamental way. Carter was only recognizing reality when he asked the Senate to withhold temporarily consideration of SALT II ratification.

Conclusions

As an exercise in executive-congressional relations, the MTN was a notable success. The two branches converged on a common foreign policy outcome; the democratic dilemma was resolved; the American system worked. By this criterion, SALT II was a failure—at least as of late 1980. Why the difference? What lessons can these two contrasting experiences offer us for congressional policy making in the 1980s?

Substantively and politically, of course, the two issues were anything but identical, and in retrospect trade seems inherently more manageable. Its politics is often represented as a deep-rooted struggle between exponents of free trade and protectionism, punctuated by recurrent threats of a protectionist wave about to sweep Capitol Hill. In fact, however, both congressmen and interest groups are strikingly pragmatic about trade issues and thus are amenable to bargaining and compromise. The politics of strategic arms has a much stronger ideological component, particularly at times when the adversary's military strength is increasing and the fruits of collaboration with that adversary seem limited. In terms of congressional politics, this means that senators and congressmen will feel strong pressure, or temptation, to take a stand at variance with that of the governing administration. And more generally, of course, the SALT treaty became a pawn in a larger game, with a growing coalition of conservatives using it as a means to press for major changes in U.S. foreign and defense policy.

But it was not inevitable that a SALT II treaty which only minimally constrained U.S. forces would become the target of such a coalition. Nor should the difficulties of the MTN's context be understated. The U.S. international *economic* position was deteriorating too, much more visibly than its military position. Yet here the administration's political management proved successful. And the Congress generated procedural innovations which contributed not a little to its success.

Political Management. On trade, *the administration had a clear policy leader* who managed, simultaneously, both foreign and domestic negotiations. There was no comparable figure for SALT II. In part, the cause was personality—Robert Strauss was ideally suited to play the role of broker and bridgebuilder, and Paul Warnke was not. But institutional factors were important also. The special trade representative's office had been created and strengthened by Congress to be its interlocutor as well as executive branch coordinator. Thus a mandate was there if a Strauss could be found to seize it. The Arms Control and Disarmament Agency had no comparable mandate on strategic arms. Far from being positioned to broker and coordinate, it was created to serve as a source of advocacy for arms control within the executive branch.

On trade, *the administration—led by Strauss—developed and maintained a centrist, politically sustainable substantive position—* against import restrictions in principle but flexible in cases of genuine injury to industry or important political pressure. On SALT, the administration failed to maintain such a position. Because of its internal divisions, it "never had a clear policy toward the USSR";[25] because of certain early decisions and the way they were handled, it lacked credibility on defense, a weakness to which any Democratic administration is susceptible, a weakness that grew as the U.S. political climate shifted rightward.

On trade, *Strauss and STR were sensitive to the general congressional climate and to individual members' needs.* Strauss went out of his way to exhibit this sensitivity, scrupulously, even extravagantly, sharing the credit for successes with others, urging members to maintain their involvement even as he took care that the lead remained his. On SALT, administration negotiators did not display such sensitivity, and some were not always able to conceal their conviction that in terms of policy substance Congress was not to be taken seriously.

On trade, *Strauss successfully cultivated the image of toughness,* of readiness to go to the mat for American interests and return home with "no agreement rather than a bad agreement." And he sought cost-free opportunities for legislators to demonstrate toughness themselves. Thus when the agreements package was completed, there was a predisposition to believe that he had gotten a reasonably good deal for the United States. On SALT, the administration failed to project this kind of image even though Warnke and his deputy and successor, Ralph Earle, proved to be very effective international bargainers and achieved a treaty that was tighter and more advantageous to the United States than the draft terms Kissinger had bequeathed them.

All of these elements of successful trade management could have been applied to SALT II. The new Congress, for all its activism and assertiveness, remains responsive to strong, politically skillful executive leadership. But SALT officials were handicapped by the weakness of congressional structures and the fluidity of congressional procedures with which they had to work.

[25] Stanley Hoffman, "Muscle and Brains," *Foreign Policy*, no. 37 (Winter 1979-80), p. 3.

Congressional Structure and Process. On trade, formal congressional supremacy had generated processes designed to reconcile this with the needs of diplomacy. On arms control, past experience had not suggested the need for such processes, and none existed. Indeed, the major special procedure for SALT II—the two-thirds treaty ratification requirement—was placed in the Constitution to constrain diplomacy.

On trade, *congressional attention focused not on the text of the codes themselves but on* a separate product—*the implementing legislation.* This needed to be consistent with the Geneva package, and foreign governments sought to influence it. But it did not have to be negotiated—or renegotiated—with them. This gave legislators a vehicle for making an impact on policy without threatening to undo the international accord. The SALT II treaty, by contrast, was the target of scores of formally proposed amendments, reservations, and understandings, many of them clearly not negotiable with the Soviet Union. Senator Nunn and others tried to make the defense budget into the de facto SALT implementing legislation, a move with both substantive logic and political potential. But in defense budgeting there was no centralized congressional process tied to the SALT schedule. This made it in Nunn's interest to hold out, to refrain from endorsing SALT as long as possible (if indeed he planned an endorsement at all) in order to generate maximum movement toward his goal in a fragmented, multistage process.

On trade, *primary jurisdiction was held by traditionally strong committees at the center of the political spectrum*—Finance and Ways and Means. SALT was buffeted by conflict between traditionally liberal Foreign Relations, responsible for treaties, and conservative Armed Services, responsible for weapons. Neither was a credible broker for the Senate as a whole.

On trade, *the special procedures buttressed the primary committees.* Ways and Means's strength within the House had been declining since 1974, when Wilbur Mills left the chairmanship and reforms enlarged it, gave it subcommittees, and weakened the closed rule.[26] The Trade Act strengthened the committees on the MTN, however, by making their members and staff official advisers with complete access to executive branch communications, and even more by the no-amendment rule and the committee-centered drafting process which it generated. On SALT II, the two-thirds rule tended to weaken Foreign Relations, since the concessions required to get it out

[26] For how the committee's decline made it possible for the Hollings-Holland textile amendment to pass the House, see my "'Reforming' Trade Politics: The Weakness of Ways and Means," *Washington Post*, November 28, 1978.

of committee (by majority vote) were almost bound to be less than what those who cast votes sixty through sixty-seven on the floor would require. Thus Byrd and Cranston became the key leaders and brokers and were organizing ad hoc committees to seek consensus on the stickiest issues, long before Foreign Relations had issued its report.

On trade, *the no-amendment rule forced both branches into prior consultation*—legislators because it was the only way they could influence the bill the president submitted; executive officials because they had to minimize the risks of its rejection once submitted. This produced an informal but decisive policy-making process—the non-markups and the non-conference—in which a limited number of executive and legislative actors could strike bargains with the expectation that they would stick, as long as the administration bill kept to the decisions which the process generated. And *it allowed the new Congress—or selected members thereof—to operate as the old Congress had operated: in closed sessions* with executive branch officials included but the public excluded; with *the functional equivalent of the closed rule* once their deliberations were complete. On SALT II, by contrast, the actual markup sessions were open, though closed meetings were held intermittently to deal with classified information.

Finally, by focusing power on two committees which did not divide on party lines (at least on trade), the *procedures facilitated bipartisanship*. This was ironic because Strauss had first come to prominence as a party politician, and he returned to this role as manager of Carter's reelection campaign. The members of Carter's SALT team were not partisan in this sense, yet they found Republican backing hard to obtain.

Into the 1980s. Senate resistance to the SALT II treaty was the culmination of a decade of congressional assertiveness in foreign policy. It had many causes specific to the issue and the time, such as growing concern about U.S. defenses and Soviet world behavior and the failure of the Carter administration to position itself effectively on these problems. But broader political and institutional factors were important too—the decentralization of power on Capitol Hill; the activism of staff aides; and the erosion of presidential credibility, which meant potential political gains for those who challenged the White House on an important foreign policy issue. It was largely liberals who had profited from these factors in the first half of the decade. SALT II showed that conservatives could exploit them as well.

Trade, by contrast, was an anomaly in 1979—a turning back of the clock. Executive and congressional leaders used Trade Act procedures to return to closed markups, committee supremacy, no-amendment floor procedures—all the things that the reform movement of the 1970s had attacked!

Which represents the pattern of the eighties?

One interesting specific question is whether procedures modeled on those developed for trade might be applied to arms control agreements. One important reason SALT II had hard going is that it was particularly attractive as a vehicle for linked issues—more defense spending, guidelines for future negotiations—that senators lacked the means to control. These can be thought of as the functional equivalent for SALT of the MTN implementing legislation. Much could have been gained if there had existed a procedural system forcing the administration to consult and build consensus with a limited, representative group of senators,[27] if an up-or-down vote on the treaty had been required within a fixed period of time, and if the prime legislative target had been not the treaty itself but "implementing legislation" covering relevant defense, foreign policy, and arms control issues. The SALT II impasse could help trigger such procedural innovation, just as the congressional failure to implement the Kennedy Round agreement on American Selling Price did for trade. But defining SALT implementing legislation would be difficult, and establishing a credible central committee even more so. Neither Foreign Relations nor Armed Services seems capable of playing this role. One possibility would be to establish a new select committee on arms control, perhaps one which drew members from the major standing committees and had carefully delimited jurisdiction for reporting arms control agreements and a companion implementing resolution.

The larger question, of course, is whether the 1980s will see a continuation of congressional foreign policy activism. Will the 1970s be reinforced or reversed? As the new decade opened with crises in Iran and Afghanistan, with Congress and the American people rallying round the presidential flag, it was tempting to anticipate the latter. Congress, for example, appeared very likely to waive strong statutory restrictions on aid to Pakistan—until that government spurned the U.S. assistance offer as "peanuts." Later, it replaced the Hughes-Ryan requirements for the reporting of covert actions to Congress with a new statute allowing greater administration leeway, though it also broadened congressional oversight to include all intelligence activities. The 1980 election produced a further swing to the right; the new conservative majorities in both houses are likely to prove ideologically compatible with the Reagan administration.

[27] Or senators and representatives, if the product were an agreement rather than a treaty.

Yet one should not expect a return to the pattern of the 1960s. The Congress continues decentralized and amply staffed; the problems will continue to cross jurisdictional lines and defy easy resolution; presidents will continue to be vulnerable politically. Thus a return to presidential dominance seems unlikely. The president may well have more chances to exploit foreign exigencies in building domestic support. But the democratic dilemma will remain with us.

PART FOUR

Conclusion

11

The House and the Senate in a New Congress

Norman J. Ornstein

The essays in this book have been designed to gauge what has changed significantly in Congress and its policy and political environment over the last twenty or so years and what has not. In this final chapter, rather than summarizing the findings and conclusions already presented, I will try to use them to examine some broader facets of Congress and the American policy process.

To begin, this essay will look more closely at the patterns of change in the *two* houses of Congress. Have the House of Representatives and the Senate changed in different ways or responded differently to the changing political environment in the 1970s? Does change in one house tell us something about change—or continuity—in the other? Has the past decade created a different relationship between the two chambers or a different role for either? Past works by Lewis Froman and Nelson Polsby, which dealt with some aspects of these questions, will be used as points of reference.

Second, I will try to assess what changes have occurred in Congress's overall role in the American political system. One does not have to have read these essays to be sensitive to the dizzying array of changes that have swept Capitol Hill in the past dozen years. Certainly, these changes, or some of them, have altered in a fundamental fashion the ways in which Congress conducts its business, the internal distribution of power, the physical plant of the legislative branch, and the ways Congress communicates with constituents and others outside Capitol Hill. But has Congress *really* changed in a broader sense? Is it a more or less significant force in changing the society and affecting America's international affairs? An essay by

Helpful comments on this essay came from Michael Malbin, John Kessel, and Thomas Mann.

Samuel P. Huntington published in 1965 addressed Congress's role in the twentieth century. That essay too will serve as a point of reference as I focus on these broader questions.

The New House and the New Senate

It is natural to think and write about "Congress" as a unified body; most of the analysis in these essays does so. But one of the most interesting aspects of change in Congress is how it has affected the two houses of Congress in the same or different ways. Our essays have frequently pointed, in passing, to different processes of or reactions to change in the House and the Senate. But we have not examined the cumulative effects of change on the nature of our two separate but equal legislative chambers. In doing so, one finds both paradox and perplexity. The paradox is that a variety of forces in the 1970s have brought at the same time sharper differences between the House and Senate in their respective electoral arenas (as Thomas Mann's chapter shows)—and growing similarities between the House and Senate in their internal legislative arenas. The perplexity comes when one tries to understand what the specific, individual roles of the House and Senate in the policy process are and will be in the 1980s. Consider first the internal characteristics of our two houses, in the context of change.

The Different Nature of the House and the Senate. In the 1950s and 1960s, the accepted wisdom about Congress suggested that the House and the Senate were very different institutions. Lewis Froman in 1967 described in outline form the major differences in internal structure, style, and behavior:

House	*Senate*
Larger (435 members)	Smaller (100 members)
More formal	Less formal
More hierarchically organized	Less hierarchically organized
Acts more quickly	Acts more slowly
Rules more rigid	Rules more flexible
Power less evenly distributed	Power more evenly distributed
Longer apprentice period	Shorter apprentice period
More impersonal	More personal
Less "important" constituencies	More "important" constituencies
Less prestige	More prestige
More "conservative"	More "liberal"

Froman emphasized these differences in analyzing the operation of the two houses, focusing especially on two underlying factors: the size difference and the differing bases of representation (states versus districts).[1]

"Perhaps the most striking difference noticed by most visitors to the Capitol," he wrote, "is the apparent confusion and impersonality in the House chamber as contrasted with the relatively more informal and friendly atmosphere in the Senate."[2] He emphasized the greater insulation of House leaders from their colleagues, the greater friction and more frequent violations of the spirit of comity in the House than in the Senate.

Froman went on to underscore the marked difference in efficiency of operation between the two houses; he commented, "the 'normal' business of the House proceeds quickly. . . . It is rare, for example, for any but major bills in the House to take longer than one day for consideration," while the Senate "is a much more leisurely body."[3] He also discussed the difference between the two chambers in the internal distribution of power, with power dispersed and democratized in the Senate and more narrowly controlled in the House. Senators, on occasion, were even able to chair a subcommittee in their first year, while House members had to wait for a long, long time and had difficulty developing any base of power from which to operate. With all these differences, and especially because of the different constituencies (those of the House being narrower and less diverse), Froman noted that the House tended to be more conservative in its policy predilections than the Senate.

Some three years after Froman's work, Nelson Polsby articulated the broader policy implications of the structural and behavioral differences between the House and Senate. In "Strengthening Congress in National Policy-making," Polsby wrote,

> As institutions, the House and Senate differ markedly in their contemporary characters. The House is a highly specialized instrument for processing legislation. Its great strength is its firmly structured division of labor. This provides the House with a toehold in the policy-making process by virtue of its capacity to specialize . . . this is a consequence of the strong division of labor that the House maintains: members are generally assigned to one or two committees

[1] Lewis A. Froman, *The Congressional Process: Strategies, Rules, and Procedures* (Boston: Little, Brown, 1967).

[2] Ibid., p. 7.

[3] Ibid., p. 8.

only. Floor debate is normally limited to participation by committee members. There is an expectation that members will concentrate their energies rather than range widely over the full spectrum of public policy.[4]

Specialization in the House, said Polsby, was encouraged by the lack of publicity accorded House members vis-à-vis senators, who preened before the media as presidential hopefuls. The House built in not presidential ambitions but *career* incentives; namely, the possibility down the road of being one of the fifth or tenth of the membership to chair a committee or subcommittee or sit on a key committee like Ways and Means or Rules. With a long-term, career orientation and specialization came experience and expertise. On the other hand, wrote Polsby,

> The essence of the Senate is that it is a forum, an echo chamber, a publicity machine. Thus, passing bills, which is central to the life of the House, is peripheral to the Senate. In the Senate, the three central activities are cultivating national constituencies, formulating questions for debate and discussion on a national scale (especially in opposition to the President), and incubating new policy proposals that may at some future time find their way into legislation.[5]

Thus, two of our most astute students of Congress identified a range of institutional differences between our two legislative houses, which led to formal and informal contrasts in internal operation and to different styles and roles in national policy making.

Froman and Polsby were right, by and large. But, it is worth reexamining their insights in light of the enormous changes which have occurred during the 1970s inside Congress and in the broader polity.

I would suggest that one consequence of the changes documented in this volume has been to make the House more like the Senate, and the Senate more like the House. As a result, the unique policy roles Polsby ascribed to the two chambers have been blurred—leading to less consistent and more erratic policy outcomes.

Consider, for a moment, Froman's list of House/Senate differences, beginning on the House side. Size is one constant: the House is still larger than the Senate. But all of the other characteristics have

[4] Nelson Polsby, "Strengthening Congress in National Policy-making," *Yale Review* (Summer 1970), pp. 485-86.

[5] Ibid., p. 487.—It is, of course, a bit hyperbolic to suggest that "passing bills" is peripheral to the Senate. But Polsby's general point is that the Senate was much more concerned, in general, with the broader scope of policy and legislation than with the details.

changed during the past decade. The House, to Froman, was more formal and impersonal, more hierarchically organized, with more rigid rules. It acted more quickly than the Senate, had power less evenly distributed, and its members served a longer apprentice period. The House dealt with less "important" constituencies, had less prestige than the Senate, and was more conservative.

Since Froman wrote, the House has become *less* formal and impersonal, *less* hierarchically organized and with *more* fluid rules and procedures. The House has also become *less* able to act—much less act quickly—on policy matters. It has spread out its power and, like the Senate before it, has abandoned the notion of apprenticeship altogether. The House and House members have become better known (or, at least, more notorious) and are noticed and paid heed to by broader and more important, often national constituencies. And on most issues, even with the changes wrought by the 1980 elections, the House has become much more "liberal" than it was in the 1950s and 1960s. There are some issues, especially the social issues like abortion and busing, where the Senate (at least the 96th) remained more liberal than the House. But on balance, in 1979–1980, and in 1981–1982, the House was and is clearly the more liberal chamber of Congress.

More and more, the House is an ad hoc institution, without firm control over its own schedule or priorities—much like the Senate. With the expansion of subcommittees and chairmanships, many more individuals hold formal positions of importance in the House. Moreover, hierarchical positions, whether in the formal party leadership or at the top of committees, mean much less today than they did in the 1960s; "leadership" on specific issues can come from any of 400 or more different sources.

The Senate has changed, too—becoming in several respects more like the House. Since Froman wrote, the Senate has become much less leisurely. An average in the 1950s of 150 or so roll calls a year has more than quadrupled; so too have the number of meetings and hearings. Indeed, a crushing workload and frenetic pace have changed interpersonal relations (senators see much less of one another, for shorter periods of time) and behavior. The Senate has become *more* formal and impersonal, *more* tightly organized, through its "reformed" committee system, and has developed *more* rigid floor rules and procedures, such as the use of detailed and limiting unanimous consent agreements. The Senate has tried—albeit less than successfully—to develop ways of acting *more* quickly on policy; the tighter filibuster procedures of the late 1970s are an example. While many senators remain celebrities the rapid turnover of members—both the departure of long-time veteran powers and the influx of freshmen—have created a greater anonymity among Senate ranks. Thomas P. "Tip" O'Neill, Morris "Mo" Udall, and several other recent House members rank with Senate celebrities in public recognition and/or acclaim. (Unfortunately for Congress, so do "Ozzie" Myers, John Jenrette, and Charles Diggs.[6]) Clearly, too, the Senate has become more conservative in the late 1970s and early 1980s and, at least since 1978, has been more conservative than the House on many or most policy questions.

The Senate and House are not now identical, by any means. The size differences and unique constitutional powers ensure that we will continue to have two distinct legislative houses. But the blurring of House-Senate differences in the 1970s has significant implications for their roles in national policy making.

Recall Polsby's distinctions. The House of the 1960s, he wrote, was "a highly specialized instrument for processing legislation," with its strength being its "firmly structured division of labor," giving it the "capacity to specialize" through the committee system. Assignments were limited, only committee members could participate in debate, specialization was encouraged by the lack of public attention given to members' work (compared with senators) and by the various career incentives inside the House. The Senate, on the other hand, was a forum, not a body concerned with the details of legislation. It served as a place to formulate questions for national debate and to incubate new policy approaches for future consideration.

What of the "new" House and Senate? The contemporary House is no longer a "highly specialized instrument." Committee and subcommittee assignments have proliferated, spreading House members much thinner. It is difficult to think of House members now with a reputation for command of, say, the internal revenue code, or the details of the budget, or the ins and outs of the Pentagon approaching that of Wilbur Mills, Clarence Cannon, or Carl Vinson twenty years ago. Reforms weakening committees and encouraging floor amendments, the expansion and decentralization of staff, the influx of new members, the erosion of reciprocity and specialization norms—all have combined to erase the hegemony of committees and committee members in floor debate.

Now the House floor is often a free-for-all, rarely a ratification point for decisions pre-structured by one or two specialists. Carefully crafted legislation is not the only, or the highest, priority of the House.

[6] This is not a function of more scandal in Congress either. As Robinson clearly demonstrates—by contrasting a 1960s scandal involving a *senator* with a 1970s scandal involving a *congressman*—media coverage is much heavier now and especially for the House.

During the floor debate and amendment process, making ideological points for national groups or constituencies, protecting the interests of particular groups, asserting an individual prerogative, or altering a broader policy direction (without deep regard for the specific piece of legislation under consideration) are all competing priorities of significant rank.

It is now possible for an individual House member to become a celebrity profiled in national magazines and featured on national news shows (as Bruce Caputo, George Hansen, Henry Hyde, and Millicent Fenwick, among others, have done in recent years) or to make a credible run for the presidency—witness Mo Udall, John Anderson, and Phil Crane. With the exceptions of Udall and Anderson, all of the above have made their mark through flashy, extralegislative, extra- or anti-committee activity that has captured a national constituency or captivated the networks. None has faced sanctions inside the House for their perfidy.

Career incentives have changed or disappeared, too. Polsby wrote of the incentive for members to accept the House system, biding their time for a decade or two until they, too, could achieve the hefty power of a subcommittee chairmanship or, with a little more patience, the even greater power of a full committee gavel. Reforms, turnover, and subcommittee inflation have changed all that. These days, a subcommittee chairmanship is easy to come by and often quickly achieved —in the 96th Congress, a *freshman* even chaired an Appropriations subcommittee! There is no need or incentive to wait patiently; "those who stand and wait" get no more or better internal rewards than those who do not. Large staffs, which give House members independence, expertise, and the opportunity for notoriety—and which once were the exclusive perquisite of senior leaders and committee honchos —come automatically to all, even the lowliest minority freshmen.[7] Many in the current House—many more than in the past—see their position not as the *capstone* of their careers, but as a *steppingstone* to a Senate seat or state house, to a national political career, to a lucrative position in law, lobbying, or business. The incentive thus is to establish an independent name and reputation as quickly as possible in as many policy areas as possible, with little regard for committee boundaries or subject matter experience. While this incentive existed for the ambitious in the past, the atmosphere and opportunities did not. As the incentive for quick recognition has broadened and been encouraged by new opportunities, the formerly widespread pride in legislative craftsmanship has steadily declined.

[7] See chapter 4 in this volume.

Sounds like the "old" Senate, doesn't it? Indeed, the House, as its structures, members, and norms have become more like the Senate's, has seen its policy behavior move in that direction as well.

As the TV cameras blink red, the House floor is a passable forum for discussing national policy, tilting with the president, cultivating national constituencies. The lengthy debate in the House in 1979 over the fiscal 1980 budget—replete with histrionics, bitter rhetoric, and a plethora of amendments—was a good example. The concern in the House was not with passing a tight and consistent budget—not with passing a budget at all. The House instead wanted to put on a national debate over policy choices and priorities.

The "new" House has other Senate-like features. Legions of aggressive and ambitious House subcommittee leaders, with savvy, aggressive, and ambitious staffs, searching for new areas or initiatives to call their own, serve as marvelous incubators for policy proposals that are before their time.

The Senate. What of the "new" Senate? It too has changed its policy role. As Senate activity in the past ten years has mushroomed,[8] steps have been taken to bring more coherence and regularity to Senate behavior and scheduling. As these steps—such as more disciplined rules for amendment offering and floor debate—have been taken, the essential character of the Senate, as a deliberative body, has disappeared. A sharp increase in workload is difficult for a small institution based on comity and informal, flexible procedures to handle. It has the same effect as a substantial increase in membership size. More formal and rigid floor procedures cause tension and shift some legislative activity to other arenas that remain flexible—like subcommittees. Staffs expand to cope with additional work but often serve to provide new work—more bills, more ideas for hearings, more amendments. As Michael Malbin has shown, when staffs become bargaining agents for senators, the informal senator-to-senator relationship changes, becoming less significant, less informal, less close. Expanding committee and subcommittee obligations exacerbate this trend—senators are always on the run, from one subcommittee hearing to another, to the floor to vote (quickly so as to make another meeting or hearing), back to the office, over to another hearing . . . and have fewer and fewer opportunities to socialize or "schmooze" with their colleagues. "I haven't exchanged six words with half these guys," one veteran senator confided to me in 1977, referring to his colleagues

[8] See John F. Bibby, Thomas E. Mann, and Norman J. Ornstein, *Vital Statistics on Congress, 1980* (Washington, D.C.: American Enterprise Institute, 1980), chap. 8.

on the floor. With more and more bills, amendments, and other votes coming up, little time remains on the Senate floor for debate and deliberation. The "morning hour" is frequently a forum for canned speeches on constituency notables or problems. The rare biting policy speech is largely ignored.

An ironic consequence of these changes—in particular of the tremendous expansion of Senate professional staff—is that the Senate has become increasingly occupied with legislative detail. Several hundred legislative professionals in the Senate have become the "specialists" of the legislative process. They scrutinize the finest details of each piece of legislation, down to the very commas and semicolons, and draft scores of amendments in committee and on the Senate floor. They enable senators to battle the House, line item by line item, in conference committees. They force senators, busy and preoccupied with balancing their overloaded schedules, away from the sustained time necessary to focus on broader, global policy concerns or alternatives. The only option remaining is to haggle over details.

Thus, the House has become less identified with legislative carpentry and more noted for grappling with the larger issues in policy debates. The Senate has moved away from its focus on debate and deliberation, and toward a preoccupation with the legislative nitty-gritty. But neither chamber has moved wholeheartedly to embrace the other's basic policy-making role or to defer to "the other body" in its new incarnation. (Indeed, intra-cameral resentment has grown, if anything.) And, most important, neither the House nor the Senate is *capable* of executing its new role adequately. The modern, 435-member House is inherently too unwieldy, too rigid, and too fractious to be the basic forum for national policy debate. The modern, 100-member Senate is inherently too small and informal to be *the* repository of legislative expertise, and staff cannot compensate for long.

The result is that neither chamber is comfortable with its contemporary role. Both chambers are undergoing identity crises, groping to find policy roles that can accommodate their institutional strengths and limitations, in the context of a greatly changed legislature and society.

Congress in the Political System

Change has affected not just the internal characteristics and behavior of the House and Senate and how they make policy, but the broader place of Congress in the American political system. In 1965, as part of an American Assembly on "The Congress and America's Future," Samuel P. Huntington published a provocative essay on the decline of Congress in the twentieth century, which he updated in 1973. It gives us a useful place to start.

Huntington opened his original essay—published, remember, during the 89th Congress, the height of Johnson-inspired legislative activism—by saying, "Congress is a frequent source of anguish to both its friends and its foes. The critics point to its legislative failure. . . . Congress either does not legislate or legislates too little and too late."[9] On the other hand, in 1964 "the friends of Congress lamented its acquiescence to presidential dictate." Thus, Huntington suggested, "at the same time that it is an obstructive ogre to its enemies, Congress is also the declining despair of its friends." And both images, he said, are true. So a paradox ensues: "Congress can assert its power or it can pass laws; but it cannot do both." Huntington's essay was criticized, justifiably, for showing little understanding of the basic role a legislature *should* and *can* play in a democratic society—and for showing little sensitivity to the basic strengths of Congress in the American political system. But one does not have to agree with either his controversial premises or his gloomy conclusions to find merit in his essay. Huntington asserted, correctly, that Congress faced an identity crisis: it could not, itself, agree on what a "strong" Congress should do or how it should relate to the executive. And he asserted, correctly, that much of Congress's dilemma stemmed from deeper causes.

To Huntington, this legislative dilemma was the effect of the many broad changes in American society during the twentieth century—urbanization, technological change, bureaucratization of organizations, nationalization of problems, sustained international involvement. Congress faces a crisis because it has failed to adapt itself, in three ways, to the changes in the society. It has *insulated* itself from new political and social forces; it has *dispersed* power internally, rendering itself incapable of establishing national legislative priorities; and it has been forced, as a result, to focus less attention on legislating and more on *overseeing* the federal bureaucracy.

For our purposes, the appropriate question is: How do these assertions stand up in the context of changes in the 1970s? Overall, it is clear that much has changed since Huntington characterized Congress, but not all of the changes have been in the same, or expected, directions. And surprisingly much has remained the same. First, Congress has removed layer after layer of insulation, leaving itself almost totally *open* to new and shifting political and social forces. Second,

[9] Samuel P. Huntington, "Congressional Responses to the Twentieth Century," in *The Congress and America's Future*, David B. Truman, ed. (Englewood Cliffs, N.J.: Prentice-Hall, 1965; 2nd ed., 1973).

Congress has dispersed power even more dramatically—far more dramatically—since Huntington's essay than it did during the preceding sixty years. Third, Congress, as a result of a variety of internal changes, has devoted more time and resources than before to legislating—and at one and the same time has become more preoccupied than ever before with overseeing the bureaucracy. The result is a Congress which has erased one problem of adaptation, while altering other trends, and perhaps intensifying other problems.

Congressional Insulation from Power. Congressional insulation was, to Huntington, the "single most important trend in evolution during the twentieth century." As evidence of this trend he cited

1. increasing tenure of office
2. the increasing importance of seniority
3. the requirement of extended tenure for leadership
4. the absence of ambition beyond a position of leadership in Congress
5. the decline of personnel interchange between Congress and the administration
6. the small-town origins and careers of congressmen
7. the provincialism of congressmen.

These trends combined to create a Congress with little feel for contemporary problems and with scant ties to national or international social or political forces. It is worth examining these seven forces in more detail, recalling Huntington's evidence and bringing it up to date.

1. Increased tenure of office. Huntington pointed out that Congress throughout the twentieth century had been an institution in which tenure "inexorably lengthened." By 1961, "the biennial infusion of new blood had reached an all-time low." Indeed, his revision noted that by 1971, the ratio in the House of two-terms-or-less newcomers to ten-terms-plus veterans was down to 1.2 to 1, compared with a ratio in 1897 of 34 to 1! The proportion of veteran members—those elected to Congress more than once—had risen consistently since the late nineteenth century; 63 percent of House members and 40 percent of senators in 1887 fit this "veteran" category, compared with 87 percent of the House and 66 percent of the Senate in 1961 and 88 percent of the House and 65 percent of the Senate in 1971.

Huntington was correct, of course, up to 1971. But the remainder of the 1970s saw a reversal of those long-time trends. The number and proportion of veterans in Congress dropped steadily throughout the decade, while the number and proportion of junior legislators increased. By 1979 the ratio of newcomers to veterans—down to 1.2 to 1 in 1971—had more than doubled, to 2.5 to 1, and it rose to more than 3 to 1 in 1981! Granted, it is not the 1890s—but it is a substantial, junior-oriented change.

Indeed, as Congress entered the 1980s, it teemed with the young and the junior. A majority of House members had served six years or less. By 1981, 54 percent of the Senate were in their first term, while only 12 percent had served three terms or more. Astonishingly, when the 97th Congress convened on January 3, 1981, nearly a majority of its members had served in their current chambers only with Jimmy Carter residing in the White House. Perhaps even more astonishing was that a full 80 percent of the Senate and of the House had come to their chambers since Richard Nixon won the presidency in 1968. If seniority had characterized Congress in 1960 and 1970, juniority was a more appropriate term by 1980.

2. The increasingly important role of seniority. Huntington linked the increasing tenure of members to an increasingly rigid adherence to seniority practices. In his 1973 revision, he did note the nascent seniority reform movement and suggested that, while the system would remain, occasional deviations might occur and be accepted.

This in fact has been the case, even following substantial reform in both houses; since 1971, only three individuals with seniority have been denied committee chairmanships, all in the House and all in 1974. But the combination of reform and extensive turnover in membership has greatly altered both the *meaning* and the *impact* of seniority. In the Congress of 1961, seniority meant not just the rigidly automatic succession to a committee chairmanship of the member with the advantage in continuous service—it meant total insulation from removal thereafter for the balance of one's congressional career. Now, in 1981, seniority means a clear edge for election to a chairmanship, but a tenuous hold on that chairmanship, with the reality of a separate secret ballot vote on your gavel every two years. Seniority now also means new and different things for subcommittee chairmanships.

Moreover, seniority no longer has the *impact* of insulating Congress from new forces. Important committees and subcommittees are often chaired these days by young, vibrant, and *junior* legislators. In the 97th Congress, several first-term senators assumed the chairmanships of important full committees, such as the Labor and Human Resources panel. In the 97th House, a large number of second-, third-, and fourth-term members chaired key subcommittees on such panels as Appropriations and Energy and Commerce.

3. *Extended tenure: a prerequisite for leadership.* Huntington noted that nearly all party and committee leaders in the House and (to a lesser extent) the Senate were "legislative veterans of long standing." In 1971, the top leaders in the House averaged 26 years in the institution and 8 years in their leadership posts; the comparable figures for the Senate were 23 years and 11 years, respectively.[10] A decade later, near-total turnover in these top leadership positions—party floor leaders plus chairmen and ranking members of three major committees—has resulted in significant reductions in average service and tenure of leaders. House leaders in 1981 averaged a still high 23 years in the House, but only 2 years in the leadership, while Senate leaders averaged 17.5 years of overall service and 3.5 years in leadership posts. These top leaders, all in all, are still selected from senior ranks, but the trend is clearly to require less service to assume a leadership position, and to serve less time in the leadership. Moreover, at the "middle management" level of leadership—caucus chairmanships, deputy whips, Policy and Steering Committee memberships, and so on—junior members are now very well represented.

4. *Leadership with Congress: a one-way street.* Huntington declared that leadership in Congress was the pinnacle of a career, not a steppingstone. With regard to the House,

> Representatives typically confront a "fourth term crisis:" if they wish to run for higher office—for governor or senator—they must usually do so by the beginning of their fourth term in the House. If they stay in the House for four or more terms, they in effect choose to make a career in the House.[11]

Writing of the Senate he added, "The most influential men in the Senate have typically been those who have looked with disdain upon the prospect of being anything but a United States Senator."[12] Neither of these generalizations could be made so easily in 1981. Eleven House members departed the institution in 1980 to run for or accept another office. Only three of the eleven had served less than four terms, while the average was five full terms. In recent years, several House party leaders and committee chairmen have run for higher office, left the House for other positions, or publicly toyed with the idea of running or departing. As for the Senate, a list of

10 Ibid., p. 12.
11 Ibid., p. 13.
12 Ibid.

the "most influential" members in the late 1970s might well include Jackson, Magnuson, Muskie, Kennedy, Dole, Baker, Byrd, Long, Church, and Javits: six of these ten have run for the presidency at least once, and at least two of the others have expressed their willingness to run.

   5. *The decline of personnel interchange between Congress and the administration.* Huntington distinguished between the frequent lateral transfers from "the Establishment" to the administration and the lack of movement between Congress and either the administration or the establishment. By contrast with the nineteenth century, few members of Congress move to the cabinet or the White House staff, or vice versa.

   In recent years, there have been a number of interesting exceptions to this trend—Daniel Patrick Moynihan moved from the administration and "the Establishment" to the Senate; Representatives Adams and Bergland and Senator Muskie gave up substantial seniority to move to the Carter cabinet; Senators Jackson and Tower indicated informally their willingness to leave the Hill for the Reagan cabinet; Senators Stevenson, Ribicoff, and Bellmon, Representatives Rogers, Moss, Mikva, and many others left Congress voluntarily to join establishment law firms, courts, or other institutions. But these are still exceptions, not broad evidence of a reversal of this trend.

   However, there is a new and interesting corollary for the 1970s: the development and vast expansion of a professional staff corps on Capitol Hill has dramatically increased the circulation of elites between Congress, the administration, and other areas of national life. The subcabinet of the Carter administration was riddled with people recruited from key staff spots on the Hill. Law firms, lobbying groups, prestigious think tanks, consulting firms, and corporations are also feeling an expanded presence of former professional staffers from Congress. This street is two-way, as well; fellowship opportunities and other avenues have brought leaders from business, the executive branch, and academia into Congress for stints of varying lengths. In this sense, Congress has become much more open to other societal elites, and vice versa.

   6. *The social origins and careers of congressmen.* Huntington pointed out that congressmen are more likely than other national leaders to come from rural and small-town backgrounds and to have begun their careers in local politics. He noted,

   Businessmen, lawyers, and bankers are found in both Congress and the administration. But those in Congress are likely to be small businessmen, small-town lawyers, and small-town bankers. . . . Administration leaders, in contrast, are far more likely to be affiliated with large national industrial corporations, with Wall Street or State Street law firms, and with New York banks.[13]

There have probably been modest changes in these career patterns since the 1950s and 1960s, but not enough to shake the basis of Huntington's point. However, staff expansion has made a clear difference here as well. Professional *staff* in Congress—for both committees and members—are quite likely to have Ivy League, Wall Street law firm, or New York bank experience and backgrounds, making Congress *as a whole* less insulated from these national institutions or organizations.

7. *The provincialism of Congress.* Points (5) and (6), said Huntington, led Congress to exhibit different policy attitudes—oriented toward "local needs and small-town ways of thought" and away from national needs and trends. As evidence, he offered the fact that congressmen are conspicuously absent from gatherings of national leaders (such as American Assembly sessions). Parochial attitudes and values, he said, were reinforced inside Congress: "The structure of Congress encourages their perpetuation. The newcomer to Congress is repeatedly warned that to get along he must go along."[14]

Few changes are as clear in Congress as the total disappearance of the norm of "going along to get along." Still a local orientation is clearly characteristic of the contemporary Congress, too, although caused less by "provincial" attitudes than by the local base of representation in our legislature (and perhaps enhanced by Congress's decentralization). But it is also true that "cosmopolitan" attitudes and backgrounds are evident among many, if not most, prominent and upcoming legislative leaders in both houses of Congress, including such legislators as Cheney, Aspin, Jones, and Solarz in the House, and Moynihan, Kassebaum, Durenberger, and Tsongas in the Senate.

It is evident, then, from cataloging these trends from the turn of the century to the beginning of the 1970s and then examining them in light of the decade just past, that Congress, in Huntington's terms, is anything but insulated from America. Not everything has changed, but enough has changed dramatically to make Congress highly responsive—many say *too* responsive—to movements and new developments in the society. The change becomes more evident if we look at the summary paragraph on this subject in Huntington's essay:

[13] Ibid., p. 17.
[14] Ibid., p. 19.

Old ideas, old values, old beliefs die hard in Congress. The structure of Congress encourages their perpetuation. The newcomer to Congress is repeatedly warned that "to get along he must go along." To go along means to adjust to the prevailing mores and attitudes of the Inner Club. The more the young congressman desires a career in the House or Senate the more readily he makes the necessary adjustments . . . on Capitol Hill the nineteenth-century ethos of the small-town, the independent farmer, and the small businessman is still entrenched behind the institutional defenses which have developed in this century to insulate Congress from the new America.[15]

These "defects" in Congress as a representative body were one key to the "decline" of Congress, asserted Huntington. No observer of the 1980s could read this characterization and recognize contemporary Capitol Hill; one important key to the *resurgence* of Congress, then, is the change in the 1970s in its behavior as a representative body.

Congressional Structure and Power. Any description of congressional change in the 1970s begins with decentralization. Indeed, our contemporary image of Congress is so infused with the importance of decentralization that it is easy to forget that the pre-reform, pre-change Congress was *also* characterized by decentralization and dispersal of power. Thus, while Congress in the past ten years has reversed a twentieth-century trend toward insulation, it has at the same time accentuated and accelerated the trend toward dispersal.

When he discussed dispersal of power, Huntington was referring, of course, to the change from the brief strong central leadership of the Reed-Cannon era (1890–1910) to the decentralized Congress dominated by standing committees and their chairmen which prevailed thereafter and which was built on the back of the seniority process. While some leaders in the post–1910 era—notably, Rayburn and Johnson—had impressive personal influence, they developed it through individual abilities more than institutional resources. Their power was personal and transitory, while the power of committees and chairmen was institutionalized.

As the chapters by Davidson, Sinclair, and others document, the 1970s brought major changes to this structure of power, through changes in formal rules, informal norms, and membership. Davidson suggests that we have moved from "committee government" to "subcommittee government." Whether or not the term "subcommittee

15 Ibid.

government" is accurate, power and initiative in Congress have indisputably shifted from committees to the much greater number of subcommittees. But a point as interesting and as important is that power and resources have expanded in other places as well. Rank-and-file members of Congress—junior or senior, Republican or Democrat, majority or minority, urban or rural, committee member or no—have each and all become more significant. As staffs have expanded and their ranks have filled with expertise, they too have increased in influence and importance. So too have party caucuses, and the respective floors of the two bodies. And so too, at least in formal powers, have the party leaders—moving back partway, in fact, toward the powers held by Reed and Cannon.

Power in Congress is not zero-sum; not all of this expansion has come out of the hides of standing committees and their chairmen. Rather, Congress has vastly expanded its scope, its activity, its physical plant, and its budget—and thus has expanded its ability to influence national policy and events, to command public attention, and to represent various interests. Its power has expanded to accommodate the panoply of forces who wanted a "piece of the action," and more. The result is the greatest degree of decentralization Congress has ever experienced and far broader dispersal of power than is found in any other legislative body on earth.

Huntington suggested in 1965 that "in both houses . . . the dispersion of power makes obstruction easy and the development of a coherent legislative program difficult."[16] These words could as easily have been written in 1981. Note that some things have changed in these areas; in the 1960s, "obstruction" as often as not meant a committee chairman killing a piece of legislation, while today, obstruction means any of 535 legislators, through subcommittee, committee, or floor procedures or amendments, altering a bill, delaying action, or tying the institution in knots for an indeterminate period of time to make a point or to stand on a principle—thus obstructing a score of bills awaiting debate and/or action. Changes in the actors and the process of obstruction have diluted further the ability of congressional party leaders to pull together a coherent legislative program. Scheduling is increasingly unpredictable and difficult. Nowadays, more bills may make it out of committee (since chairmen can no longer quash them at will)—but more bills will then enter a longer and slower-moving queue, wending their erratic way to possible consideration on the floor. Setting priorities for floor consideration has become more difficult, and the end-of-session chaos—where dozens of

16 Ibid., p. 27.

bills come up in the fateful final few days, some of which sneak through under cover of night while others die whimpering, with no particular rhyme or reason—has intensified. Dispersal of power has gone hand in hand with the removal of layers of congressional insulation. Congress has become more responsive to societal changes and to societal demands, first with the decline in seniority, tenure of office, and provincial attitudes, and second with the increase in points of access and of influence for groups and individuals. As more points of view have more frequently been heard and heeded, the routes of passage through the legislature have become ever more clogged, with few opportunities for clear and smooth sailing.

Function: The Shift to Oversight. In oversight, too, we see the continuation of a trend, not its reversal, through the 1970s. But the past decade has brought a more complicated mix of functions to Congress. The old direct and negative relationship between oversight and legislation is gone, and activity in *both* has expanded substantially.

Huntington suggested that the twentieth century had seen Congress expand and diversify its activity in overseeing administration, even as its role in legislating declined. Congress no longer served as the initiator or originator of legislation, acting only to amend or delay. Congress increasingly acted as ombudsman for individuals and as investigator and overseer for executive departments, regulators, and bureaucrats.

While Congress expanded and diversified its activity in overseeing administration, the responsibility for legislating, said Huntington, shifted to the executive. He wrote, "Today's 'aggressive spirit' is the executive branch . . . no one expects Congress to devise the important bills." Indeed, he noted, "Congress has conceded not only the initiative in originating legislation but—and perhaps inevitably as a result of losing the initiative—it has also lost the dominant influence it once had in shaping the final content of legislation."[17]

This is clearly overstatement by Huntington, as Gary Orfield, among others, has demonstrated.[18] Nevertheless, it is striking to read this 1965 essay now, in 1981—during the new era of "oversight" Congresses and right after a decade when Congress was sharply criticized for hyperactive legislating. It is clear that the 1970s *did* bring more congressional emphasis on constituent services and oversight. However, it is also the case that the 1970s brought even

[17] Ibid., p. 28.
[18] Gary Orfield, *Congressional Power: Congress and Social Change* (New York: Harcourt Brace Jovanovich, 1975).

more emphasis on legislating, in new areas and old. Congress initiated and achieved new policies in environmental control (such as the Clean Air Act), education (basic opportunity grants), pension policy (ERISA), foreign policy (the human rights initiative), and nearly every other policy area. In a newly aggressive way, Congress greatly influenced the final content of virtually every national policy decision made during the 1970s, from involvement in Angola to the Panama Canal Treaty, the Carter energy package, and the breeder reactor development decision. In the process, it drew the federal government into areas it had not even considered during prior decades.

Huntington wrote of an aggressive executive branch and a passive Congress. Today, Congress, even though it may have its own ideas and initiatives, and even though some of these, as above, may proceed to the statute books, still waits passively for many or most major policy initiatives to come down from the White House. The 97th Congress did not start in on January 3, 1981, to draft its own tax policy; it waited for President Reagan's proposal. But in the lingo of psychologists, Congress today is passive-aggressive. It reacts strongly and widely to every presidential move, and it initiates action often enough to keep the executive off balance and on guard.

For the most part, Congress's recently increased involvement in legislation has entailed shaping particulars and defining details, not drawing global guidelines. This fits with Huntington's notion of oversight: "Congress is acting where it is most competent to act: it is dealing with particulars, not general policies."[19] But it is in part precisely because Congress in the 1970s drafted the details of a huge volume of statutes that its activity in the oversight arena expanded concurrently. Congressional legislation has been complicated, often contradictory, and more than occasionally filled with gaps. The result frequently has been complicated, contradictory and gap-filled regulations issued by the executive—followed by outrage, oversight, and threats of legislative veto from Congress.

Greater activity in legislating has thus been accompanied by even greater activity in oversight. But both the House and Senate—as I suggest above—have gotten caught between the Scylla of excessive attention to legislative-administrative detail and the Charybdis of inadequate focus on the foundations of broader policy directions. More time and activity devoted to legislating and to overseeing have not translated into better quality legislation or regulation—or a Congress able to set the national policy agenda and its priorities.

[19] Huntington, "Congressional Responses," 2nd ed., p. 32.

Conclusion

Whatever the merits of his overall thesis, Huntington was correct to assert that Congress was a source of anguish to both its friends and its foes. It remains so. Whatever the changes that have swept the Capitol in the past dozen years, the identity crisis of our national legislature has deepened. Today, as before, a stronger Congress serves mainly to block presidential action, stalemating the system and calling down upon its own head demands for structural reform.[20] A weaker Congress lets a president run roughshod over it, until, when he oversteps his bounds, we wonder what became of the constitutional checks and balances and demand that Congress prevent another "imperial presidency."

Of late, we have seen this identity crisis take another form, as both the House and Senate have become more confused about their individual roles in the American political system. While the Republican takeover of the Senate in 1980 offered a unique opportunity for stepping back and reexamining the Senate's role, there were few if any signs early in the 97th Congress that the GOP would give high priority to seeking a new perspective.

We should expect another decade of concern and intermittent despair about Congress and its behavior, but they should not blind us to several fundamental truths about this particular institution and the American political system itself. First, while the changes of the 1970s have a down side, they are also fundamentally encouraging. When it had to, Congress responded, quickly and well, to its growing insulation from trends in American society and culture. Congress today is more open, democratic, and responsive to the variegated social and political forces in the country it represents than any other legislature in the world. It is now criticized, often justifiably, for being *too* responsive, particularly to single, narrow interests. But more frequently, Congress's actions or inactions represent the consensus—or lack thereof—in the country at large. It is more accurate these days to criticize the whole of the citizenry for not coalescing around a set of policy ideas or a single direction in energy, economic, or foreign policy than it is to criticize Congress for failing to do so. Where and when there has been national consensus, Congress has acted, reasonably quickly and reasonably well—at least as well as any parliament in a comparable situation. Moreover, the debate and division over an issue in Congress can and often does move the

[20] Lloyd Cutler, "To Form a Government," *Foreign Affairs*, vol. 59, no. 1 (Fall 1980).

country closer to a consensus. Congress's grappling with energy over the past five years has educated and sensitized the citizenry—and made it easier to take broad action.

In the absence of consensus, Congress either does not act or prevents the executive from acting. In a vital policy area, this can and does cause delays and problems. But over the long run, it is not necessarily better for either the process of policy formation or the quality of policy outcomes to have a system in which a legal consensus can be imposed where no public consensus exists. Indeed, often this ability results in reversals of major policies with each change in government—as the British experience with nationalization of industries and membership in the Common Market will attest.

No doubt, Congress could and can do better. No doubt, Congress at times in its history *has* done better. No doubt, there are yet structural and attitudinal changes, in House and Senate committee systems, leadership responsibilities, floor rules and customs, which would enable Congress to perform its various functions more efficiently and perhaps more wisely—and which, no doubt, would have as many *unintended* effects as the changes we have seen in the past decade. But structural changes, no matter how sweeping, in an era of intractable problems and national uncertainty, would not magically create an America strong in purpose and national defense, with high productivity and low inflation.

Indeed, given the scope and complexity of national life and international affairs, Congress has performed admirably in recent years. We can undoubtedly improve our legislature, and we should undoubtedly press it and its members to focus on their institutional limitations and to take steps to assume more responsible and proper roles in the American policy process. But there is no reason to abandon our legislative process for another. And there is good reason to laud its flexibility and vitality in a complex, diverse, and changing policy world.

Contributors

R. Douglas Arnold is assistant professor of politics and public affairs at Princeton University. He is the author of *Congress and the Bureaucracy: A Theory of Influence.*

Roger H. Davidson, on leave from the University of California, Santa Barbara, where he is professor of political science, is currently senior specialist in American government and public administration at the Congressional Research Service, Library of Congress. His writings include *Congress Against Itself, The Role of the Congressman,* and *Congress in Crisis.*

I. M. Destler, senior associate at the Carnegie Endowment for International Peace, directs a project on executive-congressional relations in foreign policy. He has written *Making Foreign Economic Policy* and *Presidents, Bureaucrats, and Foreign Policy.*

Charles O. Jones, managing editor of the *American Political Science Review,* is Maurice Falk Professor of Political Science of the University of Pittsburgh. Author of *Introduction to the Study of Public Policy, Clean Air,* and *The Minority Party in Congress,* he recently completed the manuscript for a new book on Congress.

Michael J. Malbin is a resident fellow at the American Enterprise Institute and a contributing editor to the *National Journal.* His books include *Unelected Representatives: Congressional Staff and the Future of Representative Government* and *Parties, Interest Groups, and Campaign Finance Laws.*

Thomas E. Mann is a visiting fellow and codirector of the Congress Project at the American Enterprise Institute and the executive director-designate of the American Political Science Association. He is the

385

author of *Unsafe at Any Margin: Interpreting Congressional Elections* and coauthor of *Vital Statistics on Congress, 1980.*

NORMAN J. ORNSTEIN is associate professor of politics at Catholic University, adjunct scholar at the American Enterprise Institute, and political editor of "The Lawmakers" series on public television. His books include *Congress in Change; Interest Groups, Lobbying and Policymaking;* and *Vital Statistics on Congress, 1980.*

NELSON W. POLSBY, professor of political science at the University of California, Berkeley, was editor of the *American Political Science Review* from 1972 to 1977. His books include *British Government and Its Discontents, Community Power and Political Theory, Presidential Elections,* and *Congress and the Presidency.*

MICHAEL J. ROBINSON, on leave from the faculty of Catholic University, currently directs the Media Analysis Project at George Washington University. He is the author of more than fifty articles involving media and politics and is now writing a book entitled *National Media/National Politics.*

ALLEN SCHICK is a senior specialist in American government and public administration at the Congressional Research Service, Library of Congress. The editor of *Public Budgeting and Finance,* he recently completed *Congress and Money: Budgeting, Spending, and Taxing.*

BARBARA SINCLAIR is associate professor of political science at the University of California, Riverside. She has published numerous articles on voting alignments in the House of Representatives and recently completed a manuscript on changes in congressional voting patterns during the twentieth century.

Index

Vital Statistics on Congress, 1980

John F. Bibby, Thomas E. Mann, and Norman J. Ornstein

This study provides statistics on the modern Congress that cover congressional elections, campaign finances, membership characteristics, committees, staffs, expenses, workloads, and voting patterns. In their explanatory notes, Bibby, Mann, and Ornstein highlight changes in the patterns of "safeness" and marginality in congressional seats and in the impact of contributions in congressional campaigns. Changes in the party affiliation, regional dominance, and seniority of membership in the House and Senate are also noted, together with the expansion of committees, subcommittees, and chairmanships in both houses of Congress. The authors specify the growing cost of running Congress and point out where the workload of the legislature has expanded, even as the policy outputs have declined. Most of these trends are interrelated, the authors note, and have important implications for the future role of Congress in the American political system.

1980/Political and Social Processes Study/3408–X Cloth $12.25/ 3401–2 Paper $5.25

Available from
American Enterprise Institute for Public Policy Research
1150 Seventeenth Street, N.W., Washington, D.C. 20036